THE CONSTITUTIONS OF THE USSR AND THE UNION REPUBLICS:

Analysis, Texts, Reports

A publication issued by the
Documentation Office for East European Law
University of Leyden

THE CONSTITUTIONS OF THE USSR AND THE UNION REPUBLICS:

Analysis, Texts, Reports

Edited by

F.J.M. FELDBRUGGE

SIJTHOFF & NOORDHOFF 1979
Alphen aan den Rijn—The Netherlands
Germantown, Maryland—U.S.A.

Library of Congress Catalog Card Number : 79-89780

ISBN 90 286 0489 8

Printed in The Netherlands.

TABLE OF CONTENTS

TABLE OF ABBREVIATIONS

CC	Central Committee
CDSP	*Current Digest of the Soviet Press*
CPSU	Communist Party of the Soviet Union
LG	*Literaturnaia Gazeta* [Literary Gazette]
RKP(b)	Russian Communist Party (Bolsheviks)
Rev. Soc. Law	*Review of Socialist Law*
SGiP	*Sovetskoe Gosudarstvo i Pravo* [Soviet State and Law]
SP SSSR	*Sobranie postanovlenii pravitel'stva SSSR* [Collected Decrees of the Government of the USSR]
Sots. Zak.	*Sotsialisticheskaia Zakonnost'* [Socialist Legality]
Sov. Iust.	*Sovetskaia Iustitsiia* [Soviet Justice]
Ved. SSSR	*Vedomosti Verkhovnogo Soveta SSSR* [Gazette of the Supreme Soviet of the USSR]
VMU	*Vestnik Moskovskogo Universiteta* [Herald of Moscow University]
VTsIK	(*Vserossiiskii*) *Tsentral'nyi Ispolnitel'nyi Komitet* [(All-Russian) Central Executive Committee]

PREFACE

It is undoubtedly an event of global importance when one of the most powerful states in the world adopts a new constitution. This importance cannot be defined in simple terms because, as Professors Ginsburgs and Pomorski point out in their study in this volume, the new Soviet Constitution may be looked at from different perspectives. It will have its effect on internal policies in the USSR, on Soviet law, on Soviet society, as well as on Soviet relations with the West and with the Third World. It will play a role on many stages, and whenever it does, the necessity arises of determining its precise meaning. The purpose of this volume is to be of assistance in this respect by providing a collection of such texts and documents as are the most helpful in elucidating the meaning of the new Soviet Constitution as a whole, and of its individual provisions.

Utilization of parliamentary debates and other *travaux préparatoires*, which is the most common method of interpreting constitutional texts in the West, is not applicable in the same way for the Soviet Union. The actual drafting process, when real alternatives must somehow be weighed, remains outside public observation. When the draft of the 1977 Constitution finally emerged and was published, it was submitted to a public debate of gigantic proportions and minimal depth. Nobody could doubt that, at that moment, all fundamental decisions had been taken and the only realistic suggestions to be made were those concerning editorial details.

A similar procedure was followed before the enactment of the 1936 Constitution, although the 1977 public discussion displays a few minor deviations from the established pattern. As we can see from President Brezhnev's second report, a number of proposals advocating more substantive amendments were publicly voiced, although they never had a chance of being accepted. In addition, fundamentally different views were put forward in *samizdat* form. This implies that the atmosphere of the public discussion was significantly freer than in 1936, even if the net effect of both discussions was equally modest.

In view of the peculiar nature of the public constitutional debate in the Soviet Union, comparatively small changes may acquire great meaning. In this respect one should think of changes introduced in the draft, as compared with the 1936 Constitution, and changes introduced in the final text, as compared with the draft. The former group of changes often constitutes the public reaffirmation of ideological, political, and legal developments which were already well known, such as, for instance, the position of the Communist Party (Art. 6). The present provision repeats the pronouncements of the 1961 Party Program. The differences between the draft and the final text are in many ways the most interesting, because they allow the precise definition of the regime's viewpoint on the questions concerned.

For these reasons, the text of the present USSR Constitution is printed in such a way as to enable the reader to see at a glance how this text differs from its 1936 counterpart and from the corresponding provisions in the draft Constitution of 1977.

The introductory study by Professors Ginsburgs and Pomorski centers on the basic ideological, political, and legal issues to which the Constitution addresses itself; it leaves aside the second half of the Constitution (Arts. 70–174), which deals with the organization of the Soviet state and which is, to a much greater extent, self-explanatory.

Some of the principal difficulties connected with the translation of a Russian Constitution into English are discussed in the Notes on the Translation.

Brezhnev's two main speeches on the Constitution have been included because they fulfill some of the functions of the *travaux préparatoires* in the West. The first speech was made to the Central Committee of the CPSU and it accompanied the publication of the draft. It provides an authoritative explanation of the underlying principles and motivations. With the second speech, the final text was submitted to the Supreme Soviet. Its special interest lies in its discussion of the results of the nationwide debate on the draft.

The materials on the USSR Constitution are followed by the texts of the constitutions of the fifteen union republics. These texts have been translated and prepared by Mr. William B. Simons. The format he has chosen is that of the text of the RSFSR Constitution, followed by divergent provisions in the other constitutions, which are arranged according to individual articles in the form of footnotes to the RSFSR provisions. The fact that this method was feasible demonstrates the great similarity between the constitutions of the fifteen republics. Also, this method again enables the reader to see at a glance where individual constitutions depart from the set pattern.

The translation of the 1977 Constitution of the USSR has been made by Mr. Simons and the editor, and has been published previously in the *Review of Socialist Law* (Vol. 4, 1978, pp. 57–84). The translation of the 1978 RSFSR Constitution by Mr. Simons has also been previously published in the *Review of Socialist Law* (Vol. 4, 1978, pp. 259–286). The editor is responsible for the other translations and for the Notes on the Translation. Mr. Simons and also Ms. Esselien 't Hart did a great amount of work in preparing this volume for the press; their contributions are gratefully recorded.

The Editor

CONTRIBUTORS TO THIS VOLUME

F.J.M. Feldbrugge, Professor of East European Law, Director of the Documentation Office for East European Law, University of Leyden Faculty of Law

George Ginsburgs, Professor of Law, Rutgers University School of Law, Camden, New Jersey

Stanislaw Pomorski, Professor of Law, Rutgers University School of Law, Camden, New Jersey

William B. Simons, Documentation Office for East European Law, University of Leyden Faculty of Law

ANALYSIS

A PROFILE OF THE SOVIET CONSTITUTION OF 1977*

George Ginsburgs and Stanislaw Pomorski

Introduction

The new Soviet charter may be looked at from several perspectives.

1. The Constitution is a major ideological statement. It represents a further attempt at legitimizing the political power of the CPSU *ideologically*. The document's doctrinal eloquence pursues "informational" ends as well, especially with an eye to foreign audiences. As a result, the Constitution brings dramatically into focus fundamental discrepancies between the principles of political ideology and social reality. The Preamble and Parts I and II, in particular, invite this sort of analysis. From that point of view, the Constitution is an excellent representative sample, indeed a calling card, to Soviet political culture.

2. Since the Constitution figures as the political and legal blueprint of a socialist state proclaiming its adherence to "scientific Communism" or "Marxism–Leninism",[1] one is tempted to weigh its pronouncements in light of certain basic postulates of Marxist social theory, primarily the Marxist theory of state and law.

3. The constitutional text obviously contains evidence of current policies/intentions of the Soviet leadership and must, of course, also be scrutinized for such practical signposts. While so engaged, the reader must nevertheless keep in mind that these "commitments" tend to change, sometimes quickly and abruptly, and that the probative value of the Constitution is, in the long run, limited.[2]

---

*The present essay does not deal with the historical background of the adoption of the 1977 USSR Constitution. For a fine survey and analysis of this formative stage see Robert Sharlet, *The New Soviet Constitution of 1977. Analysis and Text.* (Brunswick, Ohio: King's Court Communications, 1978), pp. 1–71.

Shirley Goldstein, a second year student at Rutgers-Camden School of Law, was of assistance in our work on this essay.

4. The Constitution may next be examined in terms of the development and evolution of Soviet constitutional doctrine.

5. Finally, the Constitution may be treated as part of a larger whole, namely, as one of a series of constitutional enactments in the Communist world. Focus on the species would naturally prompt comparison between individual components and, since the Soviet Constitution is last in line, its contents tend to reflect occasional borrowings from other recently adopted or up-dated Communist charters.[3]

Clearly, these approaches are not mutually exclusive and all can contribute toward the proper understanding of the meaning of the 1977 Fundamental Law. In some cases, several techniques can be applied concurrently; in a few instances, a particular yardstick seems most suitable. The present essay will concentrate on the first four items and will not attempt to trace the specific differences and similarities between the latest Soviet Constitution and its fellow socialist predecessors. This kind of systematic juxtaposition is a big job in itself that, in our opinion, can best be handled separately.

The range of our inquiry will likewise be limited to the Preamble and the first two parts of the charter (through Article 69), which set forth what may be called the *grands principes* of the Soviet Union's latest constitutional blueprint. There are a couple of good reasons for concentrating on that portion of the statute. First, this section recites the long-term policy commitments which will presumably stamp the operation of the entire constitutional mechanism. Second, the rest of the document deals essentially with routine technical matters of an organizational nature and so is clearly severable on grounds of focus, scope, style, and substance from the conceptual architectonic thrust of the opening segment.

Before taking a closer look at the text of the Constitution, some background data and general observations may be in order. According to Soviet sources, the nationwide discussion of the draft Constitution produced some 400,000 proposals for changes in and supplements to the original version. In the end, around 150 alterations were made, as a consequence of which one article was added and 118 articles out of an initial total of 173 were amended. Quantitatively, the process of review sounds quite impressive, although in fact the bulk of the revisions merely involved stylistic and cosmetic refinements, and significant innovations were rare at this stage of the game. At any rate, official spokesmen take considerable pleasure in discussing the physical scope of the exercise which they choose to picture as a complete and thorough debate on the merits.[4]

The 1977 Constitution is substantially longer and more explicit than its 1936 counterpart. It also has a more complex internal structure. The 1936 text featured 13 chapters comprising 146 articles. The 1977 edition is divided into 9 parts, which are further broken down into 21 chapters numbering 174 articles, and opens with a lengthy preamble. The new charter is much more eloquent, especially on points of ideology. Finally, the latest script includes many principles and rules which previously were just part of ordinary legislation and likewise deals with assorted matters which formerly were not legally regulated at all.

Several novel themes deserve to be mentioned. Most of them are introduced in the preamble and are subsequently elaborated in the body of the Constitution. In a sense, the procedure validates the editorial comment that "the function of the preamble resides in that it serves as a kind of 'key' to the constitutional text; in it are fixed the results of the path traversed, are indicated the aims and tasks of further development".[5] By the same token, however, the preamble identifies solely political and ideological landmarks as distinct from conventional constitutional models which usually contain a general statement of the values which the respective polity professes to embrace and seeks to realize. Though not strictly possessed of normative force, these "affirmations" establish superior standards the spirit of which the more technical clauses of the Constitution are then called upon to match. The preamble of the Soviet Constitution is not designed to set the legal tone for the rest of the document, but rather to sketch a profile of the Soviet experiment in its past, current, and projected incarnations.

Among the highlights, the following are worth noting. The 1977 Constitution differs from its 1936 predecessor in that it ranges far beyond the formal state structure and, instead, addresses itself to the political/social fabric of the Soviet community as a whole. Thus, it purports to be "a Constitution of the society" rather than simply "a Constitution of the state". The phenomenon is, we are told, an objective outgrowth of the advanced phase of socialism dominated by a tendency toward the steady rapprochement of state and society.[6] Some foreign critics have portrayed the trend as amounting to the "étatization" of society. Soviet legal authors reject that charge on grounds that the scope of constitutional regulation under socialism is naturally broader than in a capitalist environment. The socialist state, they point out, organizes the planning and management of the entire national economic complex, attends to the protection and expansion of public property, national education, and health, the development of culture, the distribution of material wealth, the organization of communal services, and many other facets of social life. The fact that the Constitutions of several socialist countries spell out the role of the Communist Party and civic organizations in the political system presumably does not signify the "étatization" of the society either. On the contrary—local sources claim—all this evidence attests to the "socialization of the state" for, by recognizing the separate sphere of activity of these "unofficial" bodies, the state is, so to say, compelled to take into account the position of these associations which express the interests and opinions of diverse strata of the population.[7]

Whatever the quality of this line of reasoning, there is no doubt that the regime took special pains to accentuate the social and, hence, systemic, orientation of the new charter. For example, the concluding paragraph of the preamble was ultimately amended in such a way as to affirm that the proposed Constitution recorded the principles of the USSR's social system and policy, and the rights, liberties, and duties of citizens in addition to the previous formulation that had acknowledged only the principles of organization and aims of the socialist state of all the people.[8] In a marked departure from precedent, the state's erstwhile monopoly of the constitutional scene was now ostentatiously shared by both society and the citizenry. Similar usage is encountered elsewhere. Chapter 1 is entitled "political system", and Soviet scribes themselves concede that this is the first time the concept crops up in Soviet legislation.[9] In comparable vein, the heading for Part I is "The Foundations of the Social System and the Policies of the USSR" which reportedly corresponds to the Leninist notion of the Constitution as not just a legal, but also a political document. Fitting the cardinal principles of the social system and policies into the framework of a single section is hailed as a significant step because the proximity underscores, on the one hand, the interrelationship, interaction of the economic and political strategy of the Party and the state and, on the other, the humanistic essence of Soviet domestic and foreign policy.[10] In short, if the 1936 Constitution was primarily concerned with the mechanics of government, its successor stakes out a much broader domain in a manner deliberately designed to incorporate extensive areas of community activity and set a social agenda.

Next, the new Constitution purports to be not only "a summary of achievement", but a "program for the future" as well. Not content with preserving the *status quo*, it also strives to express the "dynamic tendencies" of the Soviet society.[11] On both counts, the 1977 charter accurately reflects fresh trends in socialist constitutionalism, that is, novel developments in the constitutional doctrine[12] and the recent constitutional practices of Communist states.[13] The sense of malaise over the Stalinist dictum that socialist constitutions must function strictly as "mirror images" of the historical record had spread after its author's death, and even the earlier discussions of constitutional reform under Khrushchev suggested the existence of a consensus on the urgent need to rethink that "mistaken" proposition.[14] Thus, the decision to let the 1977 Constitution engage in prognosis and enunciate prospective guidelines appears to have met with virtually unanimous approval among Soviet commentators for whom the change means that the charter is intended to determine the direction and goals of social progression.[15] The desire to project ahead is defended as not being inconsistent with the idea of the Constitution as being true to reality by contending that the future does not lie beyond the bounds of the present, but is rooted in and can be extrapolated from the present.[16] The premise that the future is objectively cognizable logically leads to the conclusion that it is reasonable and, indeed, imperative for the Constitution to draw a rough map of the terrain still waiting to be crossed.

The tone of the 1977 Statute, one might add, is plainly conservative. The emphasis is on internal succession and stability or, as the preamble takes care to explain, the preservation of "the continuity of the ideas and principles of the first Soviet Constitution of 1918, the Constitution of the USSR of 1924, and the Constitution of the USSR of 1936". In one respect, the attitude makes good sense. Each previous generation of Soviet constitutions had coincided with watersheds in the political, social, and economic evolution of the community, and the adoption of these charters could be justified by the exigency of having to memorialize and solidify these dramatic shifts in the country's Fundamental Law. No matter how hard Brezhnev and lesser Soviet spokesmen try to alibi the latest charter in these terms, entry into the so-called stage of "developed socialism" simply does not qualify as any sort of revolutionary breakthrough. At best, what we have here is incremental "improvement" in all areas of endeavor: a higher standard of living, greater national unity, wider popular participation in public affairs, and the like.[17] The process is marked by cumulative growth, devoid of sudden leaps from one historical plateau to the next and, by that token, puts the premium on retention of past gains in order to build upward on that foundation. The regime can thus afford a mood of introspection in which the new Constitution emerges as a serene climax to a series of spasmodic convulsions, attesting to the Soviet Union's graduation from the dynamics of dialectical violence to peaceful techniques of social propulsion.

Lastly, the Constitution makes a conscious effort to advertise the internationalist flavor of the Soviet system. Note, for example, the insertion in the preamble of the clause to the effect that "the unification of the Soviet republics in the USSR multiplied the forces and possibilities of the country's peoples in the construction of socialism". Taken together with other reminders located in various parts of the charter of the "associational" origins of the USSR and the advantages allegedly accruing to all concerned from this venture, the theme could be interpreted as a reaffirmation of the "partnership" formula inviting adherence by additional members. In any event, such references keep alive the notion of the USSR as the ideal prototype of a multi-ethnic community exerting a general appeal to all peoples striving to build a world socialist order. A further attempt is made to reenforce the bid by attributing to the Soviet record a universal validity, so that Soviet history presumably holds a lesson for every society seeking to reach socialism. The 1917 Revolution, for example, affects not only Russia, but initiates the whole "worldwide historical turning-point of mankind from capitalism to socialism". Such grandiose claims recur elsewhere and, of course, their purpose is to inflate the importance of the Soviet regime's performance, canonize its experience as the established route for ascent to socialism, and elicit common deference to its tutorial authority.

The Preamble. The Political System

The preamble and Chapter 1 are inseparable, inasmuch as they both deal with the key characteristic features of the Soviet political system, chief among them the Communist Party's monopoly of political power,[18] and enunciate the official state ideology.[19] The preamble is a short recapitulation of the eschatology of "full Communism" in historical perspective as embodied in the past, present, and future of the Soviet Union. The prefatory section is clearly divided into three major parts:

1) Paragraphs 1–4 restate Soviet history since the October Revolution;
2) Paragraphs 5–11 outline the fundamental traits of the Soviet society and the Soviet state at the present stage of their career ("developed socialism");
3) Paragraph 12 sets forth "the supreme goal of the Soviet state" as well as the "main tasks of the state", obviously instrumental for the achievement of the "supreme goal".

Needless to say, "the supreme goal" of the Soviet state cannot be anything else but "the construction of the classless Communist society". This ideal society, a heaven on earth, is not described in any detail in the Constitution.[20] Still, it follows by necessary implication that every endeavor by any group, individual, or society as a whole should be judged by its relationship to the supreme goal: whether and how the enterprise brings the nation closer to paradise. Looked at from this perspective, the entire course of Soviet history ranks as a collection of unprecedented accomplishments, resulting in spectacular progress toward the ultimate goal. One need hardly mention who is the first to be credited for all these triumphs, and the Constitution does not try even for a moment to equivocate on that score: naturally, the palm belongs to the Communist Party, the Party that led the workers and peasants through the successful revolution, the Party that midwifed the Soviet state, "a state of a new type, a basic tool for construction of socialism and Communism".[21] The strength of Soviet socialism has once more been demonstrated by victory in World War II.[22] More recently, the Soviet state has become "the all-people's state" and the Party, whose leadership role has increased, has become the vanguard of the whole Soviet people.[23] Thus, the USSR now qualifies as "a developed socialist society—a necessary stage on the road to Communism".[24]

The political monopoly of leadership by the Party is finally and authoritatively broadcast in Article 6, para. 1. Paragraph 2 hastens to justify this exclusive arrangement on grounds of the Party's preemption of knowledge of Marxism–Leninism and, jointly, the preamble and Article 6 provide ideological legitimation for the Party's investiture with supreme political power. The change between the 1936 and 1977 charters in that respect is dramatic. Indeed, the old Statute relegated the Communist Party to the chapter on the rights and duties of citizens and spoke of the Party only in connection with the right of the more active and conscious elements of the working population voluntarily to band in its ranks. Hypocritical as such efforts at modesty may have been, the Party was, by deliberate decision, kept in the background in a formal "state" document. Today, however, the Party occupies a place of honor in the chapter on the USSR's political system and is openly acknowledged as "the leading and guiding force of Soviet society and the nucleus of its political system and of state and social organizations".

The sole concession here is that, while the draft version had put the Party at the heart of *all* state and social organizations, the word "all" was dropped from the final edition. As suggested by some analysts, the more cautious phrasing may well stem from tacit aquiescence in the fact that, as of late, sundry organizations have on occasion emerged and managed to operate on the Soviet scene with which the Party would in no way wish to be identified. In light of this phenomenon, an omnibus bid to assign a Party core to all social organizations (as implied in the language of the draft bill) would have forced the regime to deny the existence of these bodies or conveyed the ridiculous impression that various dissident associations were also sanctioned by an inner Party presence.[25] Otherwise, the Party no longer makes the slightest attempt to disguise its role as the absolute power behind the state throne and has even gone so far as to use the state's own charter to advertise its primacy.

For that matter, perhaps the act of self-promotion exceeded the bounds of propriety, since the leadership was then prompted to enter an official disclaimer on three counts. First, the public was told that the Party's current enhanced status conferred no special privileges on its members, but instead imposed high obligations on this "elite" corps.[26] Second, certain unnamed individuals who reportedly had advocated the transfer of state functions to Party organs were chastized for confusing the concept of the Party's will exercised *through* the competent institutions of government with direct substitution of the Party's authority for that of the governmental apparatus.[27] Practical administration of the country's affairs continued to be entrusted to the state which retained full responsibility for discharging these duties; the Party merely laid down the general policy line and reserved the right to oversee the correct application of the agenda. Third, the Constitution took pains to spell out that "all party organizations function within the framework of the Constitution of the USSR", as if to dispel the notion that the Party stands above the law or abides by a different code. Stipulating that the entire Party hierarchy is expected routinely to observe the established procedures means, of course, that it must comply with the prescribed norms of "socialist legality", thereby infusing the latter principle with an increased sense of vitality and, in insisting that the Party's activities are also regulated by its standards, asserting its total and exclusive mandate.

To justify its power, the Party is under constant pressure to record progress on the road to Communism. Moreover, the CPSU, in order to defend its claim of preeminence in the international communist movement, has to show that the Soviet Union is nearer the target of full Communism than other countries run by sister Communist parties.[28] Since the "supreme goal", once recklessly promised for about 1980, is nowhere in sight, various "intermediate stages" or intermediate scenarios registering advance toward full Communism have been invented. Khrushchev launched the "all-people's state" as evidence of the growing homogeneity of the Soviet people and, in effect, to proclaim the ideology of social solidarity. His brain-child, enshrined in the program of the CPSU at the 22nd Party Congress, is now uncritically plagiarized by the Constitution.[29] Needless to say, the "all-people's state" is a patent absurdity from the vantage point of the Marxian doctrine of state and law, a fact which the Chinese have not missed in their denunciations of the new Soviet Constitution.[30]

Stalin announced in 1936 the successful completion of the building of socialism. In the early 1960s, Khrushchev predicted that full Communism would be achieved by about 1980.[31] A later discovery of a "developed socialist society" as a "necessary stage on the road toward Communism" obviously amounts to face-saving ideological acrobatics. In that vein, the next Soviet Constitution will probably come up with something like "a highly developed socialist society" to prove that the elapsed interval had again witnessed enormous progress toward the "supreme goal".[32]

Reading the preamble along with Article 6 gives one the impression that the Constitution establishes a state religion[33] practiced under the auspices of the CPSU, the only organization privy to all the mysteries of the creed. In a manner of speaking, Article 6 is an "establishment clause": it ratifies a state religion as well as a kind of theocratic state in which the Party plays the role of the ruling church. Armed with infallible knowledge of Marxism–Leninism, the CPSU steers the Soviet people toward the millennium, that is, "full Communism".

The Constitution espouses two fundamental, and yet contradictory, political doctrines. One is the ideology of popular, participatory democracy with strong egalitarian overtones, and the need to articulate the concept suitably accounts for much of the verbal artifice encountered in this and other chapters of the Statute. A sampling of these semantic contrivances will suffice. Thus, the Soviet "all-people's state" expresses the interests and will of the "workers, peasants and intelligentsia" (Art. 1); all state power belongs to the people and is exercised either through a system of representative agencies (Arts. 2–3) or directly through referenda (Art. 5) and workers' participation in the management of the socialized economy (Art. 8). The elected government bodies have now been renamed from Soviets of Workers' Deputies to Soviets of People's Deputies to underline their inherent rapport with the entire home constituency,[34] and to confirm their superior status as repositories of popular sovereignty, all other state organs have been put under the control and rendered accountable to the network of Soviets (Art. 2).

The fundamental trend in the development of the political system calls for "the further unfolding of socialist democracy" (Art. 9). The involvement of all adult citizens in the political life of the country, based on the principle of equality, is repeatedly stressed (Arts. 34, 48). The new Constitution is much more explicit on this issue than its 1936 predecessor: the 1936 Constitution proclaimed the principle of popular democracy and its institutional implementation in two brief articles.[35] It mentioned neither direct forms of political democracy nor workers' participation in the management of the enterprises. The right of political participation was not expressly guaranteed. Articles 122 and 123 noted only the equality of rights of citizens regardless of nationality or race or sex, whereas the frame of reference of the present charter is a lot broader (Art. 34).

The accompanying organizational innovations are rather interesting. Sentiment in favor of legislative referenda seems to have been quite widespread in Soviet legal circles in recent times, and recommendations for the adoption of this procedure were fairly common.[36] Under prevailing conditions in the USSR, the technique of mass consultation is relatively innocuous and offers a safe and tame medium for staging a show of public support with a maximum of fanfare. In practical terms, the scheme rates as a high-grade promotion stunt calculated conspicuously to certify the regime's concern for popular will, at no cost or risk to its own preferences. Apart from catering, then, to the contemporary taste for democratic artifacts, the move by no stretch of the imagination signals any devolution of real authority.

More significance may attach to the decision to include in the Constitution (Art. 7) a provision that, "in accordance with their statutory functions, trade unions, the all-Union Leninist Communist Youth League, cooperative and other social organizations participate in the administration of state and public affairs and in the resolution of political, economic, and socio-cultural problems". This gesture of "co-optation" must have caused some doctrinal unease on home ground since Soviet sources have since found it advisable to deny that the step illustrated the thesis of the gradual withering away of the state through a pattern of transfer of its functions to civic bodies culminating in the inception of communist social self-management. This interpretation was faulted for being "lop-sided" in that it viewed the process as just one-way traffic along a conveyor-belt leading from state to society, whereas—so goes the claim—the Soviet state itself cannot be regarded as antipodal to or alienated from society,[37] nor can public associations be divorced from the governmental structure since their operations tightly interlock and they essentially complement each other in carrying out their assigned duties. The best solution presumably lies in getting trade unions and the rest of the social organizations to cooperate with the state apparatus in the performance of various tasks.[38]

Stripped of idle rhetoric, such a scenario envisages, of course, that the ensemble of social organizations will act in an auxiliary capacity, as an appendage of the state machine. So, once again, while the Constitution's current endorsement of their position amounts to an obvious promotion in rank for these "non-governmental" entities, the state clearly remains the dominant factor in the equation and no reversal or even appreciable adjustment in their respective roles is in the offing. The stylistic shift does, however, mark a concession to modern political fashion. Furthermore, at least on a theoretical plane, the whole experiment raises the intriguing question of how credibility is to be preserved when social units are invited to join in the job of running public affairs and yet, in practice, are then effectively denied the opportunity to do so or, if that mission turns out to be impossible and given a desire to maintain an aura of verisimilitude, the extent to which the ruling elite must compromise and let form acquire a measure of substance. In short, what starts out as a token or symbolic device could well end up, should the situation swing around, as a potent instrument for change.

Similar thoughts come to mind when contemplating the third item in the lot, to wit, the labor collectives featured in Article 8. The charter entrusts them with a comprehensive agenda which encompasses the discussion and resolution of state and public affairs, the planning of production and social development, the training and placement of personnel, the discussion and resolution of questions of the administration of enterprises and institutions, of the improvement of the conditions of labor and everyday life, and of the utilization of resources allocated for the development of production as well as for socio-cultural measures and material incentives. Labor collectives are also expected to develop socialist competition, promote the dissemination of progressive work-methods and the strengthening of labor discipline, educate their members in the spirit of communist morality, and concern themselves with raising their political awareness, culture, and professional qualifications.

Thus, their responsibilities fall principally under the heading of household chores in the domain of economic management and there is no doubt that their main function is to enhance the caliber of the Soviet Union's economic performance, *inter alia*, by providing an institutional channel designed to guarantee regular input by the labor force into the decision-making process at the grass-roots level.

Workers' sharing in industrial management is not, of course, a recent discovery and if the authors of the Constitution had been satisfied with that, the picture would have been plain enough. Note, however, that they, by their own admission, pursued far more ambitious ends. To quote Brezhnev,

> "the work collective, and the work of its Party, trade union, and Young Communist League organizations reflect the whole life of our society—economic, political, and spiritual. Indeed, this is the primary cell of the whole of our organism, both economic and political."[39]

The result was that the corresponding article, duly rewritten and amplified, was transplanted to Chapter 1 devoted to the political system.[40]

Be that as it may, learned discussions of the phenomenon focus almost exclusively on its economic dimensions, and one senses that the experiment may be suffering from an acute internal contradiction. The theme of workers' participation in the national economy today commands such universal appeal that the Soviet Union, as the self-appointed champion of the working classes, can ill afford to ignore the concept. For the sake of propaganda alone, the slogan is too valuable not to appropriate it for the USSR's personal use. Next, the Soviet economy is limping, and giving the workers a voice and a stake in organizing and monitoring its operations and a reason to identify with the successes of their respective enterprise looks like the regime's answer to the striking failure of other techniques hitherto employed to stimulate efficiency and ensure proper control over production methods. The problem, though, is that the scheme smacks dangerously of syndicalism or corporatism and in order to shield itself from that charge, the Soviet leadership took the precaution of recasting its version of "workers' collectives" in a political/economic mold. The political component is barely mentioned and is completely overshadowed by its economic counterpart both in the language of the charter and the erudite glosses on the text of the Constitution, but the arrangement does enable the USSR to mount a formal defense against possible accusations of having here succumbed to "revisionism".

Though the political rationale shows every sign of being a sham, the economic pitch sounds quite genuine, except that close analysis of what Soviet experts have to say in this connection reveals nothing startlingly original. No revolutionary change appears imminent. True, suggestions have been heard calling for wider resort to binding and not only consultative effect by the collective on key issues of the enterprise's activities. On the other hand, the proposal is immediately hedged with the caveat that such practice must be coupled with consistent and strict observance of the principle of one-man leadership in concrete questions of operational management. At the same time, the point is forcefully made that the enterprise can under no circumstances become an autonomous unit run in accordance with group interests which, moreover, would be put above general state interests, since that sort of attitude would serve to revive selfishness rooted in private possession, albeit on a group scale. While certainty is expressed that socialist practice will follow the path of further intensification of "production democracy", this process is expected to unfold within the existing mandatory framework of central planning and direction of the national economy. Participation by the workers in the administration of production, it is emphasized, can never be contraposed to their participation in the administration of the state, *i.e.* to those decisions which are adopted in the political arena as the result of exercise of popular will.[41]

The second fundamental ideological theme (the first being popular democracy) revolves around the leading role of the Communist Party (Art. 6) characterized as the "vanguard of the whole people" (preamble). The Party is elitist by nature. It is composed of the "best" representatives of the working classes. Indeed, its commitment to a tight, exclusive, and disciplined format has always been a political cornerstone of Leninism, a crucial distinctive feature of Leninism, a clear line dividing Bolsheviks from social-democrats. Hence, the Constitution is pervaded by a central contradiction between the ideology of popular, egalitarian, participatory democracy, on the one hand, and the ideology of political monopoly by an oligarchic Communist Party on the other. In this respect, the new Constitution introduces no substantive changes: the inherent incongruity of the two canonical propositions has always afflicted the world of Soviet liturgy. The present charter simply succeeds in giving the discrepancy a more pronounced and conspicuous flavor by codifying both principles in a single chapter. Needless to say, it is the ideological postulate sanctifying the "leading role of the Party", or rather the Party apparatus, that has always stamped the functional style of the Soviet state. The USSR has, in this regard, faithfully abided by the teachings of its founding fathers and, as a consequence, the latest Constitution brings dramatically into focus the inconsistency between the professed faith in mass participation and the social experience of total control by the Party/state bureaucracy.

Because the fundamental ideological precept of popular democracy is false, so are the apparent institutional embodiments of that principle. Thus, it is not in the system of Soviets that political power resides, Article 2 of the Constitution notwithstanding; for that matter, to call the Soviets "organs of state power" and "the political foundation of the USSR" (Arts. 2 and 3) is utterly misleading. The Soviets exercise no real power. To a large extent, they are devoid of any political significance, although they do retain considerable practical value in the position of instrumentalities of administration. Similarly, "democratic centralism" is not an effective norm of Soviet public life, despite what Article 3 declares. Instead, the whole pyramid of dependence works almost exactly in reverse order. The executive branches of the Party/government apparatus determine the composition of the "representative bodies". Intra-Party relations follow an identical pattern: under the Statute of the CPSU, it is the masses of Party members who elect their delegates to Party conferences and congresses; it is the delegates who elect their corresponding local/republican committees and the Central Committee; and it is the respective committees which elect their executive organs, including the Political Bureau membership and the secretariat of the Central Committee. In practice, virtually the entire procedure operates the other way round.[42]

Up till now, the business of workers' participation in the management of the enterprises has been no exception to this rule. Just a quick glance at the Statute of the Standing Production Conference is enough to figure out that the pompous declarations of Article 8 are quite unlikely to change the picture drastically,[43] unless the regime is prepared to abandon its traditional *modus operandi* and strike out in new directions. The record shows no evidence of such an appetite for enlightened reform. In fact, recent events would suggest that the contrary prediction is a much safer bet, although the last word must still await the publication of the appropriate legislative act on the rights of workers' collectives, scheduled for February 1980.[44]

In closing this survey of the section on the "political system", one ought to mention briefly that the concept of "socialist legality" gets a big play in the current charter. The Party structure, as already noted, is formally instructed to function within the framework of the Constitution of the USSR and, in comparable vein, state and social organizations and officials are at present unequivocally enjoined, *inter alia*, to observe the Constitution of the USSR and Soviet laws.[45] On paper, these pronouncements lift the principle to dizzying heights; unfortunately, in the harsh light of reality, the initial enchantment with the glossy prospectus soon vanishes without a trace.

The Economic System

The inclusion in the 1977 statute of a separate chapter dealing with the USSR's economic system rates as a major innovation in the history of Soviet constitutional legislation.[46] Such a step serves to underscore the primacy attached in Marxist thought to the role of economics in human activity in general and in the life of a socialist polity in particular. The centrality of economic matters in current Soviet affairs is a commonly acknowledged fact which Soviet sources treat as self-evident. Thus, according to a widely held view:

> "It is altogether natural that the economic role of the Soviet state should be directly reflected and consolidated in its functions, among which the organization of the economy, the creation in contemporary conditions of the material-technical basis of communism occupies first place; in the structure of the apparatus, in which the bulk of the organs are concerned with economic administration; in the legislation, in which dominate normative acts regulating socialist economic relations."[47]

Simply put, doctrine and experience have both conspired to focus attention on the economic structure and performance, and the latest Soviet national charter attests to this phenomenon by elevating the distinguishing features of the USSR's economic mechanism to constitutional rank.

In language somewhat more precise than hitherto had often been the case, the Constitution now declares that socialist ownership of the means of production is considered "the foundation of the economic system of the USSR" (Art. 10). Three "forms" of socialist ownership are identified, instead of the two mentioned in the 1936 charter.[48] The two principal forms are state ownership and collective-farm/cooperative ownership (Art. 10, para. 1). For the first time, ownership by trade unions and other social organizations also receives constitutional endorsement as a form of socialist ownership (Art. 10, para. 2). Although ignored by the 1936 Constitution and long lumped together with collective-farm/cooperative property,[49] this third category of socialist ownership has over the last several years enjoyed in Soviet civil law the status of a distinct form of ownership. The act of "emancipation" dates back to the latest Fundamental Principles of Civil Legislation and the accompanying republican civil codes.[50] Technically speaking, the change made good sense since—in stark contrast with the collective-farm/cooperative property with which it was previously bracketed for the sake of mere convenience—the property of trade unions and other social organizations consists primarily of assets of a non-productive nature intended mostly to cater to different kinds of mass consumer needs, *e.g.* vacation homes, summer camps, and so on.[51] Hence, given the earlier statutory reforms, the award of a constitutional cachet at this juncture amounts more to a question of increased prestige than of substantive promotion.

Note, too, that the draft version of the Constitution had listed the three forms of "socialist ownership"—state (all people's), collective-farm/cooperative, and property of trade unions and other social organizations—on the same footing. However, in the final edition, the clause was amended in a way that recognized the state (all people's) and collective-farm/cooperative as the essential elements of socialist ownership of the means of production and downgraded the property of trade unions and other social organizations to a subsidiary position as a supplementary form of socialist property. The revised formula is, as Brezhnev himself pointed out, "quite correct" for, in his words, "after all, it is these two forms of socialist ownership of the means of production that determine the character of our economy and the division of Soviet society into the two friendly classes of workers and peasants".[52]

On the one hand, then, the net emphasis on state and collective-farm/cooperative property accurately captures the flavor of the existing pecking-order on the Soviet economic front, and the picture would indeed have been badly distorted if through inflated reference to the property of trade unions and other social organizations all three brands of ownership had starred as co-equal. On the other hand, the decision to relegate the property of trade unions and other social organizations to secondary place, while fully justified in light of the prevailing circumstances, does cast fresh doubt on the regime's continued commitment to the once popular theme advocating the accelerated devolution of rights and responsibilities from the strictly governmental to the so-called civic sector. At least on an economic scale, social/public organizations now seem consigned to an ancillary spot so that whatever the route by which the present leadership envisages the transition from socialism to communism to proceed and the withering away of the state to occur, the scenario does not hold much promise of an impending sustained shift of economic authority from the direct and indirect sphere of state jurisdiction to effective control by "autonomous popular bodies". The Constitution's provision here is a true statement of how things actually operate, but, in ideological and practical terms, the ultimate wording of this passage plainly favors the cause of conservatism and the *status quo*.

Protection of socialist ownership and its augmentation are emphasized as one of the fundamental state functions (Art. 10, para.

3). Exploiting socialist property "for purposes of personal gain or for other selfish purposes" is explicitly prohibited (Art. 10, para. 4). The tone of this clause strikes a clearly intimidating note, made still worse by tacking on at the final stage to the initial motive of "personal gain" the infinitely stretchable concept of "other selfish" intentions. The result is a distressing melange of quasi-legal precept and moral imperative with a limitless range of applicability that invites interpretation as a sweeping constitutional mandate for severe punitive measures against "thieves of socialist property" or license for imposing harsh discipline on the bureaucracy. In any event, these newly enunciated principles possess, *inter alia*, the inherent potential of being used as an ideological weapon against the economic privileges of the elite proper should the occasion arise.[53] (Some future purges may invoke this convenient rationale and impute assorted misdeeds under this heading to a member or members of the hierarchy on the recorded evidence of a penchant for an affluent life-style ostensibly financed by routine "diversion of social resources for private ends".) Just as a general proposition, such vague phraseology tends to create ample opportunity for repressive excesses and furnishes ready ground on which periodically to mount a campaign against whatever particular breed of "economic crime" might happen to be currently singled out for special attention.

Congruent with the postulates of the Marxist social and economic canon which consider ownership of the means of production to be *the core of the economic infrastructure of every society*,[54] the Constitution puts the provisions dealing with socialist ownership in the forefront of Chapter 2 (Arts. 10–12).[55] The document emphatically endorses the etatist model of socialist ownership, which has always marked one of the cornerstones of Bolshevik economic theory and practice.[56] This view of socialization imbued the program of the Russian Communist Party (Bolsheviks) as early as March 1919[57] and thereafter remained constant.[58] One has to agree in this respect with a contemporary Soviet commentator who concludes that "the dominance of socialist ownership based on state (all people's) ownership" has been a stable feature of all Soviet constitutions.[59]

The 1977 charter not only endorses with exemplary vigor the etatist thesis of socialist ownership, but introduces further refinements and additions on that score. Thus, the Constitution manages at least twice in Chapter 2 to equate state ownership with ownership by the entire Soviet people,[60] echoing similar pronouncements found in the 1936 statute to the effect that state ownership represents the basic form of socialist ownership, superior to all other forms. By comparison, collective-farm/cooperative ownership (and, *a fortiori*, ownership by social organizations) qualified as a form of socialist ownership of secondary importance, due to the decisive role played by state ownership in the economic realm and the axiom that it spelled "the highest degree of socialization". Accordingly, the principal means of production were slated for state ownership.[61] What was well settled doctrinally under the 1936 Constitution is now explicitly formulated in the constitutional text which proclaims that "state ownership, the common heritage of the entire Soviet people, is the basic form of socialist ownership" (Art. 11, para. 1). The Constitution expressly confirms the state's monopoly as owner of "the land, natural resources, the waters and the forests", a position securely established in ordinary legislation and constitutional jurisprudence.[62] The charter also refers to the lion's share of control exercised by the state in other designated spheres of economic activity, but leaves unanswered the question of what restrictions, if any, circumscribe the state's power in these fields, that is, whether such authority must stop short of outright monopoly or, despite what the language of the charter suggests, may likewise extend to include a "radical" solution whenever that would seem a preferable alternative. Of course, the reverse contingency likewise remains unattended to, namely, the possibility that the state might at some point wish to divest itself of a portion of its present holdings in these areas and how far it is legally entitled to go in that direction.

This is the way the institution of socialist ownership officially looks today. Interestingly enough, however, the Constitution next ventures to predict what changes lie in store for that system in the near future and, in this connection, sees fit to announce (Art. 12, para. 3) that "the state promotes the development of collective-farm/cooperative ownership and *its drawing together with state ownership*" (emphasis added). The Constitution thus chooses to prophesy, in unison with the policies voiced at the 22nd, 24th, and 25th CPSU Congresses, a process of gradual transformation of collective-farm/cooperative ownership into state ownership. This pattern of rapprochement figures among the salient features deemed characteristic of "developed socialism"[63] (although, for the sake of historical accuracy, one should recall that the pitch is not so new and that the germ of the idea of a convergence along these lines can be traced back to Stalin's *Economic Problems of Socialism in the USSR* (1952)).[64]

The expectation, then, is that before too long the sole principal form of socialist ownership in the USSR will be state ownership. In substantive terms, the projected reform will not make much difference, since the party/state apparatus now exercises effective control over all the property technically owned by kolkhozes, cooperatives, and social organizations. From an economic perspective, therefore, the Soviet system of socialist ownership already complies in full with the etatist model. The proposed revision will simply adjust the rules pertaining to *legal* ownership to coincide with the blueprint.[65] Hence, in the final analysis, under the 1977 Constitution the Soviet system of socialist ownership (whether in its static aspect or in its main dynamic tendency) achieves a close approximation of the etatist paradigm.

A commentator on the new Soviet Constitution should not pass by the question of whether the Soviet etatist model of ownership corresponds with the Marxist concept of socialization of the means of production. The issue is most fundamental indeed, and disputes over it have had a long history. The issue of whether *state ownership* in Communist countries is *genuinely socialist* has been a principal platform of criticism of these systems from Marxist positions. A negative answer to the above question leads logically to the conclusion that the socio-economic system prevailing in the USSR (and elsewhere) *is not* socialist, or at least not yet such, that Communist bureaucracy has become a new ruling and exploiting class, caste or stratum. Among those who have come to such conclusions we will mention only M. Djilas (Yugoslavia), A. Sakharov (USSR), and J. Kuron and K. Modzelewski (Poland).

This current of criticism is still very much alive in the recent Marxist literature.[66] Its best representative among contemporary writers is probably Professor Wlodzimierz Brus; two relevant passages from his excellent *Socialist Ownership and Political Systems* will illustrate the line of argumentation:

> "The relatively few attempts at more rigorous definitions have started from the most general premise that ownership in an economic sense is tantamount to effective disposition over the object owned by its owner in his interests, broadly understood. Thus, by analogy with this, social ownership of the means of production would have to meet two criteria: 1) the means of production must be employed in the interests of society, and 2) society must have effective disposition over the means of production it owns. This is how socialization of the means of production was understood by Oskar Lange, and it is also the way I have formulated the problem."[67]

Having applied the above criteria to the etatist model (Soviet type), and the self-management model (Yugoslavia),[68] Brus concludes:

> "Using the criterion of socialization which we have adopted ('society has effective disposition over the means of production'), the answer to the question of whether socialization of the means of production *sensu stricto* has been achieved in the socialist countries of Eastern Europe in the period examined must be in the negative—for both models.'"[69]

Without committing ourselves to the support of Brus' theory, we suggest that his conclusions are not inconsistent with what we have said about the nature of the Soviet political system in the preceding chapter.[70]

It would probably be in order here to register a few well-known facts showing how soviet working classes perceive state/kolkhoz/cooperative property. They show that the Soviet man in the street does not conceive of himself as a co-owner of public property since he enjoys neither the rights nor the privileges of an owner. Rather, he treats public property as government property in whose protection and increase he has no interest. A phenomenon forcefully testifying to this effect is extremely widespread criminality against public property, which does not even evoke reactions of disapproval on the part of the law-abiding segments of the population. *Facts of another category*, testifying to the same effect, are the not uncommon strikes of the Soviet industrial workers. The industrial proletariat perceives its interests as opposed to those who control the means of production. Against this background, pompous declarations of the Soviet Constitution about state ownership as "the common heritage of the entire Soviet people" bring to mind a famous passage from the Preface to *A Contribution to the Critique of Political Economy*:

> "Just as our opinion of an individual is not based on what he thinks himself, so can we not judge of such a period of transformation by its own consciousness."

The charter itself, of course, keeps silent on the mechanics of the projected merger. Other sources suggest that the operation will entail the "gradual elevation" of collective-farm/cooperative ownership to the level of state ownership ending in an eventual transition from the former to the latter.[71] In a sense, the constitutional commitment to the furtherance of kolkhoz-cooperative ownership coupled with the promise of its ultimate abolition sounds quite schizoid, but on second thought a reasonable explanation can be offered to account for the apparent inconsistency. Remember that, given the total control exerted by the party/state apparatus over collective farms and cooperatives, no real difference exists even now between the two principal forms of socialist ownership. In an economic context, the Soviet state "owns" kolkhozes on an equal footing with state farms or state enterprises; the factual power of the state/party to dispose of kolkhoz assets is unlimited. Consequently, what from a technical legal position may look like two separate forms of ownership (or three, if we include ownership by social organizations) in substance boils down to a single state ownership. By that token, any reshuffling of property between socialist sectors signifies, practically speaking, as much intrinsic change as a session of pushing the home furniture around.

If so, why the excitement over the whole affair? Why advertise an essentially "paper" device as an important gain of mature socialist society? Part of the credit for the scheme may be attributed to the eschatology of "full Communism" in that the methodical progression of collective-farm/cooperative ownership to higher stages of socialization and its steady gravitation closer to and terminal conversion into state ownership serve to mark successive changes in the economic infrastructure of socialist society in its evolution toward Communism. En route to that goal, the narrow limits of group ownership are thus transcended and all people's ownership establishes its undivided hegemony, at the outset in the shape of state ownership which is then followed by a brand of uniform Communist ownership. The metamorphosis is a necessary precondition for the eradication of commodity exchange.[72] The increasing homogeneity of socialist ownership neatly corresponds to and, indeed, underlies the parallel shifts in the communal structure characteristic of societies engaged in Communist construction[73] and so, naturally enough, the "eschatological" theme of the convergence/merger provision recurs in some of the clauses of Chapter 3 on "Social Development and Culture", notably Articles 19 and 22.[74] As a feature of the "full Communism" package, the doctrine of rapprochement points the way to the attainment of the "supreme goal". Its genesis may be traced back at least to Stalin's *Economic Problems of Socialism in the USSR*[75] and the item was also one of the highlights of the 1961 Party Program.[76] which just goes to show how in Soviet conditions ideological recipes often manage to outlive the reputations of the chefs who concocted them.

In addition, Article 12, para. 3, displays a pragmatic, policy dimension. The agenda, clearly enunciated at the 24th Party Congress and vigorously promoted at the 25th Party Congress and since that time, calls for "specialization and concentration of agricultural production on the basis of interfarm cooperation and agro-industrial integration".[77] The conspicuous, and chronic, shortcomings in Soviet agricultural performance finally persuaded the leadership to pour substantial resources into a bid to modernize this branch of the national economy. Consensus that the present organizational structure is grossly inadequate has prompted a decision to create large production entities, geared to running select lines of production, lending themselves to a high degree of mechanization and automation, and capable of applying modern technology and of employing trained personnel. The simplest solution to the problem would seem to lie in the rapid amalgamation of kolkhozes and their conversion into extensive state farms, yet this prospective avenue of reform met with flat rejection.[78] Probably the leadership was determined to avoid the kind of serious disruption of agricultural production that a radical overhaul on such a scale would be bound to cause.

A country as deeply troubled by food shortages as the Soviet Union can hardly afford to gamble in the field of agriculture. Also to be avoided was the possibility that the operation would turn into a mere charade, *i.e.* a lot of outward agitation with little substantive effect, as in the case, for example, of the companion experiment in revamping the industrial table of organization. A more cautious approach was chosen: a technique of incremental assemblage of bigger agricultural or agro-industrial units by fostering cooperation between and integration of existing institutions (kolkhozes, sovkhozes, industrial enterprises, and so forth).[79] Since the practice of "interfarm cooperation" and "agro-industrial integration" involves state as well as kolkhoz organizations, the venture results in the emergence of state-kolkhoz joint enterprises and complexes (*ob"edineniia*) which embrace both kolkhozes and state corporations. That is how in fact the current program of "specialization and concentration of agricultural production" seeks to further the "drawing together" of state and collective-farm ownership,[80] and experience has spawned a variety of new types of economic specimens, only some of which have up till now received legislative recognition. The most common breed is the "interfarm enterprise", designed either to service participating farms or to process their agricultural output.[81] The associated farms function as shareholders, and the property of the interfarm enterprise is co-owned by them. In a joint kolkhoz-sovkhoz project, state and kolkhoz property is pooled.

Specialization and concentration of agricultural production by medium of interfarm cooperation and agro-industrial integration were called by Brezhnev "the principal objective of development" for agriculture. Article 12, para. 3, of the Constitution may thus be read as a very concise policy statement: the first half of the sentence seems intended to warn the cadres against contemplating the outright abolition of kolkhozes; the second half conveys in highly abstract language the regime's stake in boosting "interfarm cooperation and agro-industrial integration" as a way of raising the country's life-style to a level of affluence befitting Communist standards. Airing the issue in the Constitution suggests that the policy is considered to be of fundamental importance and that its implementation is envisaged as a long-range operation. On the other hand, the absence of any explicit reference in the statute to particular artifacts on which the regime proposed to rely to achieve these ends and especially the assorted devices already put to the test, would tend to indicate a desire on its part to retain maximum flexibility here. The preference for maintaining silence on this score stands as eloquent testimony to the leadership's resolve to preserve its options in this department, in striking contrast to the frequent calls heard during the discussion of the draft text in favor of having the Constitution contain detailed instructions on precisely this matter.[82]

Ostensibly reflecting popular demand, the final edition of the charter specifies that "the collective farms, like other land users, are obliged to use land effectively, take a solicitous attitude toward it and increase its fertility". By itself, to be sure, the constitutional formula only amounts to a general exhortation, but it may yet furnish the crucial impetus for the elaboration and adoption of concrete legislative measures designed to recast an amorphous desideratum in the shape of an enforceable norm of social conduct.

The Constitution's pronouncements on the subject of personal property pose several interesting questions as well. To begin with, the text was amended prior to enactment through insertion in the relevant Article 13 of a prefatory clause declaring that "earned income constitutes the basis of personal property of citizens of the USSR". The concept of earned/unearned income pops up again in paragraph 3 of the same article which confirms that "property in the personal ownership or use of citizens must not serve for the derivation of unearned income . . ." The whole idea of living by the fruits of one's labor lies at the heart, of course, of the socialist credo, and the fact that the maxim is prominently displayed in the current charter comes as no surprise. The ordinary meaning of the prescription is probably plain enough to be grasped by the common man at whom the admonition is aimed in any event. However, the term "earned/unearned" does create technical difficulties for members of the legal profession.

The qualification "earned/unearned" was not invented by the Constitution and already figured, for example, in the Fundamental

Principles of Civil Legislation and the latest republican civil codes. The trouble is that the criterion fails to cover all cases of malfeasance involving personal property rights. Strictly speaking, the charge would not apply in a situation where the income was obtained unlawfully, but stemmed from productive personal labor. In that respect, Brezhnev was more precise when he explained that the charter's reference to "earned income" reflected "our principled attitude to the character and origin of private ownership under socialism, where the source of growth in the well-being both of the entire people and each person is socially useful work".[83] "Work" and "socially useful work" are two quite different categories, and the second yardstick gives free rein to subjective interpretation as to what deserves to be so certified and thereby can claim title to legitimate status. Faced with the problem, some Soviet jurists have urged that the expression "unearned income" either be dropped altogether and replaced by the phrase "illegal income",[84] or broadened to extend to incidents where income was derived as a result of investment of productive labor but in conjunction with the appropriation of someone else's labor in whatever form.[85]

The authors of the Constitution chose not to adopt the "illegal income" solution, presumably out of desire to preserve linguistic symmetry, namely, since the text had mentioned "earned income", calling the contrary phenomenon "unearned income" was considered good style. In addition, the proposed change in designation, whether consciously or not, could logically lead to the criminalization of the activities thus proscribed, and one suspects that awareness of the possibility of such an outcome might have played a critical role in curbing support for the scheme within Soviet legal circles. On the whole, most Soviet lawyers sound more comfortable with the "unearned income" formula, despite its acknowledged defects, and seem confident that the available body of law is sufficiently flexible to cope with contingencies not squarely covered by the existing rules: where an individual's business affairs smack of speculation, tax assessments can be hiked to relieve him of his "ill-gotten gains"; or if, for instance, an artisan plies a forbidden trade, albeit without attracting hired labor, appropriate sanctions for this type of infraction can be discovered in the legislative record. Granted that with enough ingenuity and determination, the difficulties can be surmounted; however, it is unlikely that they will be resolved as long as the regime persists in the habit of dealing with complex matters in singularly casual fashion, often on grounds that ideological objectives have precedence. In this case, the theme of "earned income" aspires to priority on doctrinal counts, and the law incurs the cost of the ensuing ambiguities. If the "unearned income" concept is sorely afflicted by ambivalence, the companion caveat that "property in the personal ownership or use of citizens must not . . . be used to the detriment of the interests of society" is utterly immune to legal criticism because the law sheds no light on what exactly falls under the heading of "detriment to the interests of society". Needless to say, secure in their supreme wisdom the authorities can always supply an adequate answer, but, alas, this ability is not vouchsafed us mere mortals who are not privy to the omniscient Marxist key to the mysteries of the universe.

Next, the Constitution's definition of personal property has undergone considerable change. The 1936 Charter recognized the personal property of citizens and the garden plots assigned to the individual kolkhoz household as the principal forms of personal ownership, and also permitted small private undertakings of individual peasants and handicraftsmen, based on their own labor and precluding the exploitation of the labor of others. The current statute no longer talks of garden plots "owned" by the families of kolkhoz members and, instead, speaks generally of subsidiary household units, explaining that "citizens may have the use of plots of land, made available in the manner provided by law, in order to run a subsidiary household (including the keeping of livestock and fowl), to engage in fruit and vegetable gardening, and also for individual housing construction". The Constitution adds that "the state and the collective farms render aid to citizens in running the subsidiary household".[86] The absence of express reference to the kolkhoz garden plots has fueled speculation about whether they had now lost their special rank as a separate species of personal property and were henceforth reduced to an equal position with the property of workers and employees. Such a conclusion may, in fact, be premature, since the Constitution does not foresee the blanket repeal of earlier legislation, and by virtue of these laws the kolkhoz garden plots remain an institution *sui generis*. Insofar as the Constitution takes care to note that the collective farms likewise render assistance to citizens in running the subsidiary household, the old association between collective farms and the garden plots survives the amended script essentially intact.

Nevertheless, the revisions are not just stylistic and do pursue practical ends. The intention was to improvise a broad formula capable of spanning both established procedures and experiments currently in progress in a bid to preserve the text's stability. Two developments, in particular, counselled a "panoramic" approach on this occasion. First, the state had recently committed itself to assigning plots of land for purposes of husbandry, gardening, and truck-farming not only to kolkhoz households, but also to workers, employees, retired people, etc. The idea was to draw a greater proportion of the population into socially useful activities and increase the volume of agricultural production, including the stock of foodstuffs procured for sale on the open market. Second, in a number of areas kolkhozes were in the midst of being reorganized into sovkhozes, a process which entailed the transformation of kolkhoz garden plots into economic enterprises operated by workers and employees residing in rural localities. The term "subsidiary household" thus offered the advantage of being sufficiently elastic to accommodate the entire inventory.

The authors of the charter resorted to similar artifices in drafting Article 17 addressed to the subject of "individual labor activity". Again, the net was cast wide and the Constitution ended up stipulating that "individual labor activity in the spheres of trades and crafts, agriculture, serving the everyday needs of the population, as well as other forms of activity based exclusively on the individual labor of citizens and the members of their families, are permitted in the USSR in accordance with the law". In this case, too, the regime reserved the right of ultimate supervision to prevent possible abuse by appending a familiar clause to the effect that "the state regulates individual labor activity, ensuring its utilization in the interests of society". How the "interests of society" would best be promoted here was, of course, left to the unilateral discretion of the authorities, a stock feature of Soviet constitutional practice.

The "mix" contained in Article 17 is a curious one. The reference to trades, crafts, and agriculture is apparently meant to acknowledge the persistence of some vestiges of the caste of individual peasants and artisans. To be sure, the number of people still earning a livelihood in this manner is minuscule. Most Soviet commentators relegate them to the periphery of the system, consider that the property in their possession represents a marginal factor on the economic scale and conclude that the earlier concept of ownership by individual peasants and artisans as a distinct species of small personal labor property is probably ripe for burial in the archives.[87] Whether this view is valid or not, the statute prefers to play it safe by recognizing the existence of this "memorabilia". However, if this type of "individual labor activity" seems destined for "proximate extinction" and so, prima facie, does not warrant continued constitutional endorsement for fear of undermining the desired textual stability by requiring revisions once the relevant "historical phenomena" depart from the scene, the decision to let the current charter mention the item may then be due to a recent development that could succeed in fundamentally altering the old script. Indeed, the ancient, and presumably obsolete, formula could apply equally well to the work of retired folk, housewives, students, workers, and employees plying a trade in their spare time, and the record would tend to indicate that the authorities had precisely this picture in mind when they opted for a provision couched in terms ample enough to stimulate the labor activity of various segments of the population.

The perennial labor shortage may account for this unaccustomed flexibility on the part of the regime which—to extricate itself from the difficulty—appears ready to tolerate more private initiative in economic matters, within acceptable parameters set to safeguard against the excessive manifestation of entrepreneurial and, hence, acquisitive, instincts. Notwithstanding the commitment to maintain rigid limitations in this domain to keep socialist values from being swamped by bourgeois vices, the straws in the wind hinting at increased willingness to rely on the role of individual enterprise in economic affairs could portend a dramatic deceleration and even a partial reversal of the past trend toward steady expansion of state control in every direction. One can imagine in this connection Soviet authorities venturing to experiment in the near future with the technique of private franchise or licensed family business in the consumer sector where, experience shows, the state cannot handle the job and satisfy the population's demands as regards both the quantity and quality of the services rendered. The official apparatus may yet shy away from such daring innovations but, should it take that route, no amendment of the Constitution would be called for to formalize the arrangement.

The implications of the foregoing shift in accent with respect both to "subsidiary households" and "individual labor activity" can only be properly appreciated when projected against the broader background of the Marxist doctrinal canon and the Soviet policy record. The economic and legal institution of personal ownership is intimately linked to the system of economic incentives and to the basic principle of distribution premising remuneration on the norm "to each according to his work". The disbursement of income proportionately to labor contributions (inherently a non-egalitarian procedure, given differing capacity to work) was said to be an inevitable element of the period of transition, due primarily to two factors: 1) the scarcity of consumer goods/services which simply made impracticable any scheme of distribution according to need; and, 2) a low level of social consciousness which inexorably meant appeal to egotistical motivations (*i.e.* material inducement). Both defects, so theory holds, will be cured and cease to afflict the human environment in the more advanced phase of socialist development. Consequently, the new rule of income distribution "to each according to his needs" is gradually expected to supersede the present index geared to measuring work input alone. At that stage, the significance of personal ownership will decline, whereas the importance of collective consumption will rise. In a nutshell, the farther Soviet society progresses toward Communism, the more the role assigned to economic incentives and personal ownership in propelling it forward will shrink.

If one applies that standard, the conclusion is inescapable that the draftsmen of the 1977 Constitution have shelved this scenario. The language of the charter plainly concedes that the actual course of events does not seem to have followed the anticipated pattern and conveys the impression that the leadership has chosen to reconcile itself to a much more prosaic reality. The key precept of the Communist system of distribution "according to needs", for instance, is nowhere in sight. Instead of the oft-promised abundance, the Soviet population still suffers from acute lack of essential consumer goods. Lately published statistics document glaring discrepancies between "rational norms of consumption" and the actual level of consumption of basic foodstuffs.[88] The same sources picture critical inadequacies in housing, restaurant services, nursery schools, public health facilities, etc.[89] In light of the poor performance, Soviet authors have now adopted the attitude that personal ownership will have to be preserved "for an extended time" as a method of regulation of social consumption, and the Communist mechanism of distribution of the gross national product is in practice treated as a figment of the remote future.[90]

The long and eagerly awaited "upsurge" in social consciousness has likewise failed to materialize. To the contrary, the mores and ethos of Soviet society more than ever today strike the objective observer as stamped by the drive for worldly success. Items such as cars or summer houses are avidly sought not just for the sake of the creature comforts they provide, but also because they command social prestige. The results of recent public opinion polls reveal that Soviet youth assigns top priority to possession of the outward insignia of affluence.[91] The current hierarchy is apparently prepared to indulge this mentality. "Economic incentives" figure prominently on the Brezhnev team's agenda and, in fact, served as the battle-cry for the economic reforms initiated in 1965.

The charter vigorously champions this trend by further enhancing the vitality of personal ownership (Art. 13), solidifying the position of the distribution formula "to each according to his work" (Art. 14), and paying tribute to the importance of "economic accountability, profit, production costs, *and other economic levers and stimuli*" (Art. 16, para. 2; emphasis added). Under the circumstances, the references in Article 14, para. 3, to the state's "combining material and moral incentives" and promoting "the transformation of labor into the prime necessity of life of every Soviet man and woman" obviously amount to a bit of poetic license inspired by the eschatology of "full Communism" that must be savored for its intrinsic ornamental effect.

If official appreciation of the value of socialist ownership does not match popular perception on that score,[92] the higher rank awarded personal ownership is a fair reflection of popular sentiments. In general, property rights in the Soviet system, whether vested in private individuals or in "socialist organizations", are goal-oriented. The substantive content of a property right and its compass are determined by the socio-economic purpose(s) for which the right has been established.[93] The right of personal ownership is a good example. Its immediate purpose is to meet the needs of individual consumption; its broader, long-range purposes are the reproduction of labor capabilities (sold to the state) and the procurement of incentives to get the labor force to work efficiently.

The Constitution's terminology clearly demonstrates the ends-means quality of the right of personal ownership, particularly in confirming the regime's commitment to keeping its focus firmly riveted on the instrumentalities of consumption (Art. 13, para. 1).[94] For that reason, the novel right to own a subsidiary household marks a major departure from precedent and deserves a spot of analysis because—let it be emphasized—a subsidiary household is a means of production rather than a means of consumption and therefore represents a separate special category of personal ownership.[95] True, the produce of a subsidiary household serves mainly as a source of food for the owner and his family, but a substantial portion also finds its way into the open market, the freest form, incidentally, of commercial activity tolerated under Soviet conditions.[96]

The 1977 Constitution definitely elevates the rank of the subsidiary household, dispels any doubt about its legitimacy and viability in a socialist economy and, what is more, summons the party/state apparatus to render affirmative aid to its further development. In the 1936 Constitution, a subsidiary household was treated as a supplement to collectivized agriculture; the right of ownership was, in principle, limited to collective farmers, and the right of workers and employees of other sectors of the economy to own a subsidiary household was not mentioned.[97] By comparison, the 1977 Constitution has converted the subsidiary household into a general object of personal ownership, and the latest approach mirrors more accurately the dynamics of the prevailing economic situation in the country:

1) More than half of the Soviet families own subsidiary households, and the share of collective farmers in the sample has been steadily decreasing.[98] Collective farmers seem to be losing interest in running subsidiary households, and a growing percentage of kolkhozniks is either giving up subsidiary households or prefers to operate them on a reduced scale. Members of the younger generation of collective farmers appear to be the ones most reluctant to engage in this kind of "moonlighting".[99]

2) Subsidiary households play a crucial role in the nation's agriculture since they account for as much as 28% of the total agricultural output.[100] When it comes to certain products that are commonly in short supply, the subsidiary households can claim an even higher ratio.[101] Today, few will be so bold as to deny that the subsidiary household is indispensable to the well-being of Soviet society, since the public branch of the economy has repeatedly proven itself unable to feed the population, especially in the rural areas.[102]

Subsidiary households represent the only major private sector within the USSR's "official" economy. For many years, Soviet cadres looked askance at the whole phenomenon as a grudging concession to the ruthlessly exploited peasantry, devoid of any positive value. The ruling elite acted as though the subsidiary households personified an offensive non-socialist remnant of the past and viewed them with suspicion, if not naked hostility. Such attitudes reportedly still linger within the ranks of the bureaucracy. For the "collectivized" peasantry, the issue was literally a matter of life and death.[103] Not altogether surprisingly, then, one of the early post-Stalin measures instigated by Malenkov proceeded to abolish forthwith the host of "unfounded infringements" from which the subsidiary households had hitherto suffered.[104]

Soon after, Khrushchev—intoxicated by the vision of imminent "full Communism" and deliberately ignoring reality—projected the rapid "withering away" of subsidiary households and moved to cut down on their size. In quite predictable fashion, the apparatus translated the prophecy into a coercive/harassing campaign which in some regions verged on forcible expropriation. Khrushchev's more pragmatic-minded successors hastened to reverse his policy on this question. The plenary sessions of the CPSU Central Committee, held in October 1964 and March 1965, restored a more permissive climate toward subsidiary households, reinstating, in effect, the original post-Stalin line. Khrushchev's adventurism and "subjectivism" were bitterly denounced.[105] Subsequent years brought more changes in the same vein, with the result that a policy of "enlightened tolerance" gradually evolved into a policy of encouragement. A landmark in the pattern of progression was the 1969 new Model Charter of the Collective Farm, followed by other practical economic steps aimed at invigorating the performance of the country's network of subsidiary households. Brezhnev himself has on a number of recent occasions gone on record as affirming his whole-hearted commitment to the preservation and further development of the subsidiary household economy.[106]

The leadership has been seconded by the scholarly community (especially the economic experts): during the last decade, a substantial literature has sprung up dealing with subsidiary households.[107] One immediately notices that the learned writers have made a strenuous effort in this connection to prove that the subsidiary household, despite its individual character, is socialist in nature.[108] The reasoning is typical of the mentality peculiar to a theocratic state: since the leadership has given the subsidiary households its imprimatur, their ideological purity is henceforth assumed. Something approved by the Politbureau may not, by definition, bear the stigma of the capitalist past. However, the socialist label also has a utilitarian function: it serves to protect subsidiary households and their owners from assaults by "benighted" officers of the local party/state apparatus who have not yet managed to rid themselves of their old prejudices. At any rate, by ostentatiously bestowing its doctrinal blessing on the concept of subsidiary households, the regime has put an end to the aura of ambivalence that plagued the phenomenon throughout virtually its entire history and, thereupon, finally clarified the institution's status, at least for a while.

The rest of the chapter is anti-climactic, featuring a medley of resonant platitudes and solemn endorsements of fixed routine. For the first time in Soviet constitutional legislation,[109] the norm is enunciated (Art. 15) that "the highest goal of social production under socialism is the fullest possible satisfaction of the growing material and spiritual needs of the people". The thought is attractive, *i.e.* that the economic system purveys to the nation, although how the machinery's responsiveness to popular exigencies is to be secured in concrete terms given the present oligarchic structure of power is never explained. Interesting, too, is the mention here of the "spiritual needs" of the people which, of course, is meant to convey the idea that at the stage of "developed socialism" the mere gratification of physical appetites is no longer the state's primary concern and that the vast resources at its disposal not only allow, but also require, the government to cultivate the community's esthetic and intellectual talents. At this point, preoccupation with primitive consumption is neither dictated by circumstances nor, indeed, can such a focus sustain the desired pace of scientific and technological progress for a modern society. Paradoxically, what is really different on this occasion is the stylistic factor and, in this respect, the Soviet claim that these clauses of the 1977 charter are new is warranted; the component elements, though, are already identified in Stalin's last published work[110] and, even more apropos, in the 1936 Constitution (see, for example, Art. 11). Eager to ascribe special qualities to the 1977 statute, Soviet commentators have in several cases exaggerated its "pioneering" accomplishments by deliberately overlooking how much the text owes to precedent.

Next, the opening sentence of Article 14, para. 3, that "socially useful labor and its results determine the position of man in society" has a nice egalitarian (or anti-elitist) ring, but the prospects that the Soviet Union will ever function as a genuine labor meritocracy are exceedingly dim. An assessment of what psychological effect this sort of pronouncement is likely to have on the domestic audience depends on one's opinion of the level of sophistication of the average Soviet citizen: some foreign observers treat these rhetorical flourishes as idle window-dressing, with no visible impact on the tenor of local political life; others contend that propaganda, never mind how crude, leaves a residual mark on the collective consciousness and so, at least to a certain degree, does influence social behavior.

Article 16 then voices a solid commitment to the principle of central economic planning, echoing corresponding passages in the 1936 charter.[111] However, the current statute waxes somewhat more eloquent on this topic and proceeds to spell out that: 1) the economic system of the USSR "constitutes a single economic complex" (Art. 16, para. 1); and, 2) the system is managed on the basis of "state plans of economic and social development, taking into account the branch and territorial principles" (Art. 16, para. 2). The social motif recurs in that the Constitution prescribes central planning in the area of social as well as economic development on a note amounting to a strong pitch for social engineering. The rather serious demographic problems confronting the Soviet Union may explain the adjustment in emphasis. The branch and territorial format of economic organization now receives constitutional recognition. Disappointment with Khrushchev's experiment with the *sovnarkhozy* and faith in the traditional ministerial structure revived in 1965 thus find reflection in the basic law. The economic independence of the operative entities ("enterprises, associations, and other organizations") emerges as a constitutional rule, although this independence must clearly defer to the imperatives of maintaining a "centralized leadership" (Art. 16, para. 2). Nevertheless, the charter goes on to list various insignia of operational independence, especially "economic accountability" and profitability. In a substantive sense, Article 16 introduces no novelties; instead it confines itself to codifying existing procedures—underwriting the economic model adopted in 1965, alluding to later changes (*i.e.* the 1973/1974 venture into associations), and paying a modicum of tribute to the bid for "decentralization" (perhaps "deconcentration" is a better word) that set the tone for the recent economic reforms.

The chapter closes with a statement trumpeting the regime's concern for the protection of the natural environment. Ecology is a popular subject, of course, and the Soviet government's interest in advertising its commitment to the cause sounds reasonable enough. The limited space of a single paragraph can accommodate only a vow couched in the most general terms, although, we are assured, these will be suitably deciphered in the process of subsequent application.[112] On the other hand, sceptical Russia-watchers are neither particularly impressed with the Kremlin's record to date in this domain nor convinced that the Soviet leadership's fixation on numerical indicia of economic growth is in fact compatible with proper appreciation of the problems involved and objectivity in deciding among the competing priorities.[113] Be that as it may, the scenario requires that "developed socialism" show the world a "humanistic" visage alive to the issues that today agitate social conscience everywhere and, presto, the Constitution enters on cue.

Social Development and Culture

Chapter 3 is entirely new, without any counterpart in the 1936 Constitution. The tone is definitely programmatic and the contents consist of a series of sweeping pronouncements on how the state now strives and in the immediate future proposes further to transform the fabric of society and community mores to effectuate the scheduled transition to Communism. The accent here on social phenomena continues the "systemic" trend noted earlier pursuant to which the charter's frame of reference was significantly broadened in order to add civic matters to the stock items spelling out the structure and *modus operandi* of assorted components of the government apparatus. Reportedly, the shift in focus reflects a conscious realignment in priorities stemming from the realization that, in the period of developed socialism, the social activity of the state must be considered one of its fundamental functions.

The result, of course, is that the state must assume fresh responsibilities to keep pace with the enlarged agenda and sanctioning the public importance of social matters means that the state acquires a formal stake in regulating these affairs, appoints itself as a partner, and converts the whole business into a joint venture. Soviet analysts, as already mentioned, profess to discern no danger in the scheme because they posit a full concordance of interests between the two entities and, hence, refuse to see the association as posing a threat to either side (or, more precisely, the weaker member of the team—society). Others do not share that optimism and find the projected aggrandizement of the state's role disquieting in terms of promise of consequent diminution of what little room for "private" autonomy still exists in the USSR. The scope of the operation has also changed: whereas in the past the state's social calendar had concentrated almost exclusively on servicing the quotidian needs of the population, the present goals are far more ambitious, envisaging a virtual transfiguration of the matrix of society, with special emphasis on improving the "quality" of life. Law, we are told, must contribute to the common search for ways of how best to accomplish this objective, particularly since the terrain is a juridical desert and the relevant legal issues have never been satisfactorily explored.[114]

The general script is familiar to anyone versed in Marxist-Leninist scriptures. Thus, we have the state pledging itself to promote "the strengthening of the social homogeneousness of society, the effacement of class differences and of the essential differences between town and country and between mental and physical labor, and the all-round development and rapprochement of the nations and nationalities of the USSR". The only point worth recording is the curious fact that the rather perfunctory endorsement of the slogan regarding the "rapprochement of the nations and nationalities of the USSR" occurs under the heading of social development and culture. The implication is that the expected process of assimilation will follow a social and cultural route and not affect the country's political structure in the years just ahead. Indeed, if additional evidence on that count is required, Brezhnev even saw fit explicitly to rebut certain over-enthusiastic comrades who allegedly had called for

> "introducing in the Constitution the concept of an integral Soviet *nation*, eliminating the Union and Autonomous Republics or drastically curtailing the sovereignty of the Union Republics, depriving them of the right to secede from the USSR and of the right to maintain external relations. The proposals to do away with the Soviet of Nationalities and to set up a unicameral Supreme Soviet are along the same lines. I think that the erroneousness of these proposals is quite clear. The Soviet people's socio-political unity does not at all imply the disappearance of national distinctions."[115]

The institutional format expressing these distinctions will apparently not undergo surgery, and steps to solidify the unity of the Soviet people will resort on an *ad hoc* basis to other, less controversial, means of achieving that end.

Then, Article 20 restates the Marxian ideal of the self-realization of the individual.[116] This core motif of Marxist philosophy, long neglected in its Soviet incarnation, has recently been resurrected. The provision is but one of the many occasions in the charter where the status and importance of the individual are acknowledged. Since, according to the Marxist canon, such personal improvement is contingent on access to proper working conditions, the Constitution next enunciates the state's commitment to the comprehensive amelioration of the labor environment, on both a quantitative and qualitative scale. Soviet commentators like, for instance, to draw attention in this context to the changes wrought by socialism in the nature of labor, which the charter recognizes by putting a premium, "in contemporary circumstances . . . not on work in general as an investment of muscular energy, but on skilled work that increasingly approximates engineering-technical work".[117]

The staple theme of "effacement . . . of the essential differences between town and country", encountered in Article 19, recurs in Article 22 which speaks of transforming agricultural labor into a variety of industrial labor, widening in rural areas the network of institutions for public education, culture, health care, trade and public catering, services for everyday needs, and public utilities, and transforming villages into well-appointed settlements. We have heard all this before, and performance has yet to match the official picture in any of its vital details. The cryptic allusion to the desideratum of a grid of "well-appointed settlements" spanning the countryside in place of the present villages harks back to the old story about agro-cities, but whether or not this is what the regime has in mind is not clear from the Constitution's passing remark.

The charter duly records the state's pledge to foster and materially reward the growth of labor productivity and readiness to avail itself of the assistance of social organizations and labor collectives to fulfill that aim. The subject of health care, social insurance, trade and public catering, communal services, public utilities, and national education receives similar treatment. A novel feature of the 1977 Constitution is the mention of the state's concern for science, a topic neglected in previous Soviet charters. The development of Soviet society accounts for the decision to enshrine in the statute the prime role assigned to science and technology in ensuring the USSR's progress toward Communism. The state's attitude to scientific endeavor boils down to three principles: 1) to guarantee the planned development of science; 2) to guarantee the training of scientific personnel; and, 3) to organize the implementation of the results of scientific research in the national economy and in other spheres of life. In fact, the 25th Party Congress had resolved that securing practical outlets for scientific ideas was now a task equal in importance to the experience of conception proper, and up-grading the item to constitutional rank reputedly proves that the phenomenon is bound to continue to occupy a prominent position in national affairs. A major problem, however, is that special federal legislation governing the activities of scientific institutions is lacking and, instead, one must rely today on a mass of random regulations. Presumably, the situation is soon to be remedied by the enactment of an appropriate *loi-cadre*, in compliance with the animus of the Constitution.[118]

The recital closes with the familiar pitch proclaiming the system's eagerness to protect, multiply, and widely utilize spiritual values for the purpose of the moral and aesthetic upbringing of Soviet people and the lifting of their cultural level. The noble task of building Communism requires the state to bestir itself to raise a generation of individuals with the intellectual capacity to tackle the job. We are thus offered the fascinating prospect of a host of renaissance-men cadres shaping a nation of refined souls into a perfect community. Simply put, the whole chapter is a masterly summation of the mythological strains of the Communist vision; whether or not such stuff belongs in a constitutional document is a separate question, of course.

Foreign Policy

If the section on "Social Development and Culture" exudes a dream-like aura, the chapter on "Foreign Policy" amounts to a routine exercise in grand posturing—a billboard for an array of Soviet foreign policy propaganda clichés. The introductory words already set the tone for the entire scene by declaring that the USSR unswervingly conducts a Leninist peace policy, conveniently forgetting, of course, that Lenin's commitment to peace was highly selective and that he steadfastly remained an ardent advocate of war as an instrument of revolutionary change. The opening salvo is followed by equally self-serving—and dubious—assertions about the USSR standing for "consolidation of the security of peoples and broad international cooperation". Since the rest of the clauses indulge in similarly bombastic rhetoric, nothing would be gained from a micro-analysis of the script. Instead, a few salient points will be noted here.

For example, the reference (Art. 28) to the USSR's support for the struggle of peoples for national liberation and social progress smells of a deliberate attempt to win the sympathy of the Third World and influence its path of development.[119] Broadcasting in the new charter Moscow's solidarity with the aspirations of the underdeveloped countries is quite obviously calculated to portray the USSR as their staunch friend and thus reenforce their mutual ties, at the expense of the "capitalist" camp. The accompanying pledge to bring about universal and complete disarmament and to consistently implement the principle of peaceful coexistence of states with different social systems sounds a theme familiar to Soviet diplomatic oratory. Local authors take pride in assigning primacy to the Soviet regime in championing these policies and getting them top billing on the international agenda, and the current constitutional display is said to solidify the Soviet Union's status as a key exponent of these enlightened positions.[120] Furthermore, the occasion offers Soviet commentators a welcome opportunity to draw invidious comparisons between the USSR's dedication to the cause of peace and Communist China's admitted preference for war.[121] Much is also made in Soviet circles of the Constitution's outlawry of "war propaganda" in the USSR. The gesture may have some publicity value, but in substantive terms the whole affair means very little: in an international community locked in ideological conflict, what one side denounces as incitement to aggression, the other is apt to hail as a plea for peace.

Article 29 enumerates the fundamental principles which shape the relations between the USSR and other states. Although the statute speaks generally of "other states", the presumption is that the present list applies only to "non-socialist" states; "socialist" states adhere to a superior code of conduct in their intramural activities, mentioned separately in Article 30. In any event, Article 29 contains nothing new, and the vapid principles it cites belong to every modern state's stock in trade. Advertising the collection in the Constitution promises certain egregious advantages, however. First, Soviet scribes can now validly make the claim that so far the Soviet Union alone has incorporated the prescriptions formulated in the concluding act of the Helsinki conference in its organic law.[122] Second, such endorsement serves to dramatize the Soviet Union's firm adherence to the core principles of international law.[123] Third, the express stipulation concerning "inviolability of frontiers" allows the Soviets to attack the record of Communist China and West Germany on the subject of "territorial revisionism".[124] Fourth, the pitch to the effect that the Soviet system guarantees "the conscientious fulfillment of obligations arising from generally recognized principles and norms of international law and from treaties concluded by the USSR"[125] is specifically designed to protect the Soviet Union against charges of violating its international commitments. With the Constitution enjoining respect for duties owed to foreign powers, the Kremlin can henceforth be expected to argue that all its actions must, by definition, be deemed to conform to these requirements simply because the charter will not sanction anything else. The technique may be stale, but apparently the Soviets still find it useful: to wit, issue yourself an official order and then insist that whatever you do complies with the instruction and, as proof of the pudding, summon the authority of the original directive.

The final paragraph deals with the USSR's membership in the socialist community. Constitutional rank is thus conferred on the concept of socialist internationalism which, we are told, prompts the USSR to seek to develop and strengthen friendship, cooperation, and mutual comradely assistance with its partners. Presumably, that scenario includes the Brezhnev doctrine. Similar certification is bestowed on the artifacts of economic integration and the international socialist division of labor, attesting to the Soviet Union's continued faith in the Council for Mutual Economic Aid which is entrusted with the practical task of midwifing a region-wide functional union.[126]

Defense of the Socialist Fatherland

A few words will suffice to dispose of this mini-chapter, not just due to its own brevity but, more important, because of its striking lack of substantive content.[127] The essential thrust of the two relevant articles is that the military function of the Soviet state is strictly confined to devising defense measures geared to the instant repulsion of external aggression. The inference, of course, is that the Soviet Union is inherently incapable of perpetrating an aggression and, appearances notwithstanding, will in fact always be engaged in self-protection on martial occasions—a bid tantamount to filing a blanket alibi intended to establish well in advance the Soviet Union's innocence for every imaginable contingency involving resort to armed force in an international context. In theory, a mandate to purvey to the needs of defense alone would leave room for civic discussion as to whether in a given situation the specification was met and the incident genuinely qualified as a case of resistance to a foreign assailant. Going by Soviet experience, however, such a question can only elicit a positive answer, as the few brave souls who criticized their country's invasion of Czechoslovakia in 1968 learned to their great sorrow.

The State and the Individual

Part II is a new item. The prominent placement of the section devoted to the relations between the state and the individual in the Constitution's organizational table may be attributed to several motives. The decision to have this division follow the one dealing with the foundations of the social system and the policies of the USSR stems from the notion that the citizen's position *vis-à-vis* the state is objectively rooted in the community's social and economic infrastructure. Without establishing the intimate connection between the status of the individual and his political environment, one falls, according to Soviet scholars, into a metaphysical trap where the individual's rights and duties acquire a figurative and "absolutist" connotation. The philosophical premise of the inalienable or transcendental nature of human rights, divorced from their concrete setting, leads to a false picture of historical reality and reduces these freedoms to empty verbiage. By contrast, the Soviet Constitution, with its materialist outlook, claims to abide by the principle of the symbiotic unity of man and his experiential milieu and thus to invest the concept of individual rights with a superior quality: liberties understood as social phenomena are vital, tangible, genuine, plausible, and durable. Or so reads the official version.

The current format marks, of course, the promotion of the individual in the hierarchy of constitutional values, in keeping with the prevailing emphasis on the "humanistic" visage of socialism. In an indirect sense, the present arrangement also bespeaks fresh appreciation of the true complexity of the pattern of interaction between the individual and the state. Gone is the old postulate, once so pervasive in local legal and political theory, that the mere advent of socialism automatically, as it were, erases conflicts between the individual and the state. Instead, local awareness that such conflicts do exist under socialism as well seems to be spreading and, under the circumstances, the logical conclusion is that legal protection of the individual against arbitrary and oppressive state actions still is, and in the foreseeable future will continue to be, a matter of serious practical concern.[128]

USSR Citizenship. The Equality of Citizens

Even then, style generally prevails over substance, for the specific points recorded in this component chapter show no inclination to stray from the beaten path and the tone, as a whole, is timid. The subject of Soviet citizenship is now raised to constitutional level. However, the norm remains unchanged, echoing the legislative formula that a single union citizenship has been established in the USSR and that every citizen of a union republic is a citizen of the USSR. The charter adds that the grounds and the procedure for acquiring and losing Soviet citizenship are defined by the Law on Citizenship of the USSR, published in December 1978.[129] The internal contradiction between the simultaneous recognition of a single federal citizenship and an array of republican citizenships persists due to the regime's pursuit here of mutually contradictory objectives: 1) a uniform concept of citizenship ensuring central control and formally testifying to the USSR's crystallization into a coherent national entity; and, 2) individual republican citizenship designed to lend credibility to the official thesis of retention of sovereign status by the union republics within the federation. Dialectic reasoning alone can satisfactorily reconcile these opposite positions, and those of us who are not blinded by its magical properties will not be persuaded by the results of Soviet attempts to fit the two pieces together. In fact, what the rule means is that past practice will be observed in this precinct: the central government will regulate citizenship issues; the constituent republics will, for cosmetic purposes, be allowed to engage in certain ancillary administrative activities involving the *ad hoc* implementation of federal regulations.

Nevertheless, the promised enactment of a new statute on USSR citizenship (since realized) is a laudable project. The 1938 law was a bare skeleton which left a great many questions unanswered and subsequent procedures developed in rather random fashion: after forty years of improvisation, the situation in this area was chaotic, and a thorough overhaul was badly overdue.

The next three articles (34–36) address themselves to the broad theme of equality to which the 1977 Constitution devotes an inordinate amount of space. Equality is also mentioned in the title of Chapter 6 and, furthermore, the clauses in which it is discussed precede the substantive provisions on basic rights and freedoms, implying a higher priority and a general normative potency.

Article 34 distinguishes two basic aspects of equality: equality "before the law" (para. 1) and equality "in all fields of economic, political, social, and cultural life" (para. 2). The former brand can be called legal equality—equal application of the general/abstract rules of law to all citizens, whereas the latter variety can be labeled "substantive equality", or "factual equality", or equality of opportunity. A comparison of how the business of equality is treated in the 1936 Constitution with how it fares in the 1977 charter prompts several observations:

1) In the earlier document, the concept of equality enjoyed a much lower status—ending up relegated to the middle of Chapter 10, "Fundamental Rights and Duties", after economic and cultural rights.[130]

2) The 1936 charter referred solely to the substantive version of equality.

3) The previous statute had spoken only of the equality of men and women (Art. 122) and of the equality of citizens "regardless of their nationality or race", whereas the current edition covers a lot more territory in subscribing to equality

> "regardless of origin, social and property status, race or nationality, sex, education, language, attitude toward religion, type and character of occupation, place of residence, and other circumstances."

Although the above bill of particulars appears in paragraph 1 which relates to legal equality, its terms should, by logical extension, apply as well to the next paragraph which mandates factual equality.

The attitude of the 1977 Constitution in this matter may be explained on grounds of the solidaristic impulse in the official ideology to which we owe the insistent claims that Soviet society is homogenous, without major conflicts/frictions, and that the Soviet state is "the all-people's state". The reigning dogma of the 1930s preached the lessons of the "ever-sharpening class struggle" and so could not accept, say, the notion of equality "regardless of origin". Still now, though, the verbal commitment to the principle of equality clashes dramatically with massive discriminatory practices and, indeed, even sundry constitutional postulates. The Constitution itself, for instance, explicitly distinguishes between citizens who are Party members—and therefore belong to the elite or "the vanguard" (Preamble; Art. 6)—and citizens who are not Party members. The former not only monopolize political power but have preferential access to employment opportunities (*nomenklatura*) and accordingly enjoy special benefits with respect to wages, housing, availability of scarce consumer goods, health service, education, and so forth. The Soviet record of systematic discrimination against national minorities and religious believers is amply documented. Contrary to the pompous pronouncements of Article 35 of the Constitution, Soviet women bear the stigma of a double work load, inferior professional status (assignment to low-paying jobs), and extremely limited visibility in the upper echelons of the ruling apparatus despite their majority share in the country's population in general and its labor force in particular (53%).

The regime may be waking up to the "extra burden" problem. An amendment in the draft text of the charter led to the addition of two sentences expressing the authorities' determination to safeguard women's rights by, *inter alia*, "the creation of conditions enabling women to combine labor and motherhood" and "the gradual reduction of working time for women with small children". The desire to keep women in the labor pool, an important consideration in view of the USSR's nagging manpower shortage, balanced by growing awareness of the hardships occasioned by this dual role and their negative impact on family life seems to have convinced the hierarchy of the wisdom of adopting a compromise solution offering a wider choice of part-time employment. Preliminary steps have already been taken in this direction and, if the Constitution is any evidence of policy intentions, more such measures should be forthcoming.

All that talk about equality does manage to suggest, however, that the concept of equality exerts a strong attraction on the Soviet mind. The motif undeniably has a great deal of popular appeal everywhere, and the Soviet elite may be seeking to tap this vast reservoir of sympathy by officially advertising itself as a devout champion of the principle. Ideological imperatives also favor that approach, and the theme may have so deeply entered the consciousness of the Soviet people that the ruling classes must cater to the sentiment out of sheer tactical calculations.

Another interesting point concerns the Constitution's listing of the grounds which do not justify detraction from observance of the rule of equality. The rather elaborate roster hints, perhaps unwittingly, at a communal structure sufficiently differentiated for the designated phenomena to acquire significance as perceived indices of social disparity. To say, for example, as the charter does, that property status cannot be a valid reason for discrimination is to imply that distinctions in this sector are noticeable enough to spur invidious comparisons and demands for affirmative action to redress the disequilibrium. The regime, of course, is rabidly opposed to the whole idea of "economic leveling" and tries to escape the dilemma by maintaining that these dissymmetries are both temporary and harmless in that they no longer possess a class rationale. Whether such subterfuges can allay what seems to be a widespread craving for "fair" distribution of the national wealth is a difficult question to answer.

In guaranteeing the equality of citizens of the USSR of different races and nationalities, the charter mentions ensuring the possibility of using one's native language and the languages of other peoples of the USSR, an explosive issue in the Soviet Union as recent events in the Caucasus have demonstrated. A special clause (Art. 37) expressly confirms the gist of past practice in explaining that foreign citizens and stateless persons in the USSR are entitled to the rights and freedoms provided for by law, including the right to apply to a court and other state organs for the protection of the personal, property, family, and other rights which belong to them. The formula apparently puts the constitutional seal of approval on granting aliens the so-called "national regime"—hitherto strictly a policy fixture with a patchy record reflecting the fluctuations in the local political weather. The reference to the right of asylum (Art. 38) is a carry-over from the 1936 charter (Art. 129): the wording is more elaborate, but the sense is the same.

The Basic Rights, Freedoms, and Obligations of Citizens of the USSR

Chapter 7 is one of the longest, if not the longest, in the whole Constitution. It includes thirty-one articles (Arts. 39–69), that is, twice as many as the 1936 Constitution.[131] The dramatic enlargement of the chapter signals that the rhetoric of human rights has become an almost universal phenomenon, and that the majority of the Communist states have joined this international campaign.[132]

The section opens (Art. 39) with a sweeping reaffirmation of the array of rights vested in every citizen of the USSR and a pledge further to expand their scope in step with the "democratic dynamics" of steady progress forward to Communism. The entire paragraph is pure political oratory. The second paragraph, however, practically nullifies all that follows by stipulating that "in exercising their rights and freedoms, citizens may not injure the interests of society and the state or the rights of other citizens". On this score, the present statute is much more candid than its 1936 predecessor; after reading this passage, no illusions are left as to the quintessentially conditional nature of all the rights and freedoms so prominently displayed in the latest Constitution, especially when the final authority to decide what amounts to injury to the interests of society and the state, or the rights of other citizens, is the official monopoly of the governing apparatus.

Note, too, that in enumerating the rights and freedoms available to Soviet citizens, the charter observes an old Soviet/socialist tradition by putting social and economic rights ahead of political rights and freedoms. In similar vein,[133] all the provisions dealing with social, economic, and cultural rights are split into two parts: the first, as a rule, enunciates a particular right; the second adds the "guarantees" for its implementation. These "guarantees" either refer to the "material foundations" of the announced right or establish more specific, narrowly defined rights which develop/explain the general principle featured in the first portion of the article.[134] By contrast, only some of the provisions dealing with political rights/freedoms have a similar two-level structure, a piece of circumstantial corroboration (if, indeed, more such proof were needed) of their wholly ephemeral character.

The right to work logically occupies the principal position, once more hitched to the norm of "remuneration in accordance with the quantity and quality of the work". Worthy of attention is the fact that the very concept of the right to work incorporates "the right to choose a profession, occupation, and work" in accordance with the "vocation, ability, professional training, and education, taking into account the needs of society" (Art. 40, para. 1). This formulation is fairly expressive, looked at through the prism of Soviet experience:

1) True, Article 40 does not represent any major novelty inasmuch as the freedom of labor contract has been a general rule of Soviet law and labor practice during the last twenty years or so. Moreover, one must bear in mind that the "needs of society" clause still gives the regime ample mandate to control the situation here in order to push its own priorities and, in effect, to set preferential goals in the name of social exigency that would override the contrary desires of individuals in this area.

2) On the other hand, the rule of free labor contract, the freedom to choose one's job, as well as the freedom to quit, have won constitutional endorsement for the first time.[135] This elevation in rank has taken place in a country with a strong tradition of *forced labor*, not only as examplified by the Stalinist record[136] but also by the more recent anti-parasite measures and the virtual enslavement of the collective farm population.[137] The current charter certainly lends sustenance to those forces in the Soviet establishment that oppose forced-labor practices. In this sense, the stylistic accommodation equally figures as an ostensible act of compliance with the international obligations of the USSR, for the wholesale violation of which the Soviet government has so often been castigated in the international forum.[138] For their part, Soviet leaders like to attribute the change to the USSR's success in creating "an economy which makes not only a steadily growing, but also a more varied demand for labor power, for specialists" and backing it up by a "highly developed system of general and specialized education, of professional training and improvement of skills".[139]

Article 40, it should be mentioned, speaks of the right to work not just from the point of view of guaranteed employment with appropriate remuneration, but adds that this compensation must not be "lower than the minimum rate established by the state". Soviet sources consider the latter qualification a significant difference from the treatment afforded the right to work in the 1936 statute in that, "thereby, the socialist all-people's state guarantees a definite level of labor earnings by workers and employees, simultaneously expanding the social consumption funds distributed gratis".[140] Again, although a formal commitment to maintain a certain national wage-scale is *per se* laudable, the Soviet Union continues in this respect to lag substantially behind the rest of the technologically advanced members of the world community, and the conclusion on whether the pledge is apt to remain "empty talk" or means that a serious effort is going to be made to close the gap depends to a great extent on one's assessment of the Soviet Union's past performance and future prospects. A solid pinch of scepticism is thus by no means unwarranted.

The right to rest "is ensured" by observance of a "work week not exceeding 41 hours". The wording marks a tentative improvement over the language of the draft text which flatly posited a 41-hour week, so that the door is now open to a general cutback at some later date. Meanwhile, the right to non-working week-ends has been constitutionally recognized (Art. 41, para. 2). Characteristically enough, the constitutional safeguards of the right to rest do not apply to collective farmers who once more find themselves relegated to the position of second-class citizens (Art. 41, para. 3).

The constitutional rights "to health care" (Art. 42), "to housing" (Art. 44), "to use the achievements of culture" (Art. 46), as well as the guarantee of "freedom of scientific, technical, and artistic creation", did not appear in the 1936 Constitution. These increments call for a few brief comments. In the realm of housing, the real state of affairs borders on the parlous in terms of availability of apartments, waiting periods, space allocated, quality of construction, and facilities. The grim conditions have had a profound impact on the local demographic situation which, unless present trends are reversed, is pregnant with disastrous consequences. No doubt, Soviet authorities have made some effort to ameliorate the picture since, after all, national survival is at stake, but many outside observers are prone to wonder if it may not already be a case of too little and too late. The last sentence of Article 44 couples the right to housing with the duty "to treat housing carefully", an emanation of the general duty to protect socialist property (Art. 61) and also a testimonial to the high value assigned to a commodity still in desperately short supply.[141]

The right to use the achievements of culture extends, *inter alia*, to "cultural exchanges with foreign states" (Art. 46, para. 2). The gesture was probably inspired by the desire to pay lip service to the Helsinki agreement and so should be viewed in a spirit of cautious pessimism as to its likely practical effects. Article 47, guaranteeing freedom of artistic creativity, smacks of mockery in a country which deliberately killed, not so long ago, the cream of its writers, poets, artists, film-makers, theatrical directors, actors, etc., and which continues the cruel and dull persecution of its brightest minds. The recent histories of Pasternak, Brodskii, Solzhenitsyn, Rostropovich, Daniel, Siniavskii, Galich, and many others, are shining examples of how the right to creative freedom has been understood and implemented by the Soviet apparatus.

In some instances, the concept itself is not new, but the statutory basis of a right has been so thoroughly revamped that the right has thereby acquired a significantly enlarged scope and substance and, except in designation, retains little in common with its older namesake. For example, Soviet commentators point out that the 1936 charter contained a general reference to the right to education, whereas the 1977 version mentions compulsory secondary education, the extensive development of a network of higher institutions of learning, benefits to students.[142] The logistical foundations of the right to material security in old age and in the event of loss of the family breadwinner have similarly undergone a complete overhaul, and its profile has been much altered as a result of this restructuring. According to Soviet sources, a single comprehensive pension system currently operates in the USSR. The 1956 Law on State Pensions expanded considerably the radius of persons eligible to receive pensions, uniform rules were introduced regarding the payment of pensions to workers and employees, and the size of the pensions was appreciably increased. Following the enactment in 1964 of the Law on Pensions and Allowances to Kolkhoz Members, the pension system became universal. Subsequently, kolkhoz members were put on the same footing as workers and employees with respect to age for payment of old-age pensions and the manner of their computation. In 1972–1977, a series of supplementary measures were adopted for the improvement of pension services to all categories of the population.[143] Hence, we are told, the right featured in the latest Constitution in fact embraces a great deal more than its predecessor, semantic affinities notwithstanding.

Two additions to the roster of political rights (Arts. 48–52) should be noted: the right to political participation (Art. 48), and the right to submit proposals to state organs and to criticize "shortcomings in their work" (Art. 49). The former echoes a theme familiar to the Marxist and Soviet political canon which, at one level of discourse, equates "socialist democracy" with "mass involvement" in civic affairs. Citing statistics showing how many thousands of ordinary citizens had regular or *ad hoc* contact with some governmental office or community organization is a favorite Soviet pastime, and these figures purport to prove the extent to which the official apparatus functions in an ambience of responsiveness to popular wishes and, of course, also the degree of spontaneous layman interest in how the life of the nation is managed. The myth of Soviet democracy requires the perpetuation and, indeed, further amplification of the arithmetical surrogate for the substantive lack of techniques of popular control over the political decision-making process: input is gauged not by the ability to influence the ruling elite's policy choices, but by the quota of individuals drawn into formal discussions of items billed on the official agenda or the mechanics of execution of prescribed tasks.

The right to submit proposals to state organs and social organizations concerning the improvement of their activity and to criticize shortcomings in their work seems, at first blush, to strengthen considerably the position of the citizen *vis-à-vis* the "establishment". In a context where a candid exchange of opinions is an acceptable or even desirable method of forging a consensus, such procedures appear quite natural and the propriety of questioning the performance of various governmental and civic bodies is taken for granted. On the Soviet scene, however, none of these assumptions apply which gives the whole concept a very different meaning in that what is understood by the words "improvement" or "shortcomings" is seldom open to debate and only when the regime has signaled in advance what recommendations for "improvement" meet with its approval or what suggestions would, in its estimate, qualify as "constructive criticism of genuine shortcomings" is the stage set for the airing of negative views. Otherwise, the clear danger exists that publicly expressed displeasure over how a unit of the Soviet system works would lead to swift reprisal on grounds of being motivated not by the sincere urge to better the situation but a perverse intent instead "to cause trouble". One must keep in mind, too, that the regime claims full authority to impute the proper animus on these occasions and thus to determine whether the individual exercised a right duly sanctioned by the Constitution or engaged in socially abusive behavior for which specific punishment is provided: how the individual concerned perceives his conduct turns out to be largely irrelevant to what happens to him next, for, if the act of criticism which he committed is *a priori* deemed not to have been justified, then his attitude in perpetrating the offense is presumed to entail a conscious violation of the applicable rule.

The third group of rights guaranteed by the Constitution may be called "personal liberties" (Arts. 54–58). The most important of them—the inviolability of the person—has been carried over practically verbatim from the 1936 charter.[144] Characteristically, the 1977 Constitution made no modifications in the procurator's power to detain a suspect pending investigation. In this respect, Soviet law is in flagrant contravention of the international legislation on human rights.[145] No substantive changes have been introduced in the area of inviolability of the home and the secrecy of correspondence.[146]

A new right to judicial protection has been added, namely, protection "against attacks on . . . honor and dignity, . . . lives and health, and . . . personal freedom and property" (Art. 57, para. 2). The provision probably has no extra normative significance and, most likely, just codifies constitutionally the rights of the victim of unlawful acts (mainly criminal offenses) already spelled out in criminal and civil legislation.

Another novel feature, remedial in nature, is the right to bring complaints against actions by state/social agencies and their officers (Art. 58, para. 1). One's attention is drawn in particular to the apparent right to judicial protection against unlawful official actions "which infringe upon the rights of citizens" (Art. 58, para. 2). This provision is susceptible of at least two different interpretations:

1) Article 58, para. 2, merely confirms the *status quo*, since it states that such court actions may be brought "in the manner established by law". Given the fact that a number of Soviet laws currently provide for judicial review of administrative acts, the charter simply rubber-stamps routine precedent; or,

2) Article 58, para. 2, is programmatic in nature and envisages a new approach, pursuant to which:

a) violations of the constitutional rights/freedoms by official actions or inactions are to be redressed by the courts; and,

b) the legal procedure for the implementation of the rule shall be determined by ordinary legislation.

According to a further variation on the latter theme, judicial protection would not be limited to cases of infractions of constitutional rights, but would extend to legal rights of any kind.[147]

Instructions have been issued to draft a statute on the procedure for bringing complaints into court against actions of official persons commited in violation of the law, in excess of authority, or infringing on the rights of citizens, with a deadline of December 1980.[148] How much ground the projected measure will cover remains uncertain. The Soviet legal community is deeply divided on this issue. Many of its spokesmen strongly favor the expansion of judicial protection of the rights of the individual in the sphere of state administration. The step, they concede, will increase the volume of court work, which will require raising the number of people's judges and improving their qualifications. Nevertheless, this wing advocates extending the list of cases stemming from administrative law relations that would fall under the jurisdiction of the courts. All the rights and freedoms inscribed in the 1977 Constitution, they insist, must be judicially safeguarded. The champions of this view specifically urge that the courts be entrusted with hearing cases involving the loss of driving privileges and citizens' complaints against decisions of state organs and social organizations regarding the construction of installations and the performance of any other actions in the course of which harm will be done to the natural environment or the surrounding atmosphere will be polluted.[149]

Three shades of opinion may thus be distinguished within the Soviet legal profession: those who want to give the courts on an *ad hoc* basis more authority to oversee the activities of the official apparatus; those who prefer to give the courts general authority to exercise such supervisory power, subject only to a few express exemptions due to special considerations; those who straddle the fence and, while acknowledging that the new charter calls for some adjustments in this domain, want to proceed with the changes on a piecemeal basis taking into account practical needs and learning gradually from accrued experience.[150]

Finally, another part of the same provision (Art. 58, para. 3) endorses the right to compensation for torts committed by state/social organizations as well as their officers. Legislation on the subject is scheduled for completion by December 1980.[151] Again, there is material disagreement on what is intended here. Although the clause is new with reference to the 1936 Constitution, its inclusion in the latest charter may symbolize nothing more than a desire to accentuate existing Soviet practice in this domain.[152] Conversely, at least one well informed Soviet legal writer has taken the position that major revisions are at stake. The situation with regard to compensation owed to citizens for injuries caused by wrongful acts of official persons in the field of administrative management is, he claims, relatively clear: the corresponding state organs are liable on general grounds, unless the contrary is specifically provided by law.

The picture is more complicated insofar as responsibility for injury caused to citizens by wrongful service-connected acts of officials of organs of inquiry, preliminary investigation, procuracy, and judiciary is concerned. Indeed, the special law which is designed to govern such responsibility, and to which the norms of civil legislation refer, has as yet not been promulgated. Our author seems convinced that the current Constitution means to sanction civil responsibility in these cases of both kinds of institutions—administrative managerial bodies as well as law-enforcement agencies. Noting that Article 89 of the Fundamentals of Civil Legislation of the USSR and the Union Republics confirms that the organs of inquiry, preliminary investigation, procuracy, and judiciary can be held liable in instances and within limits specially established by law, he contends that without the adoption of a suitable law, the norm on responsibility must remain a dead letter. Confident in the persuasive power of Brezhnev's statement that "we created the Constitution not for decoration" and that "it must be implemented and will be implemented in all its parts",[153] he concludes that the statute in question must be enacted, presumably in the enlarged format to which he subscribes.[154]

Communist constitutions have traditionally coupled the exercise of constitutional rights by citizens with the performance by them of constitutional duties. The 1977 Soviet charter runs true to pattern in proclaiming that "the exercise of rights and freedoms is inseparable from the performance by the citizen of his duties". The peremptory tone of the pronouncement has spawned speculation that a new element has been introduced into Soviet constitutional practice whereby a citizen could forfeit his rights on grounds that he had failed to discharge his duties, *i.e.* that the enjoyment of rights automatically hinges on the fulfillment of duties. This view seems to be based on a misapprehension. No doubt Soviet party cadres and even procurators will, on occasion, virulently denounce the sort of individual who "derives benefits from membership in the socialist community without contributing his fair share to the enrichment of the common heritage". This kind of sermonizing is heard quite often and, indeed, can at times have a legal impact in that an accused flayed in those terms may meet with a harsher punishment for an imputed offense than in a stock situation where the extra weight of moral opprobrium has not been heaped upon his shoulders. However, if we are talking about a regular trial, then the difference amounts to injecting an aggravating factor by citing the defendant's dereliction of duty and definitely not to effectuating the criminalization by this artifice alone of conduct not otherwise punishable by law.

In perusing Soviet publications, one gains the impression that the treatment of this whole business of the relationship between rights and duties varies depending on whether the subject is being discussed on the pages of popular literature or technical journals. The mass media emphasize the unity of rights and duties almost *à outrance* and make it sound as if one cannot exist without the other.[155] By contrast, the available samples of legal analysis draw a careful distinction between the two aspects of the problem. The citizen, so goes the explanation, is unconditionally entitled to the ensemble of his constitutional rights and the state is obliged to guarantee him the opportunity to exercise these rights in full. Constitutional duties, on the other hand, only act as moral-ideological guidelines, unless, of course, subsidiary legislation imposes concrete sanctions for the breach of such duties, which completely changes the original equation. However, the point is stressed, nonfulfillment of a constitutional duty that is not backed by the sort of legislation just mentioned cannot by itself affect adversely the constitutional rights of the individual involved. What may very well happen is that the Constitution's bid to forge a "spiritual" link between rights and duties could lend impetus to the enactment of statutory measures fixing penalties for the breach of all or some of the duties enumerated in the charter, thus fundamentally altering the current picture.[156] Until that is done, though, there is no valid cause for alarm, except to add that the regime's choice of formula is rather disturbing for it has succeeded in creating a general climate which in essence is highly propitious to the passage of the type of punitive legislation that could make the rights-duties contingency an operational reality.

The most universal duty of all, and the one most prominently displayed, is that of loyalty to the Constitution and to Soviet law, as well as the duty to abide by "the rules of socialist community life" and "to bear with dignity the high calling of citizen of the USSR" (Art. 59, para. 2). The provision suggests that the foremost virtue of the model Soviet citizen is legalism, *i.e.* obedience to the law. The proposition fits the legality principle which now officially features among the key political indicia of the Soviet system (Art. 4).

Characteristically, the duty to work includes the freedom of choice of the field of labor. Part and parcel of the duty to work is "observance of labor discipline"—obviously a response to one of the most acute socio-economic problems in the USSR. The last sentence of Article 60 which declares that "avoiding socially useful work is incompatible with the principles of a socialist society" strikes a clearly "anti-parasite" note.

The next main substantive constitutional duty relates to socialist property, which the Soviet citizen is enjoined to "safeguard and strengthen" (Art. 61). The Constitution pulls no punches where crimes against socialist property are concerned—these crimes receive even more extensive treatment in the charter than treason.[157] The 1977 statute skips the inflated rhetoric of its 1936 predecessor which pronounced socialist property "sacred and inviolable" and branded those who committed offenses against socialist property "enemies of the people."[158] Instead, the Constitution simply recognizes that "persons infringing upon socialist property are punished according to the law"—in other words, offers a mere solemn reaffirmation of what is already the case (Art. 61, para. 2). More interesting is the companion clause that imposes upon the citizen the duty "to fight theft and waste of state and social property". Does this signify that the Constitution prescribes an affirmative legal duty? Is failure to discharge the duty punishable? A positive answer would mean sweeping criminalization of omissions in preventing crimes against socialist property. Such an interpretation does not sound plausible. A more reasonable view is that the charter articulates solely a moral and political, and not a legal, duty and, hence, does not mandate enforcement procedure through the medium of criminal law. The outspokenness of the Constitution on the subject of crimes against socialist property once more indicates that Soviet authorities themselves perceive the situation here as well-nigh critical and, with that in mind, rank the item near the top of their list of priorities.

Concluding Remarks

In seeking to pass judgment on the "policy" features of the new Soviet Constitution analyzed on the preceding pages, the claims that the document's authors have voiced on its behalf may fairly be taken into account. To the extent, for example, that the fathers of the 1977 charter have seen fit to tout it as an effective program for the final building of a Communist society in the USSR, a reader ought to be allowed to weigh its contents in the light of what sort of a future the prospectus holds in store for mankind. The glorious vision thus projected, we are sorry to say, looks rather drab when examined at close quarters.

However, proceeding on a more prosaic level and dealing with the latest statute in more routine and less extravagant terms, a milder verdict might be rendered and the current charter may even be discovered to possess a few virtues. Certainly, one of the major novel qualities attributed to the present generation of socialist constitutions is their normative function, whereas their predecessors were essentially cast in the role of political and ideological manifestoes devoid of normative significance.[159] The normative potency of the 1977 USSR Constitution is evidenced by the text itself,[160] by authoritative political statements,[161] and by the subsequent legislative record.[162]

A year has elapsed since the Constitution was promulgated and by now it is quite clear that the new charter was, *inter alia*, intended to establish a comprehensive framework for an occasion of thorough legislative house-cleaning. The task was put on the agenda by the 24th and 25th Party Congresses.[163] Economic legislation in particular is in a state of utter chaos, and the leadership has in fact repeatedly felt obliged to express its deep concern about the situation here.[164] On the other hand, the past two decades witnessed extensive revisions and codifications of the principal branches of the law and, consequently, the necessary groundwork has been laid for a further bid at systematic reorganization and reformulation of the entire legal script.

A basic program for legislative stock-taking at the federal level has been set forth in the Decree of the Presidium of the USSR Supreme Soviet of 12 December 1977.[165] The blueprint identifies four types of operations which are designed to bring the ensemble of the legislation into conformity with the Constitution. First, plans have been drawn up to draft some twenty-two new laws or "legislative acts" (*zakony/zakonodatel'nye akty*) during the period 1978–1980.[166] A precise timetable for the submission of each draft and the agencies responsible for the job have been spelled out.[167] Three prospective legislative acts on crucial aspects of the national economy[168] figure in a somewhat ambiguous position: the question of studying "the necessity of their drafting" has been entrusted to the Council of Ministers, to be taken care of in the course of 1978–1981.[169] Incidentally, some of the laws named in the Decree of 12 December 1977, have already been passed.[170]

Second, existing laws/legislative acts as well as government regulations are expected to be revised/amended to get them to comply with the Constitution.[171] Third, the terminology of the legislative acts, otherwise not in need of substantive emendation, is slated to be synchronized with the language of the Constitution.[172] Lastly, a formal roster of legislative acts that have lost effect by reason of their incompatibility with the Constitution is scheduled to be issued.[173]

The sweeping check of the accumulated inventory mandated by the Constitution is a logical precursor to the next step, to wit, a formal, official, general restatement of the corpus of laws in the shape of a *Svod zakonov SSSR*. Indeed, such a digest is due for publication beginning in 1981, that is, once the main revisions are expected to be completed.[174] The officially approved scheme of the *Svod zakonov SSSR* is visibly influenced by the overall structure and style of the Constitution,[175] and, in fact, Soviet commentators openly picture the charter as the nucleus of the projected *Svod*.[176] In short, consistent with the regime's intent, the 1977 Constitution has promptly been put to practical use as an instrument for reordering, clarifying, and straightening out the Soviet legislative system.

In this sense, the whole process, including its ultimate implementation in the *Svod zakonov SSSR*, should succeed in bringing more lucidity, stability, and predictability into Soviet legal practice. Measured by that standard, the "normative function" of the Constitution has already left a distinct mark on Soviet legal dynamics and additional progress along these lines can safely be anticipated.

Much more doubtful is the matter of a second "normative aspect" of the Constitution, to which at least one Soviet spokesman has laid claim, namely, its potential for "direct application" by law enforcement agencies. Even "direct application" in the guise of pronouncing legislative acts void or unenforceable on grounds of their incompatibility with the Constitution sounds unlikely under the conditions prevailing on the Soviet scene. Yet, elliptical hints can be found in a recently published article suggesting that, with the adoption of the 1977 charter, earlier legislation containing norms that contradict concrete constitutional prescriptions is *ipso jure* unenforceable and so must not be given effect by the organs entrusted with its application—a designation that fits the courts as well.[177] Is the author circumspectly pushing his own pet theory or "leaking" a bit of information about a debate on this issue now going on backstage? No sure answer is forthcoming at this juncture and scepticism counsels prudence, but the "straw in the wind", whatever its real meaning, does fuel interesting speculation on how strong a trend may be afoot in the Soviet Union to vest the courts with wider authority, envisaging, *inter alia*, a modest increment of powers smacking of judicial review.

"Direct application" in the affirmative version of the term, that is, freedom to cite the Constitution to override a divergent statutory directive, seems simply impossible in the absence of a suitable institutional/remedial infrastructure. This, of course, does not preclude experimentation with two lesser types of related operations. For instance, Soviet courts could, with appropriate encouragement, venture to invoke more often the Constitution's pronouncements as a guide for statutory construction whenever the need might arise to interpret the legislative message. The judiciary would thus be invited to read ordinary legislation in the light of constitutional postulates in situations requiring further elaboration of the legislative record for purposes of properly deciding specific cases. Or, the whole business might well boil down to a deliberate campaign to advertise the virtues of the Constitution by guaranteeing it greater publicity.

As pointed out in Soviet literature, the courts today tend to rely almost exclusively on statutory materials to footnote their reasoning. Instead, it is argued, the courts should, where feasible, go back to the constitutional source itself and explicitly give it credit for supplying the relevant solution. Without denying the cosmetic and psychological contribution of the proposed stratagem toward boosting the Constitution's image in the popular mind and "accenting the role of judicial practice as one of the forms of insuring the realization of constitutional guarantees",[178] the recommended procedure would still produce no perceptible juridical effect. Symbolism aside, the substantive position would remain the same if the exalted Constitution were invoked in lieu of the humble statutory measure which happened to spell out the corresponding constitutional dicta. On the other hand, in a political system like the Soviet one, symbolic gestures play an important role and our writer may not be all that naive: perhaps the initial requirement is to acquire the mental habit of attributing to the constitutional document legal validity, and this token recognition might at some later stage generate genuine impetus to treat the charter in precisely that spirit—a different conceptualization spawning fresh expectations. This "burst of optimism" coming at the close of a sustained barrage of criticism might strike the reader as incongruous, but let us take note of the fact that impressive changes in the Soviet environment have occurred since the death of Stalin and that the current leadership is fighting hard to maintain a precarious equilibrium on a slippery slope midway between authoritarian control and managed (or induced) consensus. Given this delicate balance, even minor shifts may set off significant reverberations and the bit of ephemera of the sort just discussed is no exception in that regard.

NOTES

1. The Constitution, preamble, Art. 6 [hereafter, "Article" will refer to articles of the 1977 Constitution]. The Constitution seems to use the two terms interchangeably.

2. Compare G. Brunner, "The Functions of Communist Constitutions: An Analysis of Recent Constitutional Developments", 3 *Rev. Soc. Law* 1977, p. 121, 148.

3. For a general overview, see Brunner, note 2; L. Brezhnev explicitly acknowledged the indebtedness of the Soviet draftsmen to other socialist constitutions. Brezhnev, "O proekte Konstitutsii Soiuza Sovetskikh Sotsialisticheskikh Respublik", *Pravda*, 5 June 1977; English translation on pp. 188–189 of this volume.

4. L.I. Brezhnev, *O proekte Konstitutsii* (*Osnovnogo Zakona*) *Soiuza Sovetskikh Sotsialisticheskikh Respublik i itogakh ego vsenarodnogo obsuzhdeniia*, (Moskva, 1977), pp. 5, 9, pp. 203, 207 of this volume; L. Brezhnev, "A Historic Stage on the Road to Communism", *International Affairs* 1978 No. 1, p. 8.

5. "Konstitutsiia SSSR 1977g.—vazhnaia vekha v razvitii nauki o sotsialisticheskom gosudarstve", *SGiP* 1977 No. 12, p. 7.

6. *Cf. Gosudarstvo i demokratiia v period postroeniia razvitogo sotsializma*, (Moscow, 1974), p. 79.

7. G. Kh. Shakhnazarov, "O nekotorykh tendentsiiakh razvitiia politicheskoi sistemy sotsializma", *SGiP* 1978 No. 1, p. 5.

8. Brezhnev, *O proekte*, note 4, p. 6, p. 204 of this volume.

9. "Konstitutsiia SSSR 1977g.", note 5, p. 8.

10. N. Farberov, "Vazhnoe sobytie v politicheskoi istorii strany", *Sov. Iust.* 1978 No. 5, p. 6.

11. Compare preamble, para. 6; Arts. 9, 19–27. B.N. Topornin, "Podstawowe cechy Konstytucji ZSRR z 7 października 1977 r." (Fundamental Features of the USSR Constitution of 7 October 1977), *Państwo i Prawo* 1977 No. 11, p. 6–8; Z. Jarosz, "Ogólne założenia nowej Konstytucji ZSSR" (General Assumptions of the New USSR Constitution), *Państwo i Prawo* 1977 No. 10, pp. 4–5.

12. K. Dzialocha, "Konstytucja PRL po nowelizacji z 10 II 1976. Uwagi o zmianie koncepcji konstytucji" (Constitution of the Polish People's Republic After Amendment of 10 February 1976. Remarks on the Change of the Concept of the Constitution), *Państwo i Prawo* 1977 No. 2, p. 8.

13. Brunner, note 2, p. 127; Dzialocha, note 12, p. 8.

14. See N. Farberov, note 10, p. 7. Also, G. Ginsburgs, "A Khrushchev Constitution for the Soviet Union: Projects and Prospects", *Osteuropa-Recht* 1962 No. 2, pp. 197–198.

15. G.Kh. Shakhnazarov, note 7, pp. 5–6. Also, "Konstitutsiia SSSR 1977g.", note 5, p. 7.

16. N. Farberov, note 10, p. 7.

17. Brezhnev, *O proekte*, note 4, p. 20, p. 211 of this volume; likewise, Brezhnev, "A Historic Stage", *loc. cit.*, pp. 3–4.

18. Preamble, paras. 1 and 4; Art. 6.

19. Preamble, para. 9 ("scientific Communism"); Art. 6 ("doctrine of Marxism-Leninism").

20. The preamble suggests only that in classless Communist society "communist self-government will be developed", a rather cautious statement, short of "withering away of the state" prophecies. Preamble, para. 12, first sentence. See also some references to "communist ideals", in Arts. 19–23.

21. Preamble, para. 1.

22. *Id.*, para. 3.

23. *Id.*, para. 4, last sentence.

24. *Id.*, para. 11.

25. V. Chalidze, "Human Rights in the New Soviet Constitution", *A Chronicle of Human Rights in the USSR* 1977 No. 28, p. 66, footnote.

26. "Konstitutsiia SSSR—vazhnaia vekha v zhizni sovetskoi strany, osnovopolagaiushchii dokument v deiatelnosti organov iustitsii i sudov", *Sov. Iust.* 1978 No. 5, p. 2.

27. Brezhnev, *O proekte*, note 4, p. 12, p. 209 of this volume.

28. See Editorial, "Konstitutsiia pervogo v mire obshchenarodnogo sotsialisticheskogo gosudarstva", *Vestnik Moskovskogo Universiteta* 1977 No. 6, p. 3; Topornin, note 11, p. 3.

29. Preamble, para. 4; Art. 1.

30. See "The Reactionary Essence of the New Soviet Constitution", *Peking Review* 1977 No. 25, p. 13.

31. Programma KPSS in *XXII S"ezd Kommunisticheskoi Partii Sovetskogo Soiuza. Stenograficheskii otchet* (Moskva, 1962), Vol. III, p. 276; N.S. Khrushchev, "O programme KPSS", *id.*, Vol. II, p. 167.

32. Apparently, current political literature in Communist states claims the following periodization of the process of socialist construction:

1) construction of the foundations of socialism;

2) shaping a developed socialist society; and

3) developed socialism—a period of building of the material-technical base of Communism. At some point during the second period, dictatorship of proletariat is transformed into "all-people's state". Z. Jarosz, note 11, p. 7 f.

33. "Scientific communism" (preamble); "doctrine of Marxism-Leninism" (Art. 6, para. 2).

34. G. Ginsburgs, note 14, p. 205.

35. 1936 Constitution, Arts. 2–3.

36. See G. Ginsburgs, "Referendum", in F.J.M. Feldbrugge, ed., *Encyclopedia of Soviet Law*, (New York, Leyden, 1973), Vol. 2, pp. 579–580.

37. See *Apparat upravleniia sotsialisticheskogo gosudarstva*, (Moskva, 1976), pp. 49–50; K.F. Sheremet, *Sovety deputatov trudiashchikhsia i razvitie sotsialisticheskoi demokratii*, (Moskva, 1976), p. 41.

38. G.Kh. Shakhnazarov, note 7, p. 8.

39. Brezhnev, *O proekte*, note 4, p. 6, p. 204 of this volume.

40. Note, though, that even at the time the draft Constitution was being discussed, *i.e.* before the "workers' collectives" were formally included in the "political system", a common view was that they were nevertheless part of the "general system of Soviet socialist democracy". *Cf.* I.M. Stepanov, "Konstitutsionnye osnovy sovetskoi politicheskoi sistemy", *SGiP* 1977 No. 9, p. 35; I.P. Ilinskii, *Politicheskaia organizatsiia sotsialisticheskogo obshchestva*, (Moskva, 1976).

41. G.Kh. Shakhnazarov, note 7, pp. 8–9.

42. M. Hirszowicz, *Komunistyczny Lewiatan*, (Paris, 1973), pp. 74–75; W. Brus, *Socialist Ownership and Political Systems* (London and Boston, 1975), p. 141.

43. Decree of the Council of Ministers of the USSR and the All-Union Central Council of Trade Unions, 18 June 1973, *SP SSSR* 1973 No. 15 item 80.

44. *Ved. SSSR* 1977 No. 51 item 764.

45. Iu. Lubshev, "Voploshchenie v Konstitutsii SSSR leninskikh idei o pravosudii", *Chelovek i zakon* 1978 No. 4, pp. 15–16.

46. "Novaia Konstitutsiia SSSR", *Pravovedenie* 1977 No. 6, pp. 10–11.

47. *Ibid.*, p. 10.

48. The 1936 Constitution, Art. 5.

49. Iu.K. Tolstoi, "Konstitutsiia SSSR i problemy grazhdanskogo prava", *Pravovedenie* 1977 No. 5, p. 56.

50. Fundamental Principles of Civil Legislation of the USSR and the Union Republics, 8 Dec. 1961, *Ved. SSSR* 1961 No. 50 item 525, Art. 20.

51. B.N. Topornin, note 11, p. 10.

52. L.I. Brezhnev, *O proekte*, note 4, p. 6, p. 204 of this volume.

53. Compare Art. 61, as a closely related provision.

54. From the more recent literature, compare E.A. Vladimirskii, I.P. Pavlova, *Lichnaia sobstvennost' kak ekonomicheskoe otnoshenie*, (Leningrad, 1977), pp. 6–10; W. Brus, note 42, pp. 5–7.

55. Putting the chapter on the political system before the chapter on the economic system may be considered a reflection of the Leninist theory of the primacy of politics over economics.

56. "In the etatist model socialization *boils down* to transfer of the means of production to the ownership of the socialist state", Brus, note 54, p. 33.

57. The relevant passage of the program reads: "It is essential to continue and finally complete the expropriation of the bourgeoisie, which has been begun and in principle already concluded, the transfer of the means of production and working capital to the ownership of the Soviet Republic, *that is, to the common ownership of all working people.*" Programma Rossiiskoi Kommunisticheskoi Partii (Bol'shevikov), in *Kommunisticheskaia Partiia Sovetskogo Soiuza v rezoliutsiiakh i resheniiakh s"ezdov, konferentsii i plenumov TsK*, Tom 2: 1917–1924, (Moskva, 1970), p. 50.

58. "It is true", remarks Professor Brus, commenting on the above-quoted passage from the *RKP(b)* program, "that in some of Lenin's pronouncements reservations can be found against the identification of socialization with confiscation of capitalist property and its transfer to the socialist state, but these ideas were never developed, and a mass of other formulations, identical in content with the passage cited from the programme, supports our thesis". Brus, note 42, p. 34. (The Brus thesis is that the Soviet concept of socialization corresponds to the etatist model.)

59. B.N. Topornin, note 11, p. 3.

60. Compare Art. 10, para. 1 (state ownership equals all people's ownership) and Art. 11, para. 1 ("State ownership, *the common heritage of the entire Soviet people, is the basic form of socialist ownership*".).

61. 1936 Constitution, Art. 6. For a further discussion of the doctrine of the superiority of state ownership over other forms of ownership, see S. Pomorski, "The Relationship between State Ownership and Economic Planning", (unpublished mss), and authorities cited therein.

62. In the somewhat awkward phrasing of Art. 6 of the 1936 Constitution.

63. B.N. Topornin, note 11, p. 4.

64. J.V. Stalin, "Economic Problems of Socialism in the USSR", in J.V. Stalin, *Sochineniia*, (Stanford, 1967), Vol. 3 (XVI), p. 220.

65. The doctrine of convergence (drawing together) and gradual merger of kolkhoz/cooperative ownership into state ownership is mentioned here for the limited purpose of showing full overlap with the etatist model. The "drawing together" doctrine will be discussed in greater detail later in the essay.

66. See, for example, Brus, note 42; D.M. Nuti, "Socialism and Ownership", in L. Kolakowski & S. Hampshire, eds., *The Socialist Idea. A Reappraisal*, (New York, 1974), pp. 184–196; H.M. Wachtel, "Reflections on the Theory of Socialism", (unpublished mss), February 1975.

67. Brus, note 42, p. 27.

68. *Id.*, pp. 33–94.
69. *Id.*, p. 94.
70. Here is another relevant passage from Brus' conclusions:

"It follows then from our whole analysis . . . that the problem of socialization turns on the question of the democratic evolution of the state, of the political system." *Id.* p. 95.

As Kuron and Modzelewski once aptly put it,

"State ownership can conceal different class contents depending on the class character of the state." Y. Kuron, K. Modzelewski, *List otwarty do partii* (An Open Letter to the Party) (Paris, 1966), p. 127.

71. Programma KPSS, in *XXII S"ezd KPSS, stenograficheskii otchet,* Vol. 3, (Moskva, 1962), pp. 285, 290–291; E.A. Vladimirskii, I.P. Pavlova, note 54, p. 133.
72. Programma KPSS, pp. 285, 295; M. Kozyr', "Sotsialisticheskaia sobstvennost' v perekhodnyi k kommunizmu period", *Sov. Iust.* 1961 No. 21, pp. 4–6; E.A. Vladimirskii, I.P. Pavlova, note 54, p. 133; L.V. Nikiforov, "Problemy razvitiia, sblizheniia i sozdaniia uslovii dlia sliianiia dvukh form sotsialisticheskoi sobstvennosti", in V.F. Semenov, ed., *Sotsialisticheskaia sobstvennost'—sovershenstvovanie form obshchestvennoi organizatsii proizvodstva,* (Kazan', 1974), p. 100.
73. Programma KPSS, p. 284; Postanovlenie TsK KPSS, 28 May 1976, "O dal'neishem razvitii spetsializatsii i kontsentratsii sel'skokhoziastvennogo proizvodstva na baze mezhkhoziaistvennoi kooperatsii i agropromyshlennoi integratsii", in *Resheniia Partii i pravitel'stva po khoziaistvennym voprosam,* (Moskva, 1977), Vol. 11, p. 320.
74. Art. 19: "The state promotes the strengthening of the social homogeneity of society, the effacement of class differences and of the essential differences between town and country . . ." Art. 22: "A program of transforming agricultural labor into a variety of industrial labor . . . is consistently implemented in the USSR."
75. J.V. Stalin, "Economic Problems of Socialism in the USSR", in J.V. Stalin, *Sochineniia,* note 64, p. 220.
76. Note 71, pp. 285, 290.
77. L. Brezhnev's report to the 25th Congress of the CPSU, *Pravda,* 26 Feb. 1976; A.N. Kosygin, "Osnovnye napravleniia razvitiia narodnogo khoziaistva na 1976–1980 gody", in *Materialy XXV S"ezda KPSS,* (Moskva, 1976), p. 146; Postanovlenie TsK KPSS, 28 May 1976, note 73, pp. 317–330.
78. See Postanovlenie TsK KPSS, note 73, p. 326.
79. L. Brezhnev, note 77; A.N. Kosygin, note 77; Postanovlenie TsK KPSS, note 73.
80. The close relationship between the processes of "specialization and concentration of production" and the "drawing together" (*sblizhenie*) of the two forms of socialist ownership as well as the accompanying changes in social structure have been emphasized on many occasions. See, in particular, Postanovlenie TsK KPSS, note 73, pp. 320, 323; V.F. Semenov, "Vzaimodeistvie protsessa kontsentratsii proizvodstva i razvitiia sotsialisticheskoi sobstvennosti", in V.F. Semenov, ed., note 72, pp. 55, 60.
81. Postanovlenie Soveta Ministrov SSSR, 14 April 1977, *SP SSSR* 1977 No. 13.
82. See, for instance, "Proekt novoi Konstitutsii SSSR—velikoe torzhestvo agrarnoi politiki KPSS", *SGiP* 1977 No. 8, pp. 11–13.
83. "Soobshchenie tovarishcha L.I. Brezhneva ob itogakh raboty Redaktsionnoi komissii", *Pravda,* 8 Oct. 1977.
84. *E.g.* P.P. Kask, "O poniatii 'netrudovoi dokhod'", *Uchenye zapiski Tartuskogo un-ta, trudy po pravovedeniiu,* vyp. 9, 1969, pp. 148–153.

85. For example, V.P. Gribanov, *Predely osushchestvleniia i zashchity grazhdanskikh prav*, (Moskva, 1972), pp. 118–151.

86. A. Tazetdinov, "Koordinatsiia deiatelnosti po raz"iasneniiu Konstitutsii SSSR i sovetskogo zakonodatel'stva", *Sov. Iust.* 1978 No. 5, p. 5, points out that: "Naturally, the Constitution cannot concretize the forms and methods of assistance to the owners of subsidiary households. This can be accomplished by means of adoption of corresponding laws". None of those who have had occasion to discuss the question have raised the issue of whether the collective farms can indeed be trusted to furnish appropriate assistance to the owners of the subsidiary households since they may, in fact, often be in competition for the same scarce resources. Everyone seems to be taking for granted that once the rule is enunciated, the problem has been solved.

87. Iu.K. Tolstoi, note 49, p. 66.

88. E.A. Vladimirskii, I.P. Pavlova, note 54, p. 136. One's attention is arrested particularly by the dramatically low level of consumption of meat, vegetables, and fruit.

89. *Ibid.*, pp. 136–139.

90. *Ibid.*, p. 139.

91. R.W. Mouly, "Values and Aspirations of Soviet Youth" in P. Cocks, R.V. Daniels, and N.W. Heer, eds., *The Dynamics of Soviet Politics* (Cambridge, Mass., 1976), pp. 221–238.

92. S. Pomorski, "Criminal Law Protection of Socialist Ownership in the USSR", in Barry, Ginsburgs, Maggs, eds., *Soviet Law After Stalin*, as No. 20(I) of *Law in Eastern Europe*, F.J.M. Feldbrugge, ed., (Leyden, 1977).

93. For a further discussion of the "teleological" nature of property rights in the Soviet system, see "The Relationship between State Ownership and Economic Planning", note 61, and authorities cited therein.

94. With the marked exception, as noted below, of the subsidiary households, an anomaly which may in fact explain why widespread criticism seems to have been leveled at the concept during the national discussion of the draft Constitution and why the regime saw fit to respond to these comments *expressis verbis*. See L. Brezhnev, *O proekte*, note 4, pp. 10–11, p. 208 of this volume.

95. E.A. Vladimirskii, I.P. Pavlova, note 54, pp. 109, 118.

96. In 1975, production marketed (*tovarnoe*) by subsidiary households represented 12% of all marketed agricultural production. See, E.A. Vladimirskii, I.P. Pavlova, note 54, p. 117. Reportedly, the marketed share of subsidiary household production has been decreasing in recent years. The trend has been called "undesirable". B.V. Ostrovskii, *Novyi etap v razvitii kolkhoznogo stroia*, (Moskva, 1977), p. 185.

97. 1936 Constitution, Art. 7, para. 2. The subsidiary household was also mentioned in Art. 10 as an object of personal ownership. The difference between the two Constitutions here was noted during the national discussion of the new charter. See G. Shmelev, "On Private Auxiliary Farming", *Pravda*, 10 Sept. 1977, cited after 29 *CDSP* No. 36, p. 22.

98. E.A. Vladimirskii, I.P. Pavlova, note 54, pp. 107, 111. In 1964, subsidiary households run by kolkhozniks covered about two-thirds of the whole area under cultivation, whereas in 1975 this percentage amounted to only half the area. E.A. Vladimirskii, I.P. Pavlova, note 54, p. 111, report that, as of 1977, only one-third of the total number of subsidiary households were held by collective farmers. Shmelev, note 97, reports that "in just 1965–1975 their [collective farmers'] share of total output from such farming dropped from 58% to 52%, and, numerically, they are no longer in the majority".

99. B.V. Ostrovskii, note 96, pp. 180–181; E.A. Vladimirskii, I.P. Pavlova, note 54, p.

119; S.V. Anufrienko, "O kategorii sotsialisticheskoi lichnoi formy sobstvennosti", in V.F. Semenov, ed., note 72, p. 267. See, also, from the Soviet newspapers: "Buy it at the Store or Get it from One's Household Plot", *Izvestiia*, 3 Aug. 1977, cited after 29 *CDSP* No. 31, p. 20; "On Personal Auxiliary Farming," *Pravda*, 14 June 1977, cited after 29 *CDSP* No. 24, p. 23. Nevertheless, the share of the income derived by collective farmers from their subsidiary households is still substantial; it has been estimated at about 30% of their total income. Anufrienko, p. 267; also, Ostrovskii, p. 186.

100. G. Shmelev, note 97.

101. In 1975, subsidiary households accounted for 59% of the total production of potatoes, 34% of vegetables, 31% of meat and milk. E.A. Vladimirskii, I.P. Pavlova, note 54, p. 112.

102. Anufrienko, note 99, p. 266; Ostrovskii, note 99, pp. 178–180; E.A. Vladimirskii, I.P. Pavlova, note 54, p. 110.

103. Shmelev, note 97; E.A. Vladimirskii, I.P. Pavlova, note 54, p. 112; S. Ossofsky, *Soviet Agricultural Policy Toward the Abolition of Collective Farms*, (New York, 1974), p. 157. It is enough to remember that, as late as 1960, almost half of the collective farmers' income was derived from subsidiary households. Anufrienko, note 99, p. 267.

104. Resolution of the Central Committee of the CPSU, 7 Sept. 1953, "On Measures for Further Development of the Agriculture of the USSR", in *Resheniia Partii i pravitel'stva po khoziaistvennym voprosam*, Vol. 4 (Moskva, 1968), pp. 19, 29.

105. Resolution of the Central Committee of the CPSU, 27 Oct. 1964, "On Removal of Unjustified Limitations on the Personal Subsidiary Household of Kolkhozniks, Workers, and Employees", in *Resheniia Partii i pravitel'stva po khoziaistvennym voprosam*, Vol. 5 (Moskva, 1968), p. 517.

106. See L.I. Brezhnev, "Otchetnyi doklad TsK KPSS XXIV S"ezdu Kommunisticheskoi Partii Sovetskogo Soiuza", in *XXIV S"ezd KPSS, stenograficheskii otchet*, (Moskva, 1971), p. 74, and, in particular, his speech at the plenary session of the CC CPSU, 25 Oct. 1976 (in L.I. Brezhnev, *Voprosy upravleniia ekonomikoi razvitogo sotsialisticheskogo obshchestva. Rechi, doklady, vystupleniia*, (Moskva, 1976), p. 587. See also the directives of the 23rd and 24th CPSU Congresses.

107. See the authorities collected in E.A. Vladimirskii, I.P. Pavlova, note 54, p. 107.

108. *Ibid.*, p. 114. Likewise, Shmelev, note 97.

109. "Novaia konstitutsiia SSSR", note 46, p. 11.

110. J.V. Stalin, "Economic Problems of Socialism in the USSR", note 64, p. 236. Art. 11 of the 1936 Constitution: "The economic life of the USSR shall be determined and directed by the state national-economic plan in the interests of increasing social wealth, of steadily raising the material and cultural level of the working people, of fortifying the independence of the USSR, and strengthening its defense capability."

111. M. Kirichenko, "Konstitutsiia razvitogo sotsialisticheskogo obshchestva", *Sots. Zak.* 1977 No. 8, p. 5.

112. O.S. Kolbasov, "Problemy okhrany okruzhaiushchei sredy v novoi Konstitutsii SSSR", *SGiP* 1978 No. 5, pp. 21–29.

113. See, especially, Z.L. Zile, "Soviet struggle for environmental quality: The limits of environmental law under central planning", in Barry, Butler, Ginsburgs, eds., *Contemporary Soviet Law*, (The Hague, 1974), pp. 124–157.

114. V.N. Kudriavtsev, "Konstitutsiia obshchenarodnogo gosudarstva", *SGiP* 1977 No. 11, pp. 12–13.

115. L.I. Brezhnev, *O proekte*, note 4, p. 11 (emphasis in original), p. 208 of this volume.

116. R.C. Tucker, "The Marxian Revolutionary Idea", *Nomos* VIII (1966).

117. A. Tsepin, "Pravo na trud", *Chelovek i zakon* 1978 No. 3, p. 19.

118. V.N. Kudriavtsev, note 114, p. 13.

119. I.P. Blishchenko, A.P. Glebov, *Konstitutsiia SSSR o vneshnei politike Sovetskogo gosudarstva*, (Moskva, 1978), p. 49.

120. *E.g.* N.G. Osmokesku, "Mezhdunarodnoe pravo i konstitutsii sotsialisticheskikh gosudarstv", *VMU* 1978 No. 2, p. 91.

121. I.P. Blishchenko, A.P. Glebov, note 119, p. 32.

122. "Konstitutsiia pervogo v mire obshchenarodnogo sotsialisticheskogo gosudarstva", note 28, p. 10.

123. N.G. Osmokesku, note 120, pp. 91–92.

124. V. Romanov, "Nerushimost' granits—zalog mira i bezopasnosti", *Chelovek i zakon* 1978 No. 3, pp. 34–43.

125. The term "treaty" must here be understood in its generic sense as denoting any formal international agreement, whatever its technical designation. See, for instance, V. Mironov, "Konstitutsionnye printsipy vneshnei politiki SSSR", *SGiP* 1978 No. 3, p. 19.

126. *Ibid.*, p. 16.

127. *Cf.* S. Maksimov, "Delo vsego naroda", *Chelovek i zakon* 1978 No. 2, pp. 12–23.

128. I. Szabó, *The Socialist Concept of Human Rights*, (Budapest, 1966), p. 19; *idem*, "The Theoretical Foundations of Human Rights", in *International Protection of Human Rights*, 7th Nobel Symposium, (New York-London-Sydney-Stockholm, 1968), p. 42; Michalska, *Podstawowe prawa człowieka w prawie wewnętrznym a Pakty Praw Człowieka*, (Warsaw, 1976), p. 118, and literature cited therein.

129. *Ved. SSSR* 1978 No. 49 item 816. On Soviet citizenship law in general, see G. Ginsburgs, *Soviet Citizenship Law* in Z. Szirmai, ed., No. 15 *Law in Eastern Europe*, (Leyden, 1968).

130. 1936 Constitution, Arts. 122–123.

131. The 1936 Constitution, Arts. 118–133.

132. For a further discussion, see Brunner, note 2, pp. 137ff; L. Wiśniewski, "Podstawowe prawa, wolności i obowiązki obywateli PRL na tle nowych konstytucji socjalistycznych", *Państwo i Prawo* 1977 No. 12, pp. 12–25.

133. Compare the 1936 Constitution.

134. See, for example, Art. 41: the right to rest (para. 1) and its "guarantees" (para. 2).

135. Compare the 1936 Constitution, Art. 118.

136. A. Solzhenitsyn, *The Gulag Archipelago*, Vols. 1–3 (1973–1975); Edict of 26 June 1940, *Ved. SSSR* 1940 No. 20.

137. For a useful summary see Burford, "Getting the Bugs Out of Socialist Legality: The Case of Joseph Brodsky and a Decade of Soviet Anti-Parasite Legislation", 22 *Am. J. Comp. L.* 1974, p. 465.

138. Especially by the agencies of the International Labor Organization.

139. L. Brezhnev, "A Historic Stage on the Road to Communism", *International Affairs* 1978 No. 1, p. 9.

140. A. Tsepin, note 117, p. 18.

141. *Cf.* O. Pletneva, E. Sheshenin, "Garantii prava na zhilishche", *Chelovek i zakon* 1978 No. 3, pp. 24–33.

142. *E.g.* V. Kuritsyn, "Velikii Oktiabr' i prava lichnosti", *Chelovek i zakon* 1977 No. 12, p. 13.

143. *Ibid.*, p. 14.

144. Compare the 1936 Constitution, Art. 127; the 1977 Constitution, Art. 54.

145. International Covenant on Civil and Political Rights, Art. 9. For further

analysis, see Pomorski, "Universally Accepted Norms and Their Application in National Legal Systems", (unpublished mss).

146. Compare the 1936 Constitution, Art. 128; the 1977 Constitution, Arts. 55 and 56.

147. The recently published Decree of the Presidium of the USSR Supreme Soviet of 12 Dec. 1977, strongly suggests that the latter of the two interpretations outlined above is correct. *Ved. SSSR* 1977 No. 51 item 764, Supplement, sec. 21, first sentence. The draft law is to be prepared by December 1980 by the Ministries of Justice, Internal Affairs, Finance, the Procuracy, and the USSR Supreme Court "with the participation of other interested agencies".

148. *Ved. SSSR* 1977 No. 51 item 764.

149. A. Lunev, "Sovershenstvovanie garantii prav lichnosti v sfere gosudarstvennogo upravleniia", *Sov. Iust.* 1978 No. 5, p. 21.

150. *Viz.* Iu.K. Tolstoi, note 49, pp. 62–63; S. Bratus, "Pravo na sudebnuiu zashchitu", *LG*, 3 Aug. 1977, p. 2; M.S. Strogovich, "Pravo grazhdanina", *LG*, 20 July 1977, p. 2.

151. *Ved. SSSR* 1977 No. 51 item 764.

152. The wording of the instructions for drafting a statute on the subject sheds no light on the scope of the proposed measure.

153. "Zakliuchitelnoe slovo tovarishcha L.I. Brezhneva na sessii Verkhovnogo Soveta SSSR", *Pravda*, 8 Oct. 1977.

154. Iu.K. Tolstoi, note 49, p. 63.

155. *E.g.* Editorial, "Prava i dolg grazhdanina", *Pravda*, 1 Apr. 1978, p. 1.

156. See V. Maslennikov, "Vzaimosviaz' konstitutsionnykh prav i obiazannostei grazhdan", *Sots. Zak.* 1978 No. 3, pp. 3–7.

157. Compare Arts. 61 and 62, para. 2.

158. The 1936 Constitution, Art. 131.

159. Dzialocha, note 12, p. 12.

160. The Constitution explicitly requires that certain legislative acts be passed, such, for example, as the Law on the Council of Ministers (Art. 136), on the USSR Supreme Court (Art. 153), on State Arbitrazh (Art. 163), on the USSR Procuracy (Art. 168).

161. *E.g.* L.I. Brezhnev, *O Konstitutsii*, 2nd. ed., (Moskva, 1977), p. 57.

162. See notes 165–171 below and accompanying text.

163. S.L. Zivs, "Konstitutsiia SSSR v sisteme sovetskogo zakonodatel'stva", *SGiP* 1978 No. 6, p. 14.

164. L.I. Brezhnev, *Voprosy upravleniia ekonomikoi razvitogo sotsialisticheskogo obshchestva, Rechi, doklady, vystupleniia*, (Moskva, 1976), p. 465; Decree of the CC of the CPSU and the Council of Ministers of the USSR, 25 June 1975, "O merakh po dalneishemu sovershenstvovaniiu khoziaistvennogo zakonodatelstva", *SP SSSR* 1975 No. 16 item 98.

165. See Postanovlenie Prezidiuma Verkhovnogo Soveta SSSR "Ob organizatsii raboty po privedeniiu zakonodatelstva Soiuza SSR v sootvetstvie s Konstitutsiei SSSR", *Ved. SSSR* 1977 No. 51 item 764. See also, Decree of the Council of Ministers of the USSR, 30 Dec. 1977, "Ob organizatsii raboty po privedeniiu zakonodatel'nykh aktov SSSR i reshenii Pravitel'stva SSSR v sootvetstvie s Konstitutsiei SSSR", *SP SSSR* 1978 No. 2 item 8. Analogous processes of legislative house-cleaning have been initiated at the republican level. See Decree of the Presidium of the USSR Supreme Soviet "O zavershenii raboty po podgotovke i priniatiiu novykh konstitutsii soiuznykh respublik", 16 May 1978, *Ved. SSSR* 1978 No. 21 item 326, especially section 4.

166. See Appendix to Decree of 12 Dec. 1977, note 165 above, chapter I. The only draft scheduled for a later date is the draft law on the procedure for conducting national wide voting (referendum), slated for December 1982 (*ibid.*, section 13).

167. *Ibid.*, chapter I.
168. To wit, legislative acts concerning the fundamentals of state planning, capital construction, and standardization.
169. See Appendix, note 166, chapter II.
170. Law on the Council of Ministers of the USSR, 5 July 1978, in *Pravda*, 6 July 1978, and 30 *CDSP* No. 27, p. 20; Law on International Treaties, 6 July 1978, in *Izvestiia*, 7 July 1978, and 30 *CDSP* No. 28, pp. 12ff.
171. Decree, note 165, section 3. For details, see Appendix, note 165, chapter III.
172. Decree, note 165, section 4. The preparatory work has been assigned primarily to the USSR Ministry of Justice, the Supreme Court, and the Procuracy.
173. This desk-clearing task has also been entrusted primarily to the agencies mentioned in note 172. Compare, Decree, note 165, section 4.
174. Decree of the CC CPSU, Presidium of the USSR Supreme Soviet, and USSR Council of Ministers, 23 March 1978, "Voprosy Svoda zakonov SSSR", *SP SSSR* 1978 No. 9 item 60.
175. *Ibid.*, Appendix I.
176. *Konstitutsiia razvitogo sotsializma, V pomoshch izuchaiushchim Konstitutsiiu SSSR*, (Moskva, 1978), pp. 29, 55.
177. *Cf.* S.L. Zivs, note 163, pp. 12, 15.
178. *Ibid.*, p. 15.

CONSTITUTIONS OF THE USSR: 1936 & 1977*

**Editor's Note*: The text of the Constitution of the USSR of 1977 is printed on the right-hand pages; on the left-hand pages are the corresponding provisions of the Constitution of the USSR of 5 December 1936, as it was in force on 7 October 1977. The text reproduced here is the complete text of the 1936 Constitution, as superseded by the new Constitution, *i.e.* 146 Articles minus Articles 23 and 29 which had been repealed earlier, and plus Articles 18a and 18b which had been added after 1936. The chapter headings of the 1936 Constitution have been omitted.

Differences between the texts of the present 1977 Constitution and the Draft published on 4 June 1977 are indicated in the following way:

—additions to the Draft are in italics;
—text included in the Draft but omitted in the final version of the Constitution is surrounded by square brackets;
—text which remained unchanged is in ordinary type.

Minor editorial amendments are mentioned in the footnotes.

DECREE OF THE EXTRAORDINARY VIII CONGRESS OF THE UNION OF SOVIET SOCIALIST REPUBLICS

"On the confirmation of the Constitution (Fundamental Law) of the Union of Soviet Socialist Republics"

The Extraordinary VIII Congress of the Union of Soviet Socialist Republics decrees:

to confirm the Draft Constitution (Fundamental Law) of the Union of Soviet Socialist Republics in the version submitted by the Editorial Commission of the Congress.

(Decree of 5 December 1936. *Izvestiia TsIK SSSR i VTsIK*, 6 December 1936)

CONSTITUTION (FUNDAMENTAL LAW) OF THE UNION OF SOVIET SOCIALIST REPUBLICS*

(Confirmed by the Extraordinary VIII Congress of Soviets of the Union of Soviet Socialist Republics, 5 December 1936)

*Translated by F.J.M. Feldbrugge.

DECLARATION OF THE SUPREME SOVIET OF THE UNION OF SOVIET SOCIALIST REPUBLICS

"On the enactment and promulgation of the Constitution (Fundamental Law) of the Union of Soviet Socialist Republics"

The Supreme Soviet of the Union of Soviet Socialist Republics, acting in the name of the Soviet people and expressing its sovereign will, enacts the Constitution (Fundamental Law) of the Union of Soviet Socialist Republics and proclaims its entering into effect as from 7 October 1977.

(Declaration of 7 October 1977. *Ved. SSSR* 1977 No. 41 item 616)

CONSTITUTION (FUNDAMENTAL LAW) OF THE UNION OF SOVIET SOCIALIST REPUBLICS*

(Enacted by the Special Seventh Session of the Supreme Soviet of the USSR, Ninth Convocation, 7 October 1977)

The great Socialist October Revolution, carried out by the workers and peasants of Russia under the leadership of the Communist Party, headed by V.I. Lenin, overturned the power of the capitalists and landowners, broke the chains of oppression, *established the dictatorship of the proletariat,* and created the Soviet state—a state of a new type, the basic instrument to defend the revolutionary achievements and to build socialism and communism. *The worldwide historical turning-point of mankind from capitalism to socialism began.*

Having emerged victorious in the civil war and having repulsed imperialist intervention, Soviet power has wrought the most profound socio-economic transformations, forever put an end to the exploitation of man by man and to class antagonisms and national hostility. *The association of Soviet Republics in the Union of Soviet Socialist Republics enhanced the forces and possibilities of the people of the country*

*Translated by F.J.M. Feldbrugge and William B. Simons.

for the building of socialism. Public ownership of the means of production and genuine democracy for the working masses were consolidated. For the first time in the history of mankind, a socialist society was created.

The unfading feat of the Soviet people and its Armed Forces in winning an historic victory in the Great Patriotic War has become a shining manifestation of the strength of socialism. This victory strengthened the *authority and* the international position of the USSR and opened new favorable opportunities for the growth of the forces of socialism, national liberation, democracy, and peace throughout the world.

Continuing their creative activity, the *working people of the Soviet Union* [Soviet people] have ensured the rapid and all-round development of the country and the perfection of the socialist system. The union between the working class, the collective farm peasantry, and the people's intelligentsia, and the friendship between the nations and nationalities of the USSR have been consolidated. The socio-political *and ideological* unity of Soviet society, the leading force of which is the working class, has taken shape. Having fulfilled the tasks of the dictatorship of the proletariat, the Soviet state has become an all-people's state. The leading role of the Communist Party, the vanguard of the whole people, has grown to maturity.

A developed socialist society has been built in the USSR. At this stage, as socialism is developing on its own basis, the creative forces of the new system and the advantages of the socialist way of life are becoming more and more manifest, and the working people enjoy more and more the fruits of the great revolutionary achievements:

—a society in which powerful productive forces and a progressive science and culture have been created, and in which the well-being of the people is constantly growing, and ever more and more favorable conditions for the all-round development of the individual are taking shape;

—a society of mature socialist social relationships in which, on the basis of the rapprochement of all *classes and* social strata, of the legal and factual equality of all nations and nationalities, *and of their fraternal cooperation,* a new historical community of people—the Soviet people—has *taken shape* [emerged];

—a society of working people—patriots and internationalists—who are to a high degree organized, ideologically committed, and conscious;

—a society in which the law of life is the concern of all for the *welfare* [well-being] of each and the concern of each for the *welfare* [well-being] of all;

—a society of genuine democracy, the political system of which ensures the effective administration of all public affairs, an ever more active participation of the working people in the life of the state, and the combination of genuine [human] rights and freedoms *of citizens* with *their obligations and responsibility toward society* [civic responsibility].

A developed socialist society is a necessary stage on the road to communism.

The highest goal of the Soviet state is the building of a classless communist society *in which social communist self-government will be developed.* The main tasks of the *socialist all-people's* state are: to create the material and technical base of communism; to perfect socialist social relationships and their transformation into communist relationships; to rear members of a communist society; to raise the material and cultural level of the life of the working people; to ensure the security of the country; and to promote the strengthening of peace and the development of international cooperation.

The Soviet people,

guided by the ideas of scientific communism and remaining true to their revolutionary traditions,

supported by the great socio-economic and political achievements of socialism, striving towards the further development of socialist democracy,

taking into account the international position of the USSR as a component part of the world system of socialism and recognizing their international responsibility,

preserving the continuity of the ideas and principles of the *first Soviet* Constitution [of the RSFSR] of 1918, the Constitution of the USSR of 1924, and the Constitution of the USSR of 1936,

affirm the foundations of the social system and the policies of the USSR, establish the rights, freedoms, and obligations of citizens, and the principles of organization and the aims of the socialist all-people's state, and proclaim them in this Constitution [proclaim the goals and principles, and establish the foundations of the organization of the all-people's socialist state, and consolidate them in this Constitution].

Article 1. The Union of Soviet Socialist Republics is a socialist state of workers and peasants.

Article 3. All power in the USSR belongs to the working people of city and village through the Soviets of Working People's Deputies.

Article 2. The Soviets of Working People's Deputies, which grew and became strong as a result of the overthrow of the power of the landowners and the capitalists, and of the conquest of the dictatorship of the proletariat, constitute the political foundation of the USSR.

Cf. **Article 126** (old) at **Article 51** (new)

I. THE FOUNDATIONS OF THE *SOCIAL* [SOCIO-POLITICAL AND ECONOMIC] SYSTEM *AND THE POLICIES OF THE USSR*

Chapter 1. The Political System

Article 1. The Union of Soviet Socialist Republics is a socialist all-people's state expressing the will and the interests of the *workers* [working class], the *peasants* [peasantry], and the intelligentsia, and *of the working people* of all the nations and nationalities of the country.

Article 2. All power in the USSR belongs to the people.

The people exercise state power through the Soviets of People's Deputies, which constitute the political foundation of the USSR.

All other state organs are under the control of and accountable to the Soviets *of People's Deputies.*

Article 3. The Soviet state is organized and functions in accordance with the principle of democratic centralism: all organs of state power are elected from the lowest to the highest, they are accountable to the people, and the decisions of higher organs are binding for lower organs. Democratic centralism combines unified leadership with local initiative and creative activity, and with the responsibility of every state organ and official for the tasks entrusted to them.

Article 4. The Soviet state and all its organs function on the basis of socialist legality and ensure the protection of the legal order, the interests of society, and the rights *and freedoms* of citizens.

State [institutions], *and* social organizations and officials are bound to observe the Constitution of the USSR and Soviet laws.

Article 5. The most important questions of the life of the state are submitted for nationwide discussion and are also put to a nationwide vote (referendum).

Article 6. The Communist Party of the Soviet Union is the leading and guiding force of Soviet society and the nucleus of its political system and of [all] state and social organizations. The CPSU exists for the people and serves the people.

Armed with Marxist-Leninist doctrine, the Communist Party determines the general perspective of the development of society and the course of the domestic and foreign policy of the USSR, directs the great creative activity of the Soviet people, and imparts a planned and scientifically-sound character to their struggle for the victory of communism.

All party organizations function within the framework of the Constitution of the USSR.

Article 7. In accordance with their statutory functions, trade unions, the All-Union Leninist Communist Youth League, cooperative and other [mass] social organizations participate in the administration of state and public affairs and in the resolution of political, economic, and socio-cultural problems.

Article 8. *Labor collectives participate in the discussion and resolution of state and public affairs; in the planning of production and social developments; in the training and placement of personnel; in the discussion and resolution of questions of the administration of enterprises and institutions, of the improvement of the conditions of labor and everyday life, and of the utilization of resources allocated for the development of production as well as for socio-cultural measures and material incentives.**

Labor collectives develop socialist competition; promote the dissemination of progressive work-methods, and the strengthening of labor discipline; educate their members in the spirit of communist morality; and concern themselves with raising their political awareness, culture, and professional qualifications.

Article 9[8]. The basic direction of the development of the political system of Soviet society is the further unfolding of socialist democracy: the ever-widening participation of *citizens* [the working people] in the administration of the affairs of *the state* [society] and *of society* [the state], the perfection of the state apparatus, the growth of the activity of social organizations, the strengthening of people's control, the reinforcement of the legal basis of the life of the state and of society, the extension of publicity, and permanent consideration of public opinion.

*[The first paragraph of Article 8 is based on Article 16 of Draft.]

Article 4. The socialist system of economy and socialist ownership of the instruments and means of production, which consolidated themselves as a result of the liquidation of the capitalist system of economy, the abolition of private ownership of the instruments and means of production, and the elimination of exploitation of man by man, constitute the economic basis of the USSR.

Article 5. Socialist ownership in the USSR exists either in the form of state ownership (the heritage of the whole people), or in the form of cooperative/collective-farm ownership (ownership of individual collective farms, ownership of cooperative associations).

Article 6. The land, its mineral wealth, the waters, the forests, factories, mines, rail, water, and air transport, banks, means of communication, large state-organized agricultural enterprises (state farms, machine and tractor stations, etc.), as well as municipal enterprises and the basic housing fund in cities and industrial localities, are the property of the state, *i.e.* the heritage of the whole people.

Article 7. [para. 1] The common enterprises in collective farms and cooperative organizations with their livestock and implements, the products of the collective farms and cooperative organizations, as well as their common buildings, constitute the social, socialist property of collective farms and cooperative organizations.

Article 8. The land occupied by collective farms is allocated to them for their free use and for an unlimited time, *i.e.* forever.

Chapter 2. The Economic System

Article 10[9]. The foundation of the economic system of the USSR is socialist ownership of the means of production *in the form of state (all-people's) and collective-farm/cooperative ownership.* [Socialist ownership includes state (all-people's) ownership; ownership of collective-farms and other cooperative organizations (collective-farm/cooperative ownership); ownership of trade unions and other social organizations.]

Property of trade unions and other social organizations, necessary for the realization of their statutory functions, is also socialist property.

The state protects socialist ownership and creates conditions for its increase.

No one has the right to use socialist property for purposes of personal gain *and other selfish purposes.*

Article 11[10]. State ownership, the common heritage of the entire Soviet people, is the basic form of socialist ownership.

The land, its mineral wealth, the waters, and the forests are within the exclusive ownership of the state. The state owns the basic means of production [industrial, construction, and agricultural enterprises] *in industry, construction, and agriculture,* the means of transportation and communication, [and also] the banks, *the property of* commercial, *municipal, and other* [social, and consumer-service] enterprises *organized by the state,* the basic municipal housing fund, *as well as other property necessary for the realization of the functions of the state.*

Article 12[11]. The property of collective farms and other cooperative organizations and their associations consists of the means of production and other property *necessary for* [which serves] the realization of their statutory functions.

The land occupied by collective farms is allocated to them for their free use and for an unlimited time.*

The state promotes the development of collective-farm/cooperative ownership and its drawing together with state ownership.

Collective farms, as well as other land users, are bound to utilize land efficiently, to treat it with care, and to increase its productiveness.

*[No new paragraph in Draft.]

Article 9. Along with the socialist system of economy, which is the dominant form of economy in the USSR, the law permits the small private household of individual peasants and handicraftsmen based on individual labor and excluding the exploitation of outside labor.

Article 10. The right of personal ownership of citizens in their income and savings from labor, a dwelling, the subsidiary household, articles of the household and of everyday use, articles of personal consumption and comfort, as well as the right to inherit personal property of citizens, are protected by law.

Article 7. [para. 2] Every collective farm household, in addition to its basic income from the common collective farm economy, has the personal use of a small garden plot of land, and the personal ownership of the subsidiary household on the garden plot, a dwelling, live-stock, poultry, and minor agricultural implements, in accordance with the statute of the agricultural artel.

Article 12. Labor is the duty and a matter of honor of every citizen in the USSR who is able to work, according to the principle: "He who does not work, neither shall he eat."

The principle of socialism: "From each according to his ability, to each according to his work", is realized in the USSR.

Cf. **Article 11** (old) at **Article 16** (new)

Article 13[12]. *Earned income constitutes the basis of personal property of citizens of the USSR.* [Income and savings from labor, a dwelling and the subsidiary household,] Articles of everyday use, of personal consumption and comfort, *and of the subsidiary household, a dwelling, and savings from labor* may be held in personal ownership [of citizens of the USSR]. [The right of citizens to] Personal ownership *of citizens and* [as well as] the right to its inheritance is protected by *the state* [law]. [The right of citizens to] Personal ownership *of citizens and the right* [as well as] to its inheritance *are* [is] protected *by the state* [by law].

Citizens may have the use of plots of land, made available [by the state or by collective farms] in the manner provided by law, in order to run a subsidiary household (including the keeping of livestock and fowl), to engage in fruit and vegetable gardening, and also for individual housing construction. *Citizens are bound to rationally utilize the plots of land made available to them. The state and the collective farm render aid to citizens in running the subsidiary household.*

Property in the personal ownership or use of citizens *must* [may] not serve for the derivation of unearned income or be used to the detriment *of the interests* of society.

Article 14[13]. The [free] labor of Soviet people, *free from exploitation,* is the source of the growth of public wealth and of the well-being of the people and of every Soviet citizen.

In accordance with the principle *of socialism*: "From each according to his abilities, to each according to his work", the state supervises performance and consumption. It determines the rate of [income] tax *on income subject to taxation* [and fixes the level of wages exempted from taxation].

Socially useful labor and its results determine the position of man in society. The state, combining material and moral incentives, *and encouraging inventiveness and a creative attitude to work,* furthers the transformation of labor into the prime necessity of life of every Soviet man and woman.

Article 15[14]. The highest goal of social production under socialism is the fullest possible satisfaction of the growing material and spiritual needs of the people.

Relying on the creative activity of working people and socialist competition, and on the achievements of scientific-technical progress, *and perfecting the forms and methods of economic management,* the state ensures the growth of labor productivity, the increased

Article 11. The economic life of the USSR is determined and guided by the state plan of the national economy in the interests of increasing the wealth of society, of continuously raising the material and cultural level of the working people, of consolidating the independence of the USSR, and of strengthening its defense capability.

Cf. **Article 9** (old) at **Article 13** (new)

efficiency of production and quality of work, and a dynamic, *planned,* and balanced development of the national economy.

Article 16[15]. The economic system of the USSR constitutes a single economic complex embracing all units of social production, distribution, and exchange within the territory of the country.

The economic system is managed on the basis of state plans *of economic and social development* [for the development of the national economy and of socio-cultural organization], taking into account the branch and territorial principles, and combining centralized *leadership* [management] with the economic independence and initiative of enterprises, associations, and other organizations. At the same time, economic accountability, profit, production costs, *and other economic levers and stimuli* are actively utilized.

[**Article 16.** Collectives of working people and social organizations take part in the management of enterprises and associations, and in the resolution of problems concerning the organization of labor and everyday life, and concerning the utilization of resources allocated for the development of production, as well as for socio-cultural needs and material incentives.]

Article 17. Individual labor activity in the sphere of trades and crafts, agriculture, serving the everyday needs of the population, as well as other forms of [labor] activity based exclusively on the individual labor of citizens and the members of their families are permitted in the USSR in accordance with the law. *The state regulates individual labor activity, ensuring its utilization in the interests of society.*

Article 18. In the interests of present and future generations, the necessary measures are taken in the USSR for the protection and the scientifically-sound and rational utilization of the land and its mineral wealth, *water resources,* the plant and animal world, for the preservation of the purity of air and water, for safeguarding the reproduction of natural resources, and for the improvement of the human environment.

Chapter 3. Social Development and Culture

Article 19. *The indestructible union of workers, peasants, and the intelligentsia constitutes the social foundation of the USSR.*

The [Soviet] state promotes the strengthening of the social homogeneousness of society, the effacement of *class differences and of* the essential differences between town and country and between mental and physical labor, and the *all-round* [further] development and rapprochement of the nations and nationalities of the USSR.

Article 20. In accordance with the communist ideal: "The free development of each is the condition for the free development of all", the [Soviet] state has as its goal the expansion of the actual possibilities for citizens to [develop and] apply their creative forces, abilities, and talents, and for the all-round development of the individual.

Article 21. The state concerns itself with the improvement of working conditions *and labor safety and the scientific organization of labor,* and with the reduction and, ultimately, with the complete elimination of heavy *physical* [manual] labor on the basis of the comprehensive mechanization and automation of production *processes in all branches of the national economy.*

Article 22. A program of transforming agricultural labor into a variety of industrial labor; of widening in rural areas the network of institutions for public education, culture, health care, *trade and public catering, services for everyday needs,* [trade,] and public utilities; and of transforming villages into well-appointed settlements is consistently implemented in the USSR.

Article 23. *On the basis of* [In accordance with] the growth of labor productivity, the state follows an unswerving course for raising the level of wages and the real income of working people.

Public funds for consumption are created in order to more fully satisfy the needs of *Soviet people* [the members of society]. The state, with the broad participation of social organizations and labor collectives, ensures the growth and the equitable distribution of these funds.

Article 24. State systems of health care, social insurance, [services for everyday needs,] *trade and* public catering, *services for everyday needs,* and public utilities are operated and expanded in the USSR.

The state encourages the activity of cooperative and other social organizations in *all spheres* [the field] of services to the population. *The state promotes the development of mass physical culture and sport.*

Article 25. In the USSR there exists *and is continually perfected* a single system of national education which *ensures the general educational and professional training of citizens,* serves the communist upbringing and the spiritual and physical development of young people, and prepares them for work and social activity. [Education in the USSR is free.]

Article 26. In accordance with the needs of society, the state ensures the planned development of science and the training of scientific personnel, and organizes the implementation of the results of scientific research in the national economy and in other spheres of life.

Article 27. The state concerns itself with the protection, multiplication, and broad utilization of spiritual values [of society] for the purpose of *the moral and aesthetic upbringing of Soviet people and the* raising *of their* [the] cultural level [of Soviet people].

The development of professional art and popular artistic creativeness receives every encouragement in the USSR.

Chapter 4. Foreign Policy

Article 28. The *USSR unswervingly* [Soviet state consistently] conducts a Leninist peace policy and stands for consolidation of the security of peoples and broad international cooperation.

The foreign policy of the USSR is directed at ensuring favorable international conditions for the building of communism in the USSR, *defending the state interests of the Soviet Union,* strengthening the positions of world socialism, supporting the struggle of peoples for national liberation and social progress, at preventing aggressive wars, *bringing about universal and complete disarmament,* and consistently implementing the principle of peaceful coexistence of states with different social systems.

In the USSR, war propaganda is forbidden [by law].

Article 29. Relations between the USSR and other states are shaped on the basis of the observance of the principles *of sovereign equality*; of mutual renunciation of the use of force or the threat of force; [of sovereign equality;] of the inviolability of borders; of the territorial integrity of states; of the peaceful settlement of disputes; of noninterference in internal affairs, respect for human rights and fundamental freedoms; of the equality of peoples and the right of

See also **Article 132, para. 1** (old) at **Article 63** (new)

Article 21. A single union citizenship is established for citizens of the USSR. Every citizen of a union republic is a citizen of the USSR.

peoples to decide their own destiny; of cooperation between states; and of the conscientious fulfillment of obligations arising from generally recognized principles and norms of international law and *from* treaties concluded by the USSR.

Article 30. The USSR [Soviet Union], as a component part of the world system of socialism and the socialist commonwealth, develops and strengthens friendship, cooperation, and mutual comradely assistance with the countries of socialism on the basis of *the principle of* socialist internationalism, and actively participates in economic integration and in the international socialist division of labor.

Chapter 5. Defense of the Socialist Fatherland

Article 31. Defense of the socialist Fatherland is *one of the* [a] most important *functions* [function] of the state and *is* a concern of the whole people.

In order to defend the socialist achievements, the peaceful labor of the Soviet people, and the sovereignty and territorial integrity of the state, the Armed Forces *of the USSR* have been created [in the USSR] and universal military service has been established.

The duty of the Armed Forces of the USSR to the people is reliably to defend the socialist Fatherland and to remain in constant combat readiness, guaranteeing an instant rebuff to any aggressor.

Article 32. The state ensures the security and defense capability of the country and equips the Armed Forces of the USSR with everything they require.

The duties of state organs, social organizations, officials, and citizens in ensuring the security of the country and the strengthening of its defense capability are defined by *legislation of the USSR* [law].

II. THE STATE AND THE INDIVIDUAL

Chapter 6. USSR Citizenship. The Equality of Citizens

Article 33. *A single union citizenship has been established in the USSR.* [Soviet citizenship is the same for the entire Union of Soviet Socialist Republics.] *Every citizen of a union republic is a citizen of the USSR.*

Article 122. Women are accorded equal rights with men in the USSR in all spheres of economic, state, cultural, and socio-political life.

The possibility to exercise these rights is ensured by according women an equal right with men to work, to wages, to rest, to social insurance and education, by state protection of the interests of mother and child, state aid to mothers of large families and single mothers, granting paid leave to pregnant women, and a wide network of maternity homes, nurseries, and kindergartens.

Article 123. Equality of rights of the citizens of the USSR, regardless of their nationality or race, in all spheres of economic, state, cultural, and socio-political life, is an immutable law.

Any direct or indirect restriction of rights whatsoever, or, conversely, the establishment of direct or indirect privileges for citizens on account of their race or nationality, as well as any preaching of racial or national exclusiveness, or hatred and contempt, are punished by law.

The grounds and the procedure for acquiring and losing Soviet citizenship are *defined* [established] by *the Law on Citizenship of the USSR* [the law of the USSR].

Citizens of the USSR abroad enjoy the defense and protection of the Soviet state.

Article 34. Citizens of the USSR are equal before the law regardless of origin, social and property status, *race or nationality,* [nationality or race,] sex, education, language, attitude towards religion, type and character of occupation, place of residence, and of other circumstances.

The equality of citizens of the USSR is ensured in all fields of economic, political, social, and cultural life.

Article 35. Women *and men* in the USSR have equal rights [with men].

The exercise of these rights is ensured by according women equal opportunities *with men* in receiving education and professional training, in labor, remuneration, and professional advancement, in socio-political and cultural activity, as well as by special measures for the protection of women's labor and health; *by creating conditions allowing women to combine work with motherhood*; by the legal protection of and by material and moral support for mother and child, including the granting of paid leave and other benefits to pregnant women and mothers; *and by a gradual reduction of working time for women with young children* [and by state aid to single mothers].

Article 36. [Soviet] Citizens *of the USSR* of different *races and* nationalities [and races] have equal rights.

The exercise of these rights is ensured by a policy of comprehensive development and rapprochement of all nations and nationalities of the USSR, by educating citizens in the spirit of Soviet patriotism and socialist internationalism, and by the possibility to use one's native language and the languages of other peoples of the USSR.

Any direct or indirect restriction of rights whatsoever, the establishment of direct or indirect privileges for citizens on grounds of race or nationality, as well as any preaching of racial or national exclusiveness, hostility, or contempt are punished by law.

Article 129. The USSR grants the right of asylum to foreign citizens, persecuted for defending the interests of the working people, for scientific activities, or for struggling for national liberation.

Article 118. Citizens of the USSR have the right to work, that is, the right to guaranteed employment with remuneration in accordance with the quantity and quality of the work.

The right to work is ensured by the socialist organization of the national economy, the continuous growth of the productive forces of Soviet society, the elimination of the possibility of economic crises, and the liquidation of unemployment.

Article 119. Citizens of the USSR have the right to rest.

Article 37. Foreign citizens and stateless persons in the USSR are guaranteed the rights and freedoms provided for by law, including the right to apply to a court and other state organs for the protection of the personal, property, family, and other rights which belong to them [under law].

Foreign citizens and stateless persons within the territory of the USSR are bound to respect the Constitution of the USSR and to observe Soviet laws.

Article 38. The USSR grants the right of asylum to foreigners, persecuted for defending the interests of the working people and the cause of peace, for participating in revolutionary or national liberation movements, or for progressive socio-political, scientific, or other creative activities.

Chapter 7. The Basic Rights, Freedoms, and Obligations of Citizens of the USSR

Article 39. Citizens of the USSR enjoy the full range of the socio-economic, political, and personal rights and freedoms proclaimed and guaranteed by the Constitution of the USSR and Soviet laws. The socialist system ensures the widening of rights and freedoms, and the continuous improvement of the living conditions of citizens in accordance with the fulfillment of the programs of socio-economic and cultural development.

In exercising their rights and freedoms, citizens may not injure the interests of society and the state or the rights of other citizens.

Article 40. Citizens of the USSR have the right to work, that is, to guaranteed employment with remuneration in accordance with the quantity and quality of the work, *and not lower than the minimum rate established by the state,* including the right to choose a profession, occupation, and work in accordance with their vocation, ability, professional training, and education, taking into account the needs of society.

This right is ensured by the socialist economic system, the continuous growth of the productive forces [of society], free professional training, the improvement of work skills, training in new fields, *and the development of the systems of professional guidance and job placement.*

Article 41. Citizens of the USSR have the right to rest.

The right to rest is ensured by establishing a seven-hour workday for workers and employees and by reducing the workday to six hours for a number of professions with arduous work conditions, and to four hours in shops with especially arduous work conditions; by establishing annual paid leave for workers and employees; by providing a wide network of sanatoria, rest homes, and clubs for the accommodation of the working people.

Article 120. Citizens of the USSR have the right to material security in old age, as well as in case of illness or loss of the ability to work.

This right is ensured by the extensive development of social insurance of workers and employees at the expense of the state, by free medical assistance to the working people, and by providing a wide network of health resorts for the use of the working people.

This right is ensured by *establishing* a [41-hour] workweek *not exceeding 41 hours* for workers and employees and a reduced workday for a number of professions and types of work, and by reduced working hours at night; by granting annual paid leave and weekly rest days, as well as by an expansion of the network of cultural-educational and health institutions, and the development of mass sports, physical culture, and tourism; by the creation of favorable possibilities for rest in one's place of residence, and of other conditions for a rational use of free time.

The length of working time and rest for collective farmers is regulated by the [statutes of the] collective farms.

Article 42. Citizens of the USSR have the right to health care.

This right is ensured by free professional medical assistance provided by state health institutions; by expanding the network of institutions for medical treatment and improvement of the health of citizens;* by the development and perfection of safety technology and industrial sanitation;* by taking extensive preventive measures; by measures to improve the environment; by special care for the health of the younger generation, *including* [and] the prohibition of child labor *not connected with training and labor education*; and by furthering scientific research aimed at the prevention of disease and the reduction of its incidence and at ensuring a long and active life for citizens.

Article 43. Citizens of the USSR have the right to material security in old age, in case of illness, [as well as of] complete or partial loss of the ability to work, *as well as* [or] of loss of the breadwinner.

This right is guaranteed by the social insurance of workers, employees, and collective farmers; *by allowances for temporary disability*; by *the payment of* old-age and disability pensions, and pensions for the loss of the breadwinner [and by allowances for temporary disability] *at the expense of the state and of collective farms*; by the employment of citizens who have partially lost the ability to work; by care for elderly citizens and invalids; *and by other forms of social insurance.*

Article 44. Citizens of the USSR have the right to housing.

This right is ensured by the development and protection of the state and social housing fund; by assistance to cooperative and

*[The places of these clauses were reversed in Draft.]

Article 121. Citizens of the USSR have the right to education.

This right is ensured by universal compulsory eight-year education; the extensive development of secondary general polytechnical education, professional-technical education, and secondary special and higher education on the basis of connecting learning with life and production; the all-out development of evening and correspondence courses; free education at all levels; instruction in school in one's native language; and the organization of free production, technical, and agronomic training of the working people in factories, and state and collective farms.

individual housing construction; by a fair distribution, under social supervision, of living space made available in accordance with the realization of the program for the construction of *well-built* housing; and also by moderate payments for rent *and municipal services. Citizens of the USSR are bound to treat carefully the housing made available to them.*

Article 45. Citizens of the USSR have the right to education.

This right is ensured by free education at all levels, the implementation of universal compulsory secondary education of young people, and the extensive development of professional-technical, specialized secondary, and higher education on the basis of connecting learning with life and production; by the development of correspondence and evening education; by granting state stipends and other benefits to pupils and students; by the free issue of school textbooks; by the possibility for instruction in school in one's native language; and by [the development of the system of professional guidance and] the creation of conditions for [the] self-education [of working people].

Article 46. Citizens of the USSR have the right to use the achievements of culture.

This right is ensured by the general accessibility of the treasures of national and world culture in state and public collections; by the development and balanced distribution of cultural-educational institutions within the territory of the country; *by the development of television and radio, of book publishing and the periodic press, and of the network of free libraries*; and by expanding cultural exchanges with foreign states.

Article 47. Citizens of the USSR, in accordance with the goals of communist construction, are guaranteed freedom of scientific, technical, and artistic creation. This freedom is ensured by extensively furthering scientific research and the activities of inventors and rationalizers, and by the development of *literature and* the arts. The state creates the necessary material conditions for these developments and provides support to voluntary societies and creative unions, *and organizes the introduction of inventions and rationalization proposals in the national economy and other spheres of life.*

The rights of authors, inventors, and rationalizers are protected by *the state* [law].

Article 125. In accordance with the interests of the working people and in order to strengthen the socialist system, citizens of the USSR are guaranteed by law:

a) freedom of speech;
b) freedom of the press;
c) freedom of assembly and of meetings;
d) freedom of street marches and demonstrations.

These rights of citizens are ensured by making available to the working people and their organizations printing shops, stocks of paper, public buildings, streets, means of communication, and other material conditions necessary to realize these rights.

Article 126. In accordance with the interests of the working people and in order to develop the organizational initiative and political activity of the popular masses, citizens of the USSR are ensured the

Article 48. Citizens of the USSR have the right to participate in the administration of state and public affairs, *and in the discussion and adoption of laws and decisions of general state and local significance.*

This right is ensured by the possibility to participate in elections for and to be elected to Soviets of People's Deputies and other elective state organs, and to take part in nationwide discussions and votes, in people's control, in the work of state organs, social organizations, and organs of social initiative, and in meetings of labor and residential collectives.

[Citizens of the USSR take part in elections for and may be elected to Soviets of People's Deputies, and take part in the discussion and drafting of legislative proposals and decisions of general state and local interest, in the work of state organs, cooperative, and other social organizations, in the supervision of their activities, in the management of production and the affairs of labor collectives and residential meetings.]

Article 49. Every citizen of the USSR has the right to submit proposals to state organs and social organizations concerning the improvement of their activity and to criticize shortcomings in their work.

Officials are bound to consider, within the *established* time-limits [established by law], the proposals and applications of citizens, to reply to these, and to take the measures necessary.*

Persecution on account of criticism is prohibited. *Persons engaging in persecution for criticism are held responsible.*

Article 50. In accordance with the interests of the [working] people and in order to strengthen *and develop* the socialist system, citizens of the USSR are guaranteed freedom of speech, of the press, of assembly, of meetings, and of street marches and demonstrations.

The exercise of these political freedoms is ensured by making available public buildings, streets, and squares to the working people and their organizations, by the wide dissemination of information, and by the opportunity to make use of press, television, and radio.*

Article 51. In accordance with the goals of communist construction, citizens of the USSR have the right to unite in social organizations,

*[No new paragraph in Draft.]

right to unite in social organizations: trade unions, cooperative associations, youth organizations, sports and defense organizations, cultural, technical, and scientific societies, and the most active and conscious citizens from the ranks of the working class, the working peasants, and the working intelligentsia voluntarily unite in the Communist Party of the Soviet Union, which is the vanguard of the working people in its struggle to build a communist society, and which represents the leading core of all organizations of the working people, social as well as state organizations.

Article 124. In order to ensure citizens freedom of conscience, the church in the USSR is separated from the state, and the school from the church. The freedom to perform religious rites and the freedom of anti-religious propaganda are recognized for all citizens.

Article 127. Citizens of the USSR are ensured the inviolability of the person. No one may be arrested unless according to the decision of a court or with the sanction of the procurator.

Article 128. The inviolability of the home of citizens and the secrecy of correspondence are protected by law.

which promote the development of political activity and initiative, and the satisfaction of their diverse interests.

Social organizations are guaranteed the conditions for the successful fulfillment of their statutory functions.

Article 52. *Citizens of the USSR are guaranteed* freedom of conscience [is recognized for citizens of the USSR], that is, the right to profess any religion *or to profess no religion at all,* and to perform religious rites, *or* [or not to profess any religion and] to conduct atheist propaganda. The incitement of hostility and hatred in connection with religious beliefs is prohibited.

The church in the USSR is separated from the state, and the school from the church.

Article 53. The family is under the protection of the state.

Marriage is *based on* [concluded on the basis of] the voluntary consent of the woman and the man; spouses are completely equal in family relationships.

The state *shows concern for* [aids] the family by creating and developing an extensive network of children's institutions and organizations, by organizing and perfecting everyday services and public catering, *by paying childbirth allowances,* and by granting allowances and benefits to large families [and by paying childbirth allowances], *as well as other forms of allowances and aid to the family.*

Article 54. Citizens of the USSR are guaranteed the inviolability of the person. No one may be arrested unless *on the basis of* [according to the decision of] a court *order* or with the sanction of the procurator.

Article 55. Citizens of the USSR are guaranteed the inviolability of the home. No one has the right, without lawful grounds, to enter a home against the will of the person residing therein.

Article 56. The private life of citizens and the secrecy of correspondence, telephone conversations, and telegraph messages are protected by law.

Article 130. Every citizen of the USSR is bound to observe the Constitution of the Union of Soviet Socialist Republics, to carry out the laws, to maintain labor discipline, honestly to perform his social duty, and to respect the rules of socialist community life.

[See also **Article 12, para. 1** (old) at **Article 14** (new).]

Article 131. Every citizen of the USSR is bound to safeguard and strengthen social socialist property as the sacred and inviolable foundation of the Soviet system, as the source of the wealth and the power of the motherland, and as the source of a prosperous and cultural life of all the working people.

Persons who commit crimes against social socialist property are enemies of the people.

Article 57. It is the duty of all state organs, social organizations, and officials to respect the person and to protect the rights and freedoms of *citizens* [Soviet men and women].

Citizens of the USSR have the right to judicial protection against attacks on *their honor and dignity,* their lives and health, *and their personal freedom and property* [their property and personal freedom, and their honor and dignity].

Article 58. Citizens of the USSR have the right to address complaints against actions of officials *and of* [to] state *and social* organs [and social organizations]. [These] Complaints must be considered in the manner and within the time-limits established by law.

Complaints may be brought to a court, in the manner established by law, against actions which violate the law or exceed the authority of officials and which infringe the rights of citizens.

Citizens of the USSR have the right to compensation for damages inflicted by unlawful actions of state [institutions] and social organizations, as well as of officials, in the course of the performance of their official duties [in the manner and within the limits established by law].

Article 59. The exercise of rights and freedoms is inseparable from the performance by the citizen of his duties.

The citizen of the USSR is bound to observe the Constitution of the USSR and Soviet laws, to respect the rules of socialist community life, and to bear with dignity the high calling of citizen of the USSR.

Article 60. Conscientious labor in one's chosen field of socially useful activity and [the strict] observance of labor [and production] discipline is the duty and a matter of honor for every Soviet citizen who is able to work. *Avoiding socially useful work is incompatible with the principles of a socialist society.*

Article 61. The citizen of the USSR is bound to safeguard and strengthen socialist property. It is the duty of the citizen of the USSR to fight theft and waste of state and social property, *and to treat the wealth of the people with care.*

Persons infringing upon socialist property are punished according to law.

Article 133. The defense of the fatherland is the sacred duty of every citizen of the USSR. Treason to the motherland—violation of the oath, going over to the side of the enemy, impairing the military power of the state, and espionage—are punished with all the severity of the law as the most heinous of crimes.

Article 132. Universal military service is law.

Military service in the ranks of the Armed Forces is the honorable duty of citizens of the USSR.

Article 62. The citizen of the USSR is bound to safeguard the interests of the Soviet state and to promote the growth of its power and authority.

The defense of the socialist Fatherland is the sacred duty of every citizen of the USSR.

Treason to the Motherland is the gravest crime against the people.

Article 63. Military service in the ranks of the Armed Forces of the USSR is the honorable duty of Soviet citizens.

Article 64. It is the duty of every citizen of the USSR to respect the national dignity of other citizens and to strengthen the friendship of the nations and nationalities of the multinational Soviet state.

Article 65. The citizen of the USSR is bound to respect the rights and lawful interests of other persons, to be intolerant of anti-social behavior, and to promote in every way the protection of public order.

Article 66. Citizens of the USSR are bound to show concern for the upbringing of children, to prepare them for socially useful labor, and to raise worthy members of a socialist society. *Children are bound to show concern for their parents and render them aid.*

Article 67. Citizens of the USSR are bound to protect nature and safeguard its riches.

Article 68[67]. Concern for the preservation of historical monuments and other cultural treasures is the duty *and obligation* of citizens of the USSR.*

Article 69[68]. It is the international duty of citizens of the USSR to promote the development of friendship and cooperation with peoples of other countries and the maintenance and strengthening of world peace.

*[Paragraph two of Art. 67 in Draft.]

Article 13. The Union of Soviet Socialist Republics is a federal state, formed on the basis of the voluntary association of the equal Soviet Socialist Republics:
[as in **Article 71** (new)]

Article 17. Each union republic retains the right freely to secede from the USSR.

Article 14. The jurisdiction of the Union of Soviet Socialist Republics, through its highest organ of state power and organs of state administration, encompasses:

a) representing the USSR in international relations; the conclusion, ratification, and denunciation of treaties between the USSR and other states; establishing a general procedure for the relations of union republics with foreign states;

b) questions of war and peace;

c) admitting new republics into the USSR;

III. THE NATIONAL AND STATE STRUCTURE OF THE USSR

Chapter 8. The USSR—A Federal State

Article 70[69]. The Union of Soviet Socialist Republics is a unitary, federal, multinational state, formed *on the basis of the principle of socialist federalism, and* as the result of the free self-determination of nations, and the voluntary association of equal Soviet Socialist Republics.

The USSR embodies the state unity of the Soviet people and brings together all the nations and nationalities for the purpose of jointly building communism.

Article 71[70]. In the *Union of Soviet Socialist Republics* [USSR] are united:

the Russian Soviet Federative Socialist Republic,
the Ukrainian Soviet Socialist Republic,
the Belorussian Soviet Socialist Republic,
the Uzbek Soviet Socialist Republic,
the Kazakh Soviet Socialist Republic,
the Georgian Soviet Socialist Republic,
the Azerbaidzhan Soviet Socialist Republic,
the Lithuanian Soviet Socialist Republic,
the Moldavian Soviet Socialist Republic,
the Latvian Soviet Socialist Republic,
the Kirgiz Soviet Socialist Republic,
the Tadzhik Soviet Socialist Republic,
the Armenian Soviet Socialist Republic,
the Turkmen Soviet Socialist Republic,
the Estonian Soviet Socialist Republic.

Article 72[71]. Each union republic retains the right freely to secede from the USSR.

Article 73[72]. The jurisdiction of the Union of Soviet Socialist Republics, through its highest organs of state power and administration, encompasses;

1) admitting new republics into the USSR; confirming the formation of new autonomous republics and autonomous provinces within the union republics;

2) determining the state border of the USSR and confirming changes of boundaries between union republics;

3) establishing general principles for the organization and func-

d) supervising the observance of the Constitution of the USSR and ensuring the conformity of the Constitutions of the union republics with the Constitution of the USSR;

e) confirming changes of boundaries between union republics;

f) confirming the formation of new autonomous republics and autonomous provinces within the union republics;

g) organizing the defense of the USSR, directing all the Armed Forces of the USSR, and establishing the leading principles of the organization of the military formations of the union republics;

h) foreign trade on the basis of state monopoly;

i) protection of state security;

j) establishing plans of the national economy of the USSR;

k) confirming the integrated state budget of the USSR and the report on its fulfillment, and establishing the taxes and revenues which go to form the union, republican, and local budgets;

l) administering the banks, and industrial and agricultural institutions and enterprises, as well as trading enterprises, of all-union subordination; the over-all direction of industry and construction of union republic subordination;

m) administering transportation and communications of all-union subordination;

n) directing the monetary and credit system;

o) organizing state insurance;

p) contracting and granting of loans;

q) establishing fundamental principles of land use, as well as of use of minerals, forests, and waters;

r) establishing fundamental principles in the field of education and health care;

s) organizing a uniform system of economic accounting;

t) establishing fundamental principles of labor legislation;

u) establishing fundamental principles of legislation on court organization and procedure, and fundamental principles of civil, criminal, and corrective labor legislation;

v) legislation on union citizenship; legislation on rights of foreigners;

w) establishing fundamental principles of marriage and family legislation;

x) issuing all-union acts of amnesty.

Article 19. The laws of the USSR have equal force within the territory of all the union republics.

Article 20. In the event of a discrepancy between the law of a union republic and all-union law, all-union law prevails.

tioning of republic and local organs of state power and administration;

4) ensuring the unity of legislative regulation within the entire territory of the USSR and establishing principles of legislation of the USSR and the union republics;

5) conducting a unified socio-economic policy and directing the economic system of the country; determining the basic directions of scientific-technical progress *and the general measures for a rational utilization and protection of natural resources*; formulating and confirming the *state* plans *of economic and social development* [for the development of the national economy and socio-cultural organization] of the USSR and confirming reports on their fulfillment;

6) formulating and confirming the integrated state budget of the USSR and confirming the report on its fulfillment; directing the uniform monetary and credit system; establishing the taxes and revenues which go to form the [federal, republic, and local budgets] state budget of the USSR; determining a prices and wages policy;

7) directing the branches of the national economy and the associations and enterprises of [all-]union subordination; the overall direction of the branches [associations, and enterprises] of union republic subordination;

8) questions of peace and war, the defense of the sovereignty and the protection of the state borders and territory of the USSR, organizing defense, and directing the Armed Forces *of the USSR*;

9) ensuring state security;

10) representing the USSR in international relations; the contacts of the USSR with foreign states and international organizations; establishing a general procedure for and coordination of the relations of union republics with foreign states and international organizations; foreign trade *and other forms of foreign economic activities* on the basis of the monopoly of the state;

11) Supervising the observance of the Constitution of the USSR and ensuring the conformity of the Constitutions of the union republics with the Constitution of the USSR;

12) resolving other questions of all-union importance.

Article 74[73]. The laws of the USSR have equal force within the territory of all the union republics. In the event of a discrepancy between the law of a union republic and all-union law, the law of the USSR prevails.

Article 15. The sovereignty of union republics is restricted only within the limits indicated in Article 14 of the Constitution of the USSR. Outside these limits, every union republic independently exercises state power. The USSR protects the sovereign rights of the union republics.

Article 16. Every union republic has its own Constitution, which takes account of the special character of the republic and is drawn up in full accordance with the Constitution of the USSR.

Article 18. The territory of union republics may not be altered without their consent.

Article 28. The solution of questions concerning the administrative-territorial organization of union republics into provinces and territories is within the jurisdiction of the union republics.

Article 75[74]. The territory of the Union of Soviet Socialist Republics is one and includes the territories of the union republics.

The sovereignty of the USSR extends to its entire territory.

Chapter 9. The Soviet Socialist Union Republic

Article 76[75]. A union republic is a *sovereign* Soviet socialist state which has united itself with other Soviet republics in the Union of Soviet Socialist Republics.

Outside the limits indicated in Article *73*[72] of the Constitution of the USSR, a union republic independently exercizes state power within its territory.

A union republic has its own Constitution, which conforms to the Constitution of the USSR and takes account of the special character of the republic.

Article 77[76]. A union republic participates in the resolution of questions within the jurisdiction of the USSR in the Supreme Soviet of the USSR, in the Presidium of the Supreme Soviet of the USSR, in the Government of the USSR, and in other organs of the USSR.

A union republic *ensures integrated economic and social development within its territory*, facilitates the exercise of the authority of the USSR within its territory, and implements the decisions of the *supreme* organs of state power and administration of the USSR.

With regard to questions within its jurisdiction, a union republic coordinates and supervises the activities of enterprises, institutions, and organizations of union subordination.

Article 78[77]. The territory of a union republic may not be altered without its consent. The boundaries between union republics may be altered by mutual agreement of the union republics concerned, subject to confirmation by the USSR.

Article 79[78]. A union republic determines its division into territories, provinces, areas, and districts, and resolves other questions of administrative-territorial organization.

Article 18a. Every union republic has the right to enter into direct relations with foreign states, to conclude agreements with them, and to exchange consular and diplomatic representatives.

Article 18b. Every union republic has its own republic military formations.

See last sentence of **Article 15** (old) at **Article 76** (new).

Article 92. Every autonomous republic has its own Constitution, which takes account of the special character of the autonomous republic and is drawn up in full accordance with the Constitution of the union republic.

Article 22. The Russian Soviet Federative Socialist Republic contains the Bashkir, Buriat, Dagestan, Kabardino-Balkar, Kalmyk, Karelian, Komi, Mari, Mordvinian, North Ossetian, Tatar, Tuva, Udmurt,

Article 80[79]. A union republic has the right to enter into relations with foreign states, to conclude treaties with them and to exchange diplomatic and consular representatives, and to participate in the activities of international organizations.

Article 81[80]. The sovereign rights of the union republics are protected by the USSR.

Chapter 10. The Autonomous Soviet Socialist Republic

Article 82[81]. An autonomous republic is part of a union republic.

Outside the limits of the rights of the USSR and the union republic, an autonomous republic independently resolves questions within its jurisdiction.

An autonomous republic has its own Constitution, which conforms to the Constitution of the USSR and the Constitution of the union republics, and which takes into account the special character of the autonomous republic.

Article 83[82]. An autonomous republic participates in the resolution of questions within the jurisdiction of the USSR and the union republic through the supreme organs of state power and administration of the USSR and the union republic respectively.

The autonomous republic *ensures integrated economic and social development within its territory,* facilitates the exercise within its territory of the authority of the USSR and the union republic, and implements the decisions of the *supreme* organs of state power and administration of the USSR and the union republic.

With regard to questions within its jurisdiction, an autonomous republic coordinates and supervises the activities of enterprises, institutions, and organizations of union and republic (union republic) subordination.

Article 84[83]. The territory of the autonomous republic may not be altered without its consent.

Article 85[84]. The Russian Soviet Federative Socialist Republic contains the Bashkir, Buriat, Dagestan, Kabardino-Balkar, Kalmyk, Karelian, Komi, Mari, Mordvinian, North Ossetian, Tatar, Tuva,

Chechen-Ingush, Chuvash, and Iakut Autonomous Soviet Socialist Republics; and the Adyge, Gorno-Altai, Jewish, Karachai-Cherkess, and Khakass Autonomous Provinces.

Article 26. The Uzbek Soviet Socialist Republic contains the Kara-Kalpak Autonomous Soviet Socialist Republic.

Article 25. The Georgian Soviet Socialist Republic contains the Abkhaz and Adzhar Autonomous Soviet Socialist Republics and the South Ossetian Autonomous Province.

Article 24. The Azerbaidzhan Soviet Socialist Republic contains the Nakhichevan' Autonomous Soviet Socialist Republic and the Nagorno-Karabakh Autonomous Province.

See **Article 22** (old) at **Article 85** (new).

See **Article 25** (old) at **Article 85** (new).

See **Article 24** (old) at **Article 85** (new).

Article 27. The Tadzhik Soviet Socialist Republic contains the Gorno-Badakhshan Autonomous Province.

Udmurt, Chechen-Ingush, Chuvash, and Iakut Autonomous Soviet Socialist Republics.

The Uzbek Soviet Socialist Republic contains the Kara-Kalpak Autonomous Soviet Socialist Republic.

The Georgian Soviet Socialist Republic contains the Abkhaz and Adzhar Autonomous Soviet Socialist Republics.

The Azerbaidzhan Soviet Socialist Republic contains the Nakhichevan' Autonomous Soviet Socialist Republic.

Chapter 11. The Autonomous Province and the Autonomous Area

Article 86[85]. An autonomous province is part of a union republic *or a territory.* A law on an autonomous province is adopted by the Supreme Soviet of a union republic on the recommendation of the Soviet of People's Deputies of an autonomous province.

Article 87[86]. The Russian Soviet Federative Socialist Republic contains the Adyge, Gorno-Altai, Jewish, Karachai-Cherkess, and Khakass Autonomous Provinces.

The Georgian Soviet Socialist Republic contains the South Ossetian Autonomous Province.

The Azerbaidzhan Soviet Socialist Republic contains the Nagorno-Karabakh Autonomous Province.

The Tadzhik Soviet Socialist Republic contains the Gorno-Badakhshan Autonomous Province.

Article 88[87]. An autonomous area is part of a territory or a province. A *Law* [statute] on Autonomous Areas is *adopted* [confirmed] by the Supreme Soviet of a union republic.

Article 36. The Supreme Soviet of the USSR is elected for a term of four years.

Article 58. The Supreme Soviet of the union republic is elected by the citizens of the republic for a term of four years.

The norms of representation are established by the Constitutions of the union republics.

Article 90. The Supreme Soviet of the autonomous republic is elected by the citizens of the republic for a term of four years according to norms of representation established by the Constitution of the autonomous republic.

Article 95. Soviets of Working People's Deputies of territories, provinces, autonomous provinces, areas, districts, cities, and villages (*stanitsas*, hamlets, *khutors*, *kishlaks*, *auls*) are elected by the working people of the territory, province, autonomous province, area, district, city, or village concerned, for a period of two years.

Article 54. Upon expiration of the term of office or in case of earlier dissolution of the Supreme Soviet of the USSR, the Presidium of the Supreme Soviet of the USSR calls new elections within a period of not more than two months after the day of the expiration of the term of office or the dissolution of the Supreme Soviet of the USSR.

Article 96. The norms of representation for Soviets of Working People's Deputies are determined by the Constitutions of the union republics.

IV. SOVIETS OF PEOPLE'S DEPUTIES AND THE PROCEDURE FOR THEIR ELECTION

Chapter 12. The System and Principles of Operation of the Soviets of People's Deputies

Article 89[88]. The Soviets of People's Deputies: the Supreme Soviet of the USSR; the Supreme Soviets of the union republics; the Supreme Soviets of the autonomous republics; the territorial and provincial Soviets of People's Deputies, the Soviets of People's Deputies of autonomous provinces and autonomous areas; *district,* city, [district,] city-district, settlement, and village Soviets of People's Deputies—constitute an integrated system of organs of state power.

Article 90[89]. The term of office of the Supreme Soviet of the USSR, the Supreme Soviets of the union republics, and the Supreme Soviets of autonomous republics is five years.

The term of office of *local* Soviets of People's Deputies is two and a half years.

[The term of office of territorial and provincial Soviets of People's Deputies, Soviets of People's Deputies of autonomous provinces and autonomous areas, and of city, district, city-district, settlement, and village Soviets of People's Deputies is two and a half years.]

Article 134. Elections of deputies to all Soviets of Working People's Deputies: the Supreme Soviet of the USSR, Supreme Soviets of union republics, territorial and provincial Soviets of Working

Elections for Soviets of People's Deputies are called not later than two months before the expiration of the term of office of the Soviets concerned.

Article 91[90]. The most important questions within the jurisdiction of the respective Soviets of People's Deputies are considered and resolved at their sessions.

The Soviets of People's Deputies *elect standing commissions and* create executive and administrative, as well as other organs accountable to them [and elect standing commissions].

Article 92[91]. The Soviets of People's Deputies set up organs of people's control, combining state supervision with social supervision by working people in enterprises, collective farms, institutions, and organizations.

The organs of people's control supervise the fulfillment of state plans and assignments, combat violations of state discipline, manifestations of localism, a departmental approach to business, mismanagement and wastefulness, red tape and bureaucracy, and they assist in perfecting the work of the state apparatus.

[The manner of organization and operation of the organs of people's control is defined by law.]

Article 93[92]. The Soviets of People's Deputies, directly and through organs created by them, direct all branches of state, economic, and socio-cultural construction, adopt decisions, ensure their execution, and supervise their implementation.

Article 94[93]. The activities of the Soviets of People's Deputies are based on the collective, free, and businesslike discussion and resolution of questions, on openness, on the regular accounting of executive and administrative organs, and other organs created by the Soviets, to the Soviets and to the population, and on the widespread enlistment of citizens to participate in the work of the Soviets.

The Soviets of People's Deputies and the organs created by them systematically inform the population about their work and the decisions taken.

Chapter 13. The Electoral System

Article 95[94]. Elections of deputies to all Soviets of People's Deputies are held on the basis of universal, equal, and direct suffrage by secret ballot.

People's Deputies, Supreme Soviets of autonomous republics, Soviets of Working People's Deputies of autonomous provinces, and area, district, city, and village (*stanitsa*, hamlet, *khutor, kishlak, aul*) Soviets of Working People's Deputies—are held by the voters on the basis of universal, equal, and direct suffrage by secret ballot.

Article 137. Women enjoy the right to vote and to be elected on an equal footing with men.

Article 138. Citizens serving in the ranks of the Armed Forces of the USSR enjoy the right to vote and to be elected on an equal footing with all citizens.

Article 135. Elections of deputies are universal; all citizens of the USSR who have reached the age of 18 years, irrespective of their race or nationality, sex, religion, educational qualifications, settledness, social origin, property position, and past activities, have the right to participate in elections of deputies, with the exception of persons who have, in the manner established by law, been declared insane.

Every citizen of the USSR who has reached the age of 23 years, irrespective of his race or nationality, sex, religion, educational qualifications, settledness, social origin, property position, and past activities, may be elected as a deputy to the Supreme Soviet of the USSR.

Article 136. Elections of deputies are equal: each citizen has one vote; all citizens participate in elections on an equal basis.

Article 139. Elections of deputies are direct: elections to all Soviets of Working People's Deputies, from the village and city Soviet of Working People's Deputies up to the Supreme Soviet of the USSR, are held by the citizens directly by means of direct elections.

Article 140. The voting in elections of deputies is secret.

Article 141, para. 2. The right to nominate candidates is ensured to social organizations and societies of the working people: Communist Party organizations, trade unions, cooperatives, youth organizations, and cultural societies.

Article 96[95]. Elections of deputies are universal: all citizens of the USSR who have reached the age of 18 years have the right to vote and to be elected, with the exceptic .ı of persons who have, in the manner established by law, been declared insane.

A citizen of the USSR who has reached the age of 21 years may be elected as a deputy to the Supreme Soviet.

Article 97[96]. Elections of deputies are equal: each voter has one vote; all voters participate in elections on an equal basis.

Article 98[97]. Elections of deputies are direct: the deputies of all Soviets of People's Deputies are elected directly by the citizens.

Article 99[98]. The voting in elections of deputies is secret: checking on the expression of the will of the voter is *not allowed* [is excluded].

Article 100[99]. The right to nominate candidates for election as deputies belongs to organizations of the Communist Party of the Soviet Union, of trade unions, and of the All-Union Leninist Communist League of Youth, to cooperative and other social organizations, to labor collectives, *as well as to assemblies of servicemen according to military units.*

Article 141. [para. 1] Election candidates are nominated on the basis of electoral districts.

Citizens of the USSR and social organizations are guaranteed the free and all-round discussion of the political, professional, and personal qualities of the candidates for election as deputies, as well as the right to campaign at meetings, in the press, and on television and radio.

Expenses connected with conducting elections for Soviets of People's Deputies are borne by the state.

Article 101[100]. Elections of deputies to Soviets of People's Deputies are held on the basis of electoral districts.

A citizen of the USSR may not, as a rule, be elected to more than two Soviets of People's Deputies.

Elections of deputies to Soviets of People's Deputies are conducted by electoral commissions, composed of representatives of social organizations, labor collectives,* *and assemblies of servicemen according to military units.*

The procedure for conducting elections to the Soviets of People's Deputies is defined by *laws of the USSR, the union republics, and the autonomous republics* [law].

Article 102. *The voters give mandates to their deputies.*

The appropriate Soviets of People's Deputies consider the mandates of the voters, take account of them while formulating the plans of economic and social development and drawing up of the budget, organize the implementation of mandates, and inform the citizens about their realization.

Chapter 14. The People's Deputy

Article 103[101]. Deputies are plenipotentiary representatives of the people in the Soviets of People's Deputies.

By participating in the work of the Soviets, the deputies resolve questions of state, economic, and socio-cultural construction, organize the implementation of the decisions of the Soviets, and supervise the work of state organs, enterprises, institutions, and organizations.

In his activity, a deputy is guided by the general interests of the state, takes into account the demands of the population of his constituency, and seeks to implement the mandates of his constituents.

*[No new paragraph in Draft.]

Article 142. Every deputy is obliged to report to his constituents about his work and the work of the Soviet of Working People's Deputies, and may be recalled at any time by a decision of a majority of his constituents in the manner established by law.

Article 30. The supreme organ of state power of the USSR is the Supreme Soviet of the USSR.

Article 104[102]. A deputy exercises his powers without interrupting his work in production or service.

During the sessions of the Soviet, as well as in order to *exercise* [execute] the powers of a deputy in other instances provided for by the law, the deputy is relieved from performing his duties in production or service, while retaining his average earnings at his place of permanent employment.

Article 105[103]. A deputy has the right to address inquiries to the appropriate state organs and officials, who are obliged to answer the inquiries at the session of the Soviet.

A deputy has the right to address himself to all state and social organs, enterprises, institutions, and organizations concerning questions within the scope of his activity as a deputy, and to participate in the consideration of the questions raised by him. The heads of the state and social organs, enterprises, institutions, and organizations concerned are obliged to receive the deputy without delay and to consider his proposals within the *established* time-limit [established by law].

Article 106[104]. A deputy is ensured the conditions for unhindered and effective exercise of his rights and execution of his duties.

The immunity of deputies, as well as other guarantees of a deputy's activities, are established by the Law on the Status of Deputies and by other *legislative acts* [legislation] of the USSR and the union and autonomous republics.

Article 107[105]. A deputy is obliged to report on his work and the work of the Soviet to his constituents, *as well as to the collectives and social organizations which nominated him as a candidate for election.*

A deputy, who has not justified the trust of his constituents, may at any time be recalled by a decision of a majority of his constituents in the manner established by law.

V. THE SUPREME ORGANS OF STATE POWER AND ADMINISTRATION OF THE USSR

Chapter 15. The Supreme Soviet of the USSR

Article 108[106]. The supreme organ of state power of the USSR is the Supreme Soviet of the USSR.

Article 31. The Supreme Soviet of the USSR exercises all rights attributed to the Union of Soviet Socialist Republics according to Article 14 of the Constitution, insofar as they are not, by virtue of the Constitution, within the jurisdiction of USSR organs accountable to the Supreme Soviet of the USSR: the Presidium of the Supreme Soviet of the USSR, the Council of Ministers of the USSR, and ministries of the USSR.

Article 32. The legislative power of the USSR is exercised exclusively by the Supreme Soviet of the USSR.

Article 33. The Supreme Soviet of the USSR consists of two chambers: the Soviet of the Union and the Soviet of Nationalities.

Article 37. Both chambers of the Supreme Soviet of the USSR: the Soviet of the Union and the Soviet of Nationalities, have equal rights.

Article 34. The Soviet of the Union is elected by the citizens of the USSR on the basis of electoral districts according to the norm: one deputy for every 300,000 of the population.

Article 35. The Soviet of Nationalities is elected by the citizens of the USSR by union and autonomous republics, autonomous provinces, and national areas according to the norm: 32 deputies from each union republic, 11 deputies from each autonomous republic, 5 deputies from each autonomous province, and one deputy from each national area.

The Supreme Soviet of the USSR is empowered to decide all questions assigned to the jurisdiction of the USSR by the present Constitution.

The adoption of the Constitution of the USSR and of amendments therein; the admission of new republics to the USSR and the confirmation of the formation of new autonomous republics and autonomous provinces; the confirmation of state plans *of economic and social development* [for the development of the national economy and socio-cultural organization] of the USSR, and of the state budget of the USSR and the reports on their fulfillment; and the formation of USSR organs accountable to the Supreme Soviet—are within the exclusive competence of the Supreme Soviet of the USSR.

Laws of the USSR are adopted [only] by the Supreme Soviet of the USSR, *or by a nationwide vote (referendum) conducted on the basis of a decision of the Supreme Soviet of the USSR.*

Article 109[107]. The Supreme Soviet of the USSR consists of two chambers: the Soviet of the Union and the Soviet of Nationalities.

The chambers of the Supreme Soviet have equal rights.

Article 110[108]. The Soviet of the Union and the Soviet of Nationalities consist of an equal number of deputies.

The Soviet of the Union is elected on the basis of electoral districts with an equal number of inhabitants.

The Soviet of the Nationalities is elected according to the following formula: 32 deputies from each union republic, 11 deputies from each autonomous republic, 5 deputies from each autonomous province, and one deputy from each autonomous area.

Article 50. The Soviet of the Union and the Soviet of Nationalities elect mandates commissions, which examine the credentials of the deputies of each chamber.

On the recommendation of the mandates commissions, the chambers decide either to recognize the credentials or to annul the elections of individual deputies.

Article 42. The Soviet of the Union elects a Chairman of the Soviet of the Union and four Deputy Chairmen.

Article 43. The Soviet of Nationalities elects a Chairman of the Soviet of Nationalities and four deputy Chairmen.

Article 44. The Chairmen of the Soviet of the Union and the Soviet of Nationalities preside over the meetings of the respective chambers and are in charge of their proceedings.

Article 45. The Chairmen of the Soviet of the Union and the Soviet of Nationalities alternately conduct the joint meetings of both chambers of the Supreme Soviet of the USSR.

Article 46. Sessions of the Supreme Soviet of the USSR are convened by the Presidium of the Supreme Soviet of the USSR twice a year.

Extraordinary sessions are convened by the Presidium of the Supreme Soviet of the USSR at its discretion or at the request of one of the union republics.

Article 41. Sessions of the Soviet of the Union and the Soviet of Nationalities begin and end simultaneously.

Article 38. The right of legislative initiative belongs in equal measure to the Soviet of the Union and the Soviet of Nationalities.

On the recommendation of the mandates commission elected by them, the Soviet of the Union and the Soviet of Nationalities decide on the recognition of the credentials of the deputies and, in the event of a violation of electoral legislation, on finding the election of individual deputies null and void.

Article 111[109]. Each chamber of the Supreme Soviet of the USSR elects a Chairman of the chamber and four Deputy Chairmen.

The Chairmen of the Soviet of the Union and the Soviet of Nationalities preside over the meetings of the respective chambers and are in charge of their proceedings.

The Chairmen of the Soviet of the Union and the Soviet of Nationalities alternately conduct the joint [plenary] meetings of the chambers of the Supreme Soviet of the USSR.

Article 112[110]. Sessions of the Supreme Soviet of the USSR are convened twice a year.

Extraordinary sessions are convened by the Presidium of the Supreme Soviet of the USSR at its own initiative *as well as* [or] on the proposal of *one of the union republics or of* not less than one-third of the deputies of one of the chambers [as well as at the request of one of the union republics].

A session of the Supreme Soviet of the USSR consists of separate and joint [plenary] meetings of the chambers, as well as of meetings of standing commissions of the chambers or commissions of the Supreme Soviet of the USSR held *between sessions* [during a session]. A session is opened and closed at *separate or joint* [plenary] meetings of the chambers.

[Sessions of the Soviet of the Union and the Soviet of Nationalities begin and end simultaneously.]

Article 113[111]. *The right of* legislative initiative in the Supreme Soviet of the USSR belongs to the Soviet of the Union [and] the Soviet of Nationalities, the Presidium of the Supreme Soviet of the USSR, the Council of Ministers of the USSR, the union republics

Article 39. A law is considered enacted if it is adopted by both chambers of the Supreme Soviet of the USSR by a simple majority of votes of each chamber.

Article 47. In the event of disagreement between the Soviet of the Union and the Soviet of Nationalities, the question is referred for settlement to a conciliation commission, formed by the chambers on a parity basis. If the conciliation commission does not reach agreement or if its solution does not satisfy one of the chambers, the question is examined a second time in the chambers. If both chambers fail to reach agreement, the Presidium of the Supreme Soviet of the USSR dissolves the Supreme Soviet of the USSR and calls new elections.

through their supreme organs of state power, commissions of the Supreme Soviet of the USSR and standing commissions of its chambers, deputies of the Supreme Soviet of the USSR, the Supreme Court of the USSR, and the Procurator General of the USSR.

[Mass] Social organizations, through their all-union organs, also *enjoy* [exercise] the right of legislative initiative.

Article 114[112]. *Draft bills and other questions, referred for consideration to the Supreme Soviet of the USSR, are discussed by the chambers at their separate or joint meetings. When necessary, the draft bill or, as the case may be, the question may be referred for preliminary or additional consideration to one or several commissions.* [A draft bill, after discussion at the meetings of the chambers, may be referred to one or several commissions for consideration. The chambers also have the right to discuss and vote on a draft bill without referring it to commissions.]

[Laws of the USSR, decrees, and other acts of the Supreme Soviet of the USSR are adopted at separate or joint meetings of the chambers.]

A law of the USSR is considered adopted if, in each of the chambers of the Supreme Soviet of the USSR, a majority of the total number of deputies voted in favor of it. *Decrees and other acts of the Supreme Soviet of the USSR are adopted by a majority of the total number of deputies of the Supreme Soviet of the USSR.*

Draft bills *and other highly important questions of the life of the state* may be submitted to a nationwide discussion [as well as put to a nationwide vote (referendum)] by a decision of the Supreme Soviet of the USSR or of the Presidium of the Supreme Soviet of the USSR, adopted at their own initiative, or on the proposal of *a union republic* [one of the union republics].

Article 115[113]. In the event of disagreement between the Soviet of the Union and the Soviet of Nationalities, the question is referred for settlement to a conciliation commission, formed by the chambers on a parity basis, after which the question is considered a second time by the Soviet of the Union and the Soviet of Nationalities at a joint meeting. *If even in such a case no agreement is reached, the question is carried over for consideration at the next session of the Supreme Soviet of the USSR or is submitted by the latter to a nationwide vote (referendum).*

Article 40. Laws adopted by the Supreme Soviet of the USSR are published in the languages of the union republics over the signatures of the Chairman and the Secretary of the Presidium of the Supreme Soviet.

Article 71. The Government of the USSR or a Minister of the USSR to whom an inquiry has been addressed by a deputy to the Supreme Soviet of the USSR is obliged to give an oral or written reply in the respective chamber within a period of three days.

Article 52. A deputy to the Supreme Soviet of the USSR may not be prosecuted or arrested without the consent of the Supreme Soviet of the USSR, and, during the period between the sessions of the Supreme Soviet of USSR, without the consent of the Presidium of the Supreme Soviet of the USSR.

Article 48. At a joint meeting of both chambers, the Supreme Soviet of the USSR elects the Presidium of the Supreme Soviet of the USSR consisting of the Chairman of the Presidium of the Supreme Soviet of the USSR, fifteen Deputy Chairmen—one from each Union republic, the Secretary of the Presidium, and twenty members of the Presidium of the Supreme Soviet of the USSR.

The Presidium of the Supreme Soviet of the USSR is accountable to the Supreme Soviet of the USSR in all its activities.

Article 49. The Presidium of the Supreme Soviet of the USSR:

a) convenes the sessions of the Supreme Soviet of the USSR;

b) issues edicts;

c) interprets the laws of the USSR in operation;

d) dissolves the Supreme Soviet of the USSR on the basis of Article 47 of the Constitution of the USSR and calls new elections;

e) conducts nationwide polls (referendums) on its own initiative or at the request of one of the union republics;

f) annuls decrees and resolutions of the Council of Ministers of

Article 116[114]. Laws of the USSR, decrees, and other acts of the Supreme Soviet of the USSR are published in the languages of the union republics over the signatures of the Chairman and Secretary of the Presidium of the Supreme Soviet of the USSR.

Article 117[115]. A deputy to the Supreme Soviet of the USSR has the right to address inquiries to the Council of Ministers of the USSR, and to ministers and heads of other organs formed by the Supreme Soviet of the USSR. The Council of Ministers of the USSR or the official to whom an inquiry has been addressed is obliged to give an oral or written reply at the *given* session of the Supreme Soviet of the USSR within a period of three days.

Article 118[116]. A deputy to the Supreme Soviet of the USSR may not be prosecuted, arrested, or subjected to judicially imposed administrative penalties without the consent of the Supreme Soviet of the USSR, and, during the time between its sessions, without the consent of the Presidium of the Supreme Soviet of the USSR.

Article 119[117]. At a joint meeting of the chambers, the Supreme Soviet of the USSR elects the Presidium of the Supreme Soviet of the USSR, the permanently functioning organ of the Supreme Soviet of the USSR, accountable to the latter in all its activities *and exercising, within the limits provided for by the Constitution, the functions of the supreme organ of state power of the USSR during the time between sessions of the Supreme Soviet of the USSR.*

Article 120[118]. The Presidium of the Supreme Soviet of the USSR is elected from among the deputies and consists of the Chairman of the Presidium of the Supreme Soviet, the First Deputy Chairman, fifteen Deputy Chairmen—one from each union republic, the Secretary of the Presidium, and twenty-one members of the Presidium of the Supreme Soviet of the USSR.

Article 121[119]. The Presidium of the Supreme Soviet of the USSR:

1) *calls elections to the Supreme Soviet of the USSR*;

2)[1)] convenes the sessions of the Supreme Soviet of the USSR;

3)[2)] coordinates the activities of the standing commissions of the chambers of the Supreme Soviet of the USSR;

4)[3)] supervises the observance of the Constitution of the USSR, and ensures that the Constitutions *and laws* of the union republics conform to the Constitution *and laws* of the USSR;

5)[4)] interprets the laws of the USSR;

the USSR and the Councils of Ministers of union republics where they do not conform to the law;

g) during the time between the sessions of the Supreme Soviet of the USSR, dismisses and appoints individual Ministers of the USSR on the recommendation of the Chairman of the Council of Ministers of the USSR, with the subsequent proposal for confirmation by the Supreme Soviet of the USSR;

h) institutes orders and medals of the USSR, and establishes honorary ranks of the USSR;

i) awards orders and medals of the USSR, and confers honorary ranks of the USSR;

j) exercises the right of pardon;

k) establishes military and diplomatic ranks and other special ranks;

l) appoints and replaces the high command of the Armed Forces of the USSR;

m) during the time between the sessions of the Supreme Soviet of the USSR, proclaims a state of war in the event of a military attack on the USSR or when necessary to fulfill treaty obligations concerning mutual defense against aggression;

n) proclaims general or partial mobilization;

o) ratifies and denounces treaties of the USSR;

p) appoints and recalls plenipotentiary representatives of the USSR in foreign states;

q) accepts credentials and letters of recall of diplomatic representatives of foreign states accredited to it;

r) proclaims martial law in specific localities or for the entire USSR in the interests of the defense of the USSR or for ensuring public order and state security.

6)[5)] ratifies and denounces treaties to which the USSR is a party;

7)[6)] annuls decrees and resolutions of the Council of Ministers of the USSR and of Councils of Ministers of union republics where they do not conform to the law;

8)[7)] establishes military and diplomatic ranks and other special ranks; confers military and diplomatic ranks and other special ranks;

9)[8)] institutes orders and medals of the USSR; establishes honorary titles of the USSR; awards orders and medals of the USSR; confers honorary titles of the USSR;

10)[9)] admits persons to citizenship of the USSR, and decides questions of the renunciation and deprivation of citizenship of the USSR and of granting asylum;

11)[10)] issues all-union acts of amnesty, and grants pardon;

12)[11)] appoints and recalls *diplomatic* representatives of the USSR to foreign states and at international organizations;

13)[12)] accepts credentials and letters of recall of diplomatic representatives of foreign states accredited to it;

14)[13)] forms the Council of Defense of the USSR and confirms its composition, appoints and replaces the high command of the Armed Forces of the USSR;

15)[14)] proclaims, in the interests of the defense of the USSR, martial law in specific localities or for the whole country;

16)[15)] proclaims general or partial mobilization;

17)[16)] during the time between the sessions of the Supreme Soviet of the USSR, proclaims a state of war in the event of a military attack on the USSR or when necessary to fulfill treaty obligations concerning mutual defense against aggression;

18) *exercises other powers established by the Constitution and laws of the USSR.*

Article 122[120]. The Presidium of the Supreme Soviet of the USSR, during the time between the sessions of the Supreme Soviet, and with subsequent submission for confirmation at the next session of the Supreme Soviet:

1) amends,when necessary, *legislative acts* [legislation] of the USSR in force;

2) confirms boundary changes between union republics;

3) forms and abolishes ministries of the USSR and state committees of the USSR on the proposal of the Council of Ministers of the USSR;

4) dismisses and appoints individual persons as members of the Council of Ministers of the USSR on the recommendation of the Chairman of the Council of Ministers of the USSR.

Article 53. Upon expiration of the term of office or in case of earlier dismissal of the Supreme Soviet of the USSR, the Presidium of the Supreme Soviet of the USSR retains its powers until the formation of a new Presidium of the Supreme Soviet of the USSR by the newly-elected Supreme Soviet of the USSR.

Article 55. The newly-elected Supreme Soviet of the USSR is convened by the Presidium of the outgoing Supreme Soviet of the USSR not later than three months after the election.

Article 51. The Supreme Soviet of the USSR creates, when it considers it necessary, investigative, revision, and other commissions on any question.

All institutions and officials are bound to comply with the requests of these commissions and to submit to them the necessary materials and documents.

Article 123[121]. The Presidium of the Supreme Soviet of the USSR issues edicts and adopts resolutions.

Article 124[122]. Upon expiration of the term of office of the Supreme Soviet of the USSR, the Presidium of the Supreme Soviet of the USSR retains its powers until the formation of a new Presidium by the newly-elected Supreme Soviet of the USSR.

The newly-elected Supreme Soviet of the USSR is convened by the Presidium of the outgoing Supreme Soviet of the USSR not later than two months after the elections.

Article 125[123]. The Soviet of the Union and the Soviet of Nationalities elect from among the deputies standing commissions for the preliminary consideration and preparation of questions within the jurisdiction of the Supreme Soviet of the USSR, as well as for promoting the implementation of laws of the USSR and other decisions of the Supreme Soviet of the USSR and its Presidium, and the supervision of the activities of state organs and organizations.* The chambers of the Supreme Soviet of the USSR may *also* create joint commissions on a parity basis.

[Article 125]. The Supreme Soviet of the USSR creates, when it considers it necessary, investigative, revision, and other commissions on any question.

All state *and social* organs, *organizations*, and officials are bound to comply with the requests of *the commissions of the Supreme Soviet of the USSR and of the commissions of its chambers* [these commissions], and to submit to them the necessary materials and documents.**

The recommendations of the commissions must be considered by the state and social organs, institutions, and organizations. The commissions must be informed within the established time-limit about the results of the consideration or of the measures taken.

Article 126[124]. The Supreme Soviet of the USSR supervises the activities of all state organs accountable to it.

The Supreme Soviet of the USSR sets up a Committee of People's Control of the USSR which heads the system of organs of people's control.

*[New paragraph in Draft.]

**[No new paragraph in Draft.]

Article 64. The supreme executive and administrative organ of state power of the Union of Soviet Socialist Republics is the Council of Ministers of the USSR.

Article 56. At a joint meeting of both chambers, the Supreme Soviet of the USSR sets up the Government of the USSR—the Council of Ministers of the USSR.

Article 70. The Council of Ministers is set up by the Supreme Soviet of the USSR and consists of:

the Chairman of the Council of Ministers of the USSR;

the First Deputy Chairmen of the Council of Ministers of the USSR;

the Deputy Chairmen of the Council of Ministers of the USSR;

the Ministers of the USSR;

the Chairman of the State Planning Committee of the Council of Ministers of the USSR;

the Chairman of the State Committee for Construction of the Council of Ministers of the USSR;

the Chairman of the State Committee for Material-Technical Supply of the Council of Ministers of the USSR;

the Chairman of the People's Control Committee of the USSR;

the Chairman of the State Committee for Labor and Social Questions of the Council of Ministers of the USSR;

the Chairman of the State Committee for Science and Technology of the Council of Ministers of the USSR;

the Chairman of the State Committee for Inventions and Discoveries of the Council of Ministers of the USSR;

the Chairman of the State Committee for Prices of the Council of Ministers of the USSR;

the Chairman of the State Committee for Standards of the Council of Ministers of the USSR;

The organization and manner of operation of the organs of people's control are defined by the Law on People's Control in the USSR.

Article 127[126]. The manner of operation of the Supreme Soviet of the USSR and its organs is defined by the Regulations of the Supreme Soviet of the USSR and by *other* laws of the USSR issued on the basis of the Constitution of the USSR.

Chapter 16. The Council of Ministers of the USSR

Article 128[127]. The Council of Ministers of the USSR—the Government of the USSR—is the supreme executive and administrative organ of state power of the USSR.

Article 129[128]. The Council of Ministers of the USSR is set up by the Supreme Soviet of the USSR at a joint meeting of the Soviet of the Union and the Soviet of Nationalities and is composed of [:] the Chairman of the Council of Ministers of the USSR, First Deputy Chairmen and Deputy Chairmen [of the Council of Ministers of the USSR], the ministers of the USSR, and chairmen of state committees of the USSR.

the Chairman of the State Committee for Professional-Technical Education of the Council of Ministers of the USSR;

the Chairman of the State Committee for Television and Broadcasting of the Council of Ministers of the USSR;

the Chairman of the State Committee for Cinematography of the Council of Ministers of the USSR;

the Chairman of the State Committee for the Affairs of Publishing Houses, Printing, and Book Trade of the Council of Ministers of the USSR;

the Chairman of the State Committee for Forestry of the Council of Ministers of the USSR;

the Chairman of the State Committee for Foreign Economic Relations of the Council of Ministers of the USSR;

the Chairman of the State Committee for State Security attached to the Council of Ministers of the USSR;

the Chairman of the All-Union Combine "Soiuzsel'khoztekhnika" of the Council of Ministers of the USSR;

the Chairman of the Board of the State Bank of the USSR;

the Director of the Central Statistical Administration attached to the Council of Ministers of the USSR;

the Chairmen of Union Republic Councils of Ministers are members of the Council of Ministers of the USSR by virtue of their office.

Article 65. The Council of Ministers of the USSR is responsible and accountable to the Supreme Soviet of the USSR and, during the time between the sessions of the Supreme Soviet of the USSR, to the Presidium of the Supreme Soviet of the USSR, to whom it is accountable.

The chairmen of the Councils of Ministers of the union republics are members of the Council of Ministers of the USSR by virtue of their office.

On the recommendation of the Chairman of the Council of Ministers of the USSR, the Supreme Soviet of the USSR may include the heads of other organs and organizations of the USSR as members of the Government of the USSR.

The Council of Ministers of the USSR lays down its powers before the newly-elected Supreme Soviet of the USSR at the first session of the latter.

Article 130[129]. The Council of Ministers of the USSR is responsible and accountable to the Supreme Soviet of the USSR and, during the time between the sessions of the Supreme Soviet of the USSR, to the Presidium of the Supreme Soviet of the USSR, to whom it is accountable.

The Council of Ministers of the USSR regularly reports on its work to the Supreme Soviet of the USSR.

Article 68. The Council of Ministers of the USSR

a) coordinates and directs the work of all-union and union republic Ministries of the USSR, State Committees of the Council of Ministers of the USSR, and other institutions subordinate to it;

b) takes measures to implement the national economic plan and the state budget, and to strengthen the credit and monetary system;

c) takes measures to ensure public order, to defend the interests of the state, and to protect the rights of citizens;

d) exercises general leadership in the field of relations with foreign states;

e) determines the annual contingents of citizens subject to be called up for active military service, and directs the general organization of the Armed Forces of the USSR;

f) sets up State Committees of the USSR, and also, when necessary, Special Committees and Chief Departments attached to the Council of Ministers of the USSR for matters of economic, cultural, and defense organization.

Article 131[130]. The Council of Ministers of the USSR is empowered to resolve all questions of state administration within the jurisdiction of the USSR insofar as they do not, *according to* [by virtue of] the Constitution, come within the competence of the Supreme Soviet of the USSR and the Presidium of the Supreme Soviet of the USSR.

Within the limits of its authority, the Council of Ministers of the USSR:

1) ensures the management of the national economy and socio-cultural construction [and the implementation of an integrated policy in the field of science and technology]; formulates and takes measures to ensure the growth of the well-being and culture of the people, *to develop science and technology, to rationally utilize and protect natural resources,* to strengthen the monetary and credit system, to implement a uniform policy of prices, *wages, social welfare,* and state insurance organization, and a uniform system of accounting and statistics; organizes the administration of industrial, construction, and agricultural enterprises and associations, transport and communications enterprises, banks, as well as other organizations and institutions of [all-] union subordination;

2) formulates and submits to the Supreme Soviet of the USSR current and long-range state plans of the *economic and social* development [of the national economy and socio-cultural organization] of the USSR and the state budget of the USSR; takes measures to implement [the] state *plans* [plan] and the budget; submits reports on the fulfillment of the *plans* [plan] and the budget to the Supreme Soviet of the USSR;

3) takes measures to defend the interests of the state, to protect socialist property and public order, and to safeguard and defend the rights and *freedoms* of citizens;

4) takes measures to ensure state security;

5) exercises general leadership over the organization of the Armed Forces of the USSR, and determines the annual contingents of citizens subject to be called up for active military service;

6) exercises general leadership in the field of relations with foreign states, foreign trade, and economic, scientific-technical, and cultural cooperation of the USSR with foreign countries; takes measures to ensure the fulfillment of treaties of the USSR; confirms and denounces intergovernmental treaties;

7) *sets up, when necessary, committees, chief administrations, and other departments attached to the Council of Ministers of the USSR for matters of economic, socio-cultural, and defense organization.*

Article 66. The Council of Ministers of the USSR issues decrees and resolutions on the basis and in pursuance of the laws in force and verifies their execution.

Article 67. The execution of decrees and resolutions of the Council of Ministers of the USSR is obligatory throughout the territory of the USSR.

Article 69. The Council of Ministers of the USSR has the right, in administrative and economic areas within the jurisdiction of the USSR, to suspend decrees and resolutions of the Councils of Ministers of union republics, and to annul orders and instructions of Ministers of the USSR, as well as acts of other organs subordinate to it.

See **Article 68** (old) at **Article 131** (new).

Article 74. Ministries of the USSR are either all-union or union republic ministries.

Article 72. Ministers of the USSR direct the branches of state administration within the competence of the USSR.

Article 75. All-union ministries direct the branch of state administration entrusted to them throughout the territory of the USSR, either directly or through organs created by them.

Article 76. Union republic ministries direct the branch of state administration entrusted to them, as a rule, through the identically named ministries of the union republics, and administer directly

Article 132[131]. The Presidium of the Council of Ministers of the USSR, consisting of the Chairman of the Council of Ministers of the USSR, the First Deputy Chairmen and the Deputy Chairmen, functions as a permanent organ of the Council of Ministers of the USSR for the resolution of questions connected with ensuring the management of the national economy and other questions of state administration.

[The Council of Ministers of the USSR, when necessary, sets up committees, chief administrations, and other departments attached to the Council of Ministers of the USSR for matters of economic, social, cultural, and defense organization.]

Article 133[132]. The Council of Ministers of the USSR, on the basis and in pursuance of laws of the USSR and *other decisions* [edicts of the Presidium] of the Supreme Soviet of the USSR *and its Presidium*, issues decrees and resolutions and verifies their execution. The execution of decrees and resolutions of the Council of Ministers of the USSR is obligatory throughout the territory of the USSR.

Article 134[133]. The Council of Ministers of the USSR, in questions within the jurisdiction of the USSR, has the right to suspend *the execution of* decrees and resolutions of the Councils of Ministers of the union republics, *as well as* [and] to annul acts of ministries of the USSR, state committees of the USSR, *and* [as well as] other organs subordinate to it.

Article 135[134]. The Council of Ministers of the USSR coordinates and directs the work of all-union and union republic ministries [of the USSR,] *and* state committees of the USSR, and other organs subordinate to it.

All-union ministries and state committees of the USSR direct the branches of administration entrusted to them *or exercise inter-branch control*, throughout the territory of the USSR, either directly or through organs created by them.

Union republic ministries and state committees of the USSR direct the branches of administration entrusted to them or *exercise inter-branch control*, as a rule, through the corresponding ministries, [and] only a definite and limited number of enterprises, according to a list confirmed by the Presidium of the Supreme Soviet of the USSR.

Article 73. Ministers of the USSR, within the limits of the competence of the corresponding ministries, issue orders and instructions on the basis and in pursuance of the laws in force, as well as of decrees and resolutions of the Council of Ministers of the USSR, and verify their execution.

Article 77. All-union ministries are the Ministries of:

Aviation Industry;
Automobile Industry;
Foreign Trade;
Gas Industry;
Civil Aviation;
Machine Building;
Machine Building for Animal Husbandry and Fodder Production;
Machine Building for the Light and Food Industries and for the Production of Household Appliances;
Medical Industry;
Merchant Marine;
Petroleum Industry;
Defense Industry;
General Machine Building;
Instrument Making, Means of Automation, and Control Industry;
Communications Equipment Industry;
Transportation;
Radio Industry;
Medium Machine Building;
Machine Tool and Instrument Industry;
Construction Machinery, Road-Building Machinery and Civil Engineering Machinery;
Construction of Petroleum and Gas Industry Enterprises;
Shipbuilding Industry;
Tractor and Agricultural Machinery Manufacture;
Construction of Transportation;

state committees, ***and other organs*** of the union republics, and administer directly ***individual*** enterprises and associations [enumerated on a list to be confirmed by the Presidium of the Supreme Soviet of the USSR] ***of union subordination. The manner of transferring enterprises and associations of republic or local subordination to union subordination is determined by the Presidium of the Supreme Soviet of the USSR.***

Ministries [of the USSR] and state comittees of the USSR are responsible for the state and the development of the ***spheres*** [branches] of administration entrusted to them; they issue acts within the limits of their competence and on the basis and in pursuance of the laws of the USSR, ***other decisions*** [edicts of the Presidium] of the Supreme Soviet of the USSR ***and its Presidium***, and decrees and resolutions of the Council of Ministers of the USSR; and they organize and verify their execution.

Article 136[135]. The competence of the Council of Ministers of the USSR and its Presidium, the procedure of their activity, the [mutual] relations of the Council of Ministers [of the USSR] with ***other state organs*** [ministries of the USSR and state committees of the USSR], as well as the list of all-union and union republic ministries [of the USSR] and state committees of the USSR are defined, ***on the basis of the Constitution***, by the Law on the Council of Ministers of the USSR.

Machine Building for Heavy and Transportation Industries;
Chemical and Petroleum Machine Building;
Chemical Industry;
Paper and Pulp Industry;
Electronic Industry;
Electrotechnical Industry;
Machine Building for Power Industry.

Article 78. Union republic ministries are the Ministries of:
Internal Affairs;
Higher and Specialized Secondary Education;
Geology;
Grain Procurement;
Public Health;
Foreign Affairs;
Culture;
Light Industry;
Lumber and Wood Processing Industry;
Land Improvement and Irrigation;
Assembly and Special Construction;
Meat and Dairy Industry;
Petroleum Refining and Petro-Chemical Industry;
Defense;
Food Industry;
Industrial Construction;
Building Materials Industry;
Education;
Fisheries;
Communications;
Rural Construction;
Agriculture;
Construction;
Construction of Heavy Industrial Enterprises;
Trade;
Coal Industry;
Finance;
Non-ferrous Metallurgy;
Ferrous Metallurgy;
Power and Electrification;
Justice.

Article 57. The Supreme organ of state power of a union republic is the Supreme Soviet of the union republic.

Article 60. The Supreme Soviet of the union republic:

a) adopts the Constitution of the republic and amends it in accordance with Article 16 of the Constitution of the USSR;

b) confirms the Constitutions of the autonomous republics which are part of it and defines the boundaries of their territory;

c) confirms the national economic plan and the budget of the republic;

d) enjoys the right of amnesty and pardon in respect of citizens convicted by judicial organs of the union republic;

e) establishes the representation of the union republic in international relations;

f) establishes the manner of organizing the military formations of the republic.

Article 59. The Supreme Soviet of the union republic is the only legislative organ of the republic.

Article 61. The Supreme Soviet of the union republic elects the Presidium of the Supreme Soviet of the union republic, consisting of: the Chairman of the Presidium of the Supreme Soviet of the union republic, his deputies, the Secretary of the Presidium and the members of the Presidium of the Supreme Soviet of the union republic.

The powers of the Presidium of the Supreme Soviet of the union republic are defined by the Constitution of the union republic.

Article 62. The Supreme Soviet of the union republic elects the

VI. PRINCIPLES OF THE STRUCTURE OF THE ORGANS OF STATE POWER AND ADMINISTRATION IN THE UNION REPUBLICS

Chapter 17. The Supreme Organs of State Power and Administration of a Union Republic

Article 137[136]. The supreme organ of state power of a union republic is the Supreme Soviet of the union republic.

The Supreme Soviet of a union republic is empowered to resolve all questions within the jurisdiction of the union republic by the Constitution of the USSR and the Constitution of the union republic.

The adoption of the Constitution of a union republic and of amendments therein, the confirmation of state plans of *economic and social development* [the development of the national economy and socio-cultural construction], of the state budget of the union republic *and reports on their fulfillment*; the formation of organs accountable to the Supreme Soviet of the union republic—belong to the exclusive competence of the union republic.

Laws of a union republic are adopted [only] by the Supreme Soviet of the union republic *or by a national vote (referendum) conducted on the basis of a decision of the Supreme Soviet of the union republic.*

Article 138[137]. The Supreme Soviet of a union republic elects the Presidium of the Supreme Soviet, the permanently functioning organ of the Supreme Soviet of the union republic, accountable to the latter in all its activities. The composition and powers of the Presidium of the Supreme Soviet of a union republic are defined by the Constitution of the union republic.

Chairman of the Supreme Soviet of the union republic and his deputies to conduct the meetings.

Article 63. The Supreme Soviet of a union republic sets up the Government of the union republic—the Council of Ministers of the union republic.

Article 79. The supreme executive and administrative organ of state power of a union republic is the Council of Ministers of the union republic.

Article 83. The Council of Ministers of a union republic is set up by the Supreme Soviet of the union republic and consists of:

the Chairman of the Council of Ministers of the union republic;

the deputy Chairmen of the Council of Ministers;

the Ministers;

the Chairmen of State Committees and Commissions and the heads of other departments of the Council of Ministers, set up by the Supreme Soviet of the union republic in accordance with the Constitution of the union republic.

Article 80. The Council of Ministers of a union republic is responsible and accountable to the Supreme Soviet of the union republic and, during the time between the sessions of the Supreme Soviet of the union republic, to the Presidium of the Supreme Soviet of the union republic, to whom it is accountable.

Article 81. The Council of Ministers of a union republic issues decrees and resolutions on the basis and in pursuance of the laws in force of the USSR and the union republic, and of the decrees and resolutions of the Council of Ministers of the USSR, and verifies their execution.

Article 82. The Council of Ministers of a union republic has the right to suspend decrees and resolutions of Councils of Ministers of autonomous republics, and to annul decisions and resolutions of executive committees of Soviets of Working People's Deputies of territories, provinces, and autonomous provinces.

Article 139[138]. The Supreme Soviet of a union republic sets up the Council of Ministers of the union republic—the Government of the union republic, the supreme executive and administrative organ of state power of the union republic.

The Council of Ministers of a union republic is responsible and accountable to the Supreme Soviet of the union republic and, during the time between the sessions of the Supreme Soviet, to the Presidium of the Supreme Soviet of the union republic, to whom it is accountable.

Article 140[139]. The Council of Ministers of a union republic issues decrees and resolutions on the basis and in pursuance of *legislative acts* [laws] of the USSR and the union republic, and of decrees and resolutions of the Council of Ministers of the USSR, and organizes and verifies their execution.

Article 141[140]. The Council of Ministers of a union republic has the right to suspend *the execution of* decrees and resolutions of the Councils of Ministers of autonomous republics and to annul decisions and resolutions of executive committees of territorial, provincial, and city (in cities of republican subordination) Soviets of People's Deputies, of Soviets of People's Deputies of autonomous provinces, and in union republics not divided into provinces, of executive committees of district and corresponding city Soviets of People's Deputies.

Article 84. Ministers of a union republic direct the branches of state administration within the competence of the union republic.

Article 86. Ministries of a union republic are union republic or republic ministries.

Article 87. Union republic ministries direct the branch of state administration entrusted to them, being subordinate to the Council of Ministers of the union republic, as well as to the corresponding union republic ministry of the USSR.

Article 88. Republic ministries direct the branch of state administration entrusted to them, being directly subordinate to the Council of Ministers of the union republic.

Article 85. Ministers of a union republic, within the limits of the competence of the corresponding ministries, issue orders and instructions on the basis and in pursuance of the laws of the USSR and the union republic, of decrees and resolutions of the Councils of Ministers of the USSR and the union republic, and of orders and instructions of union republic ministries of the USSR.

Article 89. The supreme organ of state power of an autonomous republic is the Supreme Soviet of the ASSR.

Article 142[141]. The Council of Ministers of a union republic coordinates and directs the work of union republic and republic ministries and state committees of the union republic, *and other organs subordinate to it.*

Union republic ministries and state committees of a union republic direct the branches of administration entrusted to them *or exercise inter-branch control,* being subordinate to the Council of Ministers of the union republic, as well as to the corresponding union republic ministry of the USSR or state committee of the USSR.

Republic ministries and state committees direct the branches of administration entrusted to them or exercise inter-branch control, being subordinate to the Council of Ministers of the union republic.

Chapter 18. The Supreme Organs of State Power and Administration of an Autonomous Republic

Article 143[142]. The supreme organ of state power of an autonomous republic is the Supreme Soviet of the autonomous republic.

The adoption of the Constitution of an autonomous republic and of amendments therein; the confirmation of state plans of *economic and social development* [the development of the national economy and socio-cultural construction], as well as of the state budget of the autonomous republic; the formation of organs accountable to the Supreme Soviet of the autonomous republic—belong to the exclusive competence of the Supreme Soviet of the autonomous republic.

Article 91. The Supreme Soviet of an autonomous republic is the only legislative organ of the ASSR.

Article 93. The Supreme Soviet of an autonomous republic elects the Presidium of the Supreme Soviet of the autonomous republic and sets up the Council of Ministers of the autonomous republic, according to its Constitution.

Article 94. The organs of state power in the territories, provinces, autonomous provinces, areas, districts, cities, villages (*stanitsas*, hamlets, *khutors*, *kishlaks*, *auls*) are the Soviets of Working People's Deputies.

Article 97. The Soviets of Working People's Deputies direct the activities of the organs of administration subordinate to them, ensure the protection of public order, the observance of laws, and the protection of the rights of citizens, direct local economic and cultural organization, and determine the local budget.

Laws of an autonomous republic are adopted [only] by the Supreme Soviet of the autonomous republic.

Article 144[143]. The Supreme Soviet of an autonomous republic elects the Presidium of the Supreme Soviet of the autonomous republic and sets up the Council of Ministers of the autonomous republic—the Government of the autonomous republic.

Chapter 19. Local Organs of State Power and Administration

Article 145[144]. The organs of state power in the territories, provinces, autonomous provinces, autonomous areas, districts, cities,* city-districts, settlements, and rural settlements are the corresponding Soviets of People's Deputies.

Article 146[145]. Local Soviets of People's Deputies resolve all questions of local importance, keeping in mind general state interests and the interests of the citizens living in the territory of the Soviet, implement the decisions of higher state organs, *direct the activity of lower-level Soviets of People's Deputies,* and also participate in the discussion of questions of republic and all-union importance, and submit proposals concerning these questions.

Within their territory, *local* Soviets of People's Deputies direct state, economic, and socio-cultural organization; confirm plans of economic and social development and the local budget; exercise leadership over the [activities of] state organs, enterprises, institutions, and organizations, subordinate to them; ensure observance of laws, the protection of state and public order and of the rights of citizens; and promote the strengthening of the defense capability of the country.

Article 147[146]. Within the limits of their authority, local Soviets of People's Deputies *ensure integrated economic and social development within their territory*; supervise the observance of legislation by enterprises, institutions, and organizations subordinate to higher bodies and located on this territory; coordinate and supervise their activities in the fields of land use, protection of nature, construction, *utilization of labor resources*, production of consumer goods, and socio-

*[The Draft has: "... cities, districts, ...".]

Article 98. The Soviets of Working People's Deputies adopt decisions and issue resolutions within the limits of the rights granted to them by the laws of the USSR and the union republic.

Article 99. The executive and administrative organs of the territorial, provincial, autonomous provincial, area, district, city, and village Soviets of Working People's Deputies are the executive committees elected by them and consisting of: a chairman, his deputy, a secretary, and members.

Article 100. The executive and administrative organs of the Soviets of Working People's Deputies in small settlements are the chairman, the deputy chairman, and the secretary, elected by the Soviet of Working People's Deputies.

Article 101. The executive organs of the Soviets of Working People's Deputies are directly accountable to the Soviet of Working People's Deputies which has elected them, as well as to the executive organ of the higher Soviet of Working People's Deputies.

Article 102. Justice in the USSR is administered by the Supreme Court of the USSR, the Supreme Courts of union republics, territorial and provincial courts, courts of autonomous republics and autonomous provinces, area courts, special USSR courts, created by decision of the Supreme Soviet of the USSR, and people's courts.

cultural services, services for everyday needs, and other services for the population.

Article 148[147]. Local Soviets of People's Deputies adopt decisions within the limits of the *authority* [rights] granted to them by the *legislation* [laws] of the USSR, the union republic, and the autonomous republic. The execution of decisions of local Soviets is obligatory for all enterprises, institutions, and organizations located on the territory of the Soviet, as well as for officials and citizens.

Article 149[148]. The executive committees elected by the local Soviets from among their deputies are the executives and administrative organs of the local Soviets of People's Deputies.

Executive committees report at least once a year to the Soviets which have elected them, *as well as at meetings of labor collectives and at citizens' places of residence.*

Article 150[149]. Executive committees of local Soviets of People's Deputies are directly accountable to the Soviet which has elected them, as well as to the higher executive and administrative organ.

VII. THE ADMINISTRATION OF JUSTICE, ARBITRATION, AND PROCURATORIAL SUPERVISION

Chapter 20. Courts and Arbitration

Article 151[150]. Justice in the USSR is administered only by the courts.

In the USSR function the Supreme Court of the USSR; Supreme Courts of union republics; Supreme Courts of autonomous republics; territorial, provincial, and city courts; courts of autonomous provinces; courts of autonomous areas; district (city) people's courts; as well as military tribunals in the Armed Forces.

Article 109. People's judges of district (city) people's courts are elected for a term of five years by secret ballot by the citizens of the district (city) on the basis of universal, equal, and direct suffrage.

People's assessors of district (city) people's courts are elected for a term of two years at general meetings of workers, employees, and farmers at their place of work or residence, and by servicemen according to military units.

Article 106. The Supreme Courts of union republics are elected for a term of five years by the Supreme Soviets of union republics.

Article 107. The Supreme Courts of autonomous republics are elected for a term of five years by the Supreme Soviets of autonomous republics.

Article 108. Territorial and provincial courts, courts of autonomous provinces, and area courts are elected for a term of five years by the territorial, provincial, or area Soviets of Working People's Deputies, or by the Soviets of Working People's Deputies of the autonomous provinces.

Article 104. The Supreme Court of the USSR is the supreme judicial organ. The Supreme Court of the USSR is charged with the supervision of the judicial activities of the judicial organs of the USSR, as well as of the judicial organs of the union republics within the limits established by law.

Article 105. The Supreme Court of the USSR is elected for a term of five years by the Supreme Soviet of the USSR.

The chairmen of the Supreme Courts of the union republics are members of the Supreme Court of the USSR by virtue of their office.

Article 152[151]. All courts in the USSR are formed on the principle that judges and people's assessors are elected.

People's judges of district (city) people's courts are elected for a term of five years by secret ballot by the citizens of the district (city) on the basis of universal, equal, and direct suffrage. People's assessors of district (city) people's courts are elected for a term of two and a half years by open ballot at meetings of *citizens* [working people] at their place of work or residence.

Higher courts are elected for a term of five years by the corresponding Soviets of the People's Deputies.

Judges of military tribunals are elected for a term of five years by the Presidium of the Supreme Soviet of the USSR, and people's assessors for a term of two and a half years by meetings of servicemen.

Judges and people's assessors are responsible to their constituents or to the organs which have elected them, *report to them, and may be recalled by them in the manner established by law.*

Article 153[152]. The Supreme Court of the USSR is the supreme judicial organ of the USSR and supervises the judicial activities of the courts of the USSR, as well as of the courts of the union republics within the limits established by law.

The Supreme Court of the USSR is elected by the Supreme Soviet of the USSR [for a term of five years] and consists of the chairman, his deputies, members, and people's assessors. The chairmen of the Supreme Courts of the union republics are members of the Supreme Court of the USSR by virtue of their office.

Article 103. In all courts, cases are considered with the participation of people's assessors, except in cases specially provided for by law.

Article 112. Judges are independent and subject only to law.

Article 111. The examination of cases in all courts of the USSR is open, insofar as the law does not provide exceptions, and the accused is ensured the right to defense.

Article 110. Judicial proceedings are conducted in the language of the union republic, autonomous republic, or autonomous province, and to persons who do not master this language, the right fully to familiarize oneself with the materials of the case through an interpreter, as well as the right to address the court in one's native language, are ensured.

The [manner of] organization and *manner of* operation of the Supreme Court of the USSR are defined by the Law on the Supreme Court of the USSR.

Article 154[153]. In all courts, civil and criminal cases are considered by a panel; [and] in the court of first instance—with the participation of people's assessors. In the administration of justice, people's assessors enjoy all the rights of a judge.

Article 155[154]. Judges and people's assessors are independent and subject only to law.

Article 156[155]. Justice is administered in the USSR on the principle of the equality of citizens before the law and the court.

Article 157[156]. The examination of cases in all courts is open. The hearing of cases in a closed session of the court is permitted only in cases established by law and with the observance of all the rules of court procedure.

Article 158[157]. The accused is ensured the right to defense.

Article 159[158]. Judicial proceedings are conducted in the language of the union republic or autonomous republic, of the autonomous province, the autonomous area, or in the language of the majority of the population of the given locality. The right fully to familiarize oneself with the materials of the case, participation in court proceedings through an interpreter, and the right to address the court in one's native language are ensured to persons who take part in a case and do not master the language in which the proceedings are conducted.

Article 160[159]. No one may be convicted of the commission of a crime *as well as* [and] be subjected to criminal punishment other than by a judgment of the court and in accordance with the [criminal] law.

Article 161[160]. There are colleges of advocates to render legal assistance to citizens and organizations. In cases provided for by *legislation* [law], citizens receive legal assistance free of charge.

The organization and manner of operation of the Bar are defined by legislation of the USSR and the union republic.

Article 113. The Procurator General of the USSR is charged with the supreme supervision over the exact execution of the law by all ministries and institutions subordinate to them, likewise by individual officials, as well as by citizens of the USSR.

Article 114. The Procurator General of the USSR is appointed by the Supreme Soviet of the USSR for a term of seven years.

Article 115. Republican, territorial, and provincial procurators, as well as procurators of autonomous republics and autonomous provinces, are appointed by the Procurator General of the USSR for a term of five years.

Article 116. Area, district, and city procurators are appointed by the procurators of the union republic with the confirmation of the Procurator General of the USSR for a term of five years.

Article 162[161]. The participation of representatives of social organizations and labor collectives is permitted in judicial proceedings in civil and criminal cases.

Article 163[162]. Economic disputes between enterprises, institutions, and organizations* are resolved by the organs of state arbitration *within the limits of their competence.*

The [manner of] organization and *manner of* operation of the organs of state arbitration are defined by *the Law on State Arbitration of the USSR* [law].**

[The State Arbitration of the USSR directs the activity of all arbitration organs and supervises it. The Chief Arbiter of the State Arbitration of the USSR is appointed for a term of five years by the Supreme Soviet of the USSR.]

Chapter 21. The Procuracy

Article 164[163]. The Procurator General of the USSR and his subordinate procurators are charged with the supreme supervision over the exact and uniform execution of the law by all ministries, state committees and departments, enterprises, institutions, and organizations, executive and administrative organs of local Soviets of People's Deputies, collective farms, cooperative and other social organizations, officials, as well as citizens.

Article 165[164]. The Procurator General of the USSR is appointed by the Supreme Soviet of the USSR, is responsible and accountable to it, and, during the time between the sessions of the Supreme Soviet, to the Presidium of the Supreme Soviet of the USSR, to whom he is accountable.

Article 166[165]. The procurators of the union republics, autonomous republics, territories, provinces, and autonomous provinces are appointed by the Procurator General of the USSR. The procurators of autonomous areas, and district and city procurators are appointed by the procurators of the union republics and confirmed by the Procurator General of the USSR.

*[The Draft has: "... organizations, institutions, and enterprises ...".]

**[No new paragraph in Draft.]

Article 117. The organs of the Procuracy exercise their functions independently from any local organs whatsoever and are subordinate only to the Procurator General of the USSR.

Article 143. The state arms of the Union of Soviet Socialist Republics consist of a sickle and hammer against a globe, represented in the rays of the sun and framed by ears of grain, with an inscription in the languages of the union republics: "Proletarians of All Countries, Unite!". Over the arms is a five-pointed star.

Article 144. The state flag of the Union of Soviet Socialist Republics consists of a red cloth, with a representation in its upper corner, near the staff, of a golden sickle and hammer, and over them a red five-pointed star, edged in gold. The ratio of the width to the length is 1:2.

Article 145. The capital of the Union of Soviet Socialist Republics is the city of Moscow.

Article 167[166]. The term of office of the Procurator General of the USSR and all procurators of lower rank is five years.

Article 168[167]. The organs of the Procuracy exercise their powers independently from any local organs whatsoever and are subordinate only to the Procurator General of the USSR.

The [manner of] organization and *manner of* operation of the organs of the Procuracy [of the USSR] are defined by the Law on *the Procuracy of* [Procuratorial Supervision in] the USSR.

VIII. THE ARMS, FLAG, ANTHEM, AND CAPITAL OF THE USSR

Article 169[168]. The state arms of the Union of Soviet Socialist Republics consists of a representation of a sickle and hammer against the background of a globe, in the rays of the sun and framed by ears of grain, with an inscription in the languages of the union republics: "Proletarians of All Countries, Unite!". There is a five-pointed star *in the upper part of* [over] the arms.

Article 170[169]. The state flag of the Union of Soviet Socialist Republics consists of a rectangular red cloth with a representation in its upper corner, near the staff, of a golden sickle and hammer, and over them a red five-pointed star, edged in gold. The ratio of the width of the flag to its length is 1:2.

Article 171[170]. The state anthem of the Union of Soviet Socialist Republics is confirmed by the Presidium of the Supreme Soviet of the USSR.

Article 172[171]. The capital of the Union of Soviet Socialist Republics is the city of Moscow.

IX. THE [PROCEDURE FOR THE] OPERATION [AND AMENDMENT] OF THE CONSTITUTION OF THE USSR *AND THE PROCEDURE FOR ITS AMENDMENT*

Article 173[172]. The Constitution of the USSR has supreme legal force. All laws and other acts of state organs are issued on the basis of and in accordance with the Constitution of the USSR.

Article 146. The Constitution of the USSR is amended only by a decision of the Supreme Soviet of the USSR, adopted by a majority of not less than two-thirds of the votes in each of its chambers.

[The Constitution of the USSR takes effect from the moment of its adoption.]

Article 174[173]. The Constitution of the USSR is amended by a decision of the Supreme Soviet of the USSR, adopted by a majority of not less than two-thirds of the total number of deputies of each of its chambers.

LAW OF THE UNION OF SOVIET SOCIALIST REPUBLICS

"On the putting into effect of the Constitution (Fundamental Law) of the USSR"

The Supreme Soviet of the Union of Soviet Socialist Republics resolves:

Article 1. Laws of the USSR, laws of union and autonomous republics, and other acts of state organs passed before 7 October 1977 retain their effect, insofar as they do not contradict the new Constitution of the USSR.

Article 2. The Supreme Soviet of the USSR, the Supreme Soviets of the union republics, and the Supreme Soviets of the autonomous republics, elected before the enactment of the Constitution of the USSR of 1977, exercise all powers granted to Supreme Soviets by the new Constitution of the USSR.

Local organs of state power, elected before the enactment of the Constitution of the USSR of 1977, are named, accordingly, territorial and provincial Soviets of People's Deputies, Soviets of People's Deputies of autonomous provinces and autonomous areas, and district, city, city-district, settlement, and village Soviets of People's Deputies, and exercise all powers granted to local Soviets of People's Deputies by the new Constitution of the USSR.

The terms of office of Soviets of People's Deputies, established by Article 90 of the Constitution of the USSR of 1977, are applicable to Soviets elected before its enactment.

The Presidium of the Supreme Soviet of the USSR shall determine the time for conducting the next elections for the Supreme Soviet of the USSR, and the Presidiums of the Supreme Soviets of the union and autonomous republics—the time for conducting the next elections for the corresponding Supreme Soviets of the union republics, the Supreme Soviets of the autonomous republics, and the local Soviets of People's Deputies.

Article 3. The executive and administrative organs of Soviets of People's Deputies, the ministries and departments, the organs of people's control, the courts, the organs of the state arbitration and of the Procuracy, and other state organs, created in accordance with the Constitution of the USSR of 1936, exercise the powers granted to them by the new Constitution, and also, until the enactment of legislative acts pursuant to the new Constitution of the USSR, by legislation passed before the enactment of the new Constitution.

Article 4. The Presidium of the Supreme Soviet of the USSR shall formulate and submit for examination by the Supreme Soviet of the USSR a draft Law on Elections for the Supreme Soviet of the USSR and draft Regulations of the Supreme Soviet of the USSR, and shall also define the manner of organizing the work for bringing the legislation of the USSR into conformity with the new Constitution of the USSR.

Article 5. The Council of Ministers of the USSR shall formulate and submit for examination by the Supreme Soviet of the USSR:
—a draft Law on the Council of Ministers of the USSR;
—a draft Law on People's Control of the USSR;
—a draft Law on the State Arbitration of the USSR.

Article 6. In connection with the Law of the USSR of 7 October 1977 "On declaring the day of enactment of the Constitution (Fundamental Law) of the USSR a nationwide holiday", the words "7 October—the Day of the Constitution of the USSR" shall be added after the words "9 May—Victory Day" in Article 31 of the Principles of Labor Legislation of the USSR and the Union Republics, excluding from this Article the words "5 December—the Day of the Constitution of the USSR".

Article 7. The Soviets of People's Deputies, their executive and administrative organs, the ministries and departments, and the heads of other state and social organs shall examine the proposals and observations made by citizens, in connection with the nationwide discussion of the draft of the Constitution of the USSR, on questions connected with the activities of these organs, and shall take measures for their realization.

(Law of 7 October 1977. *Ved. SSSR* 1977 No. 41 item 619)

NOTES ON THE TRANSLATION

F.J.M. Feldbrugge

1. General Observations

Purpose of this translation

The translation was made on the basis of the draft Constitution, approved by the Central Committee of the CPSU on 24 May 1977 and published immediately afterwards in the Soviet press. By the time we were working on the translation, two English translations were already available. One was supplied by *TASS* and published widely soon after the draft had been made public (we have used the text as printed in *The Times* of 6 June 1977). The other English translation was made by *The Current Digest of the Soviet Press* and appeared in Vol. XXIX No. 22 of 29 June 1977. In the *TASS* translation, English rather than American idiom is used; also, the translation is occasionally less literal (*e.g.* "intending spouses" for "woman and man", and "matrimonial relationships" for "family relationships" in Article 53, para. 2; "the rules of socialist behavior" for "the rules of socialist community life" in Article 59).

In contrast, the idiom of the *CDSP* translation is American and its terminology is more precise than in the *TASS* translation, although one gets the impression that the American translators have consulted and followed the *TASS* translation on a number of controversial or problematic points (*e.g.* "law and order" in Article 4, where we have preferred "legal order").

Generally speaking, both translations are competently executed and reliable. The rationale for the present translation lies in the consideration that the proper character of a translation should also be determined by its audience. A document such as the Constitution of the USSR may have a number of quite diverse audiences in the English speaking world: the educated public, politicians, political scientists, lawyers, etc. What has been attempted in the present translation is to offer a text which is of the greatest usefulness for the lawyer. The chief consequence of this policy is that wherever there appeared to be a conflict between precision and readability, the former has prevailed. This preference operates also where a more literal translation is indicated, not so much to record as precisely as possible the legal implications of a rule, but rather to convey the stylistic flavor of the original. Some of the most important peculiarities of the style of the Soviet Constitution are discussed below.

Sovietisms

Soviet political culture has a language of its own. Indeed it can be argued that if it is true that Marxist–Leninist political ideology is moribund as a genuine social force, its function is predominantly linguistic. The Soviet political debate, whatever there is of it, is carried on in the language of Marxism–Leninism because its participants do not know any other language, not because they are Marxists–Leninists. That such a thing is possible is proved by developments in the West, where Marxist political terminology ("capitalism", "exploitation", "alienation", "class struggle", etc.) has become part of the general vocabulary of politics.

Some of the most important political terms of Marxism–Leninism have inevitably found their way into the Soviet Constitution. Among such terms there are comparatively new formations, as well as older Russian words which have acquired a specific meaning in Soviet political parlance.

One of the key terms in Soviet ideology which is often encountered in the present Constitution is the adjective *vsenarodnyi* or *obshchenarodnyi*: "of the whole people". This term has become extremely popular after the new Party Program, accepted at the 22nd Party Congress in 1961, proclaimed that the Soviet state had become an "all-people's state". To be sure, it is not new; after the Revolution it was used several times in statements concerning land and forests. These were taken away from private owners and became "of the whole people". Curiously enough, it would seem that at that time "being of the whole people" was not quite the same as "being nationalized". This is borne out by Article 3 of the first Soviet Constitution of 1918, point b) of which provided that all land became the heritage of the whole people (*obshchenarodnym dostoianiem*) and was handed over to the working people; point c) then added that forests, minerals, and waters were proclaimed the heritage of the nation (*natsional'nym dostoianiem*). Under present conditions, however, *obshchenarodnyi* has a much more specific meaning; it implies that the class struggle in the Soviet Union is over and that, consequently, the dictatorship of the proletariat has outlived itself. There are no antagonistic classes anymore, and therefore the USSR has stopped being a state of workers and peasants (as it was in its early stage) and has become a state of the entire people. For this reason, *obshchenarodnyi* and *vsenarodnyi* have been translated as "all-people's".

Another term which has acquired a rather specific meaning in the language of Soviet politics and law is *obshchestvennyi*, the adjective belonging to *obshchestvo*—society. This term may be used in a general sense, *e.g.* in *obshchestvennyi poriadok* (public order), but also more specifically in contrast with the adjective *gosudarstvennyi* (state). This is normally the case where it accompanies "property" or "organs" and appears in contrast with state property or state organs. In such cases, *obshchestvennyi* has been translated as "social".

With regard to the term *organy* itself, we have chosen to translate it as "organs" and not as "agencies" or "bodies", considering that the term is typical for Soviet legislative style.

Another frequently used term is *kontrol'*, which we have, as a rule, not translated with the obvious "control" but as "supervision". There are two reasons for this. The primary meaning of *kontrol'* in Russian (as well as its counterpart in a number of European languages) is not "direction" or (as a verb) "to direct", as in English, but "supervision" (or "to supervise, to check"). Moreover, it can be argued with good reason that a profusion of supervisory agencies is one of the most pervasive features of the Soviet legal and administrative system. Everybody is supervised, not only by administrative superiors, but also by Party agencies, by People's Control (*Narodnyi Kontrol'*), by the *Prokuratura*, by the State Bank, by the *KGB*, and by a host of other bodies.

Some of the typically Soviet terms pose impossible problems to translators. To quote two examples: *zakonomernyi* (used in the Preamble) literally means "according to law", although not the law of the state but the law of societal development as revealed by Marxist political ideology: socialist society is a *zakonomernyi* stage on the road to communism. This has been translated variously as a "logically necessary" or an "objectively necessary" stage. We have translated it simply as a "necessary" stage. Of course the German *gesetzmässig*, which happens to be the legitimate ancestor of the Soviet term, is exactly right. Another example is a pure Soviet neologism: *ideinost'* (also used in the Preamble). We have resisted the suggestion of a distinguished Slavic scholar to translate it with "the equally idiotic word 'ideahood' ", and have opted for "full of ideas". Other translations are: "ideological conviction" (*CDSP*), "ideological commitment" (*TASS*).

German origins

It has often been remarked that the language of Soviet politics and law has borrowed extensively from German. This is particularly noticeable in the class of abstract and composite nouns. This is one of the reasons why it is generally easier to translate from Russian into German than into English. One of the most prominent examples is *pravoporiadok* (German *Rechtsordnung*). As Professor Harold Berman has pointed out, *pravoporiadok* should not be translated as "law and order", but as "legal order". Other examples are *zhiznennaia potrebnost'* (*Lebensbedürfnisse*) in Article 13 and *voleiz"iavlenie* (*Willensäusserung*) in Article 98.

Rhetorical style

The Soviet Constitution is richer than most other constitutions in rhetorical embellishments which lack precise legal meaning and consequence. Examples may not only be found in the Preamble, where one would more or less expect the legislator to open the registers of self-glorification and national pride, but also in the text of the Constitution itself. They are most abundant in Chapters 1 (The Political System), 3 (Social Development and Culture), 4 (Foreign Policy), and 5 (Defense of the Socialist Fatherland). The Communist Party "directs the great creative activity of the Soviet people" (Article 6); the Soviet state conducts "a Leninist peace policy" (Article 28); "Defense of the socialist Fatherland is the sacred duty of every citizen of the USSR" (Article 62). The frequent use of the term "socialist Fatherland" itself is remarkable in many cases where "the country" or "the USSR" would have done. Article 62 even uses two emotionally evocative words to refer to the USSR: *Otechestvo* (Fatherland) and *Rodina* (Motherland), both written with a capital letter in the original.

Use of the article

The absence of the article in Russian introduces an element of ambiguity in the Russian text which the translator has to face. Does the Soviet state conduct "a Leninist peace policy" or "the Leninist peace policy" (Article 28); in other words, is there only one such policy or are several conceivable? In this case we decided to play safe and allow a plurality of Leninist peace policies by using "a", although the *TASS* translation has "the".

Socialist ownership is presumably *the* basis of the Soviet economic system (see the first sentence of Article 9); however, in the next paragraph of the same Article it is not so certain whether the state creates *the* conditions for the increase of socialist ownership (*i.e.* the state would be the exclusive promoter of such ownership), or whether it just creates conditions (implying that others may do likewise).

One question where the ambiguity is of great practical importance is the composition of the Council of Ministers (Article 128); it may safely be presumed that the Council of Ministers comprises all USSR ministers, but are also all chairmen of USSR state committees members? This would be at variance with previous practice (*cf.* Article 70 of the previous USSR Constitution), in which only certain specifically mentioned chairmen of state committees were included. We have therefore opted for "the ministers of the USSR" and "chairmen of state committees of the USSR".

Use of "and"

The elements of enumerations, which are naturally quite frequent in the Constitution, are usually separated by commas in the Russian original, even the penultimate and the final element. In all such cases we have inserted "and", preceded by a comma.

Translation of the prescriptive

The prescriptive part of a legal rule is invariably voiced in the present tense in Russian, as in most other continental European languages, but unlike English which normally uses "shall". The explanation cannot be that there is no future tense in Russian (there are in fact two, of the perfective and the imperfective of every verb), but otherwise it is a subject for fruitful speculation. Most probably biblical language, particularly the translation of the Ten Commandments, has influenced the choice of tense in legal language. (My attention was drawn to this by Professor Isaac Kisch of the University of Amsterdam.) The result is that a Russian (or German) legal document—be it a law or a contract or a will—describes a universe as if it really existed and where things happen without fail. There is only one implied basic norm underlying all these subsystems: everything shall happen as prescribed by the Law. In English, the norm is reiterated in every legal rule. Whether the difference is just a linguistic accident or whether there is a more fundamental difference behind it affecting the perception of law, is a matter which need not concern us here.

We have decided, in line with the *CDSP* translators, in favor of the present tense for two reasons. In this way, one remains closer to the Russian original and one avoids the choice between the present and the future which the "shall"-method inevitably entails in a number of cases.

Spelling

We have used American spelling, and where the choice had to be made and other considerations seemed to be in balance, American rather than English terminology.

2. Notes on the Translation of Specific Articles

Article 3. "snizu doverkhu"

The definition of democratic centralism in Article 3 is obviously borrowed from a similar definition in article 19 of the 1961 Statute of the Communist Party of the Soviet Union, which, among other things, provides that all leading Party organs are elected "*snizu doverkhu*", from the lowest to the highest. The *CDSP* and *TASS* translations have "from top to bottom" in Article 3, and this would mean that "state organs of power" at all levels are elected. In fact "at all levels" would be an acceptable translation for *snizu doverkhu*. However, in the definition of democratic centralism in the Party Statute, *snizu doverkhu* may imply more than just the elective nature of all leading Party organs. The supreme Party organs of the various levels, *i.e.* Party congresses and conferences, are always elected by the next lower level. Consequently, power in the Party—at least on paper—flows upwards: the local Party conference being elected by the primary organizations, the *raion* conference by the local conferences, the provincial conference by the *raion* conferences, the republican congresses by the provincial conferences, and the CPSU Congress by the republican congresses (I disregard the special position of the RSFSR and the small republics). In other words, *snizu doverkhu* in the Party Statute might mean additionally (or might at least allow such meaning) that leading organs are elected from the bottom upwards: "From the bottom to the top", as would be the most precise translation of *snizu doverkhu*. This interpretation of democratic centralism would make the system of Party elections look more radically democratic, by de-emphasizing the centralist element. That it does not reflect the actual state of affairs is quite another matter.

The use of *snizu doverkhu* in the definition of democratic centralism in the election of state organs does not strengthen this broad interpretation. Representative bodies in the state are elected by the electorate of the territory concerned, and not by bodies on a lower rung of the ladder. Whether *snizu doverkhu* means anything beyond "at all levels" is a question which can be answered authoritatively only by the Soviets themselves.

Article 7. "ustavnye zadachi"

"*Statutory functions*" of organizations in Article 7 (and similar expressions, *e.g.* in Articles 10 and 12) refer to functions defined by the statute (*ustav*) of the organizations concerned, not to functions defined by law in general.

Article 12. "bessrochnoe pol'zovanie"

The second paragraph of Article 12 is identical to Article 8 of the old Constitution with the last two words from the latter missing: *to-est' navechno* ("*i.e.* forever"). The question may now be asked whether "use for an unlimited time" (*bessrochnoe pol'zovanie*) has a more restricted meaning at present than under the old Article 8. If not, why have the words "*i.e.* forever" been left out? The idea that "an unlimited time" is not really quite as long as "forever" is reinforced by two statements in the new Constitution which were absent in the old Constitution: that state ownership is the basic form of socialist ownership (Article 11, para. 1) and that the state promotes the drawing together of collective-farm/cooperative ownership with state ownership (Article 12, para. 3). The avowed long-term target of the fusion of these two types of ownership in one pool of state ownership would inevitably entail the disappearance of the collective farms in their present form. "Eternal" user rights of kolkhozes concerning their land allotments would stand in the way of such a development.

Article 13. "trudovye dokhody"

The exact meaning of this term is "income from labor". Only legitimate work can produce "earned income". Income from, for instance, proscribed forms of private enterprise is not "earned". On the other hand, "income from labor" includes property inherited in the regular way, although this is not directly "earned".

Article 41. "rabochie i sluzhashchie"

This term has been translated as "workers and employees". The *TASS* translation has "industrial, office, and professional workers" and *CDSP*: "workers and office employees". The term embraces the entire workforce of the country minus the kolkhoz farmers.

Article 121. "smeniaet vysshee komandovanie"

Point 14 of this Article concerns the power of the Presidium of the Supreme Soviet of the USSR to make the most important defense appointments. Among other things, it "appoints and replaces [*smeniaet*] the high command of the Armed Forces of the USSR." The word *smeniaet* means "alters" and includes therefore not only the replacement (or "removal", in the *TASS* and *CDSP* translations) of members of the high command, but any mutations in the high command.

Articles 169 and 170. "serp i molot"

Although almost all translations use "hammer and sickle", the Soviet constitutions—already since 1918—have "sickle and hammer" in the original text.

REPORTS ON THE CONSTITUTION OF THE USSR: 1977

ON THE DRAFT CONSTITUTION OF THE UNION OF SOVIET SOCIALIST REPUBLICS*

L.I. Brezhnev

(Report at the Plenum of the Central Committee of the CPSU, 24 May 1977)

Izvestiia, 5 June 1977

Respected Comrades,

We have now to consider the draft of the new Constitution of the USSR. The Politbureau has studied this document carefully and has approved it in principle. Inasmuch as all of you are already familiar with the draft, I shall only touch upon some of the central and essential questions.

I

First question: *Why was it necessary to create a new Constitution?*

Because, comrades, far-reaching changes have taken place in our country and our society during the past four decades.

When the Constitution of 1936 was adopted, we had, in fact, just finished the laying of the foundations of socialism. The collective farm system was still quite young and not yet consolidated. The technical level of the national economy was far behind the level of the most developed industrial countries. The legacy of pre-revolutionary times still made itself felt in various spheres of life.

A developed and mature socialist society has now been built in the Soviet Union. *Great and fundamental changes have affected all aspects of social life.*

The economy of the country has changed beyond recognition. Socialist ownership reigns here now without limitations. A single

*Translated by F.J.M. Feldbrugge.

powerful organism of the national economy has taken shape and functions successfully. It is being developed on the basis of combining a scientific-technical revolution with the advantages of the socialist system.

The social make-up of our society has also changed.

Our working class now embraces two-thirds of the country's population. That is to say, tens of millions of educated, technically competent, and politically mature people. Their work is getting more and more similar to the work of engineering and technical personnel. The social activeness of workers and their participation in the administration of the state has increased considerably.

The peasantry has changed too. Today's collective farmer has been born and has grown up on the collective farm; his psychology has already been formed on the basis of socialism. He operates modern technical equipment. And his educational level and his life style are often little different from those of city dwellers.

The intelligentsia has become deeply rooted in the people and is genuinely socialist. The relative weight of the intelligentsia in our society grows along with the rising of the cultural level of the people and the unprecedented increase of the role of science in the building of communism.

Equality of the nations has become not only a legal principle, but also an actual fact in our country. All our republics, including those which formerly were economically and culturally backward, have now reached a high level of development. At the same time, the economy of every republic has become an integral part of the single complex of the national economy.

The common indicator of all these changes is the growing social homogeneousness of Soviet society. The unbreakable union of the working class, the collective farm peasantry, and the people's intelligentsia has grown even stronger. The differences between the basic social groups are gradually fading. All the nations and nationalities of our country, by the very course of their life, are drawing together more and more. A new historic community of people has emerged: the Soviet people.

With the building of a mature socialism and with the adherence by all the sections of the population to the ideological-political positions of the working class, our state itself, which emerged as a dictatorship of the proletariat, has been transformed into a state of the entire people.

All these processes in the life of the country have been guided and are guided by the Communist Party—the leading, organizing, and mobilizing force of our society from the time of the October Revolution right down to our days. The problems which it must solve have become even more complicated and varied now. Its role has become even more responsible, and the scope of its guiding influence on the entire internal life of the country and its foreign policy has grown.

Finally, also the international position of the Soviet Union and the whole socio-political structure of the world have changed drastically. The capitalist encirclement of the USSR is over. Socialism has become a world system. A mighty socialist commonwealth has emerged. The positions of world capitalism have weakened considerably. Dozens of young states, opposed to imperialism, have sprung up in the place of former colonies. The international authority and influence of our country have grown immeasurably.

As a result, the balance of forces on the global theater has changed completely. There is a real possibility now to prevent a new world war; the threat of the outbreak of such a war has already been reduced considerably, although there is still much work to be done, and a hard fight to be fought in this area.

Supported by what has been achieved, the Soviet people now, under the leadership of the Party, solves new problems: the creation of the material-technical basis of communism, the gradual transformation of socialist social relationships into communist ones, and the education of man in the spirit of communist consciousness.

These are, in short, the basic changes in our society and in the life of the country since 1936. These are the basic causes of and conditions for the creation of the new Constitution of the USSR.

II

Comrades, the draft of the new Constitution is the result of a mighty and sustained effort. It was based on clear and concrete directives of the Party. The report of the Central Committee to the 25th Congress of the CPSU said: "The new draft of the Constitution, evidently, should reflect the great victories of socialism, and should state not only the general principles of the socialist system, expressing the class essence of our state, but also the basic features of a developed socialist society and its political organization."[1] It also indicated the need to give expression to the principles of the management of the national economy, the role of the state in the spiritual life of society, and the further development of socialist democracy.

These basic requirements of the Party are expressed in the draft.

In our work on the draft, *we stood firmly on the ground of tradition.*

The characteristics of a constitution of a socialist type, outlined by V.I. Lenin himself, have been preserved and developed in it.

V. I. Lenin and the Bolshevik Party held that the Constitution is not only a legal, but also a very important political document. The Party regarded the Constitution as the confirmation of the conquests of the revolution and, at the same time, as the proclamation of the fundamental aims and objectives in the building of socialism.

Such a document was the first RSFSR Constitution of 1918, which consolidated the conquests of the October Revolution and defined the class nature of the Soviet state as a state of the dictatorship of the proletariat.

Such a document was also the Constitution of the USSR of 1924, which defined the principles of the formation of a federal socialist state.

The Constitution of 1936 provided the legislative consolidation to the victory of socialist social relationships in the USSR and it brought the entire system of organs of power and administration, as well as the system of elections, in accordance with this. The constitutional framework for the development of society as it was then worked out has stood the test of time.

Many basic provisions of the present Constitution have been preserved in the new draft, as they continue to correspond to the essence of our system and the character of our development.

In this way the draft of the new Constitution, on the one hand, summarizes the entire constitutional experience of Soviet history, and, on the other hand, enriches this experience with a new content, satisfying the requirements of the present era.

The draft is also based on the renewal and improvement of Soviet legislation which have already taken place and crowns, as it were, what has been done in this respect.

And very much has been done during recent years. Federal principles of legislation and republican codes in the majority of the most important branches of law have been put into effect. We now have statutes on the industrial enterprise and on the production association and a new Collective Farm Charter. New laws on health care, national education, pensions, and environmental protection have been adopted. The rights and duties of local Soviets have been clearly defined. The status of deputies has been regulated. All these legislative acts have been taken into account in the draft and have become like building blocks for many provisions of the new Constitution.

And one other essential factor. *The experience of the constitutional development of the fraternal socialist countries has been utilized* in the preparation of the draft. During the 1970s, new constitutions were adopted in Bulgaria, the GDR, Cuba, and several other socialist countries. There are a number of provisions in those constitutions which are of interest to us. And they have not been ignored.

In one word, comrades, the new Constitution is being constructed on a sound practical and theoretical foundation. The Politbureau believes that this will guarantee its stability and its active effect on the further progress of Soviet society.

III

Let me now discuss *the main features of the contents of the draft of the new Constitution.*

First, it should be noted that *a detailed description of the guiding and leading role of the Communist Party* is given and that the actual place of our Party in Soviet society and the state is clearly defined. This matter is expressed more broadly, and, unlike the Constitution of 1936, in a separate article.

The draft of the new Constitution also indicates that *a developed socialist society has been created in the USSR and that the highest aim of the Soviet state is the building of communism.* It emphasizes that *our state is a state of the entire people,* and that it expresses the will and the interests of the working class, the peasantry, and the intelligentsia, and of all the nations and nationalities of the country. In connection with this, it is proposed to call our Soviets: Soviets of People's Deputies.

The draft retains the fundamental provision that socialist ownership of the means of production is the basis of the economic system of the USSR. At the same time, it is proposed to introduce certain amendments which are suggested by life itself. Ownership of trade unions and other social organizations is mentioned together with state and collective farm/cooperative ownership.

Altogether, it is possible to say that *the main thrust of the innovations contained in the draft is the widening and deepening of socialist democracy.*

Above all, the democratic principles of the formation and activity of the Soviets are further developed. Their role in solving the most important problems of the life of society is strengthened.

Article 106 provides that the Supreme Soviet of the USSR is empowered to solve all problems within the jurisdiction of the USSR. Local Soviets not only solve all problems of local significance, but also supervise and coordinate, within the limits of their rights, the activities of other organizations on their territory. The systematic character of the supervision by the Soviets of the executive and administrative organs and the activities of organizations and officials is especially emphasized.

The term of office of the Supreme Soviet is extended to five years, and to two and a half years for local Soviets. The same periods will be valid for the election of judges.

The main ways for strengthening the ties of the Soviets and their deputies with the masses are indicated in the draft. They are bound to report regularly on their activities to the population, to give account of themselves before their constituents, and to examine carefully each proposal of the working people.

You know, comrades, that five years ago we adopted an important Law on the Status of Deputies to Soviets. In order to enhance the role of deputies even more, the basic powers conferred on them by this law have now been included in the text of the draft of the Constitution.

A new element has also been introduced into the electoral system. While according to the present Constitution only persons who have reached the age of 23 years have the right to be elected to the Supreme Soviet of the USSR—and 21 years, for the Supreme Soviets of union republics—it is now proposed to make this possibility available to all Soviet citizens from the age of 18. This is a genuine demonstration of our society's care for and trust in youth.

The important role played by the trade unions, the Komsomol, cooperative, and other social mass organizations in the life of the country has been widely expressed in the draft. They are granted the right to participate in the solution of political, economic, and socio-cultural questions and the right of legislative initiative. In this way, it is once again emphasized that the state of the entire people takes account of the interests of all social strata and all groups of the population.

The draft of the Constitution also includes a provision concerning the role of collectives of working people. This reflects a major policy of our party and the importance it attributes to the development of democratic principles in the management of production.

The building of developed socialism allows us to improve considerably the provisions of the Basic Law *on the Rights of Soviet Citizens*. The famous words of the 'Communist Manifesto': "The free development of each is the condition for the free development of all",[2] have actually become the basic principle of our state. And this is reflected in the draft.

The general principle of the equality of Soviet citizens is proclaimed in a special section. Additionally, the achievements of socialism in such important spheres as guaranteeing equal rights of men and women and the equal rights of citizens irrespective of their nationality or race are spelled out with all clarity.

As you know, the present Constitution provides *a broad complex* of socio-economic rights, affecting the most essential aspects of the life of people. But we know very well how their contents have deepened and to what extent the material factors guaranteeing them have become richer and more powerful. All this is reflected in the draft of the new Constitution. If, for instance, the right to work was mentioned before, then now this is complemented by the right to choose a profession, an occupation, and work in accordance with the vocation, ability, professional training, and education of the citizen, and also, which is no less important, with the requirements of society.

Furthermore, if the Constitution of 1936 mentions the right to material security in case of illness or loss of the ability to work, then now the question is posed in a wider framework: Soviet citizens are guaranteed the right to health care. If formerly the right to education was mentioned in general terms, then now compulsory universal secondary education and the wide development of professional-technical and higher education is envisaged.

The draft also mentions a right of Soviet citizens which is not registered in the present Constitution. I refer to the right to housing which will be guaranteed more fully as the program of housing construction is being realized, and also by state assistance to cooperative and individual house building. Our new Constitution is one of the first in the world to proclaim this right which is so vitally important for man.

The political rights and freedoms of citizens of the USSR are formulated much more extensively in the draft.

The right of every Soviet citizen to participate in the administration of the affairs of the state and of society is proclaimed, and concrete forms of this participation are indicated.

The freedom of speech, the press, assembly, meetings, street marches, and demonstrations, included also in the present Constitution, are fully reaffirmed. An important addition to the constitutional guarantees of the rights of the person is the right of citizens to address proposals to state and social organs, to criticize shortcomings in their work, to appeal against actions of officials to the courts, and also the right to be defended by the courts against attacks on one's life and health, property and personal freedom, honor and dignity.

Of course, comrades, the draft of the Constitution assumes that the rights and freedoms of citizens cannot and may not be used against our social system, against the interests of the Soviet people. The draft therefore states firmly that, for instance, the exercise of rights and freedoms by citizens should not harm the interests of society and the state and the rights of other citizens, and that political freedoms are granted in accordance with the interests of the working people and in order to strengthen the socialist system.

It is necessary that it should be clear to every Soviet citizen that ultimately the chief guarantee of his rights is in the strength and well-being of the Motherland. Therefore, every citizen should realize his responsibility before society and should conscientiously do his duty to the state and to the people.

For this reason, the draft of the Constitution stresses the obligation of the citizens to work honestly and conscientiously and to defend the Motherland. The character of constitutional demands is now given for the first time also to the duties to protect the interests of the Soviet state, to assist in strengthening its power and authority, to cooperate in every way in protecting public order, to fight theft and wasting of state and social property, to protect nature and safeguard its wealth, and to be concerned with the preservation of cultural treasures. The draft also obliges citizens to care for the education of children and to raise them as worthy members of a socialist society.

A special chapter of the draft "*Social development and culture*" states that the state shall concern itself with the development of education, science, and art, with improving the work conditions of citizens, raising the level of their income, and with the growth and equitable distribution of the public funds of consumption. The same chapter indicates that the state strives to reach such important milestones on our road towards communism as the effacement of essential differences between town and country, and between intellectual and physical labor, and the increasing of the social homogeneousness of society.

The further strengthening of socialist legality and the legal order are also clearly expressed in the draft of the new Constitution.

We know, comrades, that some of the years following the adoption of the present Constitution were darkened by illegal repressions and violations of the principles of socialist democracy and of the Leninist norms of Party and state life. This was in violation of the rules of the Constitution. The Party has condemned this practice unreservedly and such things must never happen again.

The great amount of work done by our Central Committee, the Supreme Soviet of the USSR, and the Soviet government in perfecting Soviet legislation and in creating reliable guarantees against any violations of the rights of citizens, abuse of power, and bureaucratic perversions is well known. As if to summarize all these guarantees, the draft stresses that observation of the Constitution and the law is the duty of all state organs and officials, social organizations, and citizens.

Comrades, *the Soviet Union is a multinational state.* Experience has shown that the basic features of the federal organization of the USSR have fully justified themselves. There is no need, therefore, to introduce any essential changes into the forms of the Soviet socialist federation.

The draft indicates, as did the Constitution of 1936, that the sovereign rights of the union republics are protected by the USSR. The guarantees of these rights have also been retained. Moreover, new ones have been added, such as the right of the republics to participate in the solution of problems within the jurisdiction of the USSR by federal organs. The union republics, represented by their supreme organs of state power, are granted the right of legislative initiative in the Supreme Soviet of the USSR.

On the other hand, the increasing rapprochement of the nations and nationalities of the USSR suggests the necessity of strengthening the federal principles of the state. This has also been reflected in the very designation of the USSR as a unitary federal multinational state (Article 69). The strengthening of the all-union principles is also reflected in several other provisions of the draft.

On the whole, the solutions of questions of national-state organization in the draft ensures a genuinely democratic combination of the general interests of the multinational union with the interests of each of the constituent republics, and ensures the all-round development and steady rapprochement of all the nations and nationalities of our country.

The draft reflects *a new stage in the development of our national economy.* It indicates that the economy of the USSR has been transformed into an integrated national economic complex, embracing all links of public production, distribution, and exchange on the territory of the country.

It also registers such an important principle of the socialist economy as the combination of planned centralized management with economic independence and initiative of enterprises and associations.

The competence of central and local state organs, ministries, and departments is spelled out in more detail in the draft of the Constitution. Unlike the present Constitution, the draft does not give a list of union and union-republic ministries and departments. Considering that, as experience has proved, their composition changed from time to time, it was regarded as more appropriate to place such a list in a special law on the Council of Ministers of the USSR, the adoption of which is provided for in Article 135 of the draft of the Constitution.

Comrades! Radical changes in the international position of the USSR, the enormous growth of its influence in world politics, and the close connection of domestic and external factors of our development have made it inevitable to include in the draft of the Constitution *a special chapter on the foreign policy of the USSR*. For the first time, such a chapter is introduced into the Constitution.

It says that the Soviet state consistently follows a Leninist peace policy and that it stands for consolidation of the security of peoples and broad international cooperation. The foreign policy of the USSR is directed at ensuring favorable international conditions for the building of communism in the USSR, strengthening the positions of world socialism, supporting the struggle of peoples for national liberation and social progress, and at preventing aggressive wars and consistently implementing the principles of peaceful coexistence of states with different social systems. For the first time, the Constitution clearly lays down that the Soviet Union is a component part of the world system of socialism and the socialist commonwealth. The Soviet Union develops and strengthens friendship, cooperation, and mutual comradely assistance with the countries of socialism on the basis of socialist internationalism.

For the first time also, a special *chapter on the defense of the socialist Fatherland* is included. Moreover, the formation of the country's Defense Council and the confirmation of its composition is mentioned among the prerogatives of the Presidium of the Supreme Soviet of the USSR.

These are, in short, the main elements characterizing the contents of the draft of the Constitution of the USSR.

IV

Allow me now to dwell on the tasks facing us in connection with the implementation of the new Constitution and on the significance which its adoption will have for the development of our country, and for strengthening the positions of the forces of socialism, peace, and progress in the international arena.

First *about the significance of the new Constitution for the internal life of the country.*

The realization of its provisions should raise to a qualitatively new level our entire state and economic activity, and all the work of the organs of power and administration.

This concerns, first of all, the ever more effective utilization of the broad powers of the elective organs—the Soviets. The enormous potential of a two-million army of deputies, representatives of all layers of the population, all professions, and all nationalities, should be used to the full. This mighty collective brain of Soviet power takes on and shall take on ever more complicated and varied tasks. It can and must exercise effective supervision over the work of executive organs of all levels.

Much will have to be done in the field of legislation. Federal laws on elections, regulations of the Supreme Soviet, and a law on the Council of Ministers will have to be drafted, and the competence of territory, provincial, and area Soviets, and of ministries and departments will have to be regulated on the basis of the Constitution. Without losing time, new Constitutions of union and autonomous republics will have to be drafted and adopted.

The new Constitution of the USSR will become the core of the Collection of Laws of the Soviet state, the compilation of which has been started in accordance with the decisions of the 25th Congress of the CPSU.

At the same time, the new Constitution should lead to a considerable improvement of the work of all organs who are charged with safeguarding the strict observance of the requirements of Soviet legislation. I refer to the Procuracy, the courts, arbitration, other administrative organs, and people's control. The Party expects from all these organs even more initiative, rectitude, and toughness in the struggle against any kind of violations of the Soviet legal order.

It is very important that the draft provides possibilities for a continuous improvement of the entire system of the socialist economy and the entire work of planning organs and other organs which direct the economy and culture. Their basic functions have been defined in the Constitution. They should be carried out fully and precisely, so that the responsibility of every organ and every official is increased.

Soviets at all levels, the government, ministries and departments, as well as the executive committees of Soviets should constantly check their work against the requirements of the Constitution. And indeed, Party organs should question communists who head state and economic organs more strictly as to how they fulfill their constitutional obligations.

The implementation of the new Constitution will allow millions and millions of Soviet citizens to take a still more active part in the management of the economy and the supervision over the work of the state apparatus.

Centralism in managing the economy is necessary and inevitable. But equally necessary is the careful consideration of the full complexity of the conditions for the development of our economy. And this is impossible without the further growth of the initiative of production collectives and the active, and I would almost say proprietorial, participation in management of the working people themselves. Under socialism, democracy has been and remains an important lever for developing the economy and all fields of the economic and cultural life of society.

Thus, an enormous creative potential resides in the Constitution. And this should be utilized creatively. ". . . . the Soviet Constitution", said V.I. Lenin, "serves and will constantly serve the working people and is a powerful weapon in the struggle for the realization of socialism."[3] Today, Vladimir Il'ich would have added: and an instrument for building communism.

There is no doubt, comrades, that the adoption of the new Constitution of the USSR, a constitution of developed socialism, a constitution of communism under construction, will not only be an historic event for our country, but also *an event of enormous international significance.* Its implementation will exercise a deep and lasting influence far from the borders of our Motherland.

Our new Constitution clearly demonstrates to the whole world how a socialist state progresses by affirming ever more strongly and deeply socialist democracy, and how this socialist democracy functions and what it really means. Our Constitution will show the diverse forms and the enormous scope of the ever-growing genuine participation of the broad popular masses in the management of the affairs of the state and of society, a thing unknown in bourgeois countries, where in fact only a small class of capitalists rules.

Reading our new Constitution, people will see even more clearly how broad and varied are the rights and freedoms of the citizens of a socialist society. In the provisions of the Constitution, the world will see a state which makes the uninterrupted growth of the well-being and the culture of the whole people and all its classes and groups without exception its goal, and which works actively towards the achievement of this goal.

Finally, our new Constitution will demonstrate more persuasively that the first state of victorious socialism has written the word "Peace" in its banner forever, as the highest principle of its foreign policy, in accordance with the interests of its own people and all other peoples of this planet.

The new Constitution of the Soviet Union will undoubtedly add considerably to the rich experience of world socialism.

The achievements of victorious socialism, reflected in it in a concentrated form, will be an inspiring example for the peoples of those countries which have recently opted for the road of socialist development.

They will add to the confidence of the working masses of the capitalist countries in their struggle for their rights and for the emancipation from the yoke of capitalist exploitation.

To an interpretation of democracy and human rights, perverted and vulgarized by bourgeois and revisionist propaganda, we oppose the most complete and genuine complex of rights and duties of the citizen of a socialist society. On the scales of history, we place the truly historical conquests of the working people, won thanks to the power of the working class under the leadership of the Communist Party.

V

Comrades! The Politbureau of the Central Committee is of the opinion that the draft of the new Constitution, approved by the Plenum, must be submitted to a nationwide discussion, as has also been suggested at the 25th Congress of the Party. This means that *we are facing a work of great scope and significance.*

A document will be presented for discussion by the Soviet people in which are reflected the basic conquests of the revolution and the road traversed in building a new society. The preparations for the celebration of the 60th anniversary of the October Revolution and the discussion of the draft of the new Constitution are therefore measures which are organically connected and which complement each other.

The task before us is: *to guarantee to the best of our ability a wide, free, and really businesslike discussion of the draft of the Constitution,* to draw the mass of the working people and the representatives of all layers of the population into this matter, and to utilize for this purpose the established forms of social activity.

It will also be necessary to create an efficient mechanism for registering the observations and proposals which will come in from the working people through all channels.

It must be borne in mind that in the course of the mass discussion of the draft of the Constitution, the practical activities of all links of the Party, Soviet, and economic apparatus will also come within the view of the working people. Pressing problems which occupy people, unsolved questions, and various shortcomings in our work will be mentioned. We should be prepared for this. We should react efficiently and realistically to criticism and proposals, and take measures where this is necessary.

We are launching the discussion of the new Constitution during a period in which the Soviet people is laboring strenuously, under the leadership of the Party, to execute the decisions of the 25th Congress of the CPSU. The nationwide discussion will help *the further invigoration of the entire social life of the country.* It should awaken new creative powers in the people, give new scope to socialist competition, and increase the responsibility of each for his entrusted task.

Party organizations and Party organs are obliged to promote the wide development of the discussion of the Constitution, and to give it a precise and clear political orientation. If they will succeed in doing this properly, then this will undoubtedly improve the political and economic results of this year, the year of adoption of the new Constitution of the USSR and the 60th anniversary of the Great October Revolution.

The discussion of the draft of the Constitution is a most vital affair for the Soviets. In organizing this work, they are called upon to reach virtually the entire adult population of the country. At this moment, the preparations for the elections to local Soviets are taking place in all republics. It is important to make proper use of this occasion. It may perhaps be useful to discuss the draft of the Constitution at the sessions of newly-elected local Soviets.

We expect an active involvement of our social mass organizations in the discussion of the new Constitution, especially of the trade unions and the Komsomol, the creative associations and organizations, and the scientific institutions.

The means of mass information must play a special role. What will be required of our press, radio, and television will be an intelligent and clear elucidation of the course of the discussion and a respectful attitude towards the voice of the working people.

In short, comrades, the discussion of the draft of the new Constitution must become a matter of prime importance for all our organizations and all our cadres.

Concluding my address, I would once more stress, comrades, that the adoption of the new Constitution of the USSR will become an important milestone in the political history of our country. It will be one more historical contribution of our Leninist Party and of the entire Soviet people to the great cause of building communism and, at the same time, to the international cause of the struggle of the working people of the whole world for freedom, for the progress of mankind, and for a lasting peace on earth.

(The report of comrade L.I. Brezhnev was repeatedly interrupted by applause from the participants of the Plenum.)

NOTES

1. L.I. Brezhnev, *Leninskim kursom. Rechi i stat'i* (Along Lenin's Course. Speeches and Articles), Vol. 5, Moskva, 1976, p. 547.
2. K. Marx, F. Engels, *Sochineniia* (Collected Works), Vol. 4, p. 447.
3. V.I. Lenin, *Polnoe sobranie sochinenii* (Complete Collection of Works), Vol. 36, p. 535.

ON THE DRAFT CONSTITUTION (FUNDAMENTAL LAW) OF THE UNION OF SOVIET SOCIALIST REPUBLICS AND THE RESULTS OF THE NATIONWIDE DISCUSSION*

L.I. Brezhnev

(Report at the Session of the Supreme Soviet of the USSR, 4 October 1977)

Izvestiia, 5 October 1977

Respected comrades deputies,

A task, which is in the full sense of the word historical, faces the present session of the Supreme Soviet: the adoption of a new constitution of the Union of Soviet Socialist Republics.

We are adopting a new Constitution on the eve of the 60th anniversary of the Great Socialist October Revolution. This is not merely a matter of two of the most important events in the life of the country coinciding in time. The connection between them is much deeper. The new Constitution, one might say, epitomizes the entire sixty years' development of the Soviet state. It is clear evidence of the fact that the ideas proclaimed by the October Revolution and the teaching of Lenin are being implemented successfully. (Applause).

The draft of the Constitution, submitted for the consideration of the Supreme Soviet, is the result of many years of hard work by a large collective of people. The Constitutional Commission set up by the Supreme Soviet of the USSR includes experienced Party and state officials, and representatives of the working class, the collective farm peasantry, and the people's intelligentsia, and of the numerous nations of our country. Eminent scientists, specialists, and officials of state organs and social organizations were involved in the formulation of the draft. The draft was considered twice at plenary sessions of the Central Committee of the CPSU.

*Translated by F.J.M. Feldbrugge.

I believe that we are entitled to say that the important tasks, which have faced us in connection with the preparation, discussion, and adoption of the Constitution, have been carried out in the most conscientious manner and with the most consistent observation of all the principles of socialist democracy.

I

The nationwide discussion of the draft of the Constitution has been the decisive test of the quality of all the preparatory work. It lasted almost four months and was in the true sense of the word nationwide. Altogether *more than 140,000,000 people,* i.e. *more than four-fifths of the adult population of our country,* took part in it. *A popular activity of such scope has never before been seen in our country.*

The main political result of the nationwide discussion is that Soviet people said: "Yes, this is the Fundamental Law which we expected. It correctly reflects our conquests, our dreams and hopes, and correctly defines our rights and obligations." It confirms what has been achieved and opens a perspective of further development in the building of communism.

About 1,500,000 meetings of working people in enterprises and collective farms, in military units and places of residence have been devoted to an examination of the draft. It was discussed in general assemblies, seminars, and meetings of trade unions, the Komsomol, cooperative associations, and creative organizations. Our whole Party took part in its discussion. More than 450,000 open Party meetings took place, at which more than three million people spoke. The draft was examined by all Soviets, from the village Soviets to the Supreme Soviets of the union republics, *i.e.* by more than two million deputies, representing our whole people. At all these forums, the draft of the Constitution was approved.

Finally, there was an endless stream of letters from Soviet people.

What was characteristic of the overwhelming majority of these letters was the patriotism, the wholehearted approval of the policy of our Party and the Soviet government, the breadth of vision and the maturity of judgment, and the high standards they set to themselves and their comrades. Their authors, as well as the participants in the discussions at meetings—people of the most diverse professions and ages, nations and nationalities, communists and non-Party members—have carefully analyzed the draft of the Constitution, as masters of the country, and have expressed their proposals concerning improvements in the text, as well as other considerations concerning various aspects of life in our society.

Considering these statements and letters, one reaches the conclusion that they reflect an enormous victory of socialism: a new man, who does not separate himself from the state and who regards the interests of the state and of the whole people as his very own. (Applause).

Let us remember how soon after the victory of the October Revolution V.I. Lenin remarked that the system of exploitation had left us a legacy of deep distrust of the masses in anything connected with the state. "It will be very difficult", said Vladimir Lenin, "to overcome this, and only the Soviet government can do it, and even so only after a considerable length of time and a tremendous effort."[1]

The Soviet government has indeed carried out this task. This is abundantly confirmed by the enormous activities of the working people in the discussion of the draft of the new Constitution. We can say with conviction and with pride: *It is indeed the entire Soviet people which has become the true creator of the Fundamental Law of its state.* (Prolonged applause).

Allow me, comrades, on behalf of the Supreme Soviet of the USSR, to thank most cordially every participant in the nationwide discussion of the draft of the Constitution, to wish them all new successes in their work for the good of our great Motherland, and to wish them further and ever more active participation in the affairs of our socialist state! (Prolonged applause).

The Constitutional Commission reports that *the nationwide discussion has made it possible to considerably improve the draft of the Constitution and to introduce a number of useful additions, amendments, and corrections.*

Altogether about 400,000 proposals concerning changes in individual articles were received, aimed at amending, improving, and supplementing the wording of the draft. The Constitutional Commission, after studying these proposals carefully—many of them are, of course, identical—recommends amendments in 110 articles of the draft and the addition of one article. The recommendations of the Commission are in the possession of all deputies. It is my task to justify the proposals of the Commission on the most essential points.

First of all, I want to remark that the greatest number of proposals received concerns the very basic question of *the role of labor under socialism*. Many comrades propose to indicate more clearly in the Constitution the character of our society as a society of working people.

I believe that this proposal is very meaningful. All the classes and social groups of Soviet society consist exclusively of working people. Considering this, it is proposed to record in Article 1 of the Constitution that the Soviet all-people's state expresses the will and interests of the workers, the peasants, and the intelligentsia, and of *the working people* of all nations and nationalities of the country. At the same time, it seems to be proper to adopt one other proposal: to define in the Constitution not only the political basis of the USSR and the basis of our economic system, but also *the social basis of our state.* In our country this basis is now the indestructible unity of the working class, the collective-farm peasantry, and the people's intelligentsia, and it is necessary to say this clearly. (Applause).

Many comrades also proposed a more precise wording for the provision which concerns the basis of the economic system of the USSR, *which should indicate more clearly that this basis is formed by state and collective-farm/cooperative ownership.* This is correct because indeed these two forms of socialist ownership of the means of production define the character of our national economy and the division of Soviet society in two friendly classes, workers and peasants. Such an amendment has been provided for.

The article *on the role and significance of labor collectives* has been the subject of several thousand proposals. The authors of these proposals desire that the Constitution should give wider expression to the functions and rights of the labor collective, especially in such fields as the planning of production and social development, the training and placement of personnel, the improvement of labor and living conditions of workers, the raising of their qualifications, and the fostering of a communist attitude to labor. One has to agree with this.

The whole life of society, economic, political and spiritual, is reflected in the labor collective and in the work of its Party, trade union, and Komsomol organizations. In essence, this is the primary nucleus of our entire economic, as well as political organism. For that reason, those who propose that the provision on the labor collective would better be placed in the first chapter of the Constitution, devoted to our political system, are right.

Thousands of proposals have been received to state in the Constitution that *any evasion of socially useful work is incompatible with the principles of a socialist society.* People demand stricter penalties for absenteeism and for those who are fond of unearned income. One can only agree with these justified considerations.

Very many comrades have written about the need to lay particular stress in the Constitution on the obligation of citizens *to safeguard public wealth,* our socialist property, the fruits of the collective labor of our people, and the foundation of the development of the entire society. The Constitutional Commission agrees with the opinion of working people on this point and proposes to introduce an addition to the corresponding article of the Fundamental Law.

Taking into account various observations received, it is proposed to amend several other provisions in the section "The State and the Individual". For instance, the article concerning the right to housing mentions, in accordance with numerous wishes, *the obligation of citizens to treat carefully the housing made available to them.* The article devoted to the duty of citizens to show concern for the upbringing of children now also indicates *that children are also bound to show concern for their parents and to render them aid.* I want to observe that such proposals have been received not only from elderly people, but also, and this is very gratifying, from many young people.

The nationwide discussion of the draft has made it possible to improve a number of provisions aimed at the further development of socialist democracy.

Many comrades, among them deputies of local Soviets, propose to include a new article—*on voters' mandates*—in the Constitution. Mandates express the most diverse wishes of the population and reflect the actual interests of specific groups of working people and of society as a whole. Therefore, the carrying-out of mandates is an important part of the work of the Soviets and their deputies. It is sufficient to say that only during the last two years, more than 700,000 voters' mandates were carried out. This is one of the genuine manifestations of socialist democracy. It is important that not only deputies, but also heads of enterprises, collective farms, construction projects, and institutions pay serious attention to the implementation of mandates.

We also intend to take into consideration a number of other sensible and correct proposals of working people concerning the further development of the democratic foundations of our state. Thus it appears to be appropriate, as has been proposed by many people, to mention that *a citizen cannot, as a rule, be elected at the same time to more than two Soviets.* This will promote a supply of fresh forces to our state organs, and a widening of the circle of persons who participate in administering the affairs of the state.

As you know from the press, a lively debate emerged during the nationwide discussion concerning *the age, beginning at which citizens should have the right to be elected to Soviets.* The provision of the draft, according to which citizens who have reached the age of 18 years should have the right to be elected to Soviets, was widely supported. But there were also proposals to fix this age at 21, 23, and even 30 years.

The Constitutional Commission examined this question and took it for granted that labor collectives and social organizations, which were putting forward candidates, would assess their qualifications from every angle and would be very demanding in respect of the candidates. In this way, it could be reliably guaranteed that only worthy comrades would be elected to the Soviets, who would be able to adequately fulfill the heavy duties of a deputy. And, of course, there are many of such people among our youth. Therefore, an age limit of 18 years could be established for election to all Soviets, with the exception of the Supreme Soviet of the USSR. As the Supreme Soviet of the USSR takes the most important decisions which effect the whole state, the right to be elected to it should be granted to citizens at the age of 21.

Many statements and letters express the opinion that one should *even more strictly implement the principle of the responsibility and accountability of administrative organs and officials before the Soviets and the population.* This can be fully taken into account in the corresponding provisions, dealing with the duty of executive committees, deputies, and other elected officials to report systematically *to the Soviets, as well as to the labor collectives and the citizens' assemblies at their place of residence.*

Finally, many people believe that the provisions concerning the manner of examining the demands of deputies and the proposals of citizens, and concerning the responsibility of officials for violations of the law and for an incorrect attitude towards critical observations of the working people, should be worded more precisely. The Commission considers it possible to take this into account in the appropriate provisions of the Constitution.

Now, concerning a few corrections regarding *the organization and activities of state organs.*

A number of comrades would like to have a more exact statement *concerning the powers of union and autonomous republics and local Soviets in ensuring comprehensive economic and social development within their territory.* It is possible to agree with this. The Constitution is sufficiently clear about the responsibility of ministries and departments for the state of their respective sectors. It is apparently correct to be equally clear about the functions of local organs which ensure the smooth running and coordination of work, and the comprehensive development of enterprise and socio-cultural institutions within a given territory, irrespective of the latter's organizational subordination.

Several other provisions have also been made more exact, in accordance with the wishes of citizens, especially with regard to the competence of ministries and state committees, local organs of state power, courts, arbitration, and the Procuracy.

The participants in the discussion unanimously applauded the inclusion into the draft of the Constitution of a special chapter on the goals and principles of the Leninist foreign policy of the USSR. In connection with this chapter, the proposal was expressed to add that the Soviet Union is striving for *universal and complete disarmament.* This, of course, is correct. (Applause).

Altogether, the Constitutional Commission recommends that the Supreme Soviet adopt, apart from purely editorial changes, *about 150 corrections and amendments to the text of the Constitution.* In this way, in fact, the opinions expressed by a much greater number of citizens will be taken into account. It is enough to say that tens of thousands of virtually identical proposals lie behind one single amendment in the provision on the citizen's duty to work.

At the same time, comrades, among the proposals made there are some which *the Commission cannot accept.*

For instance, very many citizens propose to raise various rules, which are already to be found in our legislation, to a constitutional level by including them in the Fundamental Law: the actual terms for conducting sessions of local Soviets, the terms for reports by deputies, the powers of specific admistrative organs, and the sanctions for certain violations of the law.

Many consider it necessary that precisely their work should be dealt with in more detail in the new Constitution. Hence, a mass of proposals to mention concrete measures in the text concerning, for instance, the improvement of the legal regulation of economic life, the protection of the environment, the improvement of the work of the railways, the development of the material and technical basis of the health care system and the educational system, and so on.

All these proposals, comrades, are understandable from a psychological point of view and most of them, obviously, are correct in themselves. But, the Constitution is the Fundamental Law of the state. It records only the main and fundamental provisions which operate immediately and, at the same time, are developed and made more concrete in other laws. On the basis of these provisions, and in order to develop them, laws and regulations—in one word: the entire legislation in operation—will be drafted and improved as it appears necessary. And in the course of this work, it will be necessary to examine and consider carefully the numerous detailed statements made during the discussion of the draft of the Constitution. Incidentally, on the question of health care, the Central Committee is examining now a draft decree on a comprehensive program of measures to improve the protection of public health. (Applause).

Let me say something about *the proposals which the Constitutional Commission has considered incorrect in substance.*

Some of the proposals are clearly running too far ahead and do not take into account that the new Constitution is the Fundamental Law of a socialist state—albeit advanced socialism—and not of communism. In our country the socialist principle operates: "From each, according to his ability, to each, according to his work." One cannot bypass this principle at the present level of economic development and of the consciousness of the people. It is impossible therefore to accept proposals, for instance, for the introduction of equal wages and pensions for everyone, or for determining their size exclusively on the basis of seniority at work, without considering the qualifications of workers and the quality of their work.

There were also proposals to abolish or to restrict sharply the subsidiary households. It is well known, however, that this form of labor, unconnected with exploitation, plays a useful role in our economy at present. In our opinion therefore, those comrades are right who propose to emphasize in the Constitution that the state and the collective farms render aid to citizens in running a subsidiary household. Moreover, those who speak out against the subsidiary households are, insofar as can be judged, not so much worried by the fact of their existence, as by unfortunate instances of their abuse in order to acquire speculative income. In this case, the appropriate state organs should strictly exercise the right of supervision which the Constitution grants them, and they should check carefully whether the plots of land granted to citizens are utilized rationally and with profit for society, and whether the income from subsidiary households and from individual work is in accordance with the principles of socialism.

In the USSR, as is well known, a new historical community of people has emerged: the Soviet people. Some comrades, although very few, have drawn the wrong conclusion from this. They propose to introduce in the Constitution the concept of a single Soviet *nation* and to abolish the union and autonomous republics, or to restrict sharply the sovereign rights of the union republics, depriving them of the right of secession and the right to engage in foreign relations. Proposals to abolish the Soviet of the Nationalities and to set up a unicameral Supreme Soviet go in the same direction. I believe that the erroneousness of such proposals is clear. The social-political unity of the Soviet people does not at all signify the disappearance of national differences. Thanks to the consistent implementation of the Leninist national policy, we have built socialism and, at the same time, for the first time in history, we have successfully solved the national problem. The friendship between the Soviet peoples is unbreakable, they steadily draw closer together as communism is being built, and they mutually enrich each other's spiritual life. But we would be taking a dangerous road if we would artificially force this objective process of national rapprochement. V.I. Lenin has warned explicitly against this, and we shall not be diverted from his teachings. (Applause).

The article which establishes a two-and-a-half year term of office for local Soviets has evoked a lively discussion. There were quite a few proposals to fix this term at five years, so that the deputy would better be able to master his duties and work more effectively. But this would significantly limit the number of working people who are being trained in administering the state by being members of the Soviets. If a deputy, elected for two and a half years, works well, what is to prevent his candidacy for a second time? This, incidentally, is also what happens: more than half of the deputies are elected for a second term, which helps to maintain continuity in the work of the Soviets. It will not be necessary therefore, in our opinion, to change this provision.

The Constitutional Commission has also received letters proposing to transfer state functions directly to Party organs, to give legislative power to the Politbureau of the Central Committee of the CPSU, etc. These proposals are deeply erroneous because they introduce confusion into the understanding of the role of the Party in our society and attempt to obscure the meaning and functions of the organs of Soviet power.

Our Party, after it had become the ruling party, clearly stated at the 8th Congress, which was still directed by V.I. Lenin, that it carries out its decisions "through Soviet organs, *within the framework of the Soviet Constitution*",[2] and that, directing the work of the Soviets, it does not replace them and differentiates between the functions of Party and state organs. This Leninist principle is laid down in the Statute of the CPSU and has been reaffirmed in the decisions of the most recent Party congresses. We propose to give expression to it in the Constitution as well.

The Party implements its policy in the affairs of the state chiefly through communists who have been elected to the Soviets by the people and who work in state organs. The Party considers it one of its most important tasks to strengthen and improve the power of the Soviets in every way and to promote the further development of socialist democracy. This is our basic policy and will be so forever. (Applause).

Comrades, *the discussion of the draft of the Constitution has in many ways gone well beyond the framework of an analysis of the text itself. It has developed into an outspoken, genuinely nationwide dialogue on the most important questions of our life as they deeply concern Soviet people.* Collectives of working people and individual citizens have made justified and sometimes sharply critical observations concerning various aspects of the activities of state organs and social organizations, and they have proposed measures to improve work and to eliminate shortcomings.

Many letters call for strengthening the struggle against loafing, malicious violations of labor discipline, drunkenness, and other anti-social phenomena, which contradict the very essence of our socialist way of life. All state and social organizations should draw concrete conclusions from these insistent demands of working people.

A number of letters informs us of disgraceful instances of abuse of an official position by individual officials, of defrauding the state by falsifying records and cheating, of bribery, of a callous and bureaucratic approach to requests by working people, and of persecution for criticism.

Let me stress, comrades, that all such information received is being checked carefully in order to take the measures necessary, including the punishment of the guilty persons with all the severity of the law. And, in general, it is worth saying that restoring proper order in those places where it was violated—in production, and in state and social life—is of great benefit to the development of our society. By putting an end to such phenomena as sloppy work, wasting of socialist property, and a bureaucratic approach to business and people, we will powerfully speed up the progress of the country and the improvement of the life of our whole people. (Applause).

Many letters and statements ask for the further strengthening and improving of people's control. This is correct. This purpose will be served, in particular, by the Law on People's Control of the USSR, the adoption of which is provided for in the new Constitution.

A number of letterwriters recommend the introduction of a system of incentives by granting additional leave to persons who have worked for a long time, conscientiously and effectively, for the good of society, and for front-rankers of production. On the other hand, they propose to deduct leave from those who, so to say, have already taken it themselves at the expense of their working hours, *i.e.* to speak plainly, those who loaf about and stay away from their work. Obviously, the Committee for Labor and Social Questions and other departments, as well as the All-Union Central Council of Trade Unions, should pay attention to these considerations in preparing measures to improve the system of holidays; at the same time, they should take into account the practice of fraternal countries on this point.

Attention should be paid, in our opinion, to proposals for further improvement in the circumstances of Great Patriotic War veterans, who have taken part in battle, and including those who are now on a pension. The Party and the Soviet state have shown permanent concern for the participants of the Great Patriotic War and have already done much in this area. Would it be possible to find additional means to grant some more benefits to those who defended the freedom and independence of our Motherland in her most difficult war? I believe it would. (Prolonged applause.)

Wishes have also been expressed for additional benefits to mothers, questions have been asked about improved utilization of medical services, about a stricter housing allocation system, and many others. I believe that the Council of Ministers of the USSR, together with the All-Union Central Council of Trade Unions, should investigate carefully our present resources and the possibilities for satisfying the wishes expressed, and should report the results of its investigations to the Presidium of the Supreme Soviet of the USSR.

These, comrades, are the main points the Constitutional Commission felt obliged to report upon in connection with the nationwide discussion of the draft of the Constitution of the USSR.

II

[This section of the speech deals with foreign reactions to the draft.]

III

[This final and briefest section of the speech repeats once more that the USSR is a state of developed socialism and a state of the whole people.]

NOTES

1. V.I. Lenin, *Polnoe sobranie sochinenii* (Complete Collection of Works), Vol. 36, p. 184.

2. *KPSS v rezoliutsiiakh i resheniiakh s"ezdov, konferentsii i Plenumov TsK* (The CPSU in Resolutions and Decisions of Congresses, Conferences, and Central Committee Plenums), Vol. 2, 8th ed., p. 77.

RUSSIAN LANGUAGE TEXT OF THE 1977 USSR CONSTITUTION

КОНСТИТУЦИЯ

(ОСНОВНОЙ ЗАКОН)

СОЮЗА СОВЕТСКИХ СОЦИАЛИСТИЧЕСКИХ РЕСПУБЛИК

Великая Октябрьская социалистическая революция, совершенная рабочими и крестьянами России под руководством Коммунистической партии во главе с В. И. Лениным, свергла власть капиталистов и помещиков, разбила оковы угнетения, установила диктатуру пролетариата и создала Советское государство — государство нового типа, основное орудие защиты революционных завоеваний, строительства социализма и коммунизма. Начался всемирно-исторический поворот человечества от капитализма к социализму.

Одержав победу в гражданской войне, отразив империалистическую интервенцию, Советская власть осуществила глубочайшие социально-экономические преобразования, навсегда покончила с эксплуатацией человека человеком, с классовыми антагонизмами и национальной враждой. Объединение советских республик в Союз ССР преумножило силы и возможности народов страны в строительстве социализма. Утвердились общественная собственность на средства производства, подлинная демократия для трудящихся масс. Впервые в истории человечества было создано социалистическое общество.

Ярким проявлением силы социализма стал немеркнущий подвиг советского народа, его Вооруженных Сил, одержавших историческую победу в Великой Отечественной войне. Эта победа укрепила авторитет и международные позиции СССР, открыла новые благоприятные возможности для роста сил социализма, национального освобождения, демократии и мира во всем мире.

Продолжая свою созидательную деятельность, трудящиеся Советского Союза обеспечили быстрое и всестороннее развитие страны, совершенствование социалистического строя. Упрочились союз рабочего класса, колхозного крестьянства и народной интеллигенции, дружба наций и народностей СССР. Сложилось социально-политическое и идейное единство советского общества, ведущей силой которого выступает рабочий класс. Выполнив задачи диктатуры пролетариата, Советское государство стало общенародным. Возросла руководящая роль Коммунистической партии — авангарда всего народа.

В СССР построено развитое социалистическое общество. На этом этапе, когда социализм развивается на своей собственной основе, все полнее раскрываются созидательные силы нового строя, преимущества социалистического образа жизни, трудящиеся все шире пользуются плодами великих революционных завоеваний.

Это — общество, в котором созданы могучие производительные силы, передовая наука и культура, в котором постоянно растет благосостояние народа, складываются все более благоприятные условия для всестороннего развития личности.

Это — общество зрелых социалистических общественных отношений, в котором на основе сближения всех классов и социальных слоев, юридического и фактического равенства всех наций и народностей, их братского сотрудничества сложилась новая историческая общность людей — советский народ.

Это — общество высокой организованности, идейности и сознательности трудящихся — патриотов и интернационалистов.

Это — общество, законом жизни которого является забота всех о благе каждого и забота каждого о благе всех.

Это — общество подлинной демократии, политическая система которого обеспечивает эффективное управление всеми общественными делами, все более активное участие трудящихся в государственной жизни, сочетание реальных прав и свобод граждан с их обязанностями и ответственностью перед обществом.

Развитое социалистическое общество — закономерный этап на пути к коммунизму.

Высшая цель Советского государства — построение бесклассового коммунистического общества, в котором получит развитие общественное коммунистическое самоуправление. Главные задачи социалистического общенародного государства: создание материальнотехнической базы коммунизма, совершенствование социалистических общественных отношений и их преобразование в коммунистические, воспитание человека коммунистического общества, повышение материального и культурного уровня жизни трудящихся, обеспечение безопасности страны, содействие укреплению мира и развитию международного сотрудничества.

Советский народ,

руководствуясь идеями научного коммунизма и соблюдая верность своим революционным традициям,

опираясь на великие социально-экономические и политические завоевания социализма,

стремясь к дальнейшему развитию социалистической демократии,

учитывая международное положение СССР как составной части мировой системы социализма и сознавая свою интернациональную ответственность,

сохраняя преемственность идей и принципов первой советской Конституции 1918 года, Конституции СССР 1924 года и Конституции СССР 1936 года,

закрепляет основы общественного строя и политики СССР, устанавливает права, свободы и обязанности граждан, принципы организации и цели социалистического общенародного государства и провозглашает их в настоящей Конституции.

I. ОСНОВЫ ОБЩЕСТВЕННОГО СТРОЯ И ПОЛИТИКИ СССР

Глава 1.

Политическая система

Статья 1. Союз Советских Социалистических Республик есть социалистическое общенародное государство, выражающее волю и интересы рабочих, крестьян и интеллигенции, трудящихся всех наций и народностей страны.

Статья 2. Вся власть в СССР принадлежит народу.

Народ осуществляет государственную власть через Советы народных депутатов, составляющие политическую основу СССР.

Все другие государственные органы подконтрольны и подотчетны Советам народных депутатов.

Статья 3. Организация и деятельность Советского государства строятся в соответствии с принципом демократического централизма: выборностью всех органов государственной власти снизу доверху, подотчетностью их народу, обязательностью решений вышестоящих органов для нижестоящих. Демократический централизм сочетает единое руководство с инициативой и творческой активностью на местах, с ответственностью каждого государственного органа и должностного лица за порученное дело.

Статья 4. Советское государство, все его органы действуют на основе социалистической законности, обеспечивают охрану правопорядка, интересов общества, прав и свобод граждан.

Государственные и общественные организации, должностные лица обязаны соблюдать Конституцию СССР и советские законы.

Статья 5. Наиболее важные вопросы государственной жизни выносятся на всенародное обсуждение, а также ставятся на всенародное голосование (референдум).

Статья 6. Руководящей и направляющей силой советского общества, ядром его политической системы, государственных и общественных организаций является Коммунистическая партия Советского Союза. КПСС существует для народа и служит народу.

Вооруженная марксистско-ленинским учением, Коммунистическая партия определяет генеральную перспективу развития общества, линию внутренней и внешней политики СССР, руководит великой созидательной деятельностью советского народа, придает планомерный, научно обоснованный характер его борьбе за победу коммунизма.

Все партийные организации действуют в рамках Конституции СССР.

Статья 7. Профессиональные союзы, Всесоюзный Ленинский Коммунистический Союз Молодежи, кооперативные и другие общественные организации в соответствии со своими уставными задачами участвуют в управлении государственными и общественными делами, в решении политических, хозяйственных и социально-культурных вопросов.

Статья 8. Трудовые коллективы участвуют в обсуждении и решении государственных и общественных дел, в планировании производства и социального развития, в подготовке и расстановке кадров, в обсуждении и решении вопросов управления предприятиями и учреждениями, улучшения условий труда и быта, использования средств, предназначенных для развития производства, а также на социально-культурные мероприятия и материальное поощрение.

Трудовые коллективы развивают социалистическое соревнование, способствуют распространению передовых методов работы, укреплению трудовой дисциплины, воспитывают своих членов в духе коммунистической нравственности, заботятся о повышении их политической сознательности, культуры и профессиональной квалификации.

Статья 9. Основным направлением развития политической системы советского общества является дальнейшее развертывание социалистической демократии: все более широкое участие граждан в управлении делами государства и общества, совершенствование государственного аппарата, повышение активности общественных организаций, усиление народного контроля, укрепление правовой основы государственной и общественной жизни, расширение гласности, постоянный учет общественного мнения.

Глава 2.

Экономическая система

Статья 10. Основу экономической системы СССР составляет социалистическая собственность на средства производства в форме государственной (общенародной) и колхозно-кооперативной собственности.

Социалистической собственностью является также имущество профсоюзных и иных общественных организаций, необходимое им для осуществления уставных задач.

Государство охраняет социалистическую собственность и создает условия для ее преумножения.

Никто не вправе использовать социалистическую собственность в целях личной наживы и в других корыстных целях.

Статья 11. Государственная собственность — общее достояние всего советского народа, основная форма социалистической собственности.

В исключительной собственности государства находятся: земля, ее недра, воды, леса. Государству принадлежат основные средства производства в промышленности, строительстве и сельском хозяйстве, средства транспорта и связи, банки, имущество организованных государством торговых, коммунальных и иных предприятий, основной городской жилищный фонд, а также другое имущество, необходимое для осуществления задач государства.

Статья 12. Собственностью колхозов и других кооперативных организаций, их объединений являются средства производства и иное имущество, необходимое им для осуществления уставных задач.

Земля, занимаемая колхозами, закрепляется за ними в бесплатное и бессрочное пользование.

Государство содействует развитию колхозно-кооперативной собственности и ее сближению с государственной.

Колхозы, как и другие землепользователи, обязаны эффективно использовать землю, бережно относиться к ней, повышать ее плодородие.

Статья 13. Основу личной собственности граждан СССР составляют трудовые доходы. В личной собственности могут находиться предметы обихода, личного потребления, удобства и подсобного домашнего хозяйства, жилой дом и трудовые сбережения. Личная собственность граждан и право ее наследования охраняются государством.

В пользовании граждан могут находиться участки земли, предоставляемые в установленном законом порядке для ведения подсобного хозяйства (включая содержание скота и птицы), садоводства и огородничества, а также для индивидуального жилищного строительства. Граждане обязаны рационально использовать предоставленные им земельные участки. Государство и колхозы оказывают содействие гражданам в ведении подсобного хозяйства.

Имущество, находящееся в личной собственности или в пользовании граждан, не должно служить для извлечения нетрудовых доходов, использоваться в ущерб интересам общества.

Статья 14. Источником роста общественного богатства, благосостояния народа и каждого советского человека является свободный от эксплуатации труд советских людей.

В соответствии с принципом социализма «От каждого — по способностям, каждому — по труду» государство осуществляет контроль за мерой труда и потребления. Оно определяет размер налога на доходы, подлежащие налогообложению.

Общественно полезный труд и его результаты определяют положение человека в обществе. Государство, сочетая материальные и моральные стимулы, поощряя новаторство, творческое отношение к работе, способствует превращению труда в первую жизненную потребность каждого советского человека.

Статья 15. Высшая цель общественного производства при социализме — наиболее полное удовлетворение растущих материальных и духовных потребностей людей.

Опираясь на творческую активность трудящихся, социалистическое соревнование, достижения научно-технического прогресса, совершенствуя формы и методы руководства экономикой, государство обеспечивает рост производительности труда, повышение эффективности производства и качества работы, динамичное, планомерное и пропорциональное развитие народного хозяйства.

Статья 16. Экономика СССР составляет единый народнохозяйственный комплекс, охватывающий все звенья общественного производства, распределения и обмена на территории страны.

Руководство экономикой осуществляется на основе государственных планов экономического и социального развития, с учетом отраслевого и территориального принципов, при сочетании централизованного управления с хозяйственной самостоятельностью и инициативой предприятий, объединений и других организаций. При этом активно используются хозяйственный расчет, прибыль, себестоимость, другие экономические рычаги и стимулы.

Статья 17. В СССР в соответствии с законом допускаются индивидуальная трудовая деятельность в сфере кустарно-ремесленных промыслов, сельского хозяйства, бытового обслуживания населения, а также другие виды деятельности, основанные исключительно на личном труде граждан и членов их семей. Государство регулирует индивидуальную трудовую деятельность, обеспечивая ее использование в интересах общества.

Статья 18. В интересах настоящего и будущих поколений в СССР принимаются необходимые меры для охраны и научно обоснованного, рационального использования земли и ее недр, водных ресурсов, растительного и животного мира, для сохранения в чистоте воздуха и воды, обеспечения воспроизводства природных богатств и улучшения окружающей человека среды.

Глава 3.

Социальное развитие и культура

Статья 19. Социальную основу СССР составляет нерушимый союз рабочих, крестьян и интеллигенции.

Государство способствует усилению социальной однородности общества — стиранию классовых различий, существенных различий между городом и деревней, умственным и физическим трудом, всестороннему развитию и сближению всех наций и народностей СССР.

Статья 20. В соответствии с коммунистическим идеалом «Свободное развитие каждого есть условие свободного развития всех» государство ставит своей целью расширение реальных возможностей для применения гражданами своих творческих сил, способностей и дарований, для всестороннего развития личности.

Статья 21. Государство заботится об улучшении условий и охране труда, его научной организации, о сокращении, а в дальнейшем и полном вытеснении тяжелого физического труда на основе комплексной механизации и автоматизации производственных процессов во всех отраслях народного хозяйства.

Статья 22. В СССР последовательно претворяется в жизнь программа превращения сельскохозяйственного труда в разновидность индустриального; расширения в сельской местности сети учреждений народного образования, культуры, здравоохранения, торговли и общественного питания, бытового обслуживания и коммунального хозяйства; преобразования сел и деревень в благоустроенные поселки.

Статья 23. На основе роста производительности труда государство неуклонно осуществляет курс на повышение уровня оплаты труда, реальных доходов трудящихся.

В целях более полного удовлетворения потребностей советских людей создаются общественные фонды потребления. Государство при широком участии общественных организаций и трудовых коллективов обеспечивает рост и справедливое распределение этих фондов.

Статья 24. В СССР действуют и развиваются государственные системы здравоохранения, социального обеспечения, торговли и общественного питания, бытового обслуживания и коммунального хозяйства.

Государство поощряет деятельность кооперативных и других общественных организаций во всех сферах обслуживания населения. Оно содействует развитию массовой физической культуры и спорта.

Статья 25. В СССР существует и совершенствуется единая система народного образования, которая обеспечивает общеобразовательную и профессиональную подготовку граждан, служит коммунистическому воспитанию, духовному и физическому развитию молодежи, готовит ее к труду и общественной деятельности.

Статья 26. В соответствии с потребностями общества государство обеспечивает планомерное развитие науки и подготовку научных кадров, организует внедрение результатов научных исследований в народное хозяйство и другие сферы жизни.

Статья 27. Государство заботится об охране, преумножении и широком использовании духовных ценностей для нравственного и эстетического воспитания советских людей, повышения их культурного уровня.

В СССР всемерно поощряется развитие профессионального искусства и народного художественного творчества.

Глава 4.

Внешняя политика

Статья 28. СССР неуклонно проводит ленинскую политику мира, выступает за упрочение безопасности народов и широкое международное сотрудничество.

Внешняя политика СССР направлена на обеспечение благоприятных международных условий для построения коммунизма в СССР, защиту государственных интересов Советского Союза, укрепление позиций мирового социализма, поддержку борьбы народов за национальное освобождение и социальный прогресс, на предотвращение агрессивных войн, достижение всеобщего и полного разоружения и последовательное осуществление принципа мирного сосуществования государств с различным социальным строем.

В СССР пропаганда войны запрещается.

Статья 29. Отношения СССР с другими государствами строятся на основе соблюдения принципов суверенного равенства; взаимного отказа от применения силы или угрозы силой; нерушимости границ; территориальной целостности государств; мирного урегулирования споров; невмешательства во внутренние дела; уважения прав человека и основных свобод; равноправия и права народов распоряжаться своей судьбой; сотрудничества между государствами; добросовестного выполнения обязательств, вытекающих из общепризнанных принципов и норм международного права, из заключенных СССР международных договоров.

Статья 30. СССР как составная часть мировой системы социализма, социалистического содружества развивает и укрепляет дружбу и сотрудничество, товарищескую взаимопомощь со странами социализма на основе принципа социалистического интернационализма, активно участвует в экономической интеграции и в международном социалистическом разделении труда.

Глава 5.

Защита социалистического Отечества

Статья 31. Защита социалистического Отечества относится к важнейшим функциям государства и является делом всего народа.

В целях защиты социалистических завоеваний, мирного труда советского народа, суверенитета и территориальной целостности государства созданы Вооруженные Силы СССР и установлена всеобщая воинская обязанность.

Долг Вооруженных Сил СССР перед народом — надежно защищать социалистическое Отечество, быть в постоянной боевой готовности, гарантирующей немедленный отпор любому агрессору.

Статья 32. Государство обеспечивает безопасность и обороноспособность страны, оснащает Вооруженные Силы СССР всем необходимым.

Обязанности государственных органов, общественных организаций, должностных лиц и граждан по обеспечению безопасности страны и укреплению ее обороноспособности определяются законодательством Союза ССР.

II. ГОСУДАРСТВО И ЛИЧНОСТЬ

Глава 6.

Гражданство СССР. Равноправие граждан

Статья 33. В СССР установлено единое союзное гражданство. Каждый гражданин союзной республики является гражданином СССР.

Основания и порядок приобретения и утраты советского гражданства определяются Законом о гражданстве СССР.

Граждане СССР за границей пользуются защитой и покровительством Советского государства.

Статья 34. Граждане СССР равны перед законом независимо от происхождения, социального и имущественного положения, расовой и национальной принадлежности, пола, образования, языка, отношения к религии, рода и характера занятий, места жительства и других обстоятельств.

Равноправие граждан СССР обеспечивается во всех областях экономической, политической, социальной и культурной жизни.

Статья 35. Женщина и мужчина имеют в СССР равные права.

Осуществление этих прав обеспечивается предоставлением женщинам равных с мужчинами возможностей в получении образования и профессиональной подготовки, в труде, вознаграждении за него и продвижении по работе, в общественно-политической и культурной деятельности, а также специальными мерами по охране труда и здоровья женщин; созданием условий, позволяющих женщинам сочетать труд с материнством; правовой защитой, материальной и моральной поддержкой материнства и детства, включая предоставление оплачиваемых отпусков и других льгот беременным женщинам и матерям, постепенное сокращение рабочего времени женщин, имеющих малолетних детей.

Статья 36. Граждане СССР различных рас и национальностей имеют равные права.

Осуществление этих прав обеспечивается политикой всестороннего развития и сближения всех наций и народностей СССР, воспитанием граждан в духе советского патриотизма и социалистического интернационализма, возможностью пользоваться родным языком и языками других народов СССР.

Какое бы то ни было прямое или косвенное ограничение прав, установление прямых или косвенных преимуществ граждан по расовым и национальным признакам, равно как и всякая проповедь расовой или национальной исключительности, вражды или пренебрежения — наказываются по закону.

Статья 37. Иностранным гражданам и лицам без гражданства в СССР гарантируются предусмотренные законом права и свободы, в том числе право на обращение в суд и иные государственные органы для защиты принадлежащих им личных, имущественных, семейных и иных прав.

Находящиеся на территории СССР иностранные граждане и лица без гражданства обязаны уважать Конституцию СССР и соблюдать советские законы.

Статья 38. СССР предоставляет право убежища иностранцам, преследуемым за защиту интересов трудящихся и дела мира, за участие в революционном и национально-освободительном движении, за прогрессивную общественно-политическую, научную или иную творческую деятельность.

Глава 7.

Основные права, свободы и обязанности граждан СССР

Статья 39. Граждане СССР обладают всей полнотой социально-экономических, политических и личных прав и свобод, провозглашенных и гарантируемых Конституцией СССР и советскими законами. Социалистический строй обеспечивает расширение прав и свобод, непрерывное улучшение условий жизни граждан по мере выполнения программ социально-экономического и культурного развития.

Использование гражданами прав и свобод не должно наносить ущерб интересам общества и государства, правам других граждан.

Статья 40. Граждане СССР имеют право на труд,— то есть на получение гарантированной работы с оплатой труда в соответствии с его количеством и качеством и не ниже установленного государством минимального размера,— включая право на выбор профессии, рода занятий и работы в соответствии с призванием, способностями, профессиональной подготовкой, образованием и с учетом общественных потребностей.

Это право обеспечивается социалистической системой хозяйства, неуклонным ростом производительных сил, бесплатным профессиональным обучением, повышением трудовой квалификации и обучением новым специальностям, развитием систем профессиональной ориентации и трудоустройства.

Статья 41. Граждане СССР имеют право на отдых.

Это право обеспечивается установлением для рабочих и служащих рабочей недели, не превышающей 41 часа, сокращенным рабочим днем для ряда профессий и производств, сокращенной продолжительностью работы в ночное время; предоставлением ежегодных оплачиваемых отпусков, дней еженедельного отдыха, а также расширением сети культурно-просветительных и оздоровительных учреждений, развитием массового спорта, физической культуры и туризма; созданием благоприятных возможностей для отдыха по месту жительства и других условий рационального использования свободного времени.

Продолжительность рабочего времени и отдыха колхозников регулируется колхозами.

Статья 42. Граждане СССР имеют право на охрану здоровья.

Это право обеспечивается бесплатной квалифицированной медицинской помощью, оказываемой государственными учреждениями здравоохранения; расширением сети учреждений для лечения и укрепления здоровья граждан; развитием и совершенствованием техники безопасности и производственной санитарии; проведением широких профилактических мероприятий; мерами по оздоровлению окружающей среды; особой заботой о здоровье подрастающего поколения, включая запрещение детского труда, не связанного с обучением и трудовым воспитанием; развертыванием научных исследований, направленных на предупреждение и снижение заболеваемости, на обеспечение долголетней активной жизни граждан.

Статья 43. Граждане СССР имеют право на материальное обеспечение в старости, в случае болезни, полной или частичной утраты трудоспособности, а также потери кормильца.

Это право гарантируется социальным страхованием рабочих, служащих и колхозников, пособиями по временной нетрудоспособности; выплатой за счет государства и колхозов пенсий по возрасту, инвалидности и по случаю потери кормильца; трудоустройством граждан, частично утративших трудоспособность; заботой о престарелых гражданах и об инвалидах; другими формами социального обеспечения.

Статья 44. Граждане СССР имеют право на жилище.

Это право обеспечивается развитием и охраной государственного и общественного жилищного фонда, содействием кооперативному и индивидуальному жилищному строительству, справедливым распределением под общественным контролем жилой площади, предоставляемой по мере осуществления программы строительства благоустроенных жилищ, а также невысокой платой за квартиру и коммунальные услуги. Граждане СССР должны бережно относиться к предоставленному им жилищу.

Статья 45. Граждане СССР имеют право на образование.

Это право обеспечивается бесплатностью всех видов образования, осуществлением всеобщего обязательного среднего образования молодежи, широким развитием профессионально-технического, среднего специального и высшего образования на основе связи обучения с жизнью, с производством; развитием заочного и вечернего образования; предоставлением государственных стипендий и льгот учащимся и студентам; бесплатной выдачей школьных учебников; возможностью обучения в школе на родном языке; созданием условий для самообразования.

Статья 46. Граждане СССР имеют право на пользование достижениями культуры.

Это право обеспечивается общедоступностью ценностей отечественной и мировой культуры, находящихся в государственных и общественных фондах; развитием и равномерным размещением культурно-просветительных учреждений на территории страны; развитием телевидения и радио, книгоиздательского дела и периодической печати, сети бесплатных библиотек; расширением культурного обмена с зарубежными государствами.

Статья 47. Гражданам СССР в соответствии с целями коммунистического строительства гарантируется свобода научного, технического и художественного творчества. Она обеспечивается широким развертыванием научных исследований, изобретательской и рационализаторской деятельности, развитием литературы и искусства. Государство создает необходимые для этого материальные условия, оказывает поддержку добровольным обществам и творческим союзам, организует внедрение изобретений и рационализаторских предложений в народное хозяйство и другие сферы жизни.

Права авторов, изобретателей и рационализаторов охраняются государством.

Статья 48. Граждане СССР имеют право участвовать в управлении государственными и общественными делами, в обсуждении и принятии законов и решений общегосударственного и местного значения.

Это право обеспечивается возможностью избирать и быть избранными в Советы народных депутатов и другие выборные государственные органы, принимать участие во всенародных обсуждениях и голосованиях, в народном контроле, в работе государственных органов, общественных организаций и органов общественной самодеятельности, в собраниях трудовых коллективов и по месту жительства.

Статья 49. Каждый гражданин СССР имеет право вносить в государственные органы и общественные организации предложения об улучшении их деятельности, критиковать недостатки в работе.

Должностные лица обязаны в установленные сроки рассматривать предложения и заявления граждан, давать на них ответы и принимать необходимые меры.

Преследование за критику запрещается. Лица, преследующие за критику, привлекаются к ответственности.

Статья 50. В соответствии с интересами народа и в целях укрепления и развития социалистического строя гражданам СССР гарантируются свободы: слова, печати, собраний, митингов, уличных шествий и демонстраций.

Осуществление этих политических свобод обеспечивается предоставлением трудящимся и их организациям общественных зданий, улиц и площадей, широким распространением информации, возможностью использования печати, телевидения и радио.

Статья 51. В соответствии с целями коммунистического строительства граждане СССР имеют право объединяться в общественные организации, способствующие развитию политической активности и самодеятельности, удовлетворению их многообразных интересов.

Общественным организациям гарантируются условия для успешного выполнения ими своих уставных задач.

Статья 52. Гражданам СССР гарантируется свобода совести, то есть право исповедовать любую религию или не исповедовать никакой, отправлять религиозные культы или вести атеистическую пропаганду. Возбуждение вражды и ненависти в связи с религиозными верованиями запрещается.

Церковь в СССР отделена от государства и школа — от церкви.

Статья 53. Семья находится под защитой государства.

Брак основывается на добровольном согласии женщины и мужчины; супруги полностью равноправны в семейных отношениях.

Государство проявляет заботу о семье путем создания и развития широкой сети детских учреждений, организации и совершенствования службы быта и общественного питания, выплаты пособий по случаю рождения ребенка, предоставления пособий и льгот многодетным семьям, а также других видов пособий и помощи семье.

Статья 54. Гражданам СССР гарантируется неприкосновенность личности. Никто не может быть подвергнут аресту иначе как на основании судебного решения или с санкции прокурора.

Статья 55. Гражданам СССР гарантируется неприкосновенность жилища. Никто не имеет права без законного основания войти в жилище против воли проживающих в нем лиц.

Статья 56. Личная жизнь граждан, тайна переписки, телефонных переговоров и телеграфных сообщений охраняются законом.

Статья 57. Уважение личности, охрана прав и свобод граждан — обязанность всех государственных органов, общественных организаций и должностных лиц.

Граждане СССР имеют право на судебную защиту от посягательств на честь и достоинство, жизнь и здоровье, на личную свободу и имущество.

Статья 58. Граждане СССР имеют право обжаловать действия должностных лиц, государственных и общественных органов. Жалобы должны быть рассмотрены в порядке и в сроки, установленные законом.

Действия должностных лиц, совершенные с нарушением закона, с превышением полномочий, ущемляющие права граждан, могут быть в установленном законом порядке обжалованы в суд.

Граждане СССР имеют право на возмещение ущерба, причиненного незаконными действиями государственных и общественных организаций, а также должностных лиц при исполнении ими служебных обязанностей.

Статья 59. Осуществление прав и свобод неотделимо от исполнения гражданином своих обязанностей.

Гражданин СССР обязан соблюдать Конституцию СССР и советские законы, уважать правила социалистического общежития, с достоинством нести высокое звание гражданина СССР.

Статья 60. Обязанность и дело чести каждого способного к труду гражданина СССР — добросовестный труд в избранной им области общественно полезной деятельности, соблюдение трудовой дисциплины. Уклонение от общественно полезного труда несовместимо с принципами социалистического общества.

Статья 61. Гражданин СССР обязан беречь и укреплять социалистическую собственность. Долг гражданина СССР — бороться с хищениями и расточительством государственного и общественного имущества, бережно относиться к народному добру.

Лица, посягающие на социалистическую собственность, наказываются по закону.

Статья 62. Гражданин СССР обязан оберегать интересы Советского государства, способствовать укреплению его могущества и авторитета.

Защита социалистического Отечества есть священный долг каждого гражданина СССР.

Измена Родине — тягчайшее преступление перед народом.

Статья 63. Воинская служба в рядах Вооруженных Сил СССР — почетная обязанность советских граждан.

Статья 64. Долг каждого гражданина СССР — уважать национальное достоинство других граждан, укреплять дружбу наций и народностей Советского многонационального государства.

Статья 65. Гражданин СССР обязан уважать права и законные интересы других лиц, быть непримиримым к антиобщественным поступкам, всемерно содействовать охране общественного порядка.

Статья 66. Граждане СССР обязаны заботиться о воспитании детей, готовить их к общественно полезному труду, растить достойными членами социалистического общества. Дети обязаны заботиться о родителях и оказывать им помощь.

Статья 67. Граждане СССР обязаны беречь природу, охранять ее богатства.

Статья 68. Забота о сохранении исторических памятников и других культурных ценностей — долг и обязанность граждан СССР.

Статья 69. Интернациональный долг гражданина СССР — содействовать развитию дружбы и сотрудничества с народами других стран, поддержанию и укреплению всеобщего мира.

III. НАЦИОНАЛЬНО-ГОСУДАРСТВЕННОЕ УСТРОЙСТВО СССР

Глава 8.

СССР — союзное государство

Статья 70. Союз Советских Социалистических Республик — единое союзное многонациональное государство, образованное на основе принципа социалистического федерализма, в результате свободного самоопределения наций и добровольного объединения равноправных Советских Социалистических Республик.

СССР олицетворяет государственное единство советского народа, сплачивает все нации и народности в целях совместного строительства коммунизма.

Статья 71. В Союзе Советских Социалистических Республик объединяются:

Российская Советская Федеративная Социалистическая Республика,

Украинская Советская Социалистическая Республика,

Белорусская Советская Социалистическая Республика,
Узбекская Советская Социалистическая Республика,
Казахская Советская Социалистическая Республика,
Грузинская Советская Социалистическая Республика,
Азербайджанская Советская Социалистическая Республика,
Литовская Советская Социалистическая Республика,
Молдавская Советская Социалистическая Республика,
Латвийская Советская Социалистическая Республика,
Киргизская Советская Социалистическая Республика,
Таджикская Советская Социалистическая Республика,
Армянская Советская Социалистическая Республика,
Туркменская Советская Социалистическая Республика,
Эстонская Советская Социалистическая Республика.

Статья 72. За каждой союзной республикой сохраняется право свободного выхода из СССР.

Статья 73. Ведению Союза Советских Социалистических Республик в лице его высших органов государственной власти и управления подлежат:

1) принятие в состав СССР новых республик; утверждение образования новых автономных республик и автономных областей в составе союзных республик;

2) определение государственной границы СССР и утверждение изменений границ между союзными республиками;

3) установление общих начал организации и деятельности республиканских и местных органов государственной власти и управления;

4) обеспечение единства законодательного регулирования на всей территории СССР, установление основ законодательства Союза ССР и союзных республик;

5) проведение единой социально-экономической политики, руководство экономикой страны; определение основных направлений научно-технического прогресса и общих мероприятий по рациональному использованию и охране природных ресурсов; разработка и утверждение государственных планов экономического и социального развития СССР, утверждение отчетов об их выполнении;

6) разработка и утверждение единого государственного бюджета СССР, утверждение отчета о его исполнении; руководство единой денежной и кредитной системой; установление налогов и доходов, поступающих на образование государственного бюджета СССР; определение политики в области цен и оплаты труда;

7) руководство отраслями народного хозяйства, объединениями и предприятиями союзного подчинения; общее руководство отраслями союзно-республиканского подчинения;

8) вопросы мира и войны, защита суверенитета, охрана государственных границ и территории СССР, организация обороны, руководство Вооруженными Силами СССР;

9) обеспечение государственной безопасности;

10) представительство СССР в международных отношениях; связи СССР с иностранными государствами и международными организациями; установление общего порядка и координация отношений союзных республик с иностранными государствами и международными организациями; внешняя торговля и другие виды внешнеэкономической деятельности на основе государственной монополии;

11) контроль за соблюдением Конституции СССР и обеспечение соответствия конституций союзных республик Конституции СССР;

12) решение других вопросов общесоюзного значения.

Статья 74. Законы СССР имеют одинаковую силу на территории всех союзных республик. В случае расхождения закона союзной республики с общесоюзным законом действует закон СССР.

Статья 75. Территория Союза Советских Социалистических Республик едина и включает территории союзных республик.

Суверенитет СССР распространяется на всю его территорию.

Глава 9.

Союзная Советская Социалистическая Республика

Статья 76. Союзная республика — суверенное советское социалистическое государство, которое объединилось с другими советскими республиками в Союз Советских Социалистических Республик.

Вне пределов, указанных в статье 73 Конституции СССР, союзная республика самостоятельно осуществляет государственную власть на своей территории.

Союзная республика имеет свою Конституцию, соответствующую Конституции СССР и учитывающую особенности республики.

Статья 77. Союзная республика участвует в решении вопросов, отнесенных к ведению Союза ССР, в Верховном Совете СССР, Президиуме Верховного Совета СССР, Правительстве СССР и других органах Союза ССР.

Союзная республика обеспечивает комплексное экономическое и социальное развитие на своей территории, способствует осуществлению на этой территории полномочий Союза ССР, проводит в жизнь решения высших органов государственной власти и управления СССР.

По вопросам, относящимся к ее ведению, союзная республика координирует и контролирует деятельность предприятий, учреждений и организаций союзного подчинения.

Статья 78. Территория союзной республики не может быть изменена без ее согласия. Границы между союзными республиками могут изменяться по взаимному соглашению соответствующих республик, которое подлежит утверждению Союзом ССР.

Статья 79. Союзная республика определяет свое краевое, областное, окружное, районное деление и решает иные вопросы административно-территориального устройства.

Статья 80. Союзная республика имеет право вступать в отношения с иностранными государствами, заключать с ними договоры и обмениваться дипломатическими и консульскими представителями, участвовать в деятельности международных организаций.

Статья 81. Суверенные права союзных республик охраняются Союзом ССР.

Глава 10.

Автономная Советская Социалистическая Республика

Статья 82. Автономная республика находится в составе союзной республики.

Автономная республика вне пределов прав Союза ССР и союзной республики самостоятельно решает вопросы, относящиеся к ее ведению.

Автономная республика имеет свою Конституцию, соответствующую Конституции СССР и Конституции союзной республики и учитывающую особенности автономной республики.

Статья 83. Автономная республика участвует в решении вопросов, отнесенных к ведению Союза ССР и союзной республики, через высшие органы государственной власти и управления соответственно Союза ССР и союзной республики.

Автономная республика обеспечивает комплексное экономическое и социальное развитие на своей территории, способствует осуществлению на этой территории полномочий Союза ССР и союзной республики, проводит в жизнь решения высших органов государственной власти и управления СССР и союзной республики.

По вопросам, относящимся к ее ведению, автономная республика координирует и контролирует деятельность предприятий, учреждений и организаций союзного и республиканского (союзной республики) подчинения.

Статья 84. Территория автономной республики не может быть изменена без ее согласия.

Статья 85. В Российской Советской Федеративной Социалистической Республике состоят автономные советские социалистические республики: Башкирская, Бурятская, Дагестанская, Кабардино-Балкарская, Калмыцкая, Карельская, Коми, Марийская, Мордовская, Северо-Осетинская, Татарская, Тувинская, Удмуртская, Чечено-Ингушская, Чувашская, Якутская.

В Узбекской Советской Социалистической Республике состоит Каракалпакская Автономная Советская Социалистическая Республика.

В Грузинской Советской Социалистической Республике состоят Абхазская и Аджарская автономные советские социалистические республики.

В Азербайджанской Советской Социалистической Республике состоит Нахичеванская Автономная Советская Социалистическая Республика.

Глава 11.

Автономная область и автономный округ

Статья 86. Автономная область находится в составе союзной республики или края. Закон об автономной области принимается Верховным Советом союзной республики по представлению Совета народных депутатов автономной области.

Статья 87. В Российской Советской Федеративной Социалистической Республике состоят автономные области: Адыгейская, Горно-Алтайская, Еврейская, Карачаево-Черкесская, Хакасская.

В Грузинской Советской Социалистической Республике состоит Юго-Осетинская автономная область.

В Азербайджанской Советской Социалистической Республике состоит Нагорно-Карабахская автономная область.

В Таджикской Советской Социалистической Республике состоит Горно-Бадахшанская автономная область.

Статья 88. Автономный округ находится в составе края или области. Закон об автономных округах принимается Верховным Советом союзной республики.

IV. СОВЕТЫ НАРОДНЫХ ДЕПУТАТОВ И ПОРЯДОК ИХ ИЗБРАНИЯ

Глава 12.

Система и принципы деятельности Советов народных депутатов

Статья 89. Советы народных депутатов — Верховный Совет СССР, Верховные Советы союзных республик, Верховные Советы автономных республик, краевые, областные Советы народных депутатов, Советы народных депутатов автономных областей и автономных округов, районные, городские, районные в городах, поселковые и сельские Советы народных депутатов — составляют единую систему органов государственной власти.

Статья 90. Срок полномочий Верховного Совета СССР, Верховных Советов союзных республик и Верховных Советов автономных республик — пять лет.

Срок полномочий местных Советов народных депутатов — два с половиной года.

Выборы в Советы народных депутатов назначаются не позднее чем за два месяца до истечения срока полномочий соответствующих Советов.

Статья 91. Важнейшие вопросы, отнесенные к ведению соответствующих Советов народных депутатов, рассматриваются и решаются на их сессиях.

Советы народных депутатов избирают постоянные комиссии, создают исполнительные и распорядительные, а также другие подотчетные им органы.

Статья 92. Советы народных депутатов образуют органы народного контроля, сочетающего государственный контроль с общественным контролем трудящихся на предприятиях, в колхозах, учреждениях и организациях.

Органы народного контроля контролируют выполнение государственных планов и заданий; ведут борьбу с нарушениями государственной дисциплины, проявлениями местничества, ведомственного подхода к делу, с бесхозяйственностью и расточительством, волокитой и бюрократизмом; способствуют совершенствованию работы государственного аппарата.

Статья 93. Советы народных депутатов непосредственно и через создаваемые ими органы руководят всеми отраслями государственного, хозяйственного и социально-культурного строительства, принимают решения, обеспечивают их исполнение, осуществляют контроль за проведением решений в жизнь.

Статья 94. Деятельность Советов народных депутатов строится на основе коллективного, свободного, делового обсуждения и решения вопросов, гласности, регулярной отчетности исполнительных и распорядительных органов, других создаваемых Советами органов перед Советами и населением, широкого привлечения граждан к участию в их работе.

Советы народных депутатов и создаваемые ими органы систематически информируют население о своей работе и принятых решениях.

Глава 13.

Избирательная система

Статья 95. Выборы депутатов во все Советы народных депутатов производятся на основе всеобщего, равного и прямого избирательного права при тайном голосовании.

Статья 96. Выборы депутатов являются всеобщими: все граждане СССР, достигшие 18 лет, имеют право избирать и быть избранными, за исключением лиц, признанных в установленном законом порядке умалишенными.

Депутатом Верховного Совета СССР может быть избран гражданин СССР, достигший 21 года.

Статья 97. Выборы депутатов являются равными: каждый избиратель имеет один голос; все избиратели участвуют в выборах на равных основаниях.

Статья 98. Выборы депутатов являются прямыми: депутаты всех Советов народных депутатов избираются гражданами непосредственно.

Статья 99. Голосование при выборах депутатов является тайным: контроль за волеизъявлением избирателей не допускается.

Статья 100. Право выдвижения кандидатов в депутаты принадлежит организациям Коммунистической партии Советского Союза, профессиональных союзов, Всесоюзного Ленинского Коммунистического Союза Молодежи, кооперативным и другим общественным организациям, трудовым коллективам, а также собраниям военнослужащих по воинским частям.

Гражданам СССР и общественным организациям гарантируется свободное и всестороннее обсуждение политических, деловых и личных качеств кандидатов в депутаты, а также право агитации на собраниях, в печати, по телевидению, радио.

Расходы, связанные с проведением выборов в Советы народных депутатов, производятся за счет государства.

Статья 101. Выборы депутатов в Советы народных депутатов производятся по избирательным округам.

Гражданин СССР не может, как правило, быть избран более чем в два Совета народных депутатов.

Проведение выборов в Советы обеспечивают избирательные комиссии, которые образуются из представителей от общественных организаций, трудовых коллективов и собраний военнослужащих по воинским частям.

Порядок проведения выборов в Советы народных депутатов определяется законами Союза ССР, союзных и автономных республик.

Статья 102. Избиратели дают наказы своим депутатам.

Соответствующие Советы народных депутатов рассматривают наказы избирателей, учитывают их при разработке планов экономического и социального развития и составлении бюджета, организуют выполнение наказов и информируют граждан об их реализации.

Глава 14.

Народный депутат

Статья 103. Депутаты являются полномочными представителями народа в Советах народных депутатов.

Участвуя в работе Советов, депутаты решают вопросы государственного, хозяйственного и социально-культурного строительства, организуют проведение решений Советов в жизнь, осуществляют контроль за работой государственных органов, предприятий, учреждений и организаций.

В своей деятельности депутат руководствуется общегосударственными интересами, учитывает запросы населения избирательного округа, добивается претворения в жизнь наказов избирателей.

Статья 104. Депутат осуществляет свои полномочия, не порывая с производственной или служебной деятельностью.

На время сессий Совета, а также для осуществления депутатских полномочий в других случаях, предусмотренных законом, депутат освобождается от выполнения производственных или служебных обязанностей с сохранением среднего заработка по месту постоянной работы.

Статья 105. Депутат имеет право запроса к соответствующим государственным органам и должностным лицам, которые обязаны дать ответ на запрос на сессии Совета.

Депутат вправе обращаться во все государственные и общественные органы, предприятия, учреждения, организации по вопросам депутатской деятельности и принимать участие в рассмотрении поставленных им вопросов. Руководители соответствующих государственных и общественных органов, предприятий, учреждений и организаций обязаны безотлагательно принимать депутата и рассматривать его предложения в установленные сроки.

Статья 106. Депутату обеспечиваются условия для беспрепятственного и эффективного осуществления его прав и обязанностей.

Неприкосновенность депутатов, а также другие гарантии депутатской деятельности устанавливаются Законом о статусе депутатов и другими законодательными актами Союза ССР, союзных и автономных республик.

Статья 107. Депутат обязан отчитываться о своей работе и работе Совета перед избирателями, а также перед коллективами и общественными организациями, выдвинувшими его кандидатом в депутаты.

Депутат, не оправдавший доверия избирателей, может быть в любое время отозван по решению большинства избирателей в установленном законом порядке.

V. ВЫСШИЕ ОРГАНЫ ГОСУДАРСТВЕННОЙ ВЛАСТИ И УПРАВЛЕНИЯ СССР

Глава 15.

Верховный Совет СССР

Статья 108. Высшим органом государственной власти СССР является Верховный Совет СССР.

Верховный Совет СССР правомочен решать все вопросы, отнесенные настоящей Конституцией к ведению Союза ССР.

Принятие Конституции СССР, внесение в нее изменений; принятие в состав СССР новых республик, утверждение образования новых автономных республик и автономных областей; утверждение государственных планов экономического и социального развития СССР, государственного бюджета СССР и отчетов об их выполнении; образование подотчетных ему органов Союза ССР осуществляются исключительно Верховным Советом СССР.

Законы СССР принимаются Верховным Советом СССР или всенародным голосованием (референдумом), проводимым по решению Верховного Совета СССР.

Статья 109. Верховный Совет СССР состоит из двух палат: Совета Союза и Совета Национальностей.

Палаты Верховного Совета СССР равноправны.

Статья 110. Совет Союза и Совет Национальностей состоят из равного числа депутатов.

Совет Союза избирается по избирательным округам с равной численностью населения.

Совет Национальностей избирается по норме: 32 депутата от каждой союзной республики, 11 депутатов от каждой автономной республики, 5 депутатов от каждой автономной области и один депутат от каждого автономного округа.

Совет Союза и Совет Национальностей по представлению избираемых ими мандатных комиссий принимают решение о признании полномочий депутатов, а в случае нарушения законодательства о выборах — о признании выборов отдельных депутатов недействительными.

Статья 111. Каждая палата Верховного Совета СССР избирает Председателя палаты и четырех его заместителей.

Председатели Совета Союза и Совета Национальностей руководят заседаниями соответствующих палат и ведают их внутренним распорядком.

Совместные заседания палат Верховного Совета СССР ведут поочередно председатели Совета Союза и Совета Национальностей.

Статья 112. Сессии Верховного Совета СССР созываются два раза в год.

Внеочередные сессии созываются Президиумом Верховного Совета СССР по его инициативе, а также по предложению союзной республики или не менее трети депутатов одной из палат.

Сессия Верховного Совета СССР состоит из раздельных и совместных заседаний палат, а также проводимых в период между ними заседаний постоянных комиссий палат или комиссий Верховного Совета СССР. Сессия открывается и закрывается на раздельных или совместных заседаниях палат.

Статья 113. Право законодательной инициативы в Верховном Совете СССР принадлежит Совету Союза, Совету Национальностей, Президиуму Верховного Совета СССР, Совету Министров СССР, союзным республикам в лице их высших органов государственной власти, комиссиям Верховного Совета СССР и постоянным комиссиям его палат, депутатам Верховного Совета СССР, Верховному Суду СССР, Генеральному прокурору СССР.

Правом законодательной инициативы обладают также общественные организации в лице их общесоюзных органов.

Статья 114. Проекты законов и другие вопросы, внесенные на рассмотрение Верховного Совета СССР, обсуждаются палатами на их раздельных или совместных заседаниях. В случае необходимости проект закона либо соответствующий вопрос может быть передан для предварительного или дополнительного рассмотрения в одну или несколько комиссий.

Закон СССР считается принятым, если в каждой из палат Верховного Совета СССР за него проголосовало большинство от общего числа депутатов палаты. Постановления и иные акты Верховного Совета СССР принимаются большинством от общего числа депутатов Верховного Совета СССР.

Проекты законов и другие наиболее важные вопросы государственной жизни решением Верховного Совета СССР либо Президиума Верховного Совета СССР, принятым по их инициативе или по предложению союзной республики, могут быть вынесены на всенародное обсуждение.

Статья 115. В случае разногласия между Советом Союза и Советом Национальностей вопрос передается на разрешение согласительной комиссии, образуемой палатами на паритетных началах, после чего вопрос вторично рассматривается Советом Союза и Советом Национальностей на совместном заседании. Если и в этом случае согласие не будет достигнуто, вопрос переносится на обсуждение следующей сессии Верховного Совета СССР или передается им на всенародное голосование (референдум).

Статья 116. Законы СССР, постановления и иные акты Верховного Совета СССР публикуются на языках союзных республик за подписями Председателя и Секретаря Президиума Верховного Совета СССР.

Статья 117. Депутат Верховного Совета СССР имеет право обратиться с запросом к Совету Министров СССР, к министрам и руководителям других органов, образуемых Верховным Советом СССР. Совет Министров СССР или должностное лицо, к которому обращен запрос, обязаны дать не более чем в трехдневный срок устный или письменный ответ на данной сессии Верховного Совета СССР.

Статья 118. Депутат Верховного Совета СССР не может быть привлечен к уголовной ответственности, арестован или подвергнут мерам административного взыскания, налагаемым в судебном порядке, без согласия Верховного Совета СССР, а в период между его сессиями — без согласия Президиума Верховного Совета СССР.

Статья 119. Верховный Совет СССР избирает на совместном заседании палат Президиум Верховного Совета СССР — постоянно действующий орган Верховного Совета СССР, подотчетный ему во всей своей деятельности и осуществляющий в пределах, предусмотренных Конституцией, функции высшего органа государственной власти СССР в период между его сессиями.

Статья 120. Президиум Верховного Совета СССР избирается из числа депутатов в составе Председателя Президиума Верховного Совета, Первого заместителя Председателя, пятнадцати заместителей Председателя — по одному от каждой союзной республики, Секретаря Президиума и двадцати одного члена Президиума Верховного Совета СССР.

Статья 121. Президиум Верховного Совета СССР:

1) назначает выборы в Верховный Совет СССР;

2) созывает сессии Верховного Совета СССР;

3) координирует деятельность постоянных комиссий палат Верховного Совета СССР;

4) осуществляет контроль за соблюдением Конституции СССР и обеспечивает соответствие конституций и законов союзных республик Конституции и законам СССР;

5) дает толкование законов СССР;

6) ратифицирует и денонсирует международные договоры СССР;

7) отменяет постановления и распоряжения Совета Министров СССР и Советов Министров союзных республик в случае несоответствия их закону;

8) устанавливает воинские звания, дипломатические ранги и иные специальные звания; присваивает высшие воинские звания, дипломатические ранги и иные специальные звания;

9) учреждает ордена и медали СССР; устанавливает почетные звания СССР; награждает орденами и медалями СССР; присваивает почетные звания СССР;

10) принимает в гражданство СССР; решает вопросы о выходе из гражданства СССР и лишении гражданства СССР, о предоставлении убежища;

11) издает общесоюзные акты об амнистии и осуществляет помилование;

12) назначает и отзывает дипломатических представителей СССР в иностранных государствах и при международных организациях;

13) принимает верительные и отзывные грамоты аккредитованных при нем дипломатических представителей иностранных государств;

14) образует Совет обороны СССР и утверждает его состав, назначает и сменяет высшее командование Вооруженных Сил СССР;

15) объявляет в интересах защиты СССР военное положение в отдельных местностях или по всей стране;

16) объявляет общую или частичную мобилизацию;

17) в период между сессиями Верховного Совета СССР объявляет состояние войны в случае военного нападения на СССР или в случае необходимости выполнения международных договорных обязательств по взаимной обороне от агрессии;

18) осуществляет другие полномочия, установленные Конституцией и законами СССР.

Статья 122. Президиум Верховного Совета СССР в период между сессиями Верховного Совета с последующим представлением на его утверждение на очередной сессии:

1) вносит в случае необходимости изменения в действующие законодательные акты СССР;

2) утверждает изменения границ между союзными республиками;

3) по предложению Совета Министров СССР образует и упраздняет министерства СССР и государственные комитеты СССР;

4) по представлению Председателя Совета Министров СССР освобождает от должности и назначает отдельных лиц, входящих в состав Совета Министров СССР.

Статья 123. Президиум Верховного Совета СССР издает указы и принимает постановления.

Статья 124. По истечении полномочий Верховного Совета СССР Президиум Верховного Совета СССР сохраняет свои полномочия вплоть до образования вновь избранным Верховным Советом СССР нового Президиума.

Вновь избранный Верховный Совет СССР созывается Президиумом Верховного Совета СССР прежнего состава не позже чем через два месяца после выборов.

Статья 125. Совет Союза и Совет Национальностей избирают из числа депутатов постоянные комиссии для предварительного рассмотрения и подготовки вопросов, относящихся к ведению Верховного Совета СССР, а также для содействия проведению в жизнь законов СССР и иных решений Верховного Совета СССР и его Президиума, контроля за деятельностью государственных органов и организаций. Палаты Верховного Совета СССР могут создавать также совместные комиссии на паритетных началах.

Верховный Совет СССР создает, когда сочтет необходимым, следственные, ревизионные и иные комиссии по любому вопросу.

Все государственные и общественные органы, организации и должностные лица обязаны выполнять требования комиссий Верховного Совета СССР и комиссий его палат, представлять им необходимые материалы и документы.

Рекомендации комиссий подлежат обязательному рассмотрению государственными и общественными органами, учреждениями и организациями. О результатах рассмотрения или о принятых мерах должно быть сообщено комиссиям в установленный срок.

Статья 126. Верховный Совет СССР осуществляет контроль за деятельностью всех подотчетных ему государственных органов.

Верховный Совет СССР образует Комитет народного контроля СССР, возглавляющий систему органов народного контроля.

Организация и порядок деятельности органов народного контроля определяются Законом о народном контроле в СССР.

Статья 127. Порядок деятельности Верховного Совета СССР и его органов определяется Регламентом Верховного Совета СССР и другими законами СССР, издаваемыми на основе Конституции СССР.

Глава 16.

Совет Министров СССР

Статья 128. Совет Министров СССР — Правительство СССР — является высшим исполнительным и распорядительным органом государственной власти СССР.

Статья 129. Совет Министров СССР образуется Верховным Советом СССР на совместном заседании Совета Союза и Совета Национальностей в составе Председателя Совета Министров СССР, первых заместителей и заместителей Председателя, министров СССР, председателей государственных комитетов СССР.

В состав Совета Министров СССР входят по должности председатели Советов Министров союзных республик.

По представлению Председателя Совета Министров СССР Верховный Совет СССР может включить в состав Правительства СССР руководителей других органов и организаций СССР.

Совет Министров СССР слагает свои полномочия перед вновь избранным Верховным Советом СССР на его первой сессии.

Статья 130. Совет Министров СССР ответствен перед Верховным Советом СССР и ему подотчетен, а в период между сессиями Верховного Совета СССР — перед Президиумом Верховного Совета СССР, которому подотчетен.

Совет Министров СССР регулярно отчитывается о своей работе перед Верховным Советом СССР.

Статья 131. Совет Министров СССР правомочен решать все вопросы государственного управления, отнесенные к ведению Союза ССР, поскольку они не входят, согласно Конституции, в компетенцию Верховного Совета СССР и Президиума Верховного Совета СССР.

В пределах своих полномочий Совет Министров СССР:

1) обеспечивает руководство народным хозяйством и социально-культурным строительством; разрабатывает и осуществляет меры по обеспечению роста благосостояния и культуры народа, по развитию науки и техники, рациональному использованию и охране природных ресурсов, по укреплению денежной и кредитной системы, проведению единой политики цен, оплаты труда, социального обеспечения, организации государственного страхования и единой системы учета и статистики; организует управление промышленными, строительными, сельскохозяйственными пред-

приятиями и объединениями, предприятиями транспорта и связи, банками, а также иными организациями и учреждениями союзного подчинения;

2) разрабатывает и вносит в Верховный Совет СССР текущие и перспективные государственные планы экономического и социального развития СССР, государственный бюджет СССР; принимает меры по осуществлению государственных планов и бюджета; представляет Верховному Совету СССР отчеты о выполнении планов и исполнении бюджета;

3) осуществляет меры по защите интересов государства, охране социалистической собственности и общественного порядка, по обеспечению и защите прав и свобод граждан;

4) принимает меры по обеспечению государственной безопасности;

5) осуществляет общее руководство строительством Вооруженных Сил СССР, определяет ежегодные контингенты граждан, подлежащих призыву на действительную военную службу;

6) осуществляет общее руководство в области отношений с иностранными государствами, внешней торговли, экономического, научно-технического и культурного сотрудничества СССР с зарубежными странами; принимает меры к обеспечению выполнения международных договоров СССР; утверждает и денонсирует межправительственные международные договоры;

7) образует в случае необходимости комитеты, главные управления и другие ведомства при Совете Министров СССР по делам хозяйственного, социально-культурного и оборонного строительства.

Статья 132. Для решения вопросов, связанных с обеспечением руководства народным хозяйством, и других вопросов государственного управления в качестве постоянного органа Совета Министров СССР действует Президиум Совета Министров СССР в составе Председателя Совета Министров СССР, первых заместителей и заместителей Председателя.

Статья 133. Совет Министров СССР на основе и во исполнение законов СССР и иных решений Верховного Совета СССР и его Президиума издает постановления и распоряжения и проверяет их исполнение. Постановления и распоряжения Совета Министров СССР обязательны к исполнению на всей территории СССР.

Статья 134. Совет Министров СССР имеет право по вопросам, отнесенным к ведению Союза ССР, приостанавливать исполнение постановлений и распоряжений Советов Министров союзных республик, а также отменять акты министерств СССР, государственных комитетов СССР, других подведомственных ему органов.

Статья 135. Совет Министров СССР объединяет и направляет работу общесоюзных и союзно-республиканских министерств и государственных комитетов СССР, других подведомственных ему органов.

Общесоюзные министерства и государственные комитеты СССР руководят порученными им отраслями управления или осуществляют межотраслевое управление на всей территории СССР непосредственно либо через создаваемые ими органы.

Союзно-республиканские министерства и государственные комитеты СССР руководят порученными им отраслями управления или осуществляют межотраслевое управление, как правило, через соответствующие министерства, государственные комитеты, другие органы союзных республик и управляют непосредственно отдельными предприятиями и объединениями, находящимися в союзном подчинении. Порядок передачи предприятий и объединений из республиканского и местного подчинения в союзное определяется Президиумом Верховного Совета СССР.

Министерства и государственные комитеты СССР несут ответственность за состояние и развитие порученных им сфер управления; в пределах своей компетенции издают акты на основе и во исполнение законов СССР, иных решений Верховного Совета СССР и его Президиума, постановлений и распоряжений Совета Министров СССР; организуют и проверяют их исполнение.

Статья 136. Компетенция Совета Министров СССР и его Президиума, порядок их деятельности, отношения Совета Министров с другими государственными органами, а также перечень общесоюзных и союзно-республиканских министерств и государственных комитетов СССР определяются на основе Конституции Законом о Совете Министров СССР.

VI. ОСНОВЫ ПОСТРОЕНИЯ ОРГАНОВ ГОСУДАРСТВЕННОЙ ВЛАСТИ И УПРАВЛЕНИЯ В СОЮЗНЫХ РЕСПУБЛИКАХ

Глава 17.

Высшие органы государственной власти и управления союзной республики

Статья 137. Высшим органом государственной власти союзной республики является Верховный Совет союзной республики.

Верховный Совет союзной республики правомочен решать все вопросы, отнесенные к ведению союзной республики Конституцией СССР и Конституцией союзной республики.

Принятие Конституции союзной республики, внесение в нее изменений; утверждение государственных планов экономического и социального развития, государственного бюджета союзной республики и отчетов об их выполнении; образование подотчетных ему органов осуществляются исключительно Верховным Советом союзной республики.

Законы союзной республики принимаются Верховным Советом союзной республики или народным голосованием (референдумом), проводимым по решению Верховного Совета союзной республики.

Статья 138. Верховный Совет союзной республики избирает Президиум Верховного Совета — постоянно действующий орган Верховного Совета союзной республики, подотчетный ему во всей своей деятельности. Состав и полномочия Президиума Верховного Совета союзной республики определяются Конституцией союзной республики.

Статья 139. Верховный Совет союзной республики образует Совет Министров союзной республики —

Правительство союзной республики — высший исполнительный и распорядительный орган государственной власти союзной республики.

Совет Министров союзной республики ответствен перед Верховным Советом союзной республики и ему подотчетен, а в период между сессиями Верховного Совета — перед Президиумом Верховного Совета союзной республики, которому подотчетен.

Статья 140. Совет Министров союзной республики издает постановления и распоряжения на основе и во исполнение законодательных актов СССР и союзной республики, постановлений и распоряжений Совета Министров СССР, организует и проверяет их исполнение.

Статья 141. Совет Министров союзной республики имеет право приостанавливать исполнение постановлений и распоряжений Советов Министров автономных республик, отменять решения и распоряжения исполнительных комитетов краевых, областных, городских (городов республиканского подчинения) Советов народных депутатов, Советов народных депутатов автономных областей, а в союзных республиках, не имеющих областного деления,— исполнительных комитетов районных и соответствующих городских Советов народных депутатов.

Статья 142. Совет Министров союзной республики объединяет и направляет работу союзно-республиканских и республиканских министерств, государственных комитетов союзной республики, других подведомственных ему органов.

Союзно-республиканские министерства и государственные комитеты союзной республики руководят порученными им отраслями управления или осуществляют межотраслевое управление, подчиняясь как Совету Министров союзной республики, так и соответствующему союзно-республиканскому министерству СССР или государственному комитету СССР.

Республиканские министерства и государственные комитеты руководят порученными им отраслями управления или осуществляют межотраслевое управление, подчиняясь Совету Министров союзной республики.

Глава 18.

Высшие органы государственной власти и управления автономной республики

Статья 143. Высшим органом государственной власти автономной республики является Верховный Совет автономной республики.

Принятие Конституции автономной республики, внесение в нее изменений; утверждение государственных планов экономического и социального развития, а также государственного бюджета автономной республики; образование подотчетных ему органов осуществляются исключительно Верховным Советом автономной республики.

Законы автономной республики принимаются Верховным Советом автономной республики.

Статья 144. Верховный Совет автономной республики избирает Президиум Верховного Совета автономной республики и образует Совет Министров автономной республики — Правительство автономной республики.

Глава 19.

Местные органы государственной власти и управления

Статья 145. Органами государственной власти в краях, областях, автономных областях, автономных округах, районах, городах, районах в городах, поселках, сельских населенных пунктах являются соответствующие Советы народных депутатов.

Статья 146. Местные Советы народных депутатов решают все вопросы местного значения, исходя из общегосударственных интересов и интересов граждан, проживающих на территории Совета, проводят в жизнь решения вышестоящих государственных органов, руководят деятельностью нижестоящих Советов народных депутатов, участвуют в обсуждении вопросов республиканского и общесоюзного значения, вносят по ним свои предложения.

Местные Советы народных депутатов руководят на своей территории государственным, хозяйственным и социально-культурным строительством; утверждают планы экономического и социального развития и местный бюджет; осуществляют руководство подчиненными им государственными органами, предприятиями, учреждениями и организациями; обеспечивают соблюдение законов, охрану государственного и общественного порядка, прав граждан; содействуют укреплению обороноспособности страны.

Статья 147. В пределах своих полномочий местные Советы народных депутатов обеспечивают комплексное экономическое и социальное развитие на их территории; осуществляют контроль за соблюдением законодательства расположенными на этой территории предприятиями, учреждениями и организациями вышестоящего подчинения; координируют и контролируют их деятельность в области землепользования, охраны природы, строительства, использования трудовых ресурсов, производства товаров народного потребления, социально-культурного, бытового и иного обслуживания населения.

Статья 148. Местные Советы народных депутатов принимают решения в пределах полномочий, предоставленных им законодательством Союза ССР, союзной и автономной республики. Решения местных Советов обязательны для исполнения всеми расположенными на территории Совета предприятиями, учреждениями и организациями, а также должностными лицами и гражданами.

Статья 149. Исполнительными и распорядительными органами местных Советов народных депутатов являются избираемые ими из числа депутатов исполнительные комитеты.

Исполнительные комитеты не реже одного раза в год отчитываются перед избравшими их Советами, а также на собраниях трудовых коллективов и по месту жительства граждан.

Статья 150. Исполнительные комитеты местных Советов народных депутатов непосредственно подотчетны как Совету, их избравшему, так и вышестоящему исполнительному и распорядительному органу.

VII. ПРАВОСУДИЕ, АРБИТРАЖ И ПРОКУРОРСКИЙ НАДЗОР

Глава 20.

Суд и арбитраж

Статья 151. Правосудие в СССР осуществляется только судом.

В СССР действуют Верховный Суд СССР, Верховные Суды союзных республик, Верховные Суды автономных республик, краевые, областные, городские суды, суды автономных областей, суды автономных округов, районные (городские) народные суды, а также военные трибуналы в Вооруженных Силах.

Статья 152. Все суды в СССР образуются на началах выборности судей и народных заседателей.

Народные судьи районных (городских) народных судов избираются гражданами района (города) на основе всеобщего, равного и прямого избирательного права при тайном голосовании сроком на пять лет. Народные заседатели районных (городских) народных судов избираются на собраниях граждан по месту их работы или жительства открытым голосованием сроком на два с половиной года.

Вышестоящие суды избираются соответствующими Советами народных депутатов сроком на пять лет.

Судьи военных трибуналов избираются Президиумом Верховного Совета СССР сроком на пять лет, а народные заседатели — собраниями военнослужащих сроком на два с половиной года.

Судьи и народные заседатели ответственны перед избирателями или избравшими их органами, отчитываются перед ними и могут быть ими отозваны в установленном законом порядке.

Статья 153. Верховный Суд СССР является высшим судебным органом СССР и осуществляет надзор за судебной деятельностью судов СССР, а также судов союзных республик в пределах, установленных законом.

Верховный Суд СССР избирается Верховным Советом СССР в составе Председателя, его заместителей, членов и народных заседателей. В состав Верховного

Суда СССР входят по должности председатели Верховных Судов союзных республик.

Организация и порядок деятельности Верховного Суда СССР определяются Законом о Верховном Суде СССР.

Статья 154. Рассмотрение гражданских и уголовных дел во всех судах осуществляется коллегиально; в суде первой инстанции — с участием народных заседателей. Народные заседатели при осуществлении правосудия пользуются всеми правами судьи.

Статья 155. Судьи и народные заседатели независимы и подчиняются только закону.

Статья 156. Правосудие в СССР осуществляется на началах равенства граждан перед законом и судом.

Статья 157. Разбирательство дел во всех судах открытое. Слушание дел в закрытом заседании суда допускается лишь в случаях, установленных законом, с соблюдением при этом всех правил судопроизводства.

Статья 158. Обвиняемому обеспечивается право на защиту.

Статья 159. Судопроизводство ведется на языке союзной или автономной республики, автономной области, автономного округа или на языке большинства населения данной местности. Участвующим в деле лицам, не владеющим языком, на котором ведется судопроизводство, обеспечивается право полного ознакомления с материалами дела, участие в судебных действиях через переводчика и право выступать в суде на родном языке.

Статья 160. Никто не может быть признан виновным в совершении преступления, а также подвергнут уголовному наказанию иначе как по приговору суда и в соответствии с законом.

Статья 161. Для оказания юридической помощи гражданам и организациям действуют коллегии адвокатов. В случаях, предусмотренных законодательством, юридическая помощь гражданам оказывается бесплатно.

Организация и порядок деятельности адвокатуры определяются законодательством Союза ССР и союзных республик.

Статья 162. В судопроизводстве по гражданским и уголовным делам допускается участие представителей общественных организаций и трудовых коллективов.

Статья 163. Разрешение хозяйственных споров между предприятиями, учреждениями и организациями осуществляется органами государственного арбитража в пределах их компетенции.

Организация и порядок деятельности органов государственного арбитража определяются Законом о государственном арбитраже в СССР.

Глава 21.

Прокуратура

Статья 164. Высший надзор за точным и единообразным исполнением законов всеми министерствами, государственными комитетами и ведомствами, предприятиями, учреждениями и организациями, исполнительными и распорядительными органами местных Советов народных депутатов, колхозами, кооперативными и иными общественными организациями, должностными лицами, а также гражданами возлагается на Генерального прокурора СССР и подчиненных ему прокуроров.

Статья 165. Генеральный прокурор СССР назначается Верховным Советом СССР, ответствен перед ним и ему подотчетен, а в период между сессиями Верховного Совета — перед Президиумом Верховного Совета СССР, которому подотчетен.

Статья 166. Прокуроры союзных республик, автономных республик, краев, областей и автономных областей назначаются Генеральным прокурором СССР. Прокуроры автономных округов, районные и городские прокуроры назначаются прокурорами союзных республик и утверждаются Генеральным прокурором СССР.

Статья 167. Срок полномочий Генерального прокурора СССР и всех нижестоящих прокуроров — пять лет.

Статья 168. Органы прокуратуры осуществляют свои полномочия независимо от каких бы то ни было местных органов, подчиняясь только Генеральному прокурору СССР.

Организация и порядок деятельности органов прокуратуры определяются Законом о прокуратуре СССР.

VIII. ГЕРБ, ФЛАГ, ГИМН И СТОЛИЦА СССР

Статья 169. Государственный герб Союза Советских Социалистических Республик представляет собой изображение серпа и молота на фоне земного шара, в лучах солнца и в обрамлении колосьев, с надписью на языках союзных республик: «Пролетарии всех стран, соединяйтесь!». В верхней части герба — пятиконечная звезда.

Статья 170. Государственный флаг Союза Советских Социалистических Республик представляет собой красное прямоугольное полотнище с изображением в его верхнем углу, у древка, золотых серпа и молота и над ними красной пятиконечной звезды, обрамленной золотой каймой. Отношение ширины флага к его длине — 1 : 2.

Статья 171. Государственный гимн Союза Советских Социалистических Республик утверждается Президиумом Верховного Совета СССР.

Статья 172. Столицей Союза Советских Социалистических Республик является город Москва.

IX. ДЕЙСТВИЕ КОНСТИТУЦИИ СССР И ПОРЯДОК ЕЕ ИЗМЕНЕНИЯ

Статья 173. Конституция СССР обладает высшей юридической силой. Все законы и иные акты государственных органов издаются на основе и в соответствии с Конституцией СССР.

Статья 174. Изменение Конституции СССР производится решением Верховного Совета СССР, принятым большинством не менее двух третей от общего числа депутатов каждой из его палат.

CONSTITUTIONS OF THE UNION REPUBLICS: 1978*

**Translator's Note*: There are different ways of presenting the texts of the fifteen union republic constitutions in a comparative context. Because of the differences in language reflecting local history and conditions, I have translated, in full below, the preambles to all fifteen republic constitutions. This is followed by a complete translation of the constitution of the "mother republic"—the Russian Soviet Federative Socialist Republic (RSFSR). The numbering and text of the remaining fourteen republic constitutions are identical to the RSFSR text (except for the name of the republic), unless there is a notation to the contrary in the translation of the RSFSR text following the particular part, chapter, or article concerned. These notations are of three kinds: (1) differences in numbering of parts, chapters, or articles, which are given first; (2) any deviations from the RSFSR text are reproduced as footnotes to the relevant passage; and (3) the symbol *NP* in a footnote indicates that the constitution of the republic(s) indicated do(es) not contain that particular portion of the RSFSR text (NP = Not Present).

References to the texts of the union republic constitutions are abbreviated as follows:

Ar (Armenia), *Az* (Azerbaidzhan), *B* (Belorussia), *E* (Estonia), *G* (Georgia), *Ka* (Kazakhstan), *Ki* (Kirgizia), *La* (Latvia), *Li* (Lithuania), *M* (Moldavia), *Ta* (Tadzhikistan), *Tu* (Turkmenistan), *Uk* (Ukraine), and *Uz* (Uzbekistan).

CONSTITUTION (FUNDAMENTAL LAW) OF THE RUSSIAN SOVIET FEDERATIVE SOCIALIST REPUBLIC*

Sovetskaia Rossiia, 13 April 1978, 1–4.

The Great Socialist October Revolution, carried out by the workers and peasants of Russia under the leadership of the Communist Party, headed by V.I. Lenin, overturned the power of the capitalists and landowners, established the dictatorship of the proletariat, and created the Soviet state—the basic instrument to defend the revolutionary achievements and to build socialism and communism.

Soviet power has guaranteed equality and free self-determination for all the peoples of Russia, and has provided genuine democratic rights and freedoms for the working people. The formation of the RSFSR has provided the Russian people, and all nations and nationalities of the Russian Federation, favorable conditions for the all-round economic, social, and cultural development, taking into account their national character in the fraternal family of Soviet peoples.

The association of the RSFSR with other Soviet republics in the Union of Soviet Socialist Republics enhanced the forces and possibilities of the people of the country for the realization of basic socio-economic reforms.

As a result of the creative activity of the Soviet people under the leadership of the Communist Party, a developed socialist society has been built in the USSR—a society of genuine freedom of people and labor in which powerful productive forces have been created, the well-being and culture of the people is continuously increasing, and the indestructible union of the working class, the collective farm peasantry, and the people's intelligentsia is being strengthened.

The Russian Soviet Federative Socialist Republic is an equal republic in the Union of Soviet Socialist Republics, which reflects the state unity of the Soviet people and brings together all nations and nationalities for the combined construction of communism.

*Translated by William B. Simons and based upon the translation of the 1977 USSR Constitution by F.J.M. Feldbrugge and William B. Simons.

The people of the Russian Soviet Federative Socialist Republic,
—guided by the ideas of scientific communism,
—recognizing themselves as an integral part of the whole Soviet people,
—preserving the continuity of the ideas and principles of the Constitution of the RSFSR of 1918, the Constitution of the RSFSR of 1925, and the Constitution of the RSFSR of 1937, and in accordance with the Constitution (Fundamental Law) of the USSR, which has affirmed the foundations of the social system and the policies of the USSR, and established the rights, freedoms, and obligations of citizens, and the principles of organization and the aims of the socialist all-people's state, adopt and proclaim the present Constitution.

CONSTITUTION (FUNDAMENTAL LAW) OF THE ARMENIAN SOVIET SOCIALIST REPUBLIC

Kommunist, 15 April 1978, 1–4.

The Great Socialist October Revolution, carried out by the workers and peasants of Russia under the leadership of the Communist Party, headed by V.I. Lenin, marked a historical turning-point for the Armenian people, as well as for other peoples of the country, from which began its new history—a social and national revival, and the confirmation of its socialist state government.

As a result of the victory of the Great Socialist October Revolution and the establishment of the power of Soviets, the working people of our country under the leadership of the Communist Party, have realized basic socio-economic reforms, defended the achievements of socialism, and built a developed socialist society—a society of genuine freedom of people and labor in which powerful productive forces have been created, the well-being and culture of the people is continuously increasing, and the indestructible union of the working class, the collective farm peasantry, and the people's intelligentsia is strengthened.

The Armenian Soviet Socialist Republic is an equal republic in the Union of Soviet Socialist Republics, which reflects the state unity of the Soviet people and brings together all nations and nationalities for the combined construction of communism.

Guided by the high ideals of communism and in accordance with the Constitution (Fundamental Law) of the Union of Soviet Socialist Republics, which has affirmed the foundations of the social system and policies of the USSR, and established the rights, freedoms, and obligations of citizens, and the principles of organization and the aims of the socialist all-people's state, the people of the Armenian Soviet Socialist Republic proclaim the present Constitution.

CONSTITUTION (FUNDAMENTAL LAW) OF THE AZERBAIDZHAN SOVIET SOCIALIST REPUBLIC

Bakinskii Rabochii, 23 April 1978, 1–4.

The Great Socialist October Revolution, carried out by the workers and peasants of Russia under the leadership of the Communist Party, headed by V.I. Lenin, laid the beginning of a new era in the history of mankind and marked a basic turning-point in the fate of the peoples of our multinational country.

Under the banner of Great October, the working class and working peasantry of Azerbaidzhan overturned the power of the landowners and capitalists, broke the chains of oppression, established the dictatorship of the proletariat, and created for the first time in history its own socialist state—the Azerbaidzhan Soviet Socialist Republic.

The Azerbaidzhan SSR, expressing the will of the Azerbaidzhan people, joined together with other equal Soviet republics in the Union of Soviet Socialist Republics—a unitary federal state. The formation of the USSR has enhanced the forces and possibilities of the people of the country to build socialism.

In the strong union of fraternal Soviet republics, and owing to the great historical advantages of the socialist social system, and actively implementing the Leninist nationalities policy of the CPSU, the working people of the Azerbaidzhan SSR have achieved notable successes in all fields of economic, political, and socio-cultural life.

As a result of the creative activity of the Soviet people under the leadership of the Communist Party, a developed socialist society has been built in the USSR—a society of genuine freedom of people and labor in which powerful productive forces have been created, mature socialist social relationships have been affirmed, the well-being and culture of the people is continuously increasing, and the indestructible union of the working class, the collective farm peasantry, and the people's intelligentsia is being strengthened.

The people of the Azerbaidzhan Soviet Socialist Republic, recognizing themselves as an integral part of the Soviet people, guided by the ideas of scientific communism, observing allegiance to their revolutionary and international traditions, and preserving the continuity of the ideas and principles of the Constitution of the Azerbaidzhan SSR of 1921, the Constitution of the Azerbaidzhan SSR of 1937, and in accordance with the Constitution (Fundamental Law) of the USSR, which affirms the foundations of the social system and policies of the USSR, and establishes the rights, freedoms, and obligations of citizens, and the principles of organization and the aims of the socialist all-people's state, adopt and proclaim the present Constitution.

CONSTITUTION (FUNDAMENTAL LAW) OF THE BELORUSSIAN SOVIET SOCIALIST REPUBLIC

Sovetskaia Belorussiia, 16 April 1978, 1–4.

The Great Socialist October Revolution, carried out by the workers and peasants of Russia under the leadership of the Communist Party, headed by V.I. Lenin, overturned the power of the capitalists and landowners, established the dictatorship of the proletariat, and created the Soviet state—the basic instrument to defend the revolutionary achievements and to build socialism and communism.

As a result of the creative activity of the Soviet people under the leadership of the Communist Party, a developed socialist society has been built in the USSR—a society of genuine freedom of people and labor in which powerful productive forces have been created, mature socialist social relationships have been affirmed, the well-being and culture of the people is continuously increasing, the indestructible union of the working class, the collective farm peasantry, and the people's intelligentsia has been consolidated, and a new historical community of people—the Soviet people—has taken shape.

Great October marked a basic turning-point in the fate of all nations and nationalities of our country. Having set out upon the road of the socialist revolution, the workers and peasants of Belorussia, with the assistance of the Russian proletariat, for the first time in history founded their own state government and formed the Belorussian Soviet Socialist Republic.

The association of the Belorussian SSR and the other Soviet republics in a unitary federal state—the Union of Soviet Socialist Republics—enhanced the forces and possibilities of the people of our country for the realization of basic socio-economic reforms, the building of socialism, and for the defense of its great achievements.

Under the conditions of socialism, owing to the active implementation of the Leninist nationalities policy of the Party, and supported by the full fraternal assistance of the Great Russian people and the peoples of all the Soviet republics, the working people of Belorussia have achieved huge successes in the development of the economy, science, and culture.

The Belorussian Soviet Socialist Republic is an equal republic in the Union of Soviet Socialist Republics, which reflects the state unity of the Soviet people and brings together all nations and nationalities for the combined construction of communism.

The people of the Belorussian Soviet Socialist Republic,

—guided by the ideas of scientific communism,

—recognizing themselves as an integral part of the whole Soviet people,

—preserving the continuity of the constitutional development of our country, and the ideas and principles of the Constitution of the Belorussian SSR of 1919, the Constitution of the Belorussian SSR of 1927, and the Constitution of the Belorussian SSR of 1937, and in accordance with the Constitution (Fundamental Law) of the Union of Soviet Socialist Republics, which has affirmed the foundations of the social system and policies of the USSR, and established the rights, freedoms, and obligations of citizens, and the principles of organization and the aims of the socialist all-people's state, adopt and proclaim the present Constitution.

CONSTITUTION (FUNDAMENTAL LAW) OF THE ESTONIAN SOVIET SOCIALIST REPUBLIC

Sovetskaia Estoniia, 15 April 1978, 1–4.

The Great Socialist October Revolution, carried out by the workers and peasants of Russia under the leadership of the Communist Party, headed by V.I. Lenin, overturned the power of the capitalists and landowners, broke the chains of oppression, established the dictatorship of the proletariat, and created the Soviet state—a state of a new type, the basic instrument to defend the revolutionary achievements and to build socialism and communism.

Soviet power was established in Estonia in October 1917.

After the defeat of the Estonian Workers' Commune, which was given birth by Great October, but which fell under the blows of the united forces of international imperialism and internal counterrevolution, the communists of Estonia, in the most difficult conditions of resistance and terror, led the struggle of the working people for the overthrow of the power of the bourgeoisie. This struggle culminated in 1940 with the establishment of Soviet power. The Estonian Soviet Socialist Republic voluntarily entered into the great family of the Soviet people.

Under the leadership of the Communist Party, the working people of our country have realized basic socio-economic reforms, the achievements of socialism have been defended, and a developed socialist society has been built—a society of genuine freedom of people and labor in which powerful productive forces have been created, the well-being and culture of the people is continuously increasing, and the indestructible union of the working class, the collective farm peasantry, and the people's intelligentsia is being strengthened.

The Estonian Soviet Socialist Republic is an equal republic in the Union of Soviet Socialist Republics, which reflects the state unity of the Soviet people and brings together all nations and nationalities for the combined construction of communism.

Guided by the high ideals of communism and in accordance with the Constitution (Fundamental Law) of the USSR, which has affirmed the foundations of the social system and policies of the USSR, and established the rights, freedoms, and obligations of citizens, and the principles of organization and the aims of the socialist all-people's state, the people of the Estonian Soviet Socialist Republic, recognizing themselves as an integral part of the whole Soviet people, adopt and proclaim the present Constitution.

CONSTITUTION (FUNDAMENTAL LAW) OF THE GEORGIAN SOVIET SOCIALIST REPUBLIC

Zaria Vostoka, 16 April 1978, 2–5.

As a result of the victory of the Great Socialist October Revolution and the establishment of the power of the Soviets, the working people of our country under the leadership of the Communist Party, created by V.I. Lenin, have realized basic socio-economic reforms, defended the achievements of socialism, and built a developed socialist society—a society of genuine freedom of people and labor in which powerful productive forces have been created, the well-being and culture of the people is continuously increasing, and the indestructible union of the working class, the collective farm peasantry, and the people's intelligentsia is being strengthened.

Great October played a decisive role in the fate of the Georgian people. Under the leadership of the Communist Party, and owing to the fraternal assistance of Soviet Russia, Soviet power was victorious in Georgia on 25 February 1921.

The voluntary association of Georgia in a unitary family of Soviet republics has brought about the all-round development and growth of the Georgian people.

The Georgian Soviet Socialist Republic is an equal republic in the Union of Soviet Socialist Republics, which reflects the state unity of the Soviet people and brings together all nations and nationalities for the combined construction of communism.

The people of the Georgian Soviet Socialist Republic,
—guided by the ideas of scientific communism,
—recognizing themselves as an integral part of the whole Soviet people,
—preserving the continuity of the ideas and principles of the Constitution of the Georgian SSR of 1922, the Constitution of the Georgian SSR of 1927, and the Constitution of the Georgian SSR of 1937, and in agreement with the Constitution (Fundamental Law) of the USSR, which has affirmed the foundations of the social system and policies of the USSR, and established the rights, freedoms, and obligations of citizens, and the principles of organization and the aims of the socialist all-people's state, adopt and proclaim the present Constitution.

CONSTITUTION (FUNDAMENTAL LAW) OF THE KAZAKH SOVIET SOCIALIST REPUBLIC

Kazakhstanskaia Pravda, 21 April 1978, 1–4.

As a result of the victory of the Great Socialist October Revolution and the establishment of the power of the Soviets, the working people of our country, under the leadership of the Communist Party, have realized basic socio-economic reforms, defended the achievements of socialism, and built a developed socialist society—a society of genuine freedom of people and labor in which powerful productive forces have been created, the well-being and culture of the people is continuously increasing, and the indestructible union of the working class, the collective farm peasantry, and the people's intelligentsia is being strengthened.

The Kazakh Soviet Socialist Republic is an equal republic in the Union of Soviet Socialist Republics, which reflects the state unity of the Soviet people and brings together all nations and nationalities for the combined construction of communism.

Guided by the high ideals of communism and in accordance with the Constitution (Fundamental Law) of the USSR, which has affirmed the foundations of the social system and policies of the USSR, and established the rights, freedoms, and obligations of citizens, and the principles of organization and the aims of the socialist all-people's state, the people of the Kazakh Soviet Socialist Republic proclaim the present Constitution.

CONSTITUTION (FUNDAMENTAL LAW) OF THE KIRGIZ SOVIET SOCIALIST REPUBLIC

Sovetskaia Kirgiziia, 21 April 1978, 1–4.

As a result of the victory of the Great Socialist October Revolution and the establishment of the power of the Soviets, the working people of our country, under the leadership of the Communist Party, have realized basic socio-economic reforms, defended the achievements of socialism, and built a developed socialist society—a society of genuine freedom of people and labor in which powerful productive forces have been created, the well-being and culture of the people is continuously increasing, and the indestructible union of the working class, the collective farm peasantry, and the people's intelligentsia is being strengthened.

The Kirgiz Soviet Socialist Republic is an equal republic in the Union of Soviet Socialist Republics, which reflects the state unity of the Soviet people and brings together all nations and nationalities for the combined construction of communism.

Guided by the high ideals of communism and in accordance with the Constitution (Fundamental Law) of the USSR, which has affirmed the foundations of the social system and policies of the USSR, and established the rights, freedoms, and obligations of citizens, and the principles of organization and the aims of the socialist all-people's state, the people of the Kirgiz Soviet Socialist Republic proclaim the present Constitution.

CONSTITUTION (FUNDAMENTAL LAW) OF THE LATVIAN SOVIET SOCIALIST REPUBLIC

Sovetskaia Latviia, 19 April 1978, 1–4.

As a result of the victory of the Great Socialist October Revolution and the establishment of the power of the Soviets, the working people of our country under the leadership of the Communist Party, created by V.I. Lenin, have realized basic socio-economic reforms, defended the achievements of socialism, and built a developed socialist society—a society of genuine freedom of people and labor in which powerful productive forces have been created, the well-being and culture of the people is continuously increasing, and the indestructible union of the working class, the collective farm peasantry, and the people's intelligentsia is being strengthened.

The working people of Latvia actively took part in the joint revolutionary struggle of the people of Russia for the victory of Great October and the creation of the Soviet state. Their struggle was completed with the formation of the Socialist Soviet Republic of Latvia. However, under the pressure of international imperialism and the national bourgeoisie, it was not possible to defend the revolutionary achievements at that time. The working people of Latvia, in the conditions of the bourgeois dictatorship and under the leadership of the Communist Party, carried out the selfless struggle for the restoration of Soviet power. The success of socialist construction in the USSR gave them inspiration for this. This struggle culminated in the victory of the socialist revolution in 1940 and the restoration of Soviet power. The Latvian Soviet Socialist Republic was formed, which, on the basis of self-determination of its people, voluntarily entered the Union of Soviet Socialist Republics.

The Latvian Soviet Socialist Republic is an equal republic in the Union of Soviet Socialist Republics, which reflects the state unity of the Soviet people and brings together all nations and nationalities for the combined construction of communism.

Guided by the ideals of scientific communism, recognizing themselves as an integral part of the whole Soviet people, preserving the continuity of the constitutional development of our Soviet country, and the ideas and principles of the Constitution of the Socialist Soviet Republic of Latvia of 1919 and the Constitution of the Latvian SSR of 1940, and in accordance with the Constitution (Fundamental Law) of the USSR, which has affirmed the foundations of the social system and policies of the USSR, and established the rights, freedoms, and obligations of citizens, and the principles of organization and aims of the socialist all-people's state, the people of the Latvian Soviet Socialist Republic adopt and proclaim the present Constitution.

CONSTITUTION (FUNDAMENTAL LAW) OF THE LITHUANIAN SOVIET SOCIALIST REPUBLIC

Sovetskaia Litva, 21 April 1978, 1–4.

As a result of the victory of the Great Socialist October Revolution and the establishment of the power of the Soviets, the working people of our country, under the leadership of the Communist Party, have realized basic socio-economic reforms, defended the achievements of socialism, and built a developed socialist society—a society of genuine freedom of people and labor in which powerful productive forces have been created, the well-being and culture of the people is continuously increasing, and the indestructible union of the working class, the collective farm peasantry, and the people's intelligentsia is being strengthened.

Inspired by the victory of Great October, the workers and peasants of Lithuania proclaimed the formation of the Lithuanian Soviet Socialist Republic in December 1918. However, under the pressure of international imperialism and the national bourgeoisie, it was not possible to defend the revolutionary achievements at that time. The working people of Lithuania, led by the Communist Party, steadfastly fought against the bourgeois dictatorship and in 1940 restored Soviet power. The Lithuanian Soviet Socialist Republic, on the basis of the free self-determination of its people, voluntarily entered the USSR.

The Lithuanian Soviet Socialist Republic is an equal republic in the Union of Soviet Socialist Republics, which reflects the state unity of the Soviet people and brings together all nations and nationalities for the combined construction of communism.

The people of the Lithuanian Soviet Socialist Republic,

—guided by the ideals of scientific communism,

—recognizing themselves as an integral part of the whole Soviet people,

—developing the constitutional law of the republic, and preserving the continuity of the ideals and principles of the Constitution of the Lithuanian SSR of 1940, and in accordance with the Constitution (Fundamental Law) of the USSR, which has affirmed the foundations of the social system and policies of the USSR, and established the rights, freedoms, and obligations of citizens, and the principles of organization and aims of the socialist all-people's state, adopt and proclaim the present Constitution.

CONSTITUTION (FUNDAMENTAL LAW) OF THE MOLDAVIAN SOVIET SOCIALIST REPUBLIC

Sovetskaia Moldaviia, 16 April 1978, 1–4.

As a result of the victory of the Great Socialist October Revolution and the establishment of the power of the Soviets, the working people of our country, under the leadership of the Communist Party, have realized basic socio-economic reforms, defended the achievements of socialism, and built a developed socialist society—a society of genuine freedom of people and labor in which powerful productive forces have been created, the well-being and culture of the people is continuously increasing, and the indestructible union of the working class, the collective farm peasantry, and the people's intelligentsia is being strengthened.

The Moldavian Soviet Socialist Republic is an equal republic in the Union of Soviet Socialist Republics, which reflects the state unity of the Soviet people and brings together all nations and nationalities for the combined construction of communism.

Faithfully following the precepts of V.I. Lenin, the working people of Moldavia, owing to the great assistance of the Great Russian and other peoples of our country, defended the revolutionary achievements of Great October, founded a socialist state, and achieved great successes in economic, social, and cultural development.

Guided by the high ideals of communism and in accordance with the Constitution (Fundamental Law) of the Union of Soviet Socialist Republics, which has affirmed the foundations of the social system and policies of the USSR, and established the rights, freedoms, and obligations of citizens, and the principles of organization and aims of the socialist all-people's state, the people of the Moldavian Soviet Socialist Republic proclaim the present Constitution.

CONSTITUTION (FUNDAMENTAL LAW) OF THE TADZHIK SOVIET SOCIALIST REPUBLIC

Kommunist Tadzhikistana, 15 April 1978, 2–4.

As a result of the victory of the Great Socialist October Revolution and the establishment of the power of the Soviets, the working people of our country, under the leadership of the Communist Party, have realized basic socio-economic reforms, defended the achievements of socialism, and built a developed socialist society—a society of genuine freedom of people and labor in which powerful productive forces have been created, the well-being and culture of the people is continuously increasing, and the indestructible union of the working class, the collective farm peasantry, and the people's intelligentsia is being strengthened.

The Tadzhik Soviet Socialist Republic is an equal republic in the Union of Soviet Socialist Republics, which reflects the state unity of the Soviet people and brings together all nations and nationalities for the combined construction of communism.

Guided by the high ideals of communism and in accordance with the Constitution (Fundamental Law) of the Union of Soviet Socialist Republics, which has affirmed the foundations of the social system and policies of the USSR, and established the rights, freedoms, and obligations of citizens, and the principles of organization and aims of the socialist all-people's state, the people of the Tadzhik Soviet Socialist Republic proclaim the present Constitution.

CONSTITUTION (FUNDAMENTAL LAW) OF THE TURKMEN SOVIET SOCIALIST REPUBLIC

Turkmenskaia Iskra, 18 April 1978, 1–4.

As a result of the victory of the Great Socialist October Revolution, carried out under the leadership of the Communist Party, headed by V.I. Lenin, the establishment of the power of the Soviets, and the consistent implementation of the Leninist nationalities policy, the working people of our country have realized basic socio-economic reforms, defended the achievements of socialism, and built a developed socialist society—a society of genuine freedom of people and labor in which powerful productive forces have been created, the well-being and culture of the people is continuously increasing, and the indestructible union of the working class, the collective farm peasantry, and the people's intelligentsia is being strengthened.

With the victory of Great October, the Turkmen people for the first time founded a national state, and, in a historically short period, liquidated their centuries old backwardness. In the fraternal family of Soviet peoples, Turkmenistan has been turned into an industrial–agrarian socialist republic with a highly developed industry and agriculture, and a progressive science and culture.

The Turkmen Soviet Socialist Republic is an equal republic in the Union of Soviet Socialist Republics, which reflects the state unity of the Soviet people and brings together all nations and nationalities for the combined construction of communism.

The people of the Turkmen Soviet Socialist Republic,

—guided by the high ideals of communism,

—recognizing themselves as an integral part of the whole Soviet people,

—and preserving the continuity of ideas and principles of the Constitution of the Turkmen SSR of 1927, and the Constitution of the Turkmen SSR of 1937, and in accordance with the Constitution (Fundamental Law) of the Union of Soviet Socialist Republics, which has affirmed the foundations of the social system and policies of the USSR, and established the rights, freedoms, and obligations of citizens, and the principles of organization and aims of the socialist all-people's state, adopt and proclaim the present Constitution.

CONSTITUTION (FUNDAMENTAL LAW) OF THE UKRAINIAN SOVIET SOCIALIST REPUBLIC

Pravda Ukrainy, 21 April 1978, 2–5.

The Great Socialist October Revolution, carried out by the workers and peasants of Russia under the leadership of the Communist Party, headed by V.I. Lenin, overturned the power of the capitalists and landowners, established the dictatorship of the proletariat, and created the Soviet state—the basic instrument to defend the revolutionary achievements and to build socialism and communism. Soviet power has freed the peoples of Russia from social and national oppression, and guaranteed them equality and the right to free self-determination.

As a result of the creative activity of the working people, led by the Communist Party, a developed socialist society has been built in our country—a society of genuine freedom of people and labor in which powerful productive forces have been created, mature socialist social relationships have been affirmed, the well-being and culture of the people is continuously increasing, the indestructible union of the working class, the collective farm peasantry, and the people's intelligentsia is being strengthened, and a new historical community of people—the Soviet people—has taken shape. Owing to the consistent implementation of the Leninist nationalities policy and the construction of socialism in the USSR, for the first time in history the nationalities question has been successfully resolved.

Great October also marked a basic turning-point in the fate of the Ukrainian people. Having set out upon the road of the socialist revolution, the workers and peasants of the Ukraine, with the fraternal assistance of the Russian proletariat, smashed the exploitive system, crushed the bourgeois-nationalist counterrevolution, and for the first time in history created their own state—the Ukrainian Soviet Socialist Republic.

The association of the fraternal Soviet republics in a unitary federal state—the Union of Soviet Socialist Republics—enhanced the forces and possibilities in our country for the realization of basic socio-economic reforms and the defense of the great revolutionary achievements of socialism. A way had opened up for the working people of the Ukraine for rapid progress in all fields of social life and for the unprecedented rise of the economy and the flowering of culture. The Ukrainian people joined together in a unitary Soviet socialist state.

The Ukrainian Soviet Socialist Republic is an equal republic in the Union of Soviet Socialist Republics, which reflects the state unity of the Soviet people and brings together all nations and nationalities for the purpose of jointly constructing communism.

The people of the Ukrainian Soviet Socialist Republic,
—guided by the ideals of scientific communism,
—recognizing themselves as an integral part of the whole Soviet people,
—preserving the continuity of constitutional development of our country, and the ideas and principles of the Constitution of the Ukrainian SSR of 1919, the Constitution of the Ukrainian SSR of 1929, and the Constitution of the Ukrainian SSR of 1937, and in accordance with the Constitution (Fundamental Law) of the Union of Soviet Socialist Republics, which has affirmed the foundations of the social system and policies of the USSR, and established the rights, freedoms, and obligations of citizens, and the principles of organization and aims of the socialist all-people's state, adopt and proclaim the present Constitution.

CONSTITUTION (FUNDAMENTAL LAW) OF THE UZBEK SOVIET SOCIALIST REPUBLIC

Pravda Vostoka, 20 April 1978, 1–4.

The Great Socialist October Revolution, carried out by the workers and peasants of Russia under the leadership of the Communist Party, headed by V.I. Lenin, was a great historical event in the life of the peoples of the Soviet country, and also marked a basic turning-point in the fate of the people of Uzbekistan.

Having set out upon the road of the socialist revolution, the working people of Uzbekistan, with the fraternal assistance of the Russian proletariat, smashed the exploitive system, for the first time in history founded their own state, and set out on the road of transformation from feudalism to socialism, passing capitalism.

The formation of the Uzbek SSR and its voluntary association with other Soviet republics in the unitary multinational Soviet socialist state—the USSR—has immeasurably enhanced the forces and possibilities of the working people of the republic for the building of a new society.

Under the leadership of the Communist Party, the working people of our country have realized basic reforms, defended the achievements of socialism, and built a developed socialist society—a society of genuine freedom of people and labor in which powerful productive forces have been created, the well-being and culture of the people is continuously increasing, the indestructible union of the working class, the collective farm peasantry, and the people's intelligentsia is being strengthened, and a new historical community of people—the Soviet people—has taken shape.

The Uzbek Soviet Socialist Republic is an equal republic in the Union of Soviet Socialist Republics, which reflects the state unity of the Soviet people and brings together all nations and nationalities for the combined construction of communism.

Guided by the high ideals of communism, recognizing themselves as an integral part of the whole Soviet people, and preserving the continuity of constitutional development of our country, and the ideas and principles of the Constitution of the Uzbek SSR of 1927 and the Constitution of the Uzbek SSR of 1937, and in accordance with the Constitution (Fundamental Law) of the Union of Soviet Socialist Republics of

1977, which has affirmed the foundations of the social system and policies of the USSR, and established the rights, freedoms, and obligations of citizens, and the principles of organization and aims of the socialist all-people's state, the people of the Uzbek Soviet Socialist Republic adopt and proclaim the present Constitution.

I. THE FOUNDATIONS OF THE SOCIAL SYSTEM AND THE POLICIES OF THE RSFSR

Chapter 1. The Political System

Article 1. The Russian Soviet Federative Socialist Republic is a socialist all-people's state expressing the will and the interests of the workers, the peasants, and the intelligentsia, and of the working people of all the nations and nationalities of the republic.[1]

[1]**Ar,B,E,Ka,Ki,La,Li,M,Ta,Uk** the peasants, and the intelligentsia, and of the working people of all the nationalities of the republic. **Tu** the peasants, and of the intelligentsia of all the nationalities of the republic.

Article 2. All power in the RSFSR belongs to the people.

The people exercise state power through the Soviets of People's Deputies, which constitute the political foundation of the RSFSR.

All other state organs are under the control of and accountable to the Soviets of People's Deputies.

Article 3. The Soviet state is organized and functions in accordance with the principle of democratic centralism: all organs of state power are elected from the lowest to the highest, they are accountable to the people, and the decisions of higher organs are binding for lower organs. Democratic centralism combines unified leadership with local initiative, creative activity, and with the responsibility of every state organ and official for the tasks entrusted to them.

Article 4. The Soviet state and all its organs function on the basis of socialist legality and ensure the protection of the legal order, the interests of society, and the rights and freedoms of citizens.

State and social organizations and officials are bound to observe the Constitution of the USSR, the Constitution of the RSFSR, and Soviet laws.

Article 5. The most important questions of the life of the state are submitted for nationwide discussion and are also put to a nationwide vote (referendum).

Article 6. The Communist Party of the Soviet Union is the leading and guiding force of Soviet society and the nucleus of its political system and of state and social organizations. The CPSU exists for the people and serves the people.

Armed with Marxist–Leninist doctrine, the Communist Party determines the general perspective of the development of society and the course of the domestic and foreign policy of the USSR, directs the great creative activity of the Soviet people, and imparts a planned and scientifically-sound character to their struggle for the victory of communism.

All party organizations function within the framework of the Constitution of the USSR.

Article 7. In accordance with their statutory functions, trade unions, the All-Union Leninist Communist Youth League, cooperative and other social organizations participate in the administration of state and public affairs and in the resolution of political, economic, and socio-cultural problems.

Article 8. Labor collectives participate in the discussion and resolution of state and public affairs; in the planning of production and social development; in the training and placement of personnel; in the discussion and resolution of questions of the administration of enterprises and institutions, of the improvement of the conditions of labor and everyday life, and of the utilization of resources allocated for the development of production as well as for socio-cultural measures and material incentives.

Labor collectives develop socialist competition; promote the dissemination of progressive work-methods, and the strengthening of labor discipline; educate their members in the spirit of communist morality; and concern themselves with raising their political awareness, culture, and professional qualifications.

Article 9. The basic direction of the development of the political system of Soviet society is the further unfolding of socialist democracy: the ever-widening participation of citizens in the administration of the affairs of the state and of society, the perfection of the state apparatus, the growth of the activity of social organizations, the strengthening of people's control, the reinforcement of the legal basis of the life of the state and of society, the extension of publicity, and permanent consideration of public opinion.

Chapter 2. The Economic System

Article 10. The foundation of the economic system of the RSFSR is socialist ownership of the means of production in the form of state (all-people's) and collective-farm/cooperative ownership.

Property of trade unions and other social organizations, necessary for the realization of their statutory functions, is also socialist property.

The state protects socialist ownership and creates conditions for its increase.

No one has the right to use socialist property for purposes of personal gain and other selfish purposes.

Article 11. State ownership, the common heritage of the entire Soviet people, is the basic form of socialist ownership.

The land, its mineral wealth, the waters, and the forests are within the exclusive ownership of the state. The state owns the basic means of production in industry, construction, and agriculture, the means of transportation and communication, the banks, the property of commercial, municipal, and other enterprises organized by the state, the basic municipal housing fund, as well as other property necessary for the realization of the functions of the state.

Article 12. The property of collective farms, and other cooperative organizations and their associations, consists of the means of production and other property necessary for the realization of their statutory functions.

The land occupied by collective farms is allocated to them for their free use and for an unlimited time.

The state promotes the development of collective-farm/cooperative ownership and its drawing together with state ownership.

Collective farms, as well as other land users, are bound to utilize land efficiently, to treat it with care, and to increase its productiveness.

Article 13. Earned income constitutes the basis of personal property of citizens of the RSFSR. Articles of everyday use, of personal consumption and comfort, and of the subsidiary household, a dwelling, and savings from labor may be held in personal ownership. Personal ownership of citizens and the right to its inheritance are protected by the state.

Citizens may have the use of plots of land, made available in the manner provided by law, in order to run a subsidiary household (including the keeping of livestock and fowl), to engage in fruit and vegetable gardening, and also for individual housing construction. Citizens are bound to rationally utilize the plots of land made available to them. The state and the collective farm render aid to citizens in running the subsidiary household.

Property in the personal ownership or use of citizens must not serve for the derivation of unearned income or be used to the detriment of the interests of society.

Article 14. The labor of Soviet people, free from exploitation, is the source of the growth of public wealth and of the well-being of the people and of every Soviet citizen.

In accordance with the principle of socialism: "From each according to his abilities, to each according to this work", the state supervises performance and consumption. It determines the rate of tax on income subject to taxation.

Socially useful labor and its results determine the position of man in society. The state, combining material and moral incentives, and encouraging inventiveness and a creative attitude to work, furthers the transformation of labor into the prime necessity of life of every Soviet man and woman.

Article 15. The highest goal of social production under socialism is the fullest possible satisfaction of the growing material and spiritual needs of the people.

Relying on the creative activity of working people and socialist competition, and on the achievements of scientific-technical progress, and perfecting the forms and methods of economic management, the state ensures the growth of labor productivity, the increased efficiency of production and quality of work, and a dynamic, planned, and balanced development of the national economy.

Article 16. The economic system of the RSFSR constitutes a component part of the single economic complex embracing all units of social production, distribution, and exchange within the territory of the USSR.

The economic system is managed[1] on the basis of state plans of economic and social development, taking into account the branch and territorial principles, and combining centralized leadership with the economic independence and initiative of enterprises, associations, and other organizations. At the same time, economic accountability, profit, production costs, and other economic levers and stimuli are actively utilized.

[1]**Ar** The economic system in the Armenian SSR is managed

Article 17. Individual labor activity in the sphere of trades and crafts, agriculture, serving the everyday needs of the population, as well as other forms of activity based exclusively on the individual labor of citizens and the members of their families, are permitted in the RSFSR in accordance with the law. The state regulates individual labor activity, ensuring its utilization in the interests of society.

Article 18. In the interests of present and future generations, the necessary measures are taken in the RSFSR for the protection and the scientifically-sound and rational utilization of the land and its mineral wealth, water resources, the plant and animal world, for the preservation of the purity of air and water, for safeguarding the reproduction of natural resources, and for the improvement of the human environment.

Chapter 3. Social Development and Culture

Article 19. The indestructible union of workers, peasants, and the intelligentsia constitutes the social foundation of the RSFSR.

The state promotes the strengthening of the social homogeneousness of society, the effacement of class differences and of the essential differences between town and country and between mental and physical labor, and the all-round development and rapprochement of the nations and nationalities of the USSR.

Article 20. In accordance with the communist ideal: "The free development of each is the condition for the free development of all", the state has as its goal the expansion of the actual possibilities for citizens to apply their creative forces, abilities, and talents, and for the all-round development of the individual.

Article 21. The state concerns itself with the improvement of working conditions and labor safety and the scientific organization of labor, and with the reduction and, ultimately, with the complete elimination of heavy physical labor on the basis of the comprehensive mechanization and automation of production processes in all branches of the national economy.

Article 22. A program of transforming agricultural labor into a variety of industrial labor; of widening in rural areas the network of institutions for public education, culture, health care, trade and public catering, services for everyday needs, and public utilities; and of transforming villages[1] into well-appointed settlements[2] is consistently implemented in the RSFSR.

[1]**E,La,Li** and of transforming rural settlements and villages **Ka** and of transforming *auls* [a type of village in the Caucasus and Central Asia] and villages **Ta** and of transforming *kishlaks* [a type of village in Central Asia] **Uz** and of transforming villages, *kishlaks*, and *auls* [2]**Ki** into well-appointed settlements; and of the further development and improvement of cultural-everyday centers for cattle-breeders on mountainous and distant pastures

Article 23. On the basis of the growth of labor productivity, the state follows an unswerving course for raising the level of wages and the real income of working people.

Public funds for consumption are created in order to more fully satisfy the needs of Soviet people. The state, with the broad participation of social organizations and labor collectives, ensures the growth and the equitable distribution of these funds.

Article 24. State systems of health care, social insurance, trade and public catering, services for everyday needs, and public utilities are operated and expanded in the RSFSR.

The state encourages the activity of cooperative and other social organizations in all spheres of services to the population. The state promotes the development of mass physical culture and sport.

Article 25. In the RSFSR there exists and is continually perfected a single system of public education which ensures the general educational and professional training of citizens, serves the communist upbringing and the spiritual and physical development of young people, and prepares them for work and social activity.

Article 26. In accordance with the needs of society, the state ensures the planned development of science and the training of scientific personnel, and organizes the implementation of the results of scientific research in the national economy and in other spheres of life.

Article 27. The state concerns itself with the protection, multiplication, and broad utilization of spiritual values for the purpose of the moral and aesthetic upbringing of Soviet people and the raising of their cultural level.

The development of professional art and popular artistic creativeness receives every encouragement in the RSFSR.

Chapter 4. Foreign Policy and the Defense of the Socialist Fatherland

Article 28. In foreign policy activities, the RSFSR is guided by the goals, tasks, and principles of the foreign policy defined by the Constitution of the USSR.

In the RSFSR, war propaganda is forbidden.

Article 29. In accordance with the Constitution of the USSR, the defense of the socialist Fatherland is one of the most important functions of the state and is a concern of the whole people.

In order to defend the socialist achievements, the peaceful labor of the Soviet people, and the sovereignty and territorial integrity of the state, the Armed Forces of the USSR have been created and universal military service has been established.

The duty of the Armed Forces of the USSR to the people is reliably to defend the socialist Fatherland and to remain in constant combat readiness, guaranteeing an instant rebuff to any aggressor.

Article 30. The RSFSR participates in ensuring the security and defense capability of the country and equipping the Armed Forces of the USSR with everything they require.

The duties of state organs, social organizations, officials, and citizens in ensuring the security of the country and the strengthening of its defense capability are defined by legislation of the USSR.

II. THE STATE AND THE INDIVIDUAL

Chapter 5. RSFSR Citizenship. The Equality of Citizens

Article 31. In accordance with the single union citizenship established in the USSR, every citizen of the RSFSR is a citizen of the USSR.

The grounds and the procedure for acquiring and losing Soviet citizenship are defined by the Law on Citizenship of the USSR.

Within the territory of the RSFSR, citizens of other union republics enjoy equal rights with citizens of the RSFSR.

Citizens of the RSFSR abroad enjoy the defense and protection of the Soviet state.

Article 32. Citizens of the RSFSR are equal before the law regardless of origin, social and property status, race or nationality, sex, education, language, attitude towards religion, type and character of occupation, place of residence, and of other circumstances.

The equality of citizens of the RSFSR is ensured in all fields of economic, political, social, and cultural life.

Article 33. Women and men in the RSFSR have equal rights.

The exercise of these rights is ensured by according women equal opportunities with men in receiving education and professional training, in labor, remuneration, and professional advancement, in socio-political and cultural activity, as well as by special measures for the protection of women's labor and health; by creating conditions allowing women to combine work with motherhood; by the legal protection of and by material and moral support for mother and child, including the granting of paid leave and other benefits to pregnant women and mothers; and by a gradual reduction of working time for women with young children.[1]

[1]In the following five republic texts, a third paragraph has been added to the equivalent of RSFSR Art. 33: **Ka,Ki,Ta,Tu,Uz**(para. 3): A violation of the equality of women, connected with the infringement of their rights to education, to the choice of a profession, or to the participation in state, social, and cultural life, as well as in the family and everyday life, is punished by law.

Article 34. Citizens of the RSFSR of different races and nationalities have equal rights.

The exercise of these rights is ensured by a policy of comprehensive development and rapprochement of all nations and nationalities of the USSR, by educating citizens in the spirit of Soviet patriotism and socialist internationalism, and by the possibility to use one's native language and the languages of other peoples of the USSR.

Any direct or indirect restriction of rights whatsoever, the establishment of direct or indirect privileges for citizens on grounds of race or nationality, as well as any preaching of racial or national exclusiveness, hostility, or contempt are punished by law.

Article 35. Foreign citizens and stateless persons in the RSFSR are guaranteed the rights and freedoms provided for by law, including the right to apply to a court and other state organs for the protection of the personal, property, family, and other rights which belong to them.

Foreign citizens and stateless persons within the territory of the RSFSR are bound to respect the Constitution of the USSR, the Constitution of the RSFSR, and to observe Soviet laws.

Article 36. The RSFSR grants the right of asylum to foreigners, persecuted for defending the interests of the working people and the cause of peace, for participating in revolutionary or national liberation movements, or for progressive socio-political, scientific, or other creative activities.

Chapter 6. The Basic Rights, Freedoms, and Obligations of Citizens of the RSFSR

Article 37. Citizens of the RSFSR enjoy the full range of the socio-economic, political, and personal rights and freedoms proclaimed and guaranteed by the Constitution of the USSR, the Constitution of the RSFSR, and Soviet laws. The socialist system ensures the widening of rights and freedoms and the continuous improvement of the living conditions of citizens in accordance with the fulfillment of the programs of socio-economic and cultural development.

In exercising their rights and freedoms, citizens may not injure the interests of society and the state or the rights of other citizens.

Article 38. Citizens of the RSFSR have the right to work, that is, to guaranteed employment with remuneration in accordance with the quantity and quality of the work, and not lower than the minimum rate established by the state, including the right to choose a profession, occupation, and work in accordance with their vocation, ability, professional training, and education, taking into account the needs of society.

This right is ensured by the socialist economic system, the continuous growth of the productive forces, free professional training, the improvement of work skills, training in new fields, and the development of the systems of professional guidance and job placement.

Article 39. Citizens of the RSFSR have the right to rest.

This right is ensured by establishing a workweek not exceeding 41 hours for workers and employees, and a reduced workday for a number of professions and types of work, and by reduced working hours at night; by granting annual paid leave and weekly rest days, as well as by an expansion of the network of cultural-educational and health institutions and the development of mass sports, physical culture, and tourism; by the creation of favorable possibilities for rest in one's place of residence and of other conditions for a rational use of free time.

The length of working time and rest for collective farmers is regulated by the collective farms.

Article 40. Citizens of the RSFSR have the right to health care.

This right is ensured by free professional medical assistance provided by state health institutions; by expanding the network of institutions for medical treatment and improvement of the health of citizens; by the development and perfection of safety technology and industrial sanitation; by taking extensive preventive measures; by measures to improve the environment; by special care for the health of the younger generation, including the prohibition of child labor not connected with training and labor education; and by furthering scientific research aimed at the prevention of disease and the reduction of its incidence and at ensuring a long and active life for citizens.

Article 41. Citizens of the RSFSR have the right to material security in old age, in case of illness, complete or partial loss of the ability to work, as well as of loss of the breadwinner.

This right is guaranteed by the social insurance of workers, employees, and collective farmers; by allowances for temporary disability; by the payment of old-age and disability pensions, and pensions for the loss of the breadwinner at the expense of the state and of collective farms; by the employment of citizens who have partially lost the ability to work; by care for elderly citizens and invalids; and by other forms of social insurance.

Article 42. Citizens of the RSFSR have the right to housing.

This right is ensured by the development and protection of the state and social housing fund, by assistance to cooperative and individual housing construction, by a fair distribution, under social supervision, of living space made available in accordance with the realization of the program for the construction of well-built housing, and also by moderate payments for rent and municipal services. Citizens of the RSFSR are bound to treat carefully the housing made available to them.

Article 43. Citizens of the RSFSR have the right to education.

This right is ensured by free education at all levels, the implementation of universal compulsory secondary education of young people, and the extensive development of professional-technical, specialized secondary, and higher education on the basis of connecting learning with life and production; by the development of correspondence and evening education; by granting state stipends and other benefits to pupils and students; by the free issue of school textbooks, by the possibility for instruction in school in one's native language; and by the creation of conditions for self-education.

Article 44. Citizens of the RSFSR have the right to use the achievements of culture.

This right is ensured by the general accessibility of the treasures of national and world culture in state and public collections; by the development[1] and balanced distribution of cultural-educational institutions within the territory of the republic; by the development of television and radio, of book publishing and the periodic press, and of the network of free libraries; and by expanding cultural exchanges with foreign states.

[1]**B,Uk** and distribution of cultural-educational institutions; **Uz** and distribution of cultural-educational institutions within the territory of the Uzbek SSR;

Article 45. Citizens of the RSFSR, in accordance with the goals of communist construction, are guaranteed freedom of scientific, technical, and artistic creation. This freedom is ensured by extensively furthering scientific research and the activities of inventors and rationalizers, and by the development of literature and the arts. The state creates the necessary material conditions for these developments and provides support to voluntary societies and creative unions, and organizes the introduction of inventions and rationalization proposals in the national economy and other spheres of life.

The rights of authors, inventors, and rationalizers are protected by the state.

Article 46. Citizens of the RSFSR have the right to participate in the administration of state and public affairs, and in the discussion and adoption of laws and decisions of general state and local significance.

This right is ensured by the possibility to participate in elections for and to be elected to Soviets of People's Deputies and other elective state organs, and to take part in nationwide discussions and votes, in people's control, in the work of state organs, social organizations, and organs of social initiative, and in meetings of labor and residential collectives.

Article 47. Every citizen of the RSFSR has the right to submit proposals to state organs and social organizations concerning the improvement of their activity and to criticize shortcomings in their work.

Officials are bound to consider, within the established time-limits, the proposals and applications of citizens, to reply to these, and to take the measures necessary.

Persecution on account of criticism is prohibited. Persons engaging in persecution for criticism are held responsible.

Article 48. In accordance with the interests of the people and in order to strengthen and develop the socialist system, citizens of the RSFSR are guaranteed freedom of speech, of the press, of assembly, of meetings and of street marches, and demonstrations.

The exercise of these political freedoms is ensured by making available public buildings, streets, and squares to the working people and their organizations, by the wide dissemination of information, and by the opportunity to make use of press, television, and radio.

Article 49. In accordance with the goals of communist construction, citizens of the RSFSR have the right to unite in social organizations, which promote the development of political activity and initiative and the satisfaction of their diverse interests.

Social organizations are guaranteed the conditions for the successful fulfillment of their statutory functions.

Article 50. Citizens of the RSFSR are guaranteed freedom of conscience, that is, the right to profess any religion or to profess no religion at all, and to perform religious rites, or to conduct atheist propaganda. The incitement of hostility and hatred in connection with religious beliefs is prohibited.

The church in the RSFSR is separated from the state, and the school from the church.[1]

[1]**Ka** The mosque and the church in the Kazakh SSR are separated from the state, and the school from the mosque and the church.

Article 51. The family is under the protection of the state.

Marriage is based on the voluntary consent of the woman and the man; spouses are completely equal in family relationships.

The state shows concern for the family by creating and developing an extensive network of children's institutions and organizations, by organizing and perfecting everyday services and public catering, by paying childbirth allowances, and by granting allowances and benefits to large families, as well as other forms of allowances and aid to the family.

Article 52. Citizens of the RSFSR are guaranteed inviolability of the person. No one may be arrested unless on the basis of a court order or with the sanction of the procurator.

Article 53. Citizens of the RSFSR are guaranteed inviolability of the home. No one has the right, without lawful grounds, to enter a home against the will of the persons residing therein.

Article 54. The private life of citizens and the secrecy of correspondence, telephone conversations, and telegraph messages are protected by law.

Article 55. It is the duty of all state organs, social organizations, and officials to respect the person and to protect the rights and freedoms of citizens.

Citizens of the RSFSR have the right to judicial protection against attacks on their honor and dignity, their lives and health, and their personal freedom and property.

Article 56. Citizens of the RSFSR have the right to address complaints against actions of officials and of state and social organs. Complaints must be considered in the manner and within the time-limits established by law.

Complaints may be brought to a court, in the manner established by law, against actions which violate the law or exceed the authority of officials and which infringe the rights of citizens.

Citizens of the RSFSR have the right to compensation for damages inflicted by unlawful actions of state and social organizations, as well as of officials, in the course of the performance of their official duties.

Article 57. The exercise of rights and freedoms is inseparable from the performance by the citizen of his duties.

The citizen of the RSFSR is bound to observe the Constitution of the USSR, the Constitution of the RSFSR, and Soviet laws, to respect the rules of socialist community life, and to bear with dignity the high calling of a Soviet citizen.

Article 58. Conscientious labor in one's chosen field of socially useful activity and observance of labor discipline is the duty and a matter of honor for every citizen of the RSFSR who is able to work. Avoiding socially useful work is incompatible with the principles of a socialist society.

Article 59. The citizen of the RSFSR is bound to safeguard and strengthen socialist property. It is the duty of the citizen of the RSFSR to fight theft and waste of state and social property, and to treat the wealth of the people with care.

Persons infringing upon socialist property are punished according to law.

Article 60. The citizen of the RSFSR is bound to safeguard the interests of the Soviet state and to promote the growth of its power and authority.

The defense of the socialist Fatherland is the sacred duty of every citizen of the RSFSR.

Treason to the Motherland is the gravest crime against the people.

Article 61. Military service in the ranks of the Armed Forces of the USSR is the honorable duty of citizens of the RSFSR.

Article 62. It is the duty of every citizen of the RSFSR to respect the national dignity of other citizens and to strengthen the friendship of the nations and nationalities of the multinational Soviet state.

Article 63. The citizen of the RSFSR is bound to respect the rights and lawful interests of other persons, to be intolerant of anti-social behavior, and to promote in every way the protection of public order.

Article 64. Citizens of the RSFSR are bound to show concern for the upbringing of children, to prepare them for socially useful labor, and to raise worthy members of a socialist society. Children are bound to show concern for their parents and render them aid.

Article 65. Citizens of the RSFSR are bound to protect nature and safeguard its riches.

Article 66. Concern for the preservation of historical monuments and other cultural treasures is the duty and obligation of citizens of the RSFSR.

Article 67. It is the international duty of citizens of the RSFSR to promote the development of friendship and cooperation with people of other countries and the maintenance and strengthening of world peace.

III. THE NATIONAL-STATE AND ADMINISTRATIVE-TERRITORIAL STRUCTURE OF THE RSFSR

Chapter 7. The RSFSR—A Union Republic as Part of the USSR[1]

[1]In the following republics, a new article on the use of the national language(s) has been added as a part of Chapter 7.

Ar72 The state language of the Armenian Soviet Socialist Republic is the Armenian language.

The Armenian SSR exercises official encouragement for the all-round development of the Armenian language and ensures its use in state and social organs, in institutions of culture and education, and in other institutions.

The unrestricted use in these organs and institutions of the Russian and other languages, used by the population, is provided for in the Armenian SSR.

Any privileges or restrictions whatsoever in the use of these or other languages are not permitted.

Az73 The state language of the Azerbaidzhan Soviet Socialist Republic is the Azerbaidzhan language.

The Azerbaidzhan SSR ensures the use of the Azerbaidzhan language in state and social organs, institutions of culture and education, and in other institutions, and exercises official encouragement for its all-round development.

On the basis of equality, the unrestricted use in these organs and institutions of the Russian language, as well as of other languages of the population, used by it, is provided for in the Azerbaidzhan SSR.

Any privileges or restrictions whatsoever in the use of these or other languages are not permitted.

G75 The state language of the Georgian Soviet Socialist Republic is the Georgian language.

The Georgian SSR exercises official encouragement for the all-round development of the Georgian language and ensures its use in state and social organs, in institutions of culture and education, and in other institutions.

The unrestricted use in these organs and institutions of the Russian and other languages, used by the population, is provided for in the Georgian SSR Any privileges or restrictions whatsoever in the use of these or other languages are not permitted.

Article 68. The Russian Soviet Federative Socialist Republic is a sovereign Soviet socialist state. In order to successfully build a communist society, to strengthen economic and political unity, and to ensure the security and defense of the country, the Russian Soviet Federative Socialist Republic has united—as a result of the free self-determination of nations[1] and on a voluntary and equal basis—together with the Soviet Socialist Republics: the Ukrainian Soviet Socialist Republic, the Belorussian Soviet Socialist Republic, the Uzbek Soviet Socialist Republic, the Kazakh Soviet Socialist Republic, the Georgian Soviet Socialist Republic, the Azerbaidzhan Soviet Socialist Republic, the Lithuanian Soviet Socialist Republic, the Moldavian Soviet Socialist Republic, the Latvian Soviet Socialist

Republic, the Kirgiz Soviet Socialist Republic, the Tadzhik Soviet Socialist Republic, the Armenian Soviet Socialist Republic, the Turkmen Soviet Socialist Republic, and the Estonian Soviet Socialist Republic, in the Union of Soviet Socialist Republics—a unitary, federal, multinational state.

Proceeding from this, the RSFSR reserves for the USSR, through the latter's highest organs of state power and administration, the rights defined in Article 73 of the Constitution of the USSR.

Outside the limits indicated in Article 73 of the Constitution of the USSR, the RSFSR independently exercises state power within its territory.

[1]**Ar,Az,B,E,Ka,Ki,La,Li,M,Tu,Uk** the free self-determination of its people

Article 69. The RSFSR retains the right freely to secede from the USSR.

Article 70. The territory of the RSFSR may not be altered without its consent. The boundaries between the RSFSR and other union republics may be altered by mutual agreement with the union republics concerned, subject to confirmation by the USSR.

E,Li71, Ka,Ki,La,Tu72, B,Ta73

Article 71. The Russian Soviet Federative Socialist Republic contains the Bashkir, Buriat, Dagestan, Kabardino-Balkar, Kalmyk, Karelian, Komi, Mari, Mordvinian, North Ossetian, Tatar, Tuva, Udmurt, Chechen-Ingush, Chuvash, and Iakut Autonomous Soviet Socialist Republics.

In the RSFSR there are

territories: Altai, Krasnodar, Krasnoiarsk, Primor'e, Stavropol', and Khabarovsk;

provinces: Amur, Arkhangel'sk, Astrakhan', Belgorod, Briansk, Vladimir, Volgograd, Vologda, Voronezh, Gorkii, Ivanovo, Irkutsk, Kaliningrad, Kalinin, Kaluga, Kamchatka, Kemerovo, Kirov, Kostroma, Kuibyshev, Kurgan, Leningrad, Lipetsk, Magadan, Moscow, Murmansk, Novgorod, Novosibirsk, Omsk, Orenburg, Orel, Penza, Perm', Pskov, Rostov, Riazan', Saratov, Sakhalin, Sverdlovsk, Smolensk, Tambov, Tomsk, Tula, Tiumen', Ulianovsk, Cheliabinsk, Chita, Iaroslavl';

cities of republican subordination: Moscow and Leningrad;

autonomous provinces as parts of territories: Adyge, Gorno-Altai, Jewish, Karachai-Cherkess, and Khakass;

autonomous areas as parts of territories or provinces: Aga Buriat,

Komi-Permiak, Koriak, Nenets, Taimyr (Dolgano-Nenets), Ust'-Orda Buriat, Khanty-Mansi, Chukchi, Evenki, Iamal-Nenets.[1]

Ta70, G71, Uz73, Li74, B,E,Ka,Ki,La,M,Tu,Uk77, Ar,Az78

[1]**Ta70** In the Tadzhik Soviet Socialist Republic there are: Kuliab, Kurgan-Tiube, and Leninabad provinces, and the Garm, Gissar, Dzhirgatal', Komsomolabad, Lenin, Ordzhonikidzeabad, Regar, and Faizabad districts, and cities of republican subordination: Dushanbe and Nurek.

The Gorno-Badakhshan Autonomous Province is also a part of the Tadzhik Soviet Socialist Republic.

G71 The Georgian SSR contains the Abkhaz Autonomous Soviet Socialist Republic, the Adzhar Autonomous Soviet Socialist Republic, and the South Ossetian Autonomous Province.

In the Georgian SSR there are districts: Abasha, Adigeni, Ambrolauri, Aspindza, Akhalkalaki, Akhaltsikhe, Akhmeta, Bogdanovka, Bolnisi, Borzhomi, Vani, Gardabani, Gegechkori, Gori, Gurdzhaani, Dmanisi, Dusheti, Zestafoni, Zugdidi, Kazbegi, Kareli, Kaspi, Kvareli, Lagodekhi, Lanchkhuti, Lentekhi, Marneuli, Makharadze, Maiakovskii, Mestiia, Mtskheta, Oni, Ordzhonikidze, Sagaredzho, Samtredia, Sachkhere, Signakhi, Telavi, Terzhola, Tetri-Tsarko, Tianeti, Khashuri, Khobi, Tsageri, Tsalendzhikha, Tsalka, Tsiteli-Tsarko, Tsulukidze, Tskhakaev, Chokhatauri, and Chkhorotsku, and cities of republican subordination: Tbilisi, Gori, Zugdidi, Kutaisi, Poti, Rustavi, Tkibuli, Tskhaltubo, and Chiaturi.

Uz73 The Uzbek Soviet Socialist Republic contains the Kara-Kalpak Autonomous Soviet Socialist Republic. In the Uzbek SSR there are provinces: Andizhan, Bukhara, Dzhizak, Kashkadar'ia, Namangan, Samarkand, Surkhandar'ia, Sydar'ia, Tashkent, Fergane, and Khorezm, and the city of republican subordination—Tashkent.

Li74 In the Lithuanian Soviet Socialist Republic there are
—districts: Akmenė, Alytus, Anikščai, Biržai, Varėna, Vilkaviškis, Vilnius, Zarasai, Ignalina, Ionava, Ioniškis, Kaišiadōrys, Kapsukas, Kaunas, Kėdainiai, Kelmė, Klaipėda, Kretinga, Kupiškis, Lazdijai, Mažeikiai, Molėtai, Pakruois, Panevėžys, Pasvalys, Plungė, Prenai, Radviliškis, Raseiniai, Rokiškis, Skuodas, Tauragė, Telšiai, Trakai, Ukmėrgė, Utena, Šakiai, Šalčininkai, Švenčionys, Šilale, Šilutė, Širvintos, Šiauliai, and Jurbarkas;
—cities of republican subordination: Vilnius, Alytus, Birštonas, Druskininkai, Kapsukas, Kaunas, Klaipėda, Neringa, Palanga, Panevėžys, and Šiauliai.

Az78 The Azerbaidzhan Soviet Socialist Republic contains the Nakhichevan' Autonomous Soviet Socialist Republic, and the Nagorno-Karabakh Autonomous Province.

In the Azerbaidzhan SSR there are districts: Agdam, Agdash, Agdzhabedi, Apsheronsk, Astara, Akhsu, Barda, Belokany, Vartashen, Geokchai, Dashkesan, Dzhalilabad, Dzhebrail, Divichi, Evlakh, Zhdanovsk, Zakataly, Zangelan, Zardob, Imishli, Ismailly, Kazakh, Kasum-Ismailov, Kakhi, Kedabek, Kel'badzhar, Kubatly, Kuba, Kusary, Kutkashen, Kiurdamir, Lachin, Lenkoran', Lerik, Masally, Mir-Bashir, Neftechala, Pushkino, Saatly, Sabirabad, Sal'iany, Tauz, Udzhary, Fizuly, Khanlar, Khachmas, Shamkhor, Shaumianovsk (rural), Sheki, Shemakha, and Iardymly; cities of republican subordination: Ali-Bairamly, Baku, Evlakh, Kirovobad, Lenkoran', Mingechaur, Naftalan, Sumgant, and Sheki.

In the following republic constitutions, the equivalent of RSFSR Art. 71 has been made a part of Chapter 8 which, in these republics, now deals with "The Administrative-Territorial Structure of the [republic] SSR". See also the annotations to RSFSR Chapter 8 below.

Ar78 In the Armenian SSR there are districts: Abovian, Azizbekov, Amasiia, Ani, Aparan, Aragats, Ararat, Artashat, Argi, Akhurian, Ashtarak, Vardenis, Goris, Guga, Gukasian, Ekhegnadzor, Idzhevan, Kalinin, named after Kamo, Kafan, Krasnosel'sk, Martuni, Masis, Megri, Nairi, Noemberian, Oktemberian, Razdan, Sevan, Sisian, Spitak, Stepanavan, Talin, Tumanian, Shamshadin, and Echmiadzin, and cities of republican subordination: Abovian, Alaverdi, Ararat, Artashat, Artik, Ashtarak, Goris, Dzhermuk, Dilizhan, Erevan, Idzhevan, Kamo, Kafan, Kirovskaia, Leninakan, Oktemberian, Razdan, Sevan, Spitak, Stepanavan, and Echmiadzin.

B77 In the Belorussian Soviet Socialist Republic there are provinces: Brest, Vitebsk, Gomel', Grodno, Minsk, and Mogilev, and the city of republican subordination Minsk.

E77 The Estonian SSR consists of districts: Valga, Viljandi, Võru, Jõgeva, Kingisepp, Kohtla-Järve, Paide, Põlva, Pärnu, Rakvere, Rapla, Tartu, Haapsalu, Harjus, and Hjuma, and cities of republican subordination: Tallinn, Kohtla-Järve, Narva, Pärnu, Sillamäe, and Tartu.

Ka77 In the Kazakh SSR there are provinces: Aktiubinsk, Alma-Ata, Vostochno-Kazakhstan, Gur'ev, Dzhambul, Dzhezkazgan, Karagan, Kzyl-Orda, Kokchetav, Kustanai, Mangyshlak, Pavlodar, Severo-Kazakhstan, Semipalatinsk, Taldy-Kurgan, Turgai, Ural, Tselinograd, and Chimkent.

Alma-Ata is a city of republican subordination.

Ki77 The Kirgiz Soviet Socialist Republic contains the: Issyk-Kul', Naryn, and Osh provinces; Alamedin, Issykata, Kalinin, Kant, Kemin, Kirov, Leninpol', Moskva, Panfilov, Sokuluk, Talas, and Chui districts, and cities of republican subordination: Frunze, Kara-Balta, Talasa, and Tokmaka,

La77 The Latvian SSR contains the districts: Alūksne, Balvi, Bauska, Valga, Valmiera, Ventspils, Gulbene, Daugavpils, Dobele, Jekabpils, Jelgava, Krāslava, Kuldīga, Liepāja, Limbaži, Ludza, Madona, Ogre, Preiļi, Rēzekne, Rīga, Saldus, Stučka, Talsi, Tukums, and Cēsis, and cities of republican subordination: Rīga, Daugavpils, Liepāja, Jelgava, Ventspils, Rēzekne, and Jurmala.

M77 In the Moldavian Soviet Socialist Republic there are districts: Brichany, Vulkaneshti, Glodiany, Grigoriopol', Dondiushany, Drokiia, Dubossary, Edintsy, Kagul, Kalarash, Kamenka, Kantemirsk, Kaushaly, Komrat, Kotovsk, Kriuliani, Kutuzovsk, Lazovsk, Leovo, Nisporeny, Novoanensk, Oknitsa, Orgeev, Rezina, Rybnitsa, Ryshkany, Slobodzeia, Soroki, Strasheny, Suvorova, Teleneshty, Ugnev, Faleshty, Floreshty, Chadyr-Lunga, and Chimishliia; the cities: Kishinev, Bel'tsy, Bondery, Kagul, Orgeev, Rybnitsa, Soroki, Tiraspol', and Ungeny, are directly subordinate to the republican organs of the Moldavian SSR.

Tu77 In the Turkmen SSR there are
—provinces: Ashkhabad, Krasnovodsk, Mary, Tashauz, and Chardzhou;
—city of republican subordination: Ashkhabad.

Uk77 In the Ukrainian Soviet Socialist Republic there are provinces: Vinnitsa, Volyn, Voroshilovograd, Dnepropetrovsk, Donets, Zhitomir, Zakarpat, Zaporozh'e, Ivano-Frankovsk, Kiev, Kirovograd, Crimean, L'vov, Nikolaevsk, Odessa, Poltava, Rovno, Suma, Ternopol', Khar'kov, Kherson, Khmel'nitskii, Cherkassy, Chernovtsy, and Chernigov.

Cities of republican subordination in the Ukrainian SSR are Kiev and Sevastopol'.

Article 72. The jurisdiction of the Russian Soviet Federative Socialist Republic, through its highest organs of state power and administration, encompasses:

1) adopting the Constitution of the RSFSR and introducing amendments to it;[1]

2) supervising the observance of the Constitution of the RSFSR[2] and ensuring the conformity of the Constitutions of the autonomous republics with the Constitution of the RSFSR;[3]

3) submitting for confirmation, to the Supreme Soviet of the USSR, the formation of new autonomous republics and autonomous provinces of the RSFSR;[4]

4) legislation of the RSFSR;[5]

5) protecting the state order and the rights and freedoms of citizens;[6]

6) establishing the procedure for the organization and operation of republic and local organs of state power and administration;[7]

7) conducting a unified socio-economic policy and directing the economic system of the RSFSR, ensuring scientific-technical progress and implementing measures for a rational utilization and protection of natural resources;[8]

8) formulating and confirming state plans of economic and social development of the RSFSR, and the state budget of the RSFSR, and confirming reports on their fulfillment; directing the implementation of the state budgets of the autonomous republics, and the budgets of territories, provinces, and cities of republican subordination;[9]

9) establishing in accordance with the legislation of the USSR, the revenues which go to form the state budget of the RSFSR;[10]

10) directing the branches of the national economy of union republic and republic subordination, and the associations and enterprises of republic subordination;[11]

11) establishing the procedure for using the land, mineral wealth, the forests and the waters; protecting the environment;[12]

12) directing housing and municipal utilities, trade, and public catering, services for everyday needs to the population,[13] housing construction, the organization of amenities of the cities and other settlements, and railroad construction and transport;[14]

13) directing public education, cultural and scientific organizations and institutions of the RSFSR, health care, physical culture and sport, and social insurance; protecting monuments of history and culture;[15]

14) granting amnesty and pardon to citizens convicted by the courts of the RSFSR;[16]

15) representing the RSFSR in international relations;[17]

16) resolving other questions of republic importance.[18]

B,Ki,Tu70, Ar,M,Ta71, Uk72, E,La73, Uz74, Ka75, Li77; [1]**B70(1)** adopting the Constitution of the Belorussian SSR and introducing amendments to it; supervising the observance of the Constitution of the Belorussian SSR; **M71(1), E,73(1),**

Ka75(1) adopting the Constitution of the [republic] SSR, introducing amendments to it, and supervising its observance; [2]**Ki,Tu70(2), Ar,Ta71(2), Uk72(2), La73(2), Li77(2)** supervising the observance of the Constitution of the [republic] SSR; [3]**B,E,Ka,M** = NP **Az72(2)** the conformity of the Constitution of the Nakhichevan' ASSR with the Constitution of the Azerbaidzhan SSR; **G72(2)** the conformity of the Constitutions of the Abkhaz ASSR and the Adzhar ASSR with the Constitution of the Georgian SSR; **Uz74(2)** the conformity of the Constitution of the Kara-Kalpak ASSR with the Constitution of the Uzbek SSR; [4]**Ar,B,E,Ka,Ki,La,Li,M,Tu,Uk** = NP **Ta71(3)** the formation, with subsequent submission for confirmation to the Supreme Soviet of the USSR, of new autonomous provinces of the Tadzhik SSR; **G72(3)** the formation, with subsequent submission for confirmation to the Supreme Soviet of the USSR, of new autonomous republics and autonomous provinces of the Georgian SSR; **Uz74(3)** the formation, with subsequent submission for confirmation to the Supreme Soviet of the USSR, of new autonomous republics of the Uzbek SSR; [5]**B70(2), M71(2), E73(2), Ka75(2), Ki70(3), Ar,Ta71(3), Uk72(3), La73(3), Li77(3)** [6]**M71(3), E73(3), Ka75(3), B,Ki70(4), Ar,Ta71(4), Uk72(4), La73(4), Li77(4)** [7]**B70(3), M71(4), E73(4), Ka75(4), Ki70(5), Ar,Ta71(5), Uk72(5), La73(5), Li77(5)** [8]**B70(5), M71(5), Ka75(5), Ki70(6), Uk72(6), La73(6)** **Ar71(6),E73(5),Uz74(7)** and directing the economic system of the [republic] SSR; ensuring scientific-technical progress and measures for a rational utilization and protection of natural resources; **Ta71(6),Li77(6)** and directing the economic system of the republic; ensuring scientific-technical progress and measures for a rational utilization and protection of natural resources; [9]**M71(6)** **Tu70(7)** formulating and confirming state plans of economic and social development of the Turkmen SSR, and confirming reports on their fulfillment; formulating and confirming the state budget of the Turkmen SSR, and confirming reports on its execution; directing the implementation of the budgets of provinces and cities of republican subordination; **Ar71(7), E73(6)** formulating and confirming state plans of economic and social development of the [republic] SSR; confirming reports on their fulfillment; formulating and confirming the state budget of the [republic] SSR, and confirming reports on its execution; directing the implementation of the budgets of districts and cities of republican subordination; **Ta71(8)** formulating and confirming state plans of economic and social development of the Tadzhik SSR, and confirming reports on their fulfillment; formulating and confirming the state budget of the Tadzhik SSR, and confirming reports on its execution; directing the implementation of the local budgets of provinces, of the Gorno-Badakhshan Autonomous Province, and of districts and cities of republican subordination; **Uk72(7), Li77(7)** formulating and confirming state plans of economic and social development of the [republic] SSR, and confirming reports on their fulfillment; **Uk72(8)** formulating and confirming the state budget of the Ukrainian SSR, and confirming reports on its execution; directing the implementation of the budgets of provinces and cities of republican subordination; **La73(7)** formulating and confirming state plans of economic and social development of the Latvian SSR, and confirming reports on their fulfillment; formulating and confirming the state budget of the Latvian SSR, and confirming reports on its execution; directing the implementation of the local budgets of districts and cities of republican subordination; **Ka76(6)** formulating and submitting state plans of economic and social development of the Kazakh SSR, and confirming reports on their fulfillment; formulating and submitting the state budget of the Kazakh SSR, and confirming reports on its execution; implementing the budgets of provinces and of the city of Alma-Ata; **Li77(8)** formulating and confirming the state budget of the Lithuanian SSR, and confirming reports on its execution; directing the implementation of the local budgets of districts and cities of republican subordination; **B70(6)** . . . directing the implementation of the budgets of the provinces and of the city of Minsk; **Ki79(7)** . . . directing the execution of the budgets of provinces, as well as of districts and cities of republican subordination; **G72(8)** . . . directing the implementation of the state budgets of the Abkhaz ASSR and the Adzhar ASSR, and the budgets of the South Ossetian Autonomous Province, and of districts and cities of republican subordination; **Az72(8)** . . . directing the implementation of the state budget of the Nakhichevan' ASSR, and the budgets of the Nagorno-Karabakh Autonomous Province, and of provinces and cities of republican subordination; **Uz74(8)** . . . directing the implementation of the state budget of the Kara-Kalpak ASSR, and of the budgets of provinces and the city of Tashkent; [10]**B70(7), M71(7), Ka75(7), Ki,Tu70(8), Ar71(8), E,La73(8), Ta71(9), Li77(9)** [11]**E73(7), B70(8), M71(8), Ka75(8), Ki,Tu70(9), Ar71(9), La73(9), Ta71(10), Li77(10)**; **B70(8)** and the associations and enterprises of republican subordination; **Ar71(9), Ta71(10), E73(7), Ka75(8), Li77(10)** directing union republic and republic branches of the national economy, and associations and enterprises of republican subordination; [12]**B70(9), M71(9), E73(9), Ka75(9), Ki,Tu70(10), Ar71(10),La73(10), Ta71(11), Uz74(11), Li77(11), Uk72(12)** [13]**Ar71(11), Ta71(12)** directing housing and municipal utilities, services for everyday needs to the population, [14]**B70(10), M71(10), E73(10), Ka75(10), Ki,Tu70(11), Ar71(11), Uk72(11), La73(11), Ta71(12), Uz74(12), Li77(12)**; **M71(10)** and railroad construction, transportation, and communications; [15]**B70(11), M71(11), E73(11), Ka75(11), Ki,Tu70(12), Ar71(12), La73(12), Ta71(13), Uz74(13), Li77(13)**; **Ar71(12)** and social insurance; and the protection and utilization of monuments of history and culture; [16]**M71(12), E73(12), Ka75(12), N,Ki,Tu70(13), Ar71(13), La73(13), Ta71(14), Uz74(14), Li77(14)** [17]**B70(12), M71(13), E73(13), Ka75(13), Ki,Tu70(14), Ar71(14), La73(14), Ta71(15), Uz74(15), Li77(15)** [18]**B70(14), M71(14), E73(14), Ka73(14), Ki,Tu70(15), Ar71(15), La73(15), Ta71(16), Uz74(16), Li77(16)**

Article 73. The RSFSR determines its division into territories, provinces, areas, and districts,[1] and resolves other questions of administrative-territorial organization.[2]

Uz71, Ta74, B,Ka,Ki,Tu,Uk76, Az77; [1]**Uz71, Ta74** The [republic] SSR determines its division into provinces and districts, **G73, Az77** The [republic] SSR determines its division into districts, **Li73** The Lithuanian SSR determines its own administrative-territorial division,

In the following nine republic constitutions, the equivalent of RSFSR Art. 73 appears in Chapter 8 on the administrative-territorial structure of the republic: **Ar,B,E,Ka,Ki,La,M,Tu,Uk** [1]**B,Ka,Ki,Tu76** The [republic] SSR determines its division into provinces and districts, **E,La76, Ar77** The [republic] SSR determines its division into districts [2]**M73** The Moldavian SSR determines its own administrative-territorial division. (para. 2) The administrative-territorial units of the Moldavian SSR are districts, cities, city-districts, settlements of the city type, and *sel'sovety*. **Uk76** The jurisdiction of the Ukrainian Soviet Socialist Republic encompasses the determination of the division into provinces and districts, and the resolution of other questions of the administrative-territorial organization of the republic.

Article 74. The RSFSR participates in the resolution of questions within the jurisdiction of the USSR in the Supreme Soviet of the USSR, in the Presidium of the Supreme Soviet of the USSR, in the Government of the USSR, and in other organs of the USSR.

The RSFSR ensures integrated economic and social development within its territory, facilitates the exercise of the authority of the USSR within its territory, and implements the decisions of the supreme organs of state power and administration of the USSR.

With regard to questions within its jurisdiction, the RSFSR coordinates and supervises the activities of enterprises, institutions, and organizations of union subordination.

E,K,La70, Az,B,Ki,Tu71, M,Ta,Uz72, Ar,Uk73, Li75

Article 75. The RSFSR has the right to enter into relations with foreign states, to conclude treaties with them and to exchange diplomatic and consular representatives, and to participate in the activities of international organizations.

Ka71, E72, Ki,M,Tu73, Ar,Az,B,La,Uk74, G,Li,Uz76

Article 76. The laws of the USSR are binding within the territory of the RSFSR.

Li70, La,Uk71, B72, Ka73, E,Ki,M,Tu74, Ar,Az,Uz75

Article 77. In accordance with the Constitution of the USSR, the sovereign rights of the RSFSR are protected by the USSR.

Li72, Ka74, B,E,Ki,La,M,Tu,Uk75, Ar,Az76, G78

Chapter 8. The Autonomous Soviet Socialist Republic[1]

Li,Ta = NP; In the following republic constitutions, this Chapter has been renamed "The Administrative-Territorial Structure of the [republic] SSR": **Ar,B,E,Ki,Li,M,Tu,Uk,** and "Administrative-Territorial Structure" in **Ka**; for the texts of the articles contained in this renamed Chapter, see RSFSR Arts. 71 & 73 above. [1]**Az** "The Nakhichevan' Autonomous Soviet Socialist Republic" **Uz** "The Kara-Kalpak Autonomous Soviet Socialist Republic"

Article 78. An autonomous republic is a Soviet socialist state, a part of the Russian Soviet Federative Socialist Republic.

Outside the limits of the rights of the USSR and the RSFSR, an autonomous republic independently resolves questions within its jurisdiction.

An autonomous republic has its own Constitution, which conforms to the Constitution of the USSR and the Constitution of the RSFSR, and which takes into account the special character of the autonomous republic.[1]

Uz78,Az,G79; [1]**Uz78** The Kara-Kalpak Autonomous Soviet Socialist Republic is a Soviet socialist state, a part of the Uzbek Socialist Republic, and outside the limits of the rights of the USSR and the Uzbek SSR, independently resolves questions within its jurisdiction.

Article 79. An autonomous republic participates in the resolution of questions within the jurisdiction of the RSFSR and the USSR through the supreme organs of state power and administration of the RSFSR and the USSR, respectively.

The autonomous republic ensures integrated economic and social development within its territory, facilitates the exercise within its territory of the authority of the USSR and the RSFSR, and implements the decisions of the supreme organs of state power and administration of the USSR and the RSFSR.

With regard to questions within its jurisdiction, an autonomous republic coordinates and supervises the activities of enterprises, institutions, and organizations of union and republic (RSFSR) subordination.

Az,G80

Article 80. The territory of the autonomous republic may not be altered without its consent.

Az,G81

Article 81. The laws of the RSFSR are binding[1] and have equal force within the territory of all autonomous republics. In the event of a discrepancy between the law of an autonomous republic and the law of the RSFSR, the law of the RSFSR prevails.

Az,G82; [1]**Az82** are binding within the territory of the Nakhichevan' ASSR. **Uz81** are binding within the territory of the Kara-Kalpak ASSR.

Chapter 9. The Autonomous Province and the Autonomous Area[1]

Ar,B,E,Ka,Ki,La,Li,M,Tu,Uk,Uz = NP; [1]**Az** "The Nagorno-Karabakh Autonomous Province" **G** "The Autonomous Province" **Ta** "The Gorno-Badakhshan Autonomous Province"

Article 82. An autonomous province is part of the RSFSR and of a territory.

A law on an autonomous province is adopted by the Supreme Soviet of the RSFSR on the recommendation of the Soviet of People's Deputies of an autonomous province.

Ta78, Az,G83 The [. . .] Autonomous Province is a part of the [republic] Soviet Socialist Republic. **Ta79, Ar,G84** The law on the [. . .] Autonomous Province is adopted by the Supreme Soviet of the [republic] SSR on the recommendation of the Soviet of People's Deputies of the [. . .] Autonomous Province.

Article 83. The organs of state power and administration of an autonomous province are ensured the right to deal with organs of state power and administration of the RSFSR through territorial organs of state power and administration, as well as directly.

Az,G,Ta = NP

Article 84. An autonomous area is part of a territory or a province.

A Law on Autonomous Areas is adopted by the Supreme Soviet of the RSFSR.

Az,G,Ta = NP

IV. SOVIETS OF PEOPLE'S DEPUTIES AND THE PROCEDURE FOR THEIR ELECTION

Chapter 10. The System and Principles of Operation of the Soviets of People's Deputies

Li Chap8, Ar,B,E,Ka,Ki,La,M,Ta,Tu,Uk,Uz Chap9

Article 85. The Soviets of People's Deputies—the Supreme Soviet of the RSFSR; the Supreme Soviets of the autonomous republics; the territorial and provincial Soviets of People's Deputies; the Soviets of People's Deputies of autonomous provinces and autonomous areas; district, city, city-district, settlement, and village Soviets of People's Deputies[1]—constitute an integrated system of organs of state power.

B,E,Ka,Ki,La,Li,M,Tu,Uk78, Ar79, Ta80, Uz82; [1]**B,Tu,Uk78**—the Supreme Soviet of the [republic] SSR, provincial, district, city, city-district, settlement, and village Soviets of People's Deputies— **E78**—the Supreme Soviet of the Estonian SSR, district, city, districts in the city of Tallinn, settlement, and village Soviets of People's Deputies— **Ka78**—the Supreme Soviet of the Kazakh SSR, provincial Soviets of People's Deputies, district, city, city-district, settlement, village, and *aul* Soviets of People's Deputies— **Ki78**—the Supreme Soviet of the Kirgiz SSR, provincial, district, city, city-district, settlement, and village Soviets of People's Deputies— **La,M78, Ar79**—the Supreme Soviet of the [republic] SSR, district, city, city-district, settlement, and village Soviets of People's Deputies— **Li78**—the Supreme Soviet of the Lithuanian SSR, district, city, city-district, settlement, and *apilin* Soviets of People's Deputies— **Ta80**—the Supreme Soviet of the Tadzhik SSR, provincial Soviets of People's Deputies, the Soviet of People's Deputies of the Gorno-Badakhshan Autonomous Province, district, city, city-district, settlement, and *kishlak* Soviets of People's Deputies— **Uz82**—the Supreme Soviet of the Uzbek SSR, the Supreme Soviet of the Kara-Kalpak ASSR, provincial, district, city, city-district, settlement, *kishlak,* and *aul* Soviets of People's Deputies— **Az85**—the Supreme Soviet of the Azerbaidzhan SSR, the Supreme Soviet of the Nakhichevan' ASSR, the Soviet of People's Deputies of the Nagorno-Karabakh Autonomous Province, and district, city, city-district, settlement, and village Soviets of People's Deputies— **G85**—the Supreme Soviet of the Georgian SSR, the Supreme Soviets of the Abkhaz ASSR and the Adzhar ASSR, the Soviet of People's Deputies of the South Ossetian Autonomous Province, and district, city, city-district, settlement, and village Soviets of People's Deputies—

Article 86. The term of office of the Supreme Soviet of the RSFSR and the Supreme Soviets of the autonomous republics is five years.[1]

The term of office of local Soviets of People's Deputies is two and a half years.

Elections for Soviets of People's Deputies are called not later than two months before the expiration of the term of office of the Soviets concerned.

B,E,Ka,Ki,La,Li,M,Tu,Uk79, Ar80, Ta81, Uz83; [1]**B,E,Ka,Ki,La,Li,M,Tu, Uk79, Ar80, Ta81** The term of office of the Supreme Soviet of the [republic] SSR is five years. **Uz83** The term of office of the Supreme Soviet of the Uzbek SSR and of the Supreme Soviet of the Kara-Kalpak ASSR is five years. **Az86** The term of office of the Supreme Soviet of the Azerbaidzhan SSR and of the Supreme Soviet of the Nakhichevan' ASSR is five years. **G86** The term of office of the Supreme Soviet of the Georgian SSR and of the Supreme Soviets of the Abkhaz ASSR and the Adzhar ASSR is five years.

Article 87. The most important questions within the jurisdiction of the respective Soviets of People's Deputies are considered and resolved at their sessions.

The Soviets of People's Deputies elect standing commissions and create executive and administrative, as well as other organs accountable to them.

B,E,Ka,Ki,La,Li,M,Tu,Uk80, Ar81, Ta82, Uz84

Article 88. The Soviets of People's Deputies set up organs of people's control, combining state supervision with social supervision by working people in enterprises, collective farms, institutions, and organizations.

The organs of people's control supervise the fulfillment of state plans and assignments, combat violations of state discipline, manifestations of localism, a departmental approach to business, mismanagement and wastefulness, red tape and bureaucracy, and they assist in perfecting the work of the state apparatus.

B,E,Ka,Ki,La,Li,M,Tu,Uk81, Ar82, Ta83, Uz85

Article 89. The Soviets of People's Deputies, directly and through organs created by them, direct all branches of state, economic, and socio-cultural construction,[1] adopt decisions, ensure their execution, and supervise their implementation.

B,E,Ka,Ki,La,Li,M,Tu,Uk82, Ar83, Ta84, Uz86; [1]**E82, Ar83** direct all branches of state, economic, and socio-cultural construction of the [republic] SSR,

Article 90. The activities of the Soviets of People's Deputies are based on the collective, free, and businesslike discussion and resolution of questions, on openness, on the regular accounting of executive and administrative organs, and other organs created by the Soviets, to the Soviets and to the population, and on the widespread enlistment of citizens to participate in the work of the Soviets.

The Soviets of People's Deputies, and the organs created by them, systematically inform the population about their work and the decisions taken.

B,E,Ka,Ki,La,Li,M,Tu,Uk83, Ar84, Ta85, Uz87

Chapter 11. The Electoral System

Li Chap9, Ar,B,E,Ka,La,M,Ta,Tu,Uk,Uz Chap 10

Article 91. Elections of deputies to all Soviets of People's Deputies are held on the basis of universal, equal, and direct suffrage by secret ballot.

B,E,Ka,Ki,La,Li,M,Tu,Uk84, Ar85, Ta86, Uz88

Article 92. Elections of deputies are universal: all citizens of the RSFSR who have reached the age of 18 years have the right to vote and to be elected, with the exception of persons who have, in the manner established by law, been declared insane.

B,E,Ka,Ki,La,Li,M,Tu,Uk85, Ar86, Ta87, Uz89

Article 93. Elections of deputies are equal: each voter has one vote; all voters participate in elections on an equal basis.

B,E,Ka,Ki,La,Li,M,Tu,Uk86, Ar87, Ta88, Uz90

Article 94. Elections of deputies are direct: the deputies of all Soviets of People's Deputies are elected directly by the citizens.

B,E,Ka,Ki,La,Li,M,Tu,Uk87, Ar88, Ta89, Uz91

Article 95. The voting in elections of deputies is secret: checking on the expression of the will of the voter is not allowed.

B,E,Ka,Ki,La,Li,M,Tu,Uk88, Ar89, Ta90, Uz92

Article 96. The right to nominate candidates for election as deputies belongs to organizations of the Communist Party of the Soviet Union, of trade unions, and of the All-Union Leninist Communist League of Youth, to cooperative and other social organizations, to labor collectives, as well as to assemblies of servicemen according to military units.

Citizens of the RSFSR and social organizations are guaranteed the free and all-round discussion of the political, professional, and personal qualities of the candidates for election as deputies, as well as the right to campaign at meetings, in the press, and on television and radio.

Expenses connected with conducting elections for Soviets of People's Deputies are borne by the state.

B,E,Ka,Ki,La,Li,M,Tu,Uk89, Ar90, Ta91, Uz93

Article 97. Elections of deputies to Soviets of People's Deputies are held on the basis of electoral districts.

A citizen of the RSFSR may not, as a rule, be elected to more than two Soviets of People's Deputies.

Elections of deputies to Soviets of People's Deputies are conducted by electoral commissions, composed of representatives of social organizations, labor collectives, and assemblies of servicemen according to military units.

The procedure for conducting elections to the Soviets of People's Deputies is defined by laws of the USSR, the RSFSR, and the autonomous republics.[1]

B,E,Ka,Ki,La,Li,M,Tu,Uk90, Ar91, Ta92, Uz94; [1]**Li90** The norms of representation and the procedure for conducting elections to the Soviets of People's Deputies are defined by laws of the USSR and the Lithuanian SSR. **B,E,Ka,Ki,La,M,Tu,Uk90, Ar91, Ta92** is defined by laws of the USSR and the [republic] SSR. **Uz94** is defined by laws of the USSR and the Uzbek SSR, and in the Kara-Kalpak ASSR—also by laws of the Kara-Kalpak ASSR. **Az97** is defined by laws of the USSR and the Azerbaidzhan SSR, and in the Nakhichevan' ASSR—also by laws of the Nakhichevan' ASSR. **G97** is defined by laws of the USSR and the Georgian SSR, and in the Abkhaz ASSR and the Adzhar ASSR—also by laws of these autonomous republics.

Article 98. The voters give mandates to their deputies.

The appropriate Soviets of People's Deputies consider the mandates of the voters, take account of them while formulating the plans of economic and social development and drawing up of the budget, organize the implementation of mandates, and inform the citizens about their realization.

B,E,Ka,Ki,La,Li,M,Tu,Uk91, Ar92, Ta93, Uz95

Chapter 12. The People's Deputy

Li Chap10, Ar,B,E,Ka,Ki,La,Li,M,Ta,Tu,Uk,Uz Chap11

Article 99. Deputies are plenipotentiary representatives of the people in the Soviets of People's Deputies.

By participating in the work of the Soviets, the deputies resolve questions of state, economic, and socio-cultural construction, organize the implementation of the decisions of the Soviets, and supervise the work of state organs, enterprises, institutions, and organizations.

In his activity, a deputy is guided by the general interests of the state, takes into account the demands of the population of his constituency, and seeks to implement the mandates of his constituents.

B,E,Ka,Ki,La,Li,M,Tu,Uk92, Ar93, Ta94, Uz96

Article 100. A deputy exercises his powers without interrupting his work in production or service.

During the sessions of the Soviet, as well as in order to exercise the powers of a deputy in other instances provided for by law, the deputy is relieved from performing his duties in production or service, while retaining his average earnings at his place of permanent employment.

B,E,Ka,Ki,La,Li,M,Tu,Uk93, Ar94, Ta95, Uz97

Article 101. A deputy has the right to address inquiries to the appropriate state organs and officials, who are obliged to answer the inquiries at the session of the Soviet.

A deputy has the right to address himself to all state and social organs, enterprises, institutions, and organizations concerning questions within the scope of his activity as a deputy, and to participate in the consideration of the questions raised by him. The heads of the state and social organs, enterprises, institutions, and organizations concerned are obliged to receive the deputy without delay and to consider his proposals within the established time-limit.

B,E,Ka,Ki,La,Li,M,Tu,Uk94, Ar95, Ta96, Uz98

Article 102. A deputy is ensured the conditions for the unhindered and effective exercise of his rights and execution of his duties.

The immunity of deputies, as well as other guarantees of a deputy's activities, are established by the Law on the Status of Deputies and by other legislative acts of the USSR, and by legislative acts of the RSFSR and autonomous republics.[1]

B,E,Ka,Ki,La,Li,M,Tu,Uk95, Ar96, Ta97, Uz99; [1]**B,Uk95** and by other legislative acts of the USSR, and by legislative acts of the [republic] SSR. **E,Ka,Ki,La,Li,M,Tu95, Ar96, Ta97** and by other legislative acts of the USSR and the [republic] SSR. **Uz99** and by other legislative acts of the USSR and the Uzbek SSR, and in the Kara-Kalpak ASSR—also by legislative acts of the Kara-Kalpak ASSR. **Az102** and by legislative acts of the Azerbaidzhan SSR and the Nakhichevan' ASSR. **G102** and by other legislative acts of the USSR, the Georgian SSR, the Abkhaz ASSR, and the Adzhar ASSR.

Article 103. A deputy is obliged to report on his work and the work of the Soviet to his constituents, as well as to the collectives and social organizations which nominated him as a candidate for election.

A deputy, who has not justified the trust of his constituents, may at any time be recalled by a decision of a majority of his constituents in the manner established by law.

B,E,Ka,Ki,La,Li,M,Tu,Uk96, Ar97, Ta98, Uz100

V. THE SUPREME ORGANS OF STATE POWER AND ADMINISTRATION OF THE RSFSR

Chapter 13. The Supreme Soviet of the RSFSR

Li Chap11, Ar,B,E,Ka,Ki,La,Li,M,Ta,Tu,Uk,Uz Chap12

Article 104. The supreme organ of state power of the RSFSR is the Supreme Soviet of the RSFSR.

The Supreme Soviet of the RSFSR is empowered to resolve all questions assigned to the jurisdiction of the RSFSR by the Constitution of the USSR and by the[1] present Constitution.

The adoption of the Constitution of the RSFSR and of amendments therein; the submission for confirmation, to the Supreme Soviet of the USSR, of the formation of new autonomous republics and autonomous provinces of the RSFSR;[2] the confirmation of state plans of economic and social development of the RSFSR,[3] and of the state budget of the RSFSR, and the reports on their fulfillment; and the formation of organs accountable to the Supreme Soviet of the RSFSR—are within the exclusive competence of the Supreme Soviet of the RSFSR.

Laws of the RSFSR are adopted by the Supreme Soviet of the RSFSR or by a nationwide vote (referendum) conducted on the basis of a decision of the Supreme Soviet of the RSFSR.[4]

B,E,Ka,Ki,La,Li,M,Tu,Uk97, Ar98, Ta99, Uz101; [1]**E,Tu97** and by the Constitution of the [republic] SSR. [2]**G104** the formation, with subsequent submission for confirmation to the Supreme Soviet of the USSR, of new autonomous republics and autonomous provinces of the Georgian SSR; [3]**B,E,Ka,Ki,La,Li,M,Tu,Uk97, Ar98, Ta99, Uz101** The adoption of the Constitution of the [republic] SSR and of amendments therein; the confirmation of state plans of economic and social development of the [republic] SSR, [4]**Az104** Laws of the Azerbaidzhan SSR are adopted by the Supreme Soviet of the Azerbaidzhan SSR or by a nationwide vote (referendum) conducted on the basis of a decision of the Supreme Soviet of the Azerbaidzhan SSR. (para.2) Laws of the Azerbaidzhan SSR are binding on the entire territory of the Azerbaidzhan SSR.

Article 105. The Supreme Soviet of the RSFSR consists of 975[1] deputies, elected on the basis of electoral districts with an equal number of inhabitants.[2]

On the recommendation of the mandate commission elected by it, the Supreme Soviet of the RSFSR decides on the recognition of the credentials of the deputies[3] and, in the event of a violation of electoral legislation, on finding the election of individual deputies null and void.

B,E,Ka,Ki,La,Li,M,Tu,Uk98, Ar99, Ta100, Uz102; [1]**B98**, 495 deputies; **E98**, 285 deputies; **Ka98**, 510 deputies; **Ki,Li98**, 350 deputies; **La98**, 325 deputies; **M98**, 380 deputies; **Tu98**, 330 deputies; **Uk98**, 650 deputies; **Ar99**, 340 deputies; **Az105**, 450 deputies; **G105**, 440 deputies [2]**Ta100** The Supreme Soviet of the Tadzhik SSR is elected on the basis of electoral districts with an equal number of inhabitants, and consists of 350 deputies. **Uz102** The Supreme Soviet of the Uzbek SSR is elected on the basis of electoral districts with an equal number of inhabitants, and consists of 510 deputies. [3]**Uz102** of the deputies of the Supreme Soviet of the Uzbek SSR

Article 106. The Supreme Soviet of the RSFSR elects the Chairman of the Supreme Soviet of the RSFSR and eight[1] Deputy Chairmen.

The Chairman of the Supreme Soviet of the RSFSR presides over the meetings of the Supreme Soviet of the RSFSR and is in charge of its proceedings.

B,E,Ka,Ki,La,Li,M,Tu,Uk99, Ar100, Ta101, Uz103; [1]**B99** two; **E99** two; **Ka99** three; **Ki99** two; **La99** two; **Li99** four; **M99** four; **Tu99** two; **Uk99** four; **Ar100** three; **Ta101** two; **Uz103** four; **Az106** four; **G106** four;

Article 107. Sessions of the Supreme Soviet of the RSFSR are convened twice a year.[1]

Extraordinary sessions are convened by the Presidium of the Supreme Soviet of the RSFSR at its own initiative or[2] on the proposal of not less than one-third of the deputies[3] of the Supreme Soviet of the RSFSR.

A session of the Supreme Soviet of the RSFSR consists of its meetings,[4] as well as of meetings of standing and[5] other commissions of the Supreme Soviet of the RSFSR held between sessions.[6]

B,E,Ka,Ki,La,Li,M,Tu,Uk100, Ar101, Ta102, Uz104; [1]**La100** twice a year by the Presidium of the Supreme Soviet of the [2]**E,Uk100, Ar101** at its own initiative as well as [3]**La,Li100** one-third of the deputies. [4]**Li,Uk100, Uz104** consists of the meetings of the Supreme Soviet [5]**Ar101** or [6]**E100** para.NP **Ka,Ki,Tu100, Ta102** held between sessions. A session is convened and adjourned at a meeting of the Supreme Soviet of the [republic] SSR.

Article 108. The right of legislative initiative in the Supreme Soviet of the RSFSR belongs to the Presidium of the Supreme Soviet of the RSFSR, the Council of Ministers of the RSFSR, the autonomous republics through their supreme organs of state power, the standing and other commissions[1] of the Supreme Soviet of the RSFSR, deputies of the Supreme Soviet of the RSFSR, the Supreme Court of the RSFSR, and the Procurator of the RSFSR.

Social organizations, through their all-union and republic[2] organs, also enjoy the right of legislative initiative.

B,E,Ka,Ki,La,Li,M,Tu,Uk101, Ar102, Ta103, Uz105; [1]**B,E,Ka,Ki,La,Li,M,Tu, Uk101, Ta103** the Council of Ministers of the [republic] SSR, the standing and other commissions **Ar102** the Council of Ministers of the Armenian SSR, the standing commissions and other commissions **Uz105, Az108** the Council of Ministers of the Azerbaidzhan SSR, the Nakhichevan' ASSR through its supreme organ of state power, the standing and other commissions **G108** the Council of Ministers of the Georgian SSR, the Abkhaz ASSR and the Adzhar ASSR through their supreme organs of state power, the standing and other commissions **Uz105** the Council of Ministers of the Uzbek SSR, the Kara-Kalpak ASSR through its supreme organ of state power, standing and other commissions [2]**B,E,Ka,Ki,La,Li,M,Tu,Uk101, Ar102, Ta103, Uz105, Az,G108** through their republic organs

Article 109. Draft bills and other questions, referred for consideration to the Supreme Soviet of the RSFSR, are discussed at its meetings.[1] When necessary, the draft bill or, as the case may be, the question may be referred for preliminary or additional consideration to one or several commissions.

Laws of the RSFSR, and decrees, and other acts of the Supreme Soviet of the RSFSR are adopted by a majority of the total number of deputies of the Supreme Soviet of the RSFSR.[2]

Draft bills of the RSFSR and other highly important questions of the life of the state in the republic may be submitted to a national discussion[3] by a decision of the Supreme Soviet of the RSFSR or of the Presidium of the Supreme Soviet of the RSFSR.[4]

B,E,Ka,Ki,La,Li,M,Tu,Uk102, Ar103, Ta104, Uz106; [1]**E102** are discussed at meetings of the Supreme Soviet. [2]**Ki,Uk102, Ar103, Uz106** are considered adopted if a majority of the total number of the deputies of the Supreme Soviet of the [republic] SSR has voted for them. [3]**E102** a nationwide discussion [4]**La102** or of the Presidium of the Supreme Soviet of the republic. **G109** or of its Presidium.

Article 110. Laws of the RSFSR, and decrees, and other acts of the Supreme Soviet of the RSFSR are published[1] over the signature of the Chairman and Secretary of the Presidium of the Supreme Soviet of the RSFSR.

B,E,Ka,Ki,La,Li,M,Tu,Uk103, Ar104, Ta105, Uz107, Az117; [1]**B103** in the Belorussian and Russian languages **E103** in the Estonian and Russian languages **Ka103** in the Kazakh and Russian languages **Ki103** in the Kirgiz and Russian languages **La103** in the Latvian and Russian languages **Li103** in the Lithuanian and Russian languages **M103** in the Moldavian and Russian languages **Tu103** in the Turkmen and Russian languages **Uk103** in the Ukrainian and Russian languages **Ar104** in the Armenian, Russian, and Azerbaidzhan languages **Ta105** in the Tadzhik, Russian, and Uzbek languages **Uz107** in the Uzbek and Russian languages, and for the Kara-Kalpak ASSR—in the Kara-Kalpak language **G110** in the Georgian and Russian languages, and for autonomous republics and autonomous provinces, also in the language of the autonomous republic and the autonomous province **Az117** in the Azerbaidzhan, Russian, and Armenian languages

Article 111. A deputy to the Supreme Soviet of the RSFSR has the right to address inquiries to the Council of Ministers of the RSFSR, and to ministers and heads of other organs, formed by the Supreme Soviet of the RSFSR, as well as to the heads of enterprises, institutions, and organizations of union[1] subordination located within the territory of the RSFSR, concerning questions within the jurisdiction of the RSFSR. The Council of Ministers of the RSFSR, or the official to whom an inquiry has been addressed, is obliged to give an oral or written reply at the given session of the Supreme Soviet of the RSFSR.

B,E,Ka,Ki,La,Li,M,Tu,Uk104, Ar105, Ta106, Uz108, Az110; [1]**Ka104, Ta106** all-union

Article 112. A deputy to the Supreme Soviet of the RSFSR may not be prosecuted, arrested, or subjected to judicially imposed administrative penalties without the consent of the Supreme Soviet of the RSFSR, and, during the time between its sessions, without the consent of the Presidium of the Supreme Soviet of the RSFSR.

B,E,Ka,Ki,La,Li,M,Tu,Uk105, Ar106, Ta107, Uz109, Az111

Article 113. The Supreme Soviet of the RSFSR elects the Presidium of the Supreme Soviet of the RSFSR, the permanently functioning organ of the Supreme Soviet of the RSFSR, accountable to the latter in all its activities and exercising, within the limits provided for by the present Constitution,[1] the functions of the supreme organ of state power of the RSFSR during the time between sessions of the Supreme Soviet of the RSFSR.

B,E,Ka,Ki,La,Li,M,Tu,Uk106, Ar107, Ta108, Uz110, Az112; [1]**B,E,Ka,La,Li106, Ar107, Uz110** provided for by the Constitution **Ki106** provided for by the Constitution of the Kirgiz SSR

Article 114. The Presidium of the Supreme Soviet of the RSFSR is elected from among the deputies and consists of the Chairman of the Presidium of the Supreme Soviet, seventeen Deputy Chairmen, including one Deputy Chairman from each autonomous republic, the Secretary of the Presidium, and twenty members[1] of the Presidium of the Supreme Soviet of the RSFSR.

B,E,Ka,Ki,La,Li,M,Tu,Uk107, Ar108, Ta109, Uz111, Az113; [1]**B,Ki,M107, Ar108** two Deputy Chairmen, the Secretary of the Presidium, and fifteen members **E,La107** two Deputy Chairmen, the Secretary of the Presidium, and nine members **Ka107** the Deputy Chairman, the Secretary of the Presidium, and seventeen members **Li107** two Deputy Chairmen, the Secretary of the Presidium, and thirteen members **Tu107,Ta109** two Deputy Chairmen, the Secretary of the Presidium, and eleven members **Uk107** three Deputy Chairmen, the Secretary of the Presidium, and twenty members **Uz111** two Deputy Chairmen, including a Deputy Chairman from the Kara-Kalpak ASSR, the Secretary of the Presidium, and seventeen members **Az113** three Deputy Chairmen, including one Deputy Chairman each from the Nakhichevan' ASSR and the Nagorno-Karabakh Autonomous Province, the Secretary of the Presidium, and sixteen members **G114** three Deputy Chairmen, including two from the autonomous republics, the Secretary of the Presidium, and fourteen members

Article 115. The Presidium of the Supreme Soviet of the RSFSR:

1) calls elections to the Supreme Soviet of the RSFSR and to local Soviets of People's Deputies;

2) convenes the sessions of the Supreme Soviet of the RSFSR;

3) coordinates the activities of the standing commissions of the Supreme Soviet of the RSFSR;

4) supervises the observance of the Constitution of the RSFSR;[1] ensures that the Constitutions and laws of the autonomous republics conform to the Constitution and laws of the RSFSR;

5) calls elections to district (city) people's courts;[2]

6) interprets laws of the RSFSR;[3]

7) exercises leadership of the activities of local Soviets of People's Deputies;[4]

8)[5] defines[6] the procedure for resolving questions of the administrative-territorial structure of the RSFSR;[7] establishes and changes the boundaries and division into districts of territories, provinces, autonomous provinces, and autonomous areas; forms districts, cities, and city-districts; establishes the subordination of cities; conducts the re-naming of districts, cities, city-districts, workers' settlements, and other settlements;

9) confirms the area division, the formation of cities and city-districts, the change of subordination of cities, the naming and re-naming of districts, cities and city-districts, as well as the re-naming of other settlements of autonomous republics;[8]

10) annuls decrees and resolutions of the Council of Ministers of the RSFSR and the Councils of Ministers of autonomous republics, and decisions of territorial, provincial, and city (cities of republican subordination) Soviets of People's Deputies, and of Soviets of People's Deputies of autonomous provinces where they do not conform to the law;[9]

11) awards Honorary Diplomas of the Presidium of the Supreme Soviet of the RSFSR; establishes and confers honorary titles of the RSFSR;[10]

12) admits persons to citizenship of the RSFSR; decides the question of granting asylum;[11]

13) grants pardon to citizens convicted by the courts of the RSFSR;[12]

14) ratifies and denounces treaties to which the RSFSR is a party;[13]

15) appoints and recalls diplomatic representatives of the RSFSR to foreign states and at international organizations;[14]

16) accepts credentials and letters of recall of diplomatic representatives of foreign states accredited to it;[15]

17) exercises other powers established by the Constitution and laws of the RSFSR.[16]

B,E,Ka,Ki,La,Li,M,Tu,Uk108, Ar109, Ta110, Uz112, Az114;

[1]**B,E,Ka,Ki,La,Li,M,Tu,Uk108(4), Ar109(4), Ta110(4)** supervises the observance

of the Constitution of the [republic] SSR; **Uz112(4)** supervises the observance of the Constitution of the Uzbek SSR; ensures that the Constitution and laws of the Kara-Kalpak ASSR conform to the Constitution and laws of the Uzbek SSR; **Az114(4)** supervises the observance of the Constitution of the Azerbaidzhan SSR; ensures that the Constitution and laws of the Nakhichevan' ASSR conform to the Constitution and laws of the Azerbaidzhan SSR; **G115(4)** supervises the observance of the Constitution of the Georgian SSR and ensures that the [2]**Uk108(9), Li108(6)** [3]**Li108(5), Uk108(5)** [4]**Ka108(8) G115(7)**... the activities of local Soviets; [5]**M108(15), Ta110(8)** resolves questions of the administrative-territorial structure of the [republic] SSR; [6]**E,Ka,Li108(8), Ar109(8), Uz112(8)** establishes the procedure [7]**B108(8)** establishes and changes the boundaries and division into districts of provinces; forms districts, cities, city-districts, and settlements of the city type; establishes the subordination of cities; conducts the re-naming of districts, cities, city-districts, settlements of the city type, and other settlements; **E108(8)** forms cities and city-districts; establishes the subordination of cities; conducts the re-naming of cities, city-districts, settlements, and other settlements; **Ka108(7)** establishes and changes the boundaries and division into districts of provinces; forms districts, cities, and city-districts; establishes the subordination of cities; conducts the re-naming of districts, cities, city-districts, workers' settlements, and other settlements; **Ki108(8)** establishes and changes the boundaries of provinces and districts; establishes the division into districts of provinces; forms cities in districts, city-districts, settlements of the city type, and *sel'sovety*; conducts the re-naming of districts and cities in provinces, city-districts, workers' settlements, and other settlements; **La108(8)** forms city-districts, cities, city settlements, and rural settlements, and establishes and changes their boundaries; establishes the subordination of cities; conducts the naming and re-naming of districts, cities, city-districts, city settlements, and rural and other settlements; **Li108(8)** forms cities and city-districts; conducts the re-naming of cities, city-districts, settlements, *apilinki*, and other settlements; establishes and changes the boundaries of districts, cities, city-districts, settlements, and *apilinki*; resolves other questions of the administrative-territorial structure; **Tu108(8)** establishes and changes the boundaries and division into districts of provinces; forms districts **Uk108(6)** establishes and changes the boundaries and division into districts of provinces; forms districts and city-districts; reorganizes settlements into cities; establishes the subordination of cities; conducts the re-naming of districts, cities, city-districts, settlements, and other settlements; **Ar109(8)** establishes and changes the boundaries of districts and cities; forms cities in districts and city-districts, and establishes the subordination of cities; conducts the re-naming of cities in districts, city-districts, settlements, and other settlements; **Uz112(8)** confirms the area division of the Kara-Kalpak ASSR; establishes and changes the boundaries and division into districts of provinces; forms districts, cities, city-districts, city settlements, *kishlaks*, and *auls*; establishes the subordination of cities; conducts the re-naming of districts, cities, city-districts, city settlements, *kishlaks*, *auls*, and other settlements; **Az114(8)** establishes and changes the boundaries and division into districts of the Nagorno-Karabakh Autonomous Province: forms districts, cities, city-districts, and settlements; establishes the subordination of cities; conducts the re-naming of districts, cities, city-districts, settlements, and other settlements; **G115(8)** establishes and changes the boundaries and division into districts of an autonomous province; forms cities in districts and city-districts; establishes the subordination of cities; conducts the re-naming of districts, cities, city-districts, settlements, and other settlements; [8]**Ar,B,E,Ka,Ki,La,Li,M,Ta,Tu,Uk,Uz** = NP; **Az114(9)** confirms the area division, the formation of cities, the change of subordination of cities, the naming and re-naming of districts and cities, as well as the re-naming of other settlements of the Nakhichevan' ASSR; [9]**B108(9)** annuls decrees and resolutions of the Council of Ministers of the Belorussian SSR, and decisions of provincial Soviets of People's Deputies and the Minsk city Soviet of People's Deputies where they do not conform to the law; **E,La,108(9),M108(8)** annuls decrees and resolutions of the Council of Ministers of the [republic] SSR, and decisions of district and city (cities of republican subordination) Soviets of People's Deputies where they do not conform to the law; **Ka108(9)** annuls decrees and resolutions of the Council of Ministers of the Kazakh SSR, as well as decisions of provincial Soviets of People's Deputies and the Alma-Ata city Soviet of People's Deputies where they do not conform to the law; **Ki108(9)** annuls decrees and resolutions of the Council of Ministers of the Kirgiz SSR, and decisions of provincial Soviets, as well as of district and city Soviets (districts and cities of republican subordination) where they do not conform to the law; **Li108(9)** annuls decrees and resolutions of the Council of Ministers of the Lithuanian SSR, as well as decisions of district and city (cities of republican subordination) Soviets of People's Deputies where they do not conform to the law; **Tu,Uk108(9)** annuls decrees and resolutions of the Council of Ministers of the [republic] SSR, and decisions of provincial and city (cities of republican subordination) Soviets of People's Deputies where they do not conform to the law; **Ar109(9)** annuls decrees and resolutions of the Council of Ministers of the Armenian SSR, and decisions of district and city Soviets of People's Deputies of republican subordination where they do not conform to the law; **Uz112(9)** annuls decrees and resolutions of the Council of Ministers of the Uzbek SSR, and of the Council of Ministers of the Kara-Kalpak ASSR, and decisions of provincial Soviets of People's Deputies and the Tashkent city Soviet of People's Deputies where they do not conform to the law; **Az114(10)** annuls decrees and resolutions of the Council of Ministers of the Azerbaidzhan SSR, and of the Council of Ministers of the Nakhichevan' ASSR, and decisions of Soviets of People's Deputies of the Nagorno-Karabakh Autonomous Province, and of district and city (cities of republican subordination) Soviets of People's Deputies where they do not conform to the law; **G115(10)** annuls decrees and resolutions of the Council of Ministers of the Georgian SSR, and of the Council of Ministers of the autonomous republics, as well as decisions of Soviets of People's Deputies of an autonomous province, and of district and city (cities of republican subordination) Soviets of People's Deputies where they do not conform to the law; [10]**M108(9)**; **B,E,La,Li,Tu,Uk108(10), Ar109(10), Ta110(10), Uz112(10), G115(11)** establishes and confers honorary titles of the [republic] SSR; awards Honorary Diplomas of the Presidium of the Supreme Soviet of the [republic] SSR; **Ka108(10)** awards diplomas of the Supreme Soviet of the Kazakh SSR, and establishes and confers honorary titles of the Kazakh SSR; **Ki108(10)** establishes and confers honorary titles of the Kirgiz SSR; awards Honorary Diplomas and Diplomas of the Supreme Soviet of the Kirgiz SSR; [11]**M108(10), B,E,Ki,Li,Tu,Uk108(11), Ar109(11), Ta110(11), Uz112(11), Az114(12)**; **Ka108(11)** admits persons to citizenship of the Kazakh SSR, and grants the right of asylum; **La108(11)** admits persons to citizenship of the Latvian SSR; decides questions of granting asylum; [12]**M108(11), E,La,Li,Tu108(12), Ar109(12), Uz112(12)**; **B,Ka,Ki,Uk108(12), Ta110(12), Az114(13)** issues republic acts on amnesty and grants pardon to citizens convicted by courts of the [republic] SSR; [13]**M108(12), B,E,Ka,Ki,La,Li,Tu,Uk108(13), Ar109(13), Ta110(13), Uz112(13), Az114(14)** [14]**M108(13), B,E,Ka,Ki,La,Li,Tu,Uk108(14), Ar109(14), Ta110(14), Uz112(14), Az114(15)** [15]**M108(14), B,E,Ka,Ki,La,Li,Tu,Uk108(15), Ar109(15), Ta110(15), Uz112(15), Az114(16)** [16]**M108(15), B,E,Ka,Ki,La,Li,Tu,Uk108(16), Ar109(16), Ta110(16), Uz112(16), Az114(17)**

Article 116. The Presidium of the Supreme Soviet of the RSFSR, during the time between the sessions of the Supreme Soviet, and with subsequent submission for confirmation at the next session of the Supreme Soviet:

1) amends, when necessary, legislative acts of the RSFSR in force;

2) confirms boundary changes of autonomous republics, and forms new territories, provinces, and autonomous areas;[1]

3) forms and abolishes ministries and state committees of the RSFSR on the proposal of the Council of Ministers of the RSFSR;[2]

4) dismisses and appoints individual persons as members of the Council of Ministers of the RSFSR on the recommendation of the Chairman of the Council of Ministers of the RSFSR.[3]

B,E,Ka,Ki,La,Li,M,Tu,Uk109, Ar110, Ta111, Uz113, Az115; [1]**B,Tu109(2)** forms new provinces; **E109(4)** forms and abolishes districts and cities of republican subordination, establishes the republican subordination of cities, and changes the names of districts and cities of republican subordination; **Ka109(2)** forms and abolishes provinces; **Ki109(2)** forms new provinces and districts; **La109(2)** forms and abolishes districts and cities of republican subordination; **Li109(2)** forms new districts, and conducts the re-naming of and abolishes districts; establishes and abolishes the republican subordination of cities; conducts the renaming of cities of republican subordination; **M109(2)** forms and abolishes districts, and establishes the republican subordination of cities; **Uk109(2)** forms provinces; **Ar110(2)** forms districts and cities of republican subordination; **Ta111(2)** forms provinces, districts, and cities; **Uz113(2)** confirms boundary changes of the Kara-Kalpak ASSR, and forms new provinces; **Az115(2)** confirms boundary changes of the Nakhichevan' ASSR, forms new districts and cities of republican subordination; **G116(2)** confirms boundary changes of the autonomous republics; forms new districts and cities of republican subordination; [2]**E109(2); Ka,La,Tu109(3), Ta111(2), Uz112(3), G116(3)** forms and abolishes ministries of the [republic] SSR and state committees of the [republic] SSR on the proposal of the Council of Ministers of the [republic] SSR; [3]**E109(3)**

Article 117. The Presidium of the Supreme Soviet of the RSFSR issues edicts and adopts resolutions.

B,E,Ka,Ki,La,Li,M,Tu,Uk110, Ar111, Ta112, Uz114, Az116

Article 118. Upon expiration of the term of office of the Supreme Soviet of the RSFSR, the Presidium of the Supreme Soviet of the RSFSR retains its powers until the formation of a new Presidium by the newly-elected Supreme Soviet of the RSFSR.

The newly-elected Supreme Soviet of the RSFSR is convened by the Presidium of the outgoing Supreme Soviet of the RSFSR not later than two months after the elections.

B,E,Ka,Ki,La,Li,M,Tu,Uk111, Ar112, Ta113, Uz115

Article 119. The Supreme Soviet of the RSFSR elects, from among the deputies, standing commissions for the preliminary consideration and preparation of questions[1] within the jurisdiction of the Supreme Soviet of the RSFSR, as well as for promoting the implementation of laws of the RSFSR and other decisions of the Supreme Soviet of the RSFSR and its Presidium, and the supervision of the activities of state organs and organizations.

The Supreme Soviet of the RSFSR creates, when it considers it necessary, investigative, revision, and other commissions on any question.[2]

All state and social organs,[3] organizations, and officials are bound to comply with the requests of the[4] commissions of the Supreme Soviet of the RSFSR, and to submit to them the necessary materials and documents.

The recommendations of the commissions must be considered by the state and social organs, institutions, and organizations. The commissions must be informed within the established time-limit about the results of the consideration or of the measure taken.

B,E,Ka,Ki,La,Li,M,Tu,Uk112, Ar113, Ta114, Uz116; [1]**G119** questions within its jurisdiction, as well as for promoting [2]**G119** on any questions coming within its jurisdiction. [3]**La112** All state and social organs, institutions, organizations, [4]**Ka112** with the requests of the permanent and other commissions

Article 120. The Supreme Soviet of the RSFSR supervises the activities of all state organs accountable to it.

The Supreme Soviet of the RSFSR sets up a Committee of People's Control of the RSFSR which heads the system of organs of people's control of the RSFSR.[1]

B,E,Ka,Ki,La,Li,M,Tu,Uk113, Ar114, Ta115, Uz117; [1]**Ka,La,Li,Uk113, Ta115** of the republic.

Article 121. The manner of operation of the Supreme Soviet of the RSFSR and its organs is defined by the Regulations of the Supreme Soviet of the RSFSR and by other laws of the RSFSR, issued on the basis of the Constitution[1] of the RSFSR.

B,E,Ka,Ki,La,Li,Tu,Uk114, Ar115, Ta116, Uz118; [1]**K,Li114, G121** issued on the basis of the present Constitution.

Chapter 14. The Council of Ministers of the RSFSR

Li Chap12, Ar,B,E,Ka,Ki,La,M,Ta,Tu,Uk,Uz Chap13

Article 122. The Council of Ministers of the RSFSR—the Government of the RSFSR[1]—is the supreme executive and administrative organ of state power of the RSFSR.

B,E,Ka,Ki,La,Li,M,Tu,Uk115, Ar116, Ta117, Uz119; [1]**Li115**—the Government of the republic—

Article 123. The Council of Ministers of the RSFSR is set up by the Supreme Soviet of the RSFSR and is composed of: the Chairman of the Council of Ministers of the RSFSR, First Deputy Chairmen[1] and Deputy Chairmen, the ministers of the RSFSR, and chairmen of state committees of the RSFSR.

On the recommendation of the Chairman of the Council of Ministers of the RSFSR, the Supreme Soviet of the RSFSR may include the heads of other organs and organizations of the RSFSR as members of the Government of the RSFSR.[2]

The Council of Ministers of the RSFSR lays down its powers before the newly-elected Supreme Soviet of the RSFSR at the first session of the latter.[2]

B,E,Ka,Ki,La,Li,M,Tu,Uk116, Ar117, Ta118, Uz120; [1]**E,M,Tu116, Ar117, Ta118, Uz120** the First Deputy Chairman and Deputy Chairmen, **Ka116** the First Deputy Chairman and Deputy Chairman of the Council of Ministers of the Kazakh SSR, **Ki,La,Li116** the First Deputy Chairman and Deputy Chairmen of the Council of Ministers of the [republic] SSR, [2]In the following republic constitutions, a new second paragraph has been added to the equivalent of Art.123, and paras.2&3 in the RSFSR text now appear as paras.3&4 of the following three texts: **Uz120** (para.2) The Chairman of the Council of Ministers of the Kara-Kalpak ASSR is a member of the Council of Ministers of the Uzbek SSR by virtue of his office. **Az123** (para.2) The Chairman of the Council of Ministers of the Nakhichevan' ASSR is a member of the Council of Ministers of the Azerbaidzhan SSR by virtue of his office. **G123** (para.2) The Chairmen of the Councils of Ministers of the Abkhaz ASSR and the Adzhar ASSR are members of the Council of Ministers of the Georgian SSR by virtue of their office.

Article 124. The Council of Ministers of the RSFSR is responsible and accountable to the Supreme Soviet of the RSFSR and, during the time between the sessions of the Supreme Soviet of the RSFSR, to the Presidium of the Supreme Soviet of the RSFSR, to whom it is accountable.

The Council of Ministers of the RSFSR regularly reports on its work to the Supreme Soviet of the RSFSR.

B,E,Ka,Ki,La,Li,M,Tu,Uk117, Ar118, Ta119, Uz121

Article 125. The Council of Ministers of the RSFSR is empowered to resolve all questions of state administration within the jurisdiction of the RSFSR insofar as they do not, according to the Constitution,[1] come within the competence of the Supreme Soviet of the RSFSR and the Presidium of the Supreme Soviet of the RSFSR.

Within the limits of its authority, the Council of Ministers of the RSFSR:

1) ensures[2] the management of the national economy and socio-cultural construction; formulates and takes measures to ensure the growth of the well-being and culture of the people, to develop science and technology, to[3] rationally utilize and protect natural resources; promotes the implementation of measures to strengthen the monetary and credit system, and to organize state insurance and a uniform system of accounting and statistics; participates in the implementation of a uniform policy of prices, wages, and social welfare; organizes the administration of industrial, construction, and agricultural enterprises and associations, transport and communications enterprises, as well as other organizations and institutions of republic and local subordination;[4]

2) formulates and submits to the Supreme Soviet of the RSFSR current and long-range state plans of the economic and social development of the RSFSR and the state budget of the RSFSR; takes measures to implement the state plans and budget,[5] and to ensure the integrated economic and social development of the RSFSR,[6] and of economic districts, autonomous republics, territories, provinces, and cities of republican subordination; coordinates and supervises the activities of enterprises, institutions, and organizations[7] of union subordination concerning questions within the jurisdiction of the RSFSR; submits reports on the fulfillment of the plans and the execution of the budget to the Supreme Soviet of the RSFSR;

3) takes measures to defend the interests of the state, to protect socialist property and public order, and to safeguard and defend the rights and freedoms of citizens;[8]

4) takes measures, within the limits defined by the Constitution of the USSR, to ensure state security and the defense capability of the country;[9]

5) exercises leadership in the field of relations of the RSFSR with foreign states and international organizations in the manner established by the Constitution of the USSR;[10]

6) sets up, when necessary, committees, chief administrations, and other departments attached to the Council of Ministers of the RSFSR for matters of economic and socio-cultural construction;[11]

7) directs and verifies the work of the Councils of Ministers of the autonomous republics, and exercises leadership over the activities of executive committees of local Soviets of People's Deputies.[12]

B,E,Ka,Ki,La,Li,M,Tu,Uk118, Ar119, Ta120, Uz122; [1]**Ka118** according to the Constitution, come within the competence of the Supreme Soviet and the Presidium of the Supreme Soviet of the Kazakh SSR. **Ki118** according to the Constitution of the Kirgiz SSR, [2]**Li118(1)** ensures in the Lithuanian SSR the management [3]**Ta120(1)** to protect and rationally utilize natural resources:... [4]**E,La,Li118(1), Ar119(1), Ta120(1)** institutions of republic subordination; [5]**E118(2), Ar119(2)** and budget; submits reports on the fulfillment of the plans and the execution of the budget; coordinates and supervises the activities of enterprises, institutions, and organizations of union subordination concerning questions within the jurisdiction of the [republic] SSR; **Ka118(2)** and budget; submits reports on the fulfillment of the plans and the execution of the budget to the Supreme Soviet of the Kazakh SSR; **Li118(2)** and budget, and to ensure the integrated development of districts and cities;... **Uk118(2)** and budget of the republic; submits reports to the Supreme Soviet of the Ukrainian SSR on the fulfillment of the plans and the execution of the budget of the Ukrainian SSR; **Ta120(2)** and budget, and to ensure the integrated development of provinces, districts, and cities of republican subordination;... **Uz122(2)** and budget, and to ensure the integrated development of the Kara-Kalpak ASSR and of provinces;... [6]**B118(2)** social development of the Belorussian SSR, and of provinces and the city of Minsk;... **Ki118(2)** social development of the Kirgiz SSR; submits reports on the fulfillment of the plans and the execution of the budget to the Supreme Soviet of the Kirgiz SSR; coordinates and supervises the activities of enterprises, institutions, and organizations of union subordination concerning questions within the jurisdiction of the Kirgiz SSR; **La118(2)** social development of the Latvian SSR, and of districts and cities of republican subordination;... **M118(2)** social development of the Moldavian SSR, and of districts and cities of republican subordination;... **G125(2)** social development of the Georgian SSR, and of the autonomous republics, autonomous provinces, nature-economic zones, cities of republican subordination, and districts;... [7]**Az125(2)** the activities of enterprises and organizations [8]**Li118(4)**; In the following republic constitutions, a new section (3) has been added to the equivalent of RSFSR Art.125, and RSFSR Art.125(3) now appears as Art.118(4) in the following three texts: **Ka118(3)** ensures an integrated economic and social development on the territory of the Kazakh SSR; concerning questions within the jurisdiction of the Kazakh SSR, coordinates and supervises the activities of enterprises, institutions, and organizations of union subordination situated on the territory of the republic; **M118(3)** ensures the development of the specialization and concentration of agricultural production on the basis of intereconomic cooperation and agrarian industrial integration, and the further socialization of socialist production; **Uk118(3)** ensures the integrated economic and social development of the Ukrainian SSR, and of economic districts, provinces, and cities of republican subordination; coordinates and supervises the activities of enterprises, institutions, and organizations of union subordination concerning questions within the jurisdiction of the Ukrainian SSR; [9]**B,Ka,Li,M,Uk118(5); Ar119(4), G125(4)** takes measures, within the limits established by the Constitution of the USSR, to ensure state security and to strengthen the defense capability of the country; **Uz122(4)** takes measures, within the limits established by the Constitution of the USSR,... [10]**Ka,Li118(6), E,Ki,Tu118(5), Ar119(5), Ta120(5), Uz122(5)** with foreign states and international organizations, keeping in mind the procedure established by the USSR for the mutual relations of union republics with foreign states; [11]**Li,M,Uk118(7)** [17]**B118(3), Uk118(6), E,Ki,La,Tu118(7), Ar119(7), Ta120(7), M118(8)** exercises leadership over the activities of executive committees of local Soviets of People's Deputies. **Ka118(7)** exercises leadership over the activities of executive committees of provincial Soviets of People's Deputies and the Alma-Ata city Soviet of People's Deputies. **Uz122(7)** directs and verifies the work of the

Council of Ministers of the Kara-Kalpak ASSR, and exercises leadership… **Az125(7)** directs and verifies the work of the Council of Ministers of the Nakhichevan' ASSR, and exercises leadership over the activities of executive committees of the Soviet of People's Deputies of the Nagorno-Karabakh Autonomous Province, and of district and city (cities of republican subordination) Soviets of People's Deputies of the Azerbaidzhan SSR.

Article 126. The Presidium of the Council of Ministers of the RSFSR, consisting of the Chairman of the Council of Ministers of the RSFSR, the First Deputy Chairmen[1] and Deputy Chairmen of the Council of Ministers of the RSFSR, as well as other members[2] of the Government in accordance with the Law on the Council of Ministers of the RSFSR, functions as a permanent organ of the Council of Ministers of the RSFSR for the resolution of questions connected with ensuring the management of the national economy and other questions of state administration.

B,E,Ka,Ki,La,Li,M,Tu,Uk119, Ar120, Ta121, Uz123; [1]**M,Tu119, G126** the First Deputy Chairman [2]**B,E,Ki,La,Li119, Ta121, Uz123** the First Deputy Chairman and Deputy Chairmen, as well as other members **Ka,Uk119** the First Deputy Chairmen and Deputy Chairmen, as well as other members [3]**Ar120** The Presidium of the Council of Ministers of the Armenian SSR functions as a permanent organ of the Council of Ministers of the Armenian SSR for the resolution of questions connected with ensuring the management of the national economy and other questions of state administration. The Presidium of the Council of Ministers of the republic consists of the Chairman of the Council of Ministers, the First Deputy Chairman and Deputy Chairmen, as well as other members of the Government in accordance with the Law on the Council of Ministers of the republic.

Article 127. The Council of Ministers of the RSFSR issues decrees and resolutions on the basis and in pursuance of legislative acts of the USSR and the RSFSR, and of decrees and resolutions of the Council of Ministers of the USSR, and organizes and verifies their execution.[1] The execution of decrees and resolutions of the Council of Ministers of the RSFSR is obligatory throughout the territory of the RSFSR.[2]

B,E,Ka,Ki,La,Li,M,Tu,Uk120, Ar121, Ta122, Uz124; [1]**Uk120** The Council of Ministers of the Ukrainian SSR issues decrees and resolutions on the basis and in pursuance of laws and other decisions of the Supreme Soviet of the USSR and its Presidium, laws of the Ukrainian SSR and other decisions of the Supreme Soviet of the Ukrainian SSR and its Presidium, and of decrees and resolutions of the Council of Ministers of the USSR, issues decrees and resolutions, and organizes and verifies their execution. **Ar121** The Council of Ministers of the Armenian SSR, on the basis and in pursuance of legislative acts of the USSR and the Armenian SSR, and of decrees and resolutions of the Council of Ministers of the USSR, issues decrees and resolutions and organizes and verifies their execution. [2]**Li,Tu120** In these two texts, this second sentence appears as a second and separate paragraph.

Article 128. The Council of Ministers of the RSFSR, within the limits of its competence, has the right to[1] suspend the execution of decrees and resolutions of the Councils of Ministers of the autonomous republics, as well as to annul[2] decisions and resolutions of executive committees of territorial, provincial, and city (cities of republican subordination) Soviets of People's Deputies, and executive committees of Soviets of People's Deputies of autonomous provinces.

The Council of Ministers of the RSFSR has the right to annul acts of ministries and state committees of the RSFSR, and of other organs subordinate to it.[3]

B,E,Ka,Ki,La,Li,M,Tu,Uk121, Ar122, Ta123, Uz125; [1]**Az128** to suspend the execution of decrees and resolutions of the Council of Ministers of the Nakhichevan' ASSR, as well as to annul decisions and resolutions of executive committees of Soviets of People's Deputies of the Nagorno-Badakhshan Autonomous Province, and district and city (cities of republican subordination) Soviets of People's Deputies. [2]**B121** to annul decisions and resolutions of executive committees of provincial Soviets of People's Deputies and the Minsk city Soviet of People's Deputies. **E,La121** to annul acts of ministries of the [republic] SSR and state committees of the [republic] SSR, and of other organs subordinate to it, and decisions and resolutions of executive committees of district and city (cities of republican subordination) Soviets of People's Deputies. **Ka121** to annul decisions and resolutions of executive committees of provincial Soviets of People's Deputies and the Alma-Ata city Soviet of People's Deputies, and acts of ministries of the Kazakh SSR, of state committees of the Kazakh SSR, and of other organs subordinate to it. **Ki121** to annul decisions and resolutions of executive committees of provincial, district, and city (districts and cities of republican subordination) Soviets of People's Deputies. **Li121** to annul acts of ministries and state committees of the Lithuanian SSR, and of other organs subordinate to it, and decisions and resolutions of executive committees of district and city (cities of republican subordination) Soviets of People's Deputies. **M121, Ar122** to annul decisions and resolutions of executive committees of district and city (cities of republican subordination) Soviets of Peoples Deputies. **Ta121** to annul decisions and resolutions of executive committees of provincial and city (cities of republican subordination) Soviets of People's Deputies. **Uk121** to annul decisions and resolutions of executive committees of provincial and city (cities of republican subordination) Soviets of People's Deputies, and acts of ministries of the Ukrainian SSR, of state committees of the Ukrainian SSR, and of other organs subordinate to it. **Ta123** to annul decisions and resolutions of executive committees of provincial Soviets of People's Deputies, of the executive committee of the Soviet of People's Deputies of the Gorno-Badakhshan Autonomous Province, and of executive committees of district and city Soviets of People's Deputies of districts and cities of republican subordination. **G128** to annul decisions and resolutions of executive committees of the South Ossetian provincial Soviet of People's Deputies, and of district and city (cities of republican subordination) Soviets of People's Deputies. [3]**E,Ka,La,Li,Uk,Uz** = NP; **Ka,Tu121, Ar122, Ta123** The Council of Ministers of the [republic] SSR has the right to annul acts of ministries of the [republic] SSR, of state committees of the [republic] SSR, and of other organs subordinate to it.

Article 129. The Council of Ministers of the RSFSR coordinates and directs the work of union republic and republic ministries and state committees[1] of the RSFSR, and of other organs subordinate to it.

Union republic ministries and state committees[2] of the RSFSR direct the branches of administration[3] entrusted to them or exercise inter-branch control, being subordinate to the Council of Ministers of the RSFSR as well as to the corresponding union republic ministry[4] or state committee of the USSR.

Republic ministries and state committees of the RSFSR direct the branches of administration[5] entrusted to them or exercise inter-branch control, being subordinate to the Council of Ministers of the RSFSR.

Ministries and state committees of the RSFSR are responsible for[6] the state and the development of the spheres of administration entrusted to them; they issue acts within the limits of their competence and on the basis and in pursuance of laws[7] of the USSR and the RSFSR, and of other decisions of the Supreme Soviet of the USSR and its Presidium, and the Supreme Soviet of the RSFSR and its Presidium, decrees and resolutions of the Council of Ministers of the USSR and the Council of Ministers of the RSFSR,[8] and of acts of the corresponding ministries and state committees of the USSR, and they organize and verify their execution.[9]

B,E,Ka,Ki,La,Li,M,Tu,Uk122, Ar123, Ta124, Uz126; [1]**M122** union republic and republic ministries, state committees, and agrarian-industrial associations of the Moldavian SSR, [2]**M122** union republic ministries, state committees, and agrarian-industrial associations of the Moldavian SSR [3]**Ka122** direct the branches of administration of the Kazakh SSR entrusted to them [4]**La,Tu122, Ar123, Uz126, G129** as well as to the corresponding union republic ministry of the USSR or state committee of the USSR. [5]**Li122** Republic ministries and state committees direct the branches of administration [6]**Li122** Ministries and state committees of the republic are responsible for [7]**B122, G129** and on the basis and in pursuance of legislative acts of the USSR and the [republic] SSR, [8]**Uk122** and on the basis and in pursuance of laws of the USSR and its Presidium, laws of the Ukrainian SSR, and other decisions of the Supreme Soviet of the Ukrainian SSR and its Presidium, decrees and resolutions of the Council of Ministers of the USSR, decrees and resolutions of the Council of Ministers of the Ukrainian SSR, [9]**Ka122** This last and fourth paragraph of RSFSR Art.129 appears as a separate article in the Kazakh text, numbered Art.123.

Article 130. The competence of the Council of Ministers of the RSFSR and its Presidium, the procedure of their activity, and the relations of the Council of Ministers of the RSFSR with other state organs,[1] as well as the list of union republic and republic ministries and state committees[2] of the RSFSR, are defined, on the basis of the Constitution,[3] by the Law on the Council of Ministers of the RSFSR.

B,E,Ka,Ki,La,Li,M,Tu,Uk123, Ar124, Ta125, Uz127; [1]**B,Uk123, G130** and the relations of the Council of Ministers with other state organs, [2]**M123** as well as the list of union republic and republic ministries, state committees, and agrarian-industrial associations of the Moldavian SSR [3]**M123, G130** on the basis of the Constitution of the [republic] SSR,

VI. THE SUPREME ORGANS OF STATE POWER AND ADMINISTRATION OF AN AUTONOMOUS REPUBLIC[1]

Ar,B,E,Ka,Ki,La,Li,M,Ta,Tu,Uk = NP; [1]**Az** of the Nakhichevan' ASSR **Uz** of the Kara-Kalpak ASSR

Chapter 15. The Supreme Soviet of an Autonomous Republic[1]

Uz Chap14; [1]**Uz Chap14** The Supreme Soviet of the Kara-Kalpak ASSR **Az Chap15** The Supreme Soviet of the Nakhichevan' ASSR In the articles in this Chapter, whenever the words "of the (an) autonomous republic" appear in the RSFSR text, read "of the Nakhichevan' ASSR" for the Azerbaidzhan text and "of the Kara-Kalpak ASSR" for the Uzbek text.

Article 131. The supreme organ of state power of an autonomous republic is the Supreme Soviet of the autonomous republic.[1]

The Supreme Soviet of an autonomous republic is empowered to resolve all questions assigned to the jurisdiction of the autonomous republic by the Constitution of the USSR, the Constitution of the RSFSR, and the Constitution of the autonomous republic.[2]

The adoption of the Constitution of the autonomous republic and of amendments therein; the confirmation of state plans of economic and social development, and of the state budget[3] of the autonomous republic, and the reports on their fulfillment; the formation of organs accountable to the Supreme Soviet of the autonomous republic—belong to the exclusive competence of the Supreme Soviet of the autonomous republic.[4]

Laws of an autonomous republic are adopted by the Supreme Soviet of the autonomous republic.[5]

[1]**Uz128**; [1]**G131** The Supreme organs of state power of the Abkhaz ASSR and the Adzhar ASSR are the Supreme Soviets of these republics. [2]**G131** The Supreme Soviets of the Abkhaz ASSR and the Adzhar ASSR are empowered to resolve all questions assigned to the jurisdiction of the autonomous republics by the Constitution of the USSR, the Constitution of the Georgian SSR, and the Constitution of these republics. [3]**Uz128** as well as of the state budget [4]**G131** The adoption of the Constitutions of the Abkhaz ASSR and the Adzhar ASSR and of amendments therein; the confirmation of the state plans of economic and social development, and of the state budgets of these autonomous republics, and the reports on their fulfillment; the formation of organs accountable to the Supreme Soviets of the autonomous republics—belong to the exclusive competence of the Supreme Soviets of

the Abkhaz ASSR and the Adzhar ASSR. [5]**G131** Laws of the Abkhaz ASSR and the Adzhar ASSR are adopted by the Supreme Soviets of these autonomous republics.

Article 132. The Supreme Soviet of an autonomous republic elects the Presidium of the Supreme Soviet, the permanently functioning organ of the Supreme Soviet of the Autonomous republic, accountable to the latter in all its activities and exercising, within the limits provided for by the Constitution, the functions of the supreme organ of state power of the autonomous republic during the time between the sessions of the Supreme Soviet of the autonomous republic.[1]

The composition and powers of the Presidium of the Supreme Soviet of an autonomous republic are defined by the Constitution of the autonomous republic.[2]

Uz129; [1]**G131** The Supreme Soviets of the Abkhaz ASSR and the Adzhar ASSR elect the Presidia of the Supreme Soviets of these autonomous republics—the permanently functioning organs of the Supreme Soviets of the Abkhaz ASSR and the Adzhar ASSR, accountable to them in all their activities and exercising, within the limits provided for by the Constitutions, the functions of the supreme organ of state power of these autonomous republics during the time between their sessions. [2]**G131** The composition and powers of the Presidia of the Supreme Soviets of the autonomous republics are defined by the Constitutions of the Abkhaz ASSR and the Adzhar ASSR.

Chapter 16. The Council of Ministers of an Autonomous Republic[1]

Uz Chap15; [1]**Uz Chap15** The Council of Ministers of the Kara-Kalpak ASSR **Az Chap16** The Council of Ministers of the Nakhichevan' ASSR In the articles in this Chapter, whenever the words "of the (an) autonomous republic" appear in the RSFSR text, read "of the Nakhichevan' ASSR" for the Azerbaidzhan text and "of the Kara-Kalpak ASSR" for the Uzbek text.

Article 133. The Council of Ministers of an autonomous republic—the Government of the autonomous republic—the supreme executive and administrative organ of state power of the autonomous republic, is set up by the Supreme Soviet of the autonomous republic.[1]

The Council of Ministers of an autonomous republic is responsible and accountable to the Supreme Soviet of the autonomous republic and, during the time between the sessions of the Supreme Soviet of the autonomous republic, to the Presidium of the Supreme Soviet of the autonomous republic, to whom it is accountable.[2]

Uz130; [1]**Uz130** The Supreme Soviet of the Kara-Kalpak ASSR sets up the Council of Ministers of the Kara-Kalpak ASSR—the Government of the Kara-Kalpak ASSR—the supreme executive and administrative organ of state power of the Kara-

Kalpak ASSR. **G133** The Councils of Ministers of the Abkhaz ASSR and the Adzhar ASSR—the Governments of the autonomous republics—the supreme executive and administrative organs of state power of the Abkhaz ASSR and the Adzhar ASSR, are set up by the Supreme Soviets of these autonomous republics. [2]**G133** The Councils of Ministers of the Abkhaz ASSR and the Adzhar ASSR are responsible and accountable to the Supreme Soviets of these autonomous republics and, during the time between the sessions of the Supreme Soviets of these autonomous republics, to the Presidia of the Supreme Soviets of the Abkhaz ASSR and the Adzhar ASSR, to which they are accountable.

Article 134. The Council of Ministers of an autonomous republic issues decrees and resolutions on the basis and in pursuance of legislative acts of the USSR, the RSFSR, and the autonomous republic, and of decrees and resolutions of the Council of Ministers of the USSR and the Council of Ministers of the RSFSR, and organizes and verifies their execution.[1]

Uz131; [1]**G134** The Councils of Ministers of the Abkhaz ASSR and the Adzhar ASSR issue decrees and resolutions on the basis and in pursuance of legislative acts of the USSR, the Georgian SSR, and the autonomous republics, and of decrees and resolutions of the Council of Ministers of the USSR and the Council of Ministers of the Georgian SSR, and organize and verify their execution.

Article 135. The Council of Ministers of an autonomous republic, within the limits of its competence, has the right to annul decisions[1] and resolutions of executive committees of district and city (cities of republican (ASSR) subordination) Soviets of People's Deputies.[2]

The Council of Ministers of an autonomous republic has the right to annul acts of ministries and state committees of the autonomous republic, and of other organs subordinate to it.[3]

Uz132; [1]**Uz132** The Council of Ministers of the Kara-Kalpak ASSR has the right, within the limits of its competence, to annul decisions [2]**G135** The Councils of Ministers of the Abkhaz ASSR and the Adzhar ASSR, within the limits of their competence, have the right to annul decisions and resolutions of executive committees of district and city (cities of republican (ASSR) subordination) Soviets of People's Deputies. [3]**G135** The Councils of Ministers of the Abkhaz ASSR and the Adzhar ASSR have the right to annul acts of ministries and state committees of these autonomous republics, and of other organs subordinate to them.

Article 136. The Council of Ministers of an autonomous republic coordinates and directs the work of ministries and state committees of the autonomous republic, and of other organs subordinate to it.[1]

Ministries and state committees of an autonomous republic direct the branches of administration entrusted to them or exercise interbranch control, being subordinate to the Council of Ministers of the autonomous republic as well as to the corresponding ministry and state committee of the RSFSR.[2]

Uz133; [1]**Az136** and directs the work of ministries and state committees, and of other organs subordinate to it. **G136** The Councils of Ministers of the Abkhaz ASSR and the Adzhar ASSR coordinate and direct the work of ministries and state committees of the autonomous republics, and of other organs subordinate to them. [2]**Uz133** as well as to the corresponding ministries of the Uzbek SSR and the state committees of the Uzbek SSR. **G136** Ministries and state committees of the Abkhaz ASSR and the Adzhar ASSR direct the branches of administration entrusted to them or exercise inter-branch control, being subordinate to the Councils of Ministers of these republics as well as to the corresponding ministries and state committees of the Georgian SSR.

VII. LOCAL ORGANS OF STATE POWER AND ADMINISTRATION IN THE RSFSR

Ar,B,E,Ka,Ki,La,Li,M,Ta,Tu,Uk = PART VI.

Chapter 17. Local Soviets of People's Deputies

Li Chap13, Ar,B,E,Ka,Ki,La,Li,M,Ta,Tu,Uk Chap14, Uz Chap16

Article 137. The organs of state power in the territories, provinces, autonomous provinces, autonomous areas, districts,[1] cities, city-districts, settlements,[2] and rural settlements[3] are the corresponding Soviets of People's Deputies.[4]

B,E,Ki,La,Li,M,Tu,Uk124, Ar,Ka125, Ta126, Uz134; [1]**B,Ki,Tu124, Uz134** in the provinces, districts, **La,Li,M124, Ar125** in the districts, **Ta126** in the provinces, autonomous provinces, districts **Az137** in the Nagorno-Karabakh Autonomous Province, and in the districts, [2]**E124** in the districts, cities, districts in the city of Tallinn, settlements, [3]**Ka124** and *auls* **Li124** and *apilinki* **Ta126** and *kishlaks* **Uz134** settlements, *kishlaks*, and *auls* **G137** and village [4]**Uk124** The organs of state power in the provinces, districts, cities, city-districts, settlements, and villages of the Ukrainian SSR are the provincial, district, city, city-district, settlement, and village Soviets of People's Deputies.

Article 138. Local Soviets of People's Deputies resolve all questions of local importance, keeping in mind general state interests and the interests of the citizens living in the territory of the Soviet, implement the decisions of higher state organs, direct the activity of lower-level Soviets of People's Deputies, and also participate in the discussion of questions of republic and all-union importance, and submit proposals concerning these questions.

Within their territory, local Soviets of People's Deputies direct state, economic, and socio-cultural organization; confirm plans of economic and social development, and the local budget, and the reports on their fulfillment; exercise[1] leadership over the activities of state organs, enterprises, institutions, and organizations, subordinate to them; ensure observance of laws, the protection of state and public order and of the rights of citizens; and promote the strengthening of the defense capability of the country.

B,E,Ki,La,Li,M,Tu,Uk125, Ar,Ka126, Ta127, Uz135; [1]**Ar,Ka126** confirm plans of economic and social development, and the local budget; exercise

Article 139. Within the limits of their authority, local Soviets of People's Deputies ensure integrated economic and social development within their territory; supervise the observance of legislation by enterprises, institutions, and organizations subordinate to higher bodies and located on this territory; coordinate and supervise their activities in the fields of land use,[1] protection of nature, construction, utilization of labor resources,[2] production of consumer goods, and socio-cultural services, services for everyday needs, and other services for the population.

B,E,Ki,La,Li,M,Tu,Uk126, Ar,Ka127, Ta128, Uz136; [1]**Tu126, Uz136** in the fields of land and water use, [2]**Uk126** construction, amenities, utilization of labor resources

Article 140. Local Soviets of People's Deputies adopt decisions within the limits of the authority granted to them by the legislation of the USSR, the RSFSR,[1] and the autonomous republic.

The execution of decisions of local Soviets is obligatory for all enterprises, institutions, and organizations located on the territory of the Soviet, as well as for officials and citizens.[2]

E,Ki,La,Li,M,Tu,Uk127, B,Ar,Ka128, Ta129, Uz137; [1]**E,Ki,La,Li,M,Tu,Uk127, B,Ar,Ka128, Ta129** legislation of the USSR and the [republic] SSR. **Uz136** legislation of the USSR and the Uzbek SSR, and in the Kara-Kalpak ASSR—and by the legislation of the Kara-Kalpak ASSR. **Az140** legislation of the USSR, and the Azerbaidzhan SSR, and in the Nakhichevan' ASSR, by the laws of the Nakhichevan' ASSR. **G140** legislation of the USSR, and the Georgian SSR, and in the autonomous republics—also by the laws of the autonomous republics. [2]In the following republic constitutions, the second paragraph of RSFSR Art.140 becomes the second sentence in the first paragraph of the relevant article, and there is thus no second paragraph: **E,La127, B128, Ta129, Uz137**

Article 141. Sessions of territorial and provincial Soviets of People's Deputies, Soviets of People's Deputies of autonomous provinces and autonomous areas, and of district, city, and city-district Soviets of People's Deputies are convened[2] by their executive committees at least four times a year.

Sessions of settlement and rural settlement Soviets of People's Deputies are convened[3] by their executive committees at least six times a year.[4]

Local Soviets of People's Deputies are empowered to consider and resolve at sessions any questions that are assigned to their jurisdiction by legislation of the USSR, the RSFSR,[5] and the autonomous republic. A list of the questions, which are resolved exclusively at sessions,[6] is established by laws on the local Soviets of People's Deputies.[7]

B127, E,Ki,La,Li,M,Tu,Uk128, Ar,Ka,La129, Tu130, Uz138; [1]**Az141** Sessions of the Soviet of People's Deputies of the Nagorno-Karabakh Autonomous Province, [2]**B127, Tu128** Sessions of provincial, district, city, city-district, settlement, and rural Soviets of People's Deputies are convened **E,Ki,Li,Uk128, Ar129, Ta130, Uz138, G141** Sessions of local Soviets of People's Deputies are convened **La128** Sessions of district, city, city-district, settlement, and rural settlement Soviets of People's Deputies are convened **M128** Sessions of district, city, and city-district Soviets of People's Deputies are convened **Ka129** Sessions of provincial, district, city, and city-district Soviets of People's Deputies are convened [3]**Ka129** Sessions of settlement, rural settlement, and *aul* Soviets of People's Deputies are convened [4]**Ar,B,E,G,Ki,La,Li,Ta,Tu,Uk,Uz** = NP [5]**B127, E,Li,M,Tu128, Ar,Ka,La129, Ta130** by legislation of the USSR and the [republic] SSR. **Uz139** by legislation of the USSR and the Uzbek SSR, and in the Kara-Kalpak ASSR—by legislation of the Kara-Kalpak ASSR. **Az141** by legislation of the USSR, the Azerbaidzhan SSR, and the Nakhichevan' ASSR. **G141** by legislation of the USSR and the Georgian SSR, and of the corresponding autonomous republics. [6]**E,Li,Tu128, Ar129, Ta130, Uz138** the questions, to be considered and resolved exclusively at sessions, [7]**Uk128**(entire 3rd para.) The range of questions which are resolved exclusively at sessions is established by laws on the local Soviets of People's Deputies. **La129** The third paragraph of RSFSR Art.141 is a separate article (129) in the Latvian text.

Article 142. Local Soviets of People's Deputies elect[1] from among the deputies standing commissions for the preliminary consideration and preparation of questions within the jurisdiction of the local Soviets, as well as for promoting the implementation of decisions of the Soviets, and the supervision of the activities[2] of state organs, enterprises, institutions, and organizations.

The recommendations of standing commissions of local Soviets must be considered by the corresponding state and social organs, enterprises, institutions, and organizations. The commissions must be informed within the established time-limit about the results of the consideration or of the measures taken.

B,E,Ki,Li,M,Tu,Uk129, Ar,Ka,La130, Ta131, Uz140; [1]**Az142** The Soviet of People's Deputies of the Nagorno-Karabakh Autonomous Province, and district, city, city-district, settlement, and rural Soviets of People's Deputies elect [2]**Ka,Uk128** as well as for promoting the implementation of decisions of the Soviets, their executive committees, and the higher organs of state power and administration, and the supervision of the activities

Article 143. Local Soviets of People's Deputies, in exercising leadership over the activities of lower-level Soviets, have the right to annul acts of lower-level Soviets where these acts do not conform to law.[1]

B,E,Ki,Li,M,Tu,Uk130, Ar,Ka,La131, Ta132, Uz141; [1]**B,E130, Ar131, Ta132** Higher-level local Soviets have the power to annul acts of lower-level Soviets and their executive committees where these acts do not conform to the law. **Ka131** Higher-level local Soviets of People's Deputies exercise leadership over the activities of lower-level Soviets, and have the right to annul decisions of lower-level Soviets and their executive committees where they do not conform to the law. **Li,Tu130** Higher-level local Soviets of People's Deputies have the right to annul acts of lower-level Soviets and their executive committees where these acts do not conform to the law. **M,Uk130** Local Soviets of People's Deputies have the right to annul acts of lower-level Soviets where these acts do not conform to the law. **Uz141** Higher-level local Soviets of People's Deputies exercise leadership over the activities of lower-level Soviets. (para.2) Higher-level Soviets have the right to annul acts of lower-level Soviets of People's Deputies and their executive committees where these acts do not conform to the law.

Article 144. Local Soviets of People's Deputies carry out their activities[1] in close contact with social organizations and labor collectives, submit highly important questions to discussion by citizens, and involve them in the work of standing commissions, executive committees, and other organs accountable to the Soviets, promote[2] the work of local voluntary societies, and develop the social initiative of the population.[3]

B,E,Ki,Li,M,Tu,Uk131, Ar,Ka,La132, Ta133, Uz142; [1]**Tu131** Local Soviets of People's Deputies enlist citizens in the administration of state and social affairs, carry out their activities **Uz142** Local Soviets of People's Deputies widely enlist citizens in the administration of state and social affairs, carry out their activities [2]**B,E131, Ar,Ka132, Ta133, Uz141** direct the work [3]**M131** Local Soviets of People's Deputies carry out their activities in close contact with social organizations and labor collectives, promote the work of local voluntary societies, and develop the social initiative of the population, submit highly important questions to discussion by citizens, and involve them in the work of the standing commissions, executive committees, and other organs accountable to the Soviets.

Chapter 18. Executive Committees of Local Soviets of People's Deputies

Li Chap14, Ar,B,E,Ka,Ki,La,Li,M,Ta,Tu,Uk Chap15, Uz Chap17

Article 145. The executive committees elected by the local Soviets from among the deputies are the executive[1] and administrative organs of the local Soviets of People's Deputies and consist of: the chairman, deputy chairmen,[2] the secretary, and members.[3]

Executive committees report at least once a year to the Soviets which have elected them, as well as at meetings of labor collectives and at citizens' places of residence.

B,E,Ki,Li,M,Tu,Uk132, Ar,Ka,La133, Ta134, Uz143; [1]**Az145** The executive committees elected from among the deputies by the Soviet of People's Deputies of the Nagorno-Karabakh Autonomous Province, and by district, city, city-district, settlement, and rural Soviets of People's Deputies are the executive [2]**G145** the chairman, his deputies, [3]**La,Li,Uk132** the secretary, and the members of the executive committees.

Article 146. Executive committees of local Soviets of People's Deputies are directly accountable to the Soviet which has elected them, as well as to the higher executive and administrative organ.[1]

Ar,B,E,Ki,Li,M,Tu,Uk133, Ka,La134, Ta135, Uz144, Az150; [1]The text of RSFSR Art.146 appears as the third paragraph of the preceeding equivalent article (133) of the Armenian Constitution.

Article 147. Within the territory of the corresponding Soviet, executive committees of local Soviets of People's Deputies direct state, economic, and socio-cultural organization[1] on the basis of decisions of the Soviets which have elected them and of higher organs of state power and administration.[2]

Executive committees of local Soviets of People's Deputies have the right to resolve all questions, assigned to the jurisdiction of Soviets, with the exception of those questions which must be resolved only at sessions of Soviets.[3]

Executive committees convene sessions[4] of Soviets and coordinate the work of the standing commissions of Soviets; render assistance to deputies in the exercise of their powers; organize the execution[5] of decisions of Soviets and higher state organs, as well as the mandates of the voters; direct the organs of administration subordinate to them.

Ar,B,E,Ki,Li,M,Tu,Uk134, Ka,La135, Ta136, Uz145, Az146; [1]**Uz145** executive committees of local Soviets of People's Deputies exercise leadership of state, economic, and socio-cultural organization [2]**Uz134** of higher organs of state power and administration, ensure the fulfillment of these decisions, and exercise supervision over their implementation. [3]**Ar,B,E,G,Ka,Li,Ta,Uk** = NP [4]**M,Uk134, Ka135** Executive committees of local Soviets of People's Deputies convene sessions [5]**Ar,E134** Executive committees convene sessions of Soviets: coordinate the work of the standing committees of Soviets; organize the execution

Article 148. Within the limits of their competence,[1] executive committees[2] of local Soviets of People's Deputies adopt decisions and issue resolutions.[3]

Ar,B,E,Ki,Li,M,Tu,Uk135, Ka,La136, Ta137, Uz146, Az147; [1]**Ka136** of their authority, [2]**B135** Within the limits of the authority granted to them by the legislation of the USSR and the Belorussian SSR, executive committees [3]**Ar135** adopt decisions and resolutions. **Ki135** Within the limits of the rights granted to them, executive committees of Soviets of People's Deputies adopt decisions and issue resolutions which are obligatory for all enterprises, institutions, and organizations located on the territory of the Soviet, as well as for officials and citizens. **Uk135** Executive committees of local Soviets of People's Deputies adopt decisions and issue resolutions within the limits of the authority granted to them by legislation of the USSR and the Ukrainian SSR.

Article 149. Executive committees of Soviets of People's Deputies have the right[1] to annul decisions and resolutions of executive committees of lower-level[2] Soviets[3] of People's Deputies.[4]

Ar135, B,E,Ki,Li,M,Tu,Uk136, Ka,La137, Ta138, Uz147, Ar148; [1]**Li,Tu136** Executive committees of higher-level Soviets of People's Deputies have the right **Ta138, Uz147** Higher-level executive committees have the right [2]**E,Ki136** and resolutions of lower-level executive committees. [3]**Ar135, Uk136** and resolutions of executive committees of lower-level Soviets. [4] The text of RSFSR Art.149, as modified, appears as the second paragraph of the preceeding equivalent article (135) of the Armenian Constitution.

Article 150. Upon expiration of the term of office of local Soviets of People's Deputies, their executive committees[1] retain their powers until the election of executive committees by the newly-elected Soviets of People's Deputies.

Ar136, B,E,Ki,Li,M,Tu,Uk137, Ka,La138, Ta139, Uz148, Ar149, G151; [1]**Ar136, Li137, Ka138, Ta139, Uz148** the executive committees

Article 151. Departments and administrations of executive committees are set up by territorial and provincial Soviets of People's Deputies, Soviets of People's Deputies of autonomous provinces and autonomous areas, and[1] district, city, and city-district Soviets of People's Deputies, and are subordinate[2] in their activities to the Soviets and their executive committees as well as to the corresponding higher organs of state administration.[3]

A list of the departments and administrations of executive committees of local Soviets of People's Deputies, and the procedure for setting them up, are established by legislation of the USSR, the RSFSR, and the autonomous republics.[4,5]

Ar137, B,E,Ki,Li,M,Tu,Uk138, Ka,La139, Ta140, Uz149, G150; [1]**G150** Departments and administrations of executive committees are set up by the Soviet of People's Deputies of the South-Ossetian Autonomous Province, and

Az151 Departments and administrations of executive committees are set up by the Soviet of People's Deputies of the Nagorno-Karabakh Autonomous Province, and **Ta140** Departments and administrations of executive committees are set up by provincial Soviets of People's Deputies, the Soviet of People's Deputies of the Gorno-Badakhshan Autonomous Province, and [2]**B,Ki,Tu138, Ka139, Uz149** Departments and administrations of executive committees are set up by provincial, district, city, and city-district Soviets of People's Deputies, and are subordinate **E138** Departments and administrations of executive committees are set up by district, city (cities of republican subordination), and district in the city of Tallinn Soviets of People's Deputies, and are subordinate **Li138** Departments and administrations of executive committees are set up by district, city (cities of republican subordination), and city-district Soviets of People's Deputies, and are subordinate **La139** Departments and administrations of executive committees are set up by district, city, and city-district Soviets of People's Deputies, and are subordinate [3]**Ar137** District, city, and city-district Soviets of People's Deputies form departments and administrations of executive committees for the direct management of the separate branches of state administration. **M138** District and city (cities of republican subordination) as well as city-district Soviets of People's Deputies, in accordance with legislation of the Moldavian SSR and taking into account the nature of the economic and socio-cultural life of the district and city, form departments and administrations which, in their activities, are subordinate to the Soviets and their executive committees, as well as to the corresponding higher organs of state administration. **Uk138** Departments and administrations of executive committees are set up by provincial, district, city, and city-district Soviets of People's Deputies. [4]**E** = NP; **Ar,137, Li138, Ta140** A list of and the procedure for setting up the departments and administrations are defined by legislation of the USSR and the [republic] SSR. **Uk138** Departments and administrations of executive committees of Soviets of People's Deputies direct the branches of administration entrusted to them, and are subordinate in their activities to the corresponding Soviet and its executive committee, as well as to the higher branch organ of state administration. **B,Ki,M,Tu138, Ka,La139** by legislation of the USSR and the [republic] SSR. **Uz149** by legislation of the USSR and the Uzbek SSR, and in the Kara-Kalpak ASSR—also by legislation of the Kara-Kalpak ASSR. **Az151** by legislation of the USSR and the Azerbaidzhan SSR, and for local Soviets of the Nakhichevan' ASSR, also by legislation of the Nakhichevan' ASSR. [5]In the following two republic texts, a third paragraph has been added to the equivalent of RSFSR Art.151: **Ar137, Uk138** (para.3) Departments and administrations of executive committees of district, city, and city-district Soviets of People's Deputies are subordinate in their activities to the Soviets and their executive committees, as well as to the corresponding higher executive and administrative organ.

VIII. THE STATE PLAN OF THE ECONOMIC AND SOCIAL DEVELOPMENT OF THE RSFSR. THE STATE BUDGET OF THE RSFSR.[1]

Ar,B,E,Ka,Ki,La,Li,M,Ta,Tu,Uk = PART VII. [1]**G,La,Li,M,Uk** THE STATE PLAN OF THE ECONOMIC AND SOCIAL DEVELOPMENT OF THE [REPUBLIC] SSR, AND THE STATE BUDGET OF THE [REPUBLIC] SSR.

Chapter 19. The State Plan of the Economic and Social Development of the RSFSR

Li Chap15, Ar,B,E,Ka,Ki,La,Li,M,Ta,Tu,Uk Chap16, Uz Chap18

Article 152. The state plan of the economic and social development of the RSFSR is a component part of the state plan[1] of the economic and social development of the USSR.

Current and long-range state plans of the economic and social development of the RSFSR have as their goal to ensure integrated economic and social development within the territory of the republic in accordance with the fundamental tasks and directions of the economic and social development of the USSR.[2,3]

Ar138, B,E,Ki,Li,M,Tu,Uk139, Ka,La140, Ta141, Uz150; [1]**Ar138, E,Li,Tu139, Ka140, Ta141, Uz150** a component part of the unified state plan [2]**Ar138, E,Tu139, Ka140, Ta141, Uz150** Long-range and current plans of the economic and social development of the [republic] SSR are formulated in accordance with the fundamental tasks and directions of the development of the national economy of the USSR, and are directed at ensuring integrated economic and social development within the territory of the republic. **Ki139** Current and long-range plans of the economic and social development of the Kirgiz SSR are formulated in accordance with the fundamental tasks and directions of the development of the national economy of the USSR, and are directed at ensuring integrated economic and social development within the territory of the republic. [3]**Li139** Here, the text of the second paragraph of RSFSR Art.152 becomes the second sentence of the first paragraph.

Article 153. State plans of the economic and social development of the RSFSR define the tasks in the field of economic and sociocultural construction, contain entire integrated programs and plans for the development of branches of the national economy and economic districts within the territory of the RSFSR, and include plans of the economic and social development of autonomous republics, territories, provinces, autonomous provinces, and cities of republican subordination.[1]

Ar139, B,E,Ki,Li,M,Tu,Uk140, Ka,La141, Ta142, Uz151; [1]**Ar139, Li140** contain integrated programs for the development of branches of the national economy of the [republic] SSR, and include plans of ministries, state committees, and other organs of state administration, and plans of the economic and social development of districts and cities of republican subordination. **B140** contain entire integrated programs and plans for the development of branches of the national economy within the territory of the Belorussian SSR, and include plans of the economic and social development of provinces and the city of Minsk. **Ki140** contain entire integrated programs and plans for the development of branches of the national economy, and include plans of the economic and social development of provinces, as well as of districts and cities of republican subordination. **M140, La141** contain entire integrated programs and plans for the development of branches of the national economy of the [republic] SSR, and include plans of the economic and social development of districts and cities of republican subordination. **Tu140** contain integrated programs for the development of branches of the national economy of the Turkmen SSR, and include plans of ministries, state committees, and other organs of state administration, and plans of the economic and social development of provinces and cities of republican subordination. **Uk140** and include plans of the economic and social development of provinces and cities of republican subordination. **Ka141** contain integrated programs for the development of branches of the national economy and economic districts within the territory of the Kazakh SSR, and include plans of ministries, state committees, and other organs of state administration, and plans of the economic and social development of provinces and the city of Alma-Ata. **Ta142** contain integrated programs for the development of branches of the national economy and the territorial-production complexes of the Tadzhik SSR, and include plans of ministries, state committees, and other organs of state administration, and plans of the economic and social development of provinces, autonomous provinces, districts, and cities of republican subordination. **Uz151** contain integrated programs for the development of branches of the national economy within the territory of the Uzbek SSR, and include plans of ministries, state committees, and other organs of state administration, and plans of the economic and social development of the Kara-Kalpak ASSR, provinces, and the city of Tashkent. **G153** and include plans for the development of branches of the national economy and nature-economic zones within the territory of the Georgian SSR, and include plans of the economic and social development of autonomous republics, autonomous provinces, districts, and cities of republican subordination.

Article 154. Proceeding from the state plan of the economic and social development of the USSR, the state plan of the economic and social development of the RSFSR is formulated by the Council of Ministers of the RSFSR on the basis of draft plans of ministries, state committees, and other organs of state administration of the RSFSR, the Councils of Ministers of autonomous republics, and local Soviets of People's Deputies.[1]

The basic plan indices of enterprises, institutions, and organizations of union subordination, located within the territory of the RSFSR, are included in the state plan of the economic and social development of the RSFSR.[2]

The formulation of plans of economic and social development is made taking into account the proposals of collectives of enterprises, institutions, and organizations, as well as of social organizations.[3]

Ar140, B,E,Ki,Li,M,Tu,Uk141, Ka,La142, Ta143, Uz152; [1]**Ar140, Tu141, Uz152** Proceeding from general state interests and taking into account the proposals of ministries, state committees, and other organs of state administration of the [republic] SSR, of local Soviets of People's Deputies, social organizations, and collectives of enterprises and institutions, as well as of ministries and agencies of the USSR, the state plan of the economic and social development of the [republic] SSR is formulated by the Council of Ministers of the [republic] SSR, and is submitted to the Supreme Soviet of the [republic] SSR. **E141, Ka142, Ta143** Proceeding from general state interests and taking into account the proposals of ministries, state committees, and other organs of state administration of the Estonian SSR, of local Soviets of People's

Deputies, social organizations, and collectives of enterprises, institutions, and organizations, as well as of ministries and agencies of the USSR, the state plan of the economic and social development of the Estonian SSR is formulated by the Council of Ministers of the Estonian SSR and submitted to the Supreme Soviet of the Estonian SSR. **Ki141** Proceeding from the state plan of the economic and social development of the Kirgiz SSR and taking into account the proposals of ministries, state committees, and other organs of state administration of the Kirgiz SSR, and of local Soviets of People's Deputies, the state plan of the economic and social development of the Kirgiz SSR is formulated by the Council of Ministers of the Kirgiz SSR. **B,Li,Uk141, La142** on the basis of draft plans of ministries, state committees, and other organs of state administration of the [republic] SSR, and local Soviets of People's Deputies. **M141** on the basis of draft plans of ministries, state committees, and other organs of state administration of the Moldavian SSR, and of district and city (cities of republican subordination) Soviets of People's Deputies. **Az154** on the basis of draft plans of ministries, state committees, and other organs of state administration of the Azerbaidzhan SSR, the Council of Ministers of the Nakhichevan' ASSR, and local Soviets of People's Deputies. [2]**Ar,E,Ka,Ta,Tu,Uz** = NP [3]**Ar,E,Ka,Li,Ta,Tu,Uz** = NP

Article 155. The Council of Ministers of the RSFSR submits the state plan of the economic and social development of the RSFSR for consideration to the Supreme Soviet of the RSFSR.[1]

The Supreme Soviet of the RSFSR, upon the report of the Council of Ministers of the RSFSR and the conclusions of the Planning-budget and other standing commissions of the Supreme Soviet of the RSFSR, discusses and confirms the state plan of the economic and social development of the RSFSR.

Ar141, B,E,Ki,Li,M,Tu,Uk142, Ka,La143, Ta144, Uz153; [1]In the texts of the following republic constitutions, paragraph one of RSFSR Art.155 is not present, and paragraph two of RSFSR Art.155 thus becomes the first and only paragraph in the equivalent article: **Ar,E,Ka,Ki,Li,Ta,Tu,Uz**

Article 156. The Council of Ministers of the RSFSR organizes the fulfillment of the plan of the economic and social development of the RSFSR and takes measures[1] to strengthen plan discipline.

Ar142, B,E,Ki,Li,M,Tu,Uk143, Ka,La144, Ta145, Uz154; [1]**Ar142, E,Ki,Li,Tu143, Ka144, Ta145, Uz154, Az156** and takes the necessary measures

Article 157. Reports on the fulfillment of the state plans of economic and social development of the RSFSR are considered and confirmed by the Supreme Soviet of the RSFSR. Overall indices of the fulfillment of the plan are published for general information.

Ar143, B,E,Ki,Li,M,Tu,Uk144, Ka,La145, Ta146, Uz155

Chapter 20. The State Budget of the RSFSR

Li Chap16, Ar,B,E,Ka,Ki,La,Li,M,Ta,Tu,Uk Chap17, Uz Chap19

Article 158. The state budget of the RSFSR is a component part of the unified state budget of the USSR.

Ar144, B,E,Ki,Li,M,Tu,Uk145, Ka,La146, Ta147, Uz156

Article 159. The state budget of the RSFSR embraces the republic budget of the RSFSR, the state budgets of autonomous republics, and local budgets.[1]

Ar145, Li145(para.2), B,E,Ki,M,Tu,Uk146, Ka,La147, Ta148, Uz157; [1]**Ar145, B,E,Ki146, Ka147** embraces the republic budget and the local budgets of the [republic] SSR. **Li145(para.2), M146** embraces the republic budget of the [republic] SSR and local budgets of districts and cities of republican subordination. **Uk,Tu146, La147, Ta148** embraces the republic budget of the [republic] SSR and local budgets. **Uz157** embraces the republic budget of the Uzbek SSR, the state budget of the Kara-Kalpak ASSR, and local budgets. **Az159** embraces the republic budget of the Azerbaidzhan SSR, the state budget of the Nakhichevan' ASSR, and local budgets of the Nagorno-Karabakh Autonomous Province, and of districts and cities of republican subordination.

Article 160. The distribution of the revenues and expenditures of the state budget of the RSFSR between the republic budget of the RSFSR, the state budgets of autonomous republics, and local budgets is defined by the Law of the RSFSR on Budget Rights of the RSFSR, Autonomous Republics, and Local Soviets of People's Deputies.[1]

Li145(para.3), Ar146, Uk146(para.2), B,E,Ki,M,Tu147, Ka,La148, Tu149, Uz158; [1]**Ar146, E147, Ka148, Ta149** between the republic budget and local budgets is defined by the Law on Budget Rights of the [republic] SSR and Local Soviets of People's Deputies, and by other legislation of the [republic] SSR. **Li146(para.3)** between the republic budget and local budgets of districts and cities of republican subordination is defined by the Law on Budget Rights of the Lithuanian SSR and Local Soviets of People's Deputies, as well as by other legislation of the Lithuanian SSR. **B147** between the republic budget and local budgets is defined by the Law on Budget Rights of the Belorussian SSR and Local Soviets of People's Deputies of the Belorussian SSR. **Uk146(para.2), Ki147, La148** between the republic budget and local budgets is defined by the Law of the [republic] SSR on Budget Rights of the [republic] SSR and Local Soviets of People's Deputies. **M147** between the republic budget of the Moldavian SSR and local budgets is defined by the Law of the Moldavian SSR on Budget Rights of the Moldavian SSR and Local Soviets of People's Deputies. **Tu147** between the republic budget of the Turkmen SSR and local budgets is defined by the Law on Budget Rights of the Turkmen SSR and Local Soviets of People's Deputies, and by other legislation of the Turkmen SSR. **Uz158** between the republic budget of the Uzbek SSR, the state budget of the Kara-Kalpak ASSR, and local budgets is defined by the Law on Budget Rights of the Uzbek SSR, the Kara-Kalpak ASSR, and Local Soviets of People's Deputies, and by other legislation of the Uzbek SSR. **Az160** between the republic budget of the Azerbaidzhan SSR, the state budget of the Nakhichevan' ASSR, and local budgets of the Nagorno-Karabakh Autonomous Province, and districts and cities of the republic is defined by the Law of the Azerbaidzhan SSR on Budget Rights of the Azerbaidzhan SSR, the Nakhichevan' ASSR, and Local Soviets of People's Deputies.

Article 161. The state budget of the RSFSR is formulated by the Council of Ministers of the RSFSR on the basis of state plans of the economic and social development of the USSR and the RSFSR, and the state budget of the USSR, and is confirmed by the Supreme Soviet of the RSFSR upon the report of the Council of Ministers of the RSFSR, and the conclusions of the Planning-budget[1] and other standing commissions of the Supreme Soviet of the RSFSR.[2]

Li146, Ar,Li,Uk147, B,E,Ki,M,Tu148, Ka,La,Tu149, Ta150, Uz159, Uz160; [1]**B148** and the conclusion of the Planning-budget [2]**Ar147, Ta150(para.1)** The state budget of the [republic] SSR is compiled by the Council of Ministers of the [republic] SSR on the basis of state plans of the economic and social development of the USSR and the [republic] SSR, and the state budget of the USSR, and is submitted for confirmation to the Supreme Soviet of the [republic] SSR. **Ar147(para.2)** The state budget of the Armenian SSR is considered by the Supreme Soviet of the Armenian SSR upon the report of the Council of Ministers of the Armenian SSR and the conclusions of the Planning-budget and other standing commissions of the Supreme Soviet of the Armenian SSR. **Li146, E148 (para.1), Tu148, Uz159** The state budget of the [republic] SSR is formulated by the Council of Ministers of the [republic] SSR on the basis of state plans of the economic and social development of the USSR and the [republic] SSR, and the state budget of the USSR, and is submitted for confirmation to the Supreme Soviet of the [republic] SSR. **Li147, E148 (para.2)** The state budget of the [republic] SSR is considered and confirmed by the Supreme Soviet of the [republic] SSR upon the report of the Council of Ministers of the [republic] SSR and the conclusion of the Planning-budget and other standing commissions of the Supreme Soviet of the [republic] SSR. **Tu149, Ta150(para.2), Uz160** The state budget of the [republic] SSR is considered and confirmed by the Supreme Soviet of the [republic] SSR upon the report of the Council of Ministers of the [republic] SSR and the conclusions of the Planning-budget and other standing commissions of the Supreme Soviet of the [republic] SSR.

Article 162. The report on the execution of the state budget of the RSFSR is confirmed by the Supreme Soviet of the RSFSR. Overall indices of the execution of the state budget of the RSFSR are published for general information.

Ar,Li,Uk148, B,E,Ki,M149, Ka,La,Tu150, Ta151, Uz161

IX. THE ADMINISTRATION OF JUSTICE, ARBITRATION, AND PROCURATORIAL SUPERVISION

Ar,B,E,Ka,Ki,La,Li,M,Ta,Tu,Uk = PART VIII.

Chapter 21. Courts and Arbitration

Li Chap17, Ar,B,E,Ka,Ki,La,Li,M,Ta,Tu,Uk Chap18, Uz Chap20

Article 163. Justice in the RSFSR is administered only by the courts.

The courts of the RSFSR are the Supreme Court of the RSFSR; Supreme Courts of autonomous republics; territorial, provincial, and city courts; courts of autonomous provinces; courts of autonomous areas; district[1] (city) people's courts.

The organization and manner of operation of the courts of the RSFSR are defined by the laws of the USSR and the RSFSR.[2]

Ar,Li,Uk149, B,E,Ki,M150, Ka,La,Tu151, Ta152, Uz162; [1]**Ar,Li149, E,M150, La151** The courts of the [republic] SSR are the Supreme Court of the [republic] SSR, and district **Uk149** The courts of the Ukrainian SSR are the Supreme Court of the Ukrainian SSR, provincial courts, the Kiev city court, and district **B,Ki150, Ta151** The courts of the [republic] SSR are the Supreme Court of the [republic] SSR, provincial courts, and district **Ka151** The courts of the Kazakh SSR are: the Supreme Court of the Kazakh SSR, provincial courts and the Alma-Ata city courts, and district **Ta152** The courts of the Tadzhik SSR are: the Supreme Court of the Tadzhik SSR, provincial courts, the court of the Gorno-Badakhshan Autonomous Province, the Dushanbe city court, and district **Uz161** The courts of the Uzbek SSR are the Supreme Court of the Uzbek SSR, the Supreme Court of the Kara-Kalpak ASSR, provincial courts, the Tashkent city court, and district **Az163** The courts of the Azerbaidzhan SSR are the Supreme Court of the Azerbaidzhan SSR, the Supreme Court of the Nakhichevan' ASSR, the Baku city court, the provincial court of the Nagorno-Karabakh Autonomous Province, and district **G163** The court of the Georgian SSR are: the Supreme Court of the Georgian SSR, the Supreme Courts of the Abkhaz ASSR and the Adzhar ASSR, the Tbilisi city court, the provincial court of the South Ossetian Autonomous Province, and district [2]In the Estonian text, the third paragraph of RSFSR Art.163 becomes the second sentence in the second paragraph of **E150**, and there is thus no third paragraph in **E150**.

Article 164. All courts in the RSFSR are formed on the principle that judges and people's assessors are elected.

People's judges of district (city) people's courts are elected for a term of five years by secret ballot by the citizens of the district (city) on the basis of universal, equal, and direct suffrage. People's assessors of district (city) people's courts are elected for a term of two and a half years by open ballot at meetings of citizens at their place of work or residence.

Higher courts are elected for a term of five years by the corresponding Soviets of People's Deputies.[1,2]

Judges and people's assessors are responsible to their constituents or to the organs which have elected them, report to them, and may be recalled by them in the manner established by law.

Ar,Li,Uk150, B,E,Ki,M151, Ka,La,Tu152, Ta153, Uz163; [1]In the following republic constitutions, the text of RSFSR Art.164 para.3 is not present, and thus what is para.4 in the RSFSR text becomes para.3 in the equivalent articles of these constitutions: **Ar,E,Li,M** [2]**Ka152** Provincial courts and Alma-Ata city courts are elected for a term of five years by the provincial Soviets of People's Deputies and the Alma-Ata city Soviet of People's Deputies, and consist of the chairmen, deputy chairmen, members, and people's assessors. **La152** The Supreme Court of the Latvian SSR is elected for a term of five years by the Supreme Soviet of the Latvian SSR.

Article 165. The Supreme Court of the RSFSR is the supreme judicial organ of the RSFSR and supervises the judicial activities of the courts[1] of the RSFSR.[2]

The Supreme Court of the RSFSR is elected by the Supreme Soviet of the RSFSR and[3] consists of the Chairman, his deputies,[4] members, and people's assessors.[5]

Ar,Li,Uk151, B,E,Ki,M152, Ka,La,Tu153, Ta154, Uz164; [1]**E152** of all the courts [2]**Ar,Uk151** of the republic. [3]**E,M152, Ka153** elected by the Supreme Soviet of the [republic] SSR for a term of five years and **La153** The Supreme Court of the Latvian SSR is elected and [4]**Ar151, La153** Deputy Chairmen [5]**Az165(para.2)** The Supreme Court of the Azerbaidzhan SSR is elected by the Supreme Soviet of the Azerbaidzhan SSR and consists of the Chairman, his deputies, members, and people's assessors. The Chairmen of the Supreme Court of the Nakhichevan' ASSR and of the provincial court of the Nagorno-Karabakh Autonomous Province are members of the Supreme Court of the Azerbaidzhan SSR by virtue of their office.

Article 166. In all courts, civil and criminal cases are considered by a panel; in the court of first instance—with the participation of people's assessors. In the administration of justice, people's assessors enjoy all the rights of a judge.[1]

Ar,Li,Uk152, B,E,Ki,M153, Ka,La,Tu154, Ta155, Uz165; [1]**Uz165** The second sentence in RSFSR Art.166 becomes a separate second paragraph in the Uzbek constitution.

Article 167. Judges and people's assessors are independent and subject only to law.

Ar,Li,Uk153, B,E,Ki,M154, Ka,La,Tu155, Ta156, Uz166

Article 168. Justice is administered in the RSFSR on the principle of the equality of citizens before the law and the court.

Ar,Li,Uk154, B,E,Ki,M155, Ka,La,Tu156, Ta157, Uz167

Article 169. The examination of cases in all courts is open. The hearing of cases in a closed session of the court is permitted only in cases established by law and with the observance of all the rules of court procedure.

Ar,Li,Uk155, B,E,Ki,M156, Ka,La,Tu157, Ta158, Uz168

Article 170. The accused is ensured the right to defense.

Ar,Li,Uk156, B,E,Ki,M157, Ka,La,Tu158, Ta159, Uz169

Article 171. Judicial proceedings in the RSFSR are conducted in the Russian language, or in the language of the autonomous republic, the autonomous province, the autonomous area, or[1] in the language of the majority of the population of the given locality. The right fully to familiarize oneself with the materials of the case, participation in court proceedings through an interpreter, and the right to address the court in one's native language are ensured to persons who take part in a case and do not master the language in which the proceedings are conducted.

Ar,Li,Uk157, B,E,Ki,M158, Ka,La,Tu159, Ta160, Uz170; [1]**Ar,Li,Uk157, B,E,Ki158, Ka,La,Tu159, Ta160** are conducted in the [republic] language, or **M158** are conducted either in the Moldavian language, or **Uz170** are conducted in the Uzbek language, the Kara-Kalpak language, or **Az,G171** are conducted in the [republic] language, or in the language of the autonomous republic or autonomous province, or

Article 172. No one may be convicted of the commission of a crime as well as be subjected to criminal punishment other than by a judgment of the court and in accordance with the law.

Ar,Li,Uk158, B,E,Ki,M159, Ka,La,Tu160, Ta161, Uz171

Article 173. There are colleges of advocates[1] to render legal assistance to citizens and organizations. In cases provided for by legislation, citizens receive legal assistance free of charge.

The organization and manner of operation of the Bar are defined by legislation of the USSR and the RSFSR.

Ar,Li,Uk159, B,E,Ki,M160, Ka,La,Tu161, Ta162, Uz172; [1]**E160** colleges of advocates of the Estonian SSR

Article 174. The participation of representatives of social organizations and labor collectives is permitted in judicial proceedings in civil and criminal cases.

Ar,Li,Uk160, B,E,Ki,M161, Ka,La,Tu162, Ta163, Uz173

Article 175. Economic disputes between enterprises, institutions, and organizations are resolved by the organs of state arbitration within the limits of their competence.

Ar,Li,Uk161, B,E,Ki,M162, Ka,La,Tu163, Ta164, Uz174

Chapter 22. The Procuracy

Li Chap18, Ar,B,E,Ka,Ki,La,Li,M,Ta,Tu,Uk Chap19, Uz Chap21

Article 176. The Procurator General of the USSR and his subordinates, the Procurator of the RSFSR and procurators of lower rank, exercise supreme supervision over the exact and uniform execution of the law by all ministries, state committees and departments, enterprises, institutions, and organizations, executive and administrative organs of local Soviets of People's Deputies, collective farms, cooperative and other social organizations, and officials, as well as citizens within the territory of the RSFSR.

Ar,Li,Uk162, B,E,Ki,M163, Ka,La,Tu164, Ta165, Uz175

Article 177. The Procurator of the RSFSR, and the procurators of the autonomous republics, territories, provinces, and autonomous provinces are appointed[1] by the Procurator General of the USSR.

Procurators of autonomous areas and district and city procurators are appointed[2,3] by the Procurator of the RSFSR and confirmed by the Procurator General of the USSR.

Ar,Li,Uk163, B,E,Ki,Li,M164, Ka,La,Tu165, Ta166, Uz176; [1]**Ar,Li163, M164, La165,** The Procurator of the [republic] SSR is appointed **Uk163, B,Ki164, Ka,Tu165** The Procurator of the [republic] SSR and the procurators of provinces are appointed **Ta166** The Procurator of the Tadzhik SSR, the procurators of provinces, and the procurator of the Gorno-Badakhshan Autonomous Province are appointed **Uz176** The Procurator of the Uzbek SSR, the procurator of the Kara-Kalpak ASSR, and the procurators of provinces are appointed for a term of five years **Az177** The Procurator of the Azerbaidzhan SSR, and the procurators of the Nakhichevan' ASSR and the Nagorno-Karabakh Autonomous Province are appointed **G177** The Procurator of the Georgian SSR, and the procurators of the Abkhaz ASSR and the Adzhar ASSR, and of the South Ossetian Autonomous Province are appointed [2]**Ar163, B,Ki,Li164, Ka,Tu165, Ta166, Az,G177** District and city procurators are appointed In the following constitutions, the second paragraph, as modified, of RSFSR Art.177 becomes the second sentence of the first paragraph: **Uk163, E,M164, La165** District and city procurators are appointed [3]**Uz176(para.2)** District and city procurators are appointed for a term of five years

Article 178. The term of office of the Procurator of the RSFSR and all procurators of lower rank is five years.

Ar,Uk164, E164(para.2), B,Ki,Li,M165, Ka,La,Tu166, Ta167, Uz177

Article 179. The organs of the Procuracy exercise their powers independently from any local organs whatsoever and are subordinate only to the Procurator General of the USSR.

Ar,E,Uk165, B,Ki,Li,M166, Ka,La,Tu167, Ta168, Uz178

X. THE ARMS, FLAG, ANTHEM, AND CAPITAL OF THE RSFSR

Ar,B,E,Ka,Ki,La,Li,M,Ta,Tu,Uk = Part IX.

Article 180. The state arms of the Russian Soviet Federative Socialist Republic consist of a representation of a sickle and hammer against a red background, in the rays of the sun and framed by ears of grain, with an inscription "RSFSR" and "Proletarians of All Countries, Unite!". There is a five-pointed star in the upper part of the arms.[1]

Ar,E,Uk166, B,Ki,Li,M167, Ka,La,Tu168, Ta169, Uz178; [1]**Ar166** The state arms of the Armenian Soviet Socialist Republic consist of a representation of the Great and the Small Ararat, above which are placed the sickle and hammer on a five-pointed star surrounded by the rays of the sun; at the foot of the mountain, a grapevine with a cluster of leaves, and to the left and right ears of grain. Around the arms on the borders the inscription [in Armenian]: "Armenian Soviet Socialist Republic", and below against the red background the inscription in the Armenian and Russian languages: "Proletarians of All Countries, Unite!". **E166** The state arms of the Estonian Soviet Socialist Republic consist of a representation of a sickle and hammer in the rays of a rising sun, framed by a garland, which on the left is made out of coniferous branches, and on the right out of ears of rye, with the inscriptions in the Estonian and Russian languages "Proletarians of All Countries, Unite!", and below "*Eesti NSV*". There is a five-pointed star in the upper part of the arms. **Uk166** The state arms of the Ukrainian Soviet Socialist Republic consist of a representation of a sickle and hammer on a shield in the rays of the sun and framed in ears of grain, with an inscription on the ribbon: below the garland [in Ukrainian]—"Ukrainian SSR", to the right on the column [in Russian] "Proletarians of All Countries, Unite!", and to the left [in Ukrainian]—"Proletarians of All Countries, Unite!". Over the shield between the ears of grain—a five-pointed star. **B167** The state arms of the Belorussian Soviet Socialist Republic consist of the representation in the rays of a rising sun of a sickle and hammer, surrounded, on the right, by a garland made out of ears of rye bound with clover, and on the left, made out of ears of rye grain bound with flax; below, between both halves of the garland, there is part of the globe. Both halves of the garland are intertwined with red ribbon, on which are contained the inscriptions in the Belorussian and Russian languages: "Proletarians of All Countries, Unite!", and below that "BSSR". There is a five-pointed star in the upper part of the arms. **Ki167** The state arms of the Kirgiz SSR consist of a representation of a sickle and hammer in a decorated circle, a mountain range with a rising sun in a light-blue arch, framed on the right by ears of wheat, and on the left with a cotton branch, and intertwined with red ribbon. On the ribbon is an inscription—in the center part in the Kirgiz and Russian languages: "Proletarians of All Countries, Unite!", and below in the Kirgiz language "Kirgiz SSR". There is a five-pointed star in the upper part of the arms. **Li167** The state arms of the Lithuanian Soviet Socialist Republic consist of a representation of a sickle and hammer against a white background, in the rays of the sun, and framed in ears of grain and oak leaves, with an inscription in the Lithuanian and Russian languages: "Proletarians of All Countries, Unite!". [para.2] In the upper part of the arms is a five-pointed star, and in the lower part—the letters "LTSR". **M167** The state arms of the Moldavian Soviet Socialist Republic consist of a representation of a sickle and hammer in the rays of the sun and framed by ears of grain and corn, with a garland of a bunch of grapes and fruit, and with the inscriptions on a red ribbon: "Proletarians of All Countries, Unite!", and on the left side in the Moldavian language "*Proletar' din toate tserile chnitsi-ve*!". There is a five-pointed star in the upper part of the arms. **Ka168** The state arms of the Kazakh Soviet Socialist Republic consist of the representation of a sickle and hammer against a red background, in the rays of the sun and framed by ears of grain, with an inscription in the Kazakh and Russian languages: "Proletarians of All Countries, Unite!". In the upper part of the arms there is a five-pointed star, and in the lower part the letters "KSSR" and "KSSR". **La168** The state arms of the Latvian Soviet Socialist Republic consist of a representation of a sickle and hammer in the rays of a rising sun and framed in ears of grain; in the upper part of the arms there is a five-pointed star; in the lower part, the sea, and on a ribbon which joins together the ears of grain, an inscription: in the Latvian language in the center "*Latvijas PSR*", and on the sides "*Visu zenju proletarieši, savienolieties*!", and in the Russian language "Proletarians of All Countries, Unite!". **Tu168** The state arms of the Turkmen Soviet Socialist Republic consist of a representation of a sickle and hammer, buildings of an industrial enterprise, and a drilling tower against the background of the rising sun framed by ears of grain and closed balls of cotton, a rug, and bunches of grapes with an inscription on a red ribbon—on the left in the Turkmen language: "Proletarians of All Countries, Unite!", and on the right in the Russian language—"Proletarians of All Countries, Unite!". There is a five-pointed star in the upper part of the arms. **Ta169** The state arms of the Tadzhik Soviet Socialist Republic consist of a representation of a five-pointed star framed by a wreath, which is made up on the right of sheaves of wheat, and on the left from a cotton branch with closed balls, in the upper part of which there are represented a sickle and hammer in the rays of the sun. Above, the wreath is intertwined with a ribbon with inscription: "Proletarians of All Countries, Unite!" in the Tadzhik and Russian languages. In the lower portion of the circle, formed by the wreath, there is a ribbon with an inscription: "Tadzhik SSR" in the Tadzhik and Russian languages. **Uz178** The state arms of the Uzbek Soviet Socialist Republic consist of a representation of a sickle and hammer in the rays of the sun, surrounded by a garland, on the right made up of sheaves of wheat, and on the left by a cotton branch with blooms and closed cotton balls, and in the upper part of the arms there is a five-pointed star; below there is represented a part of the globe. On the ribbon of the garland there is an inscription: on the left—in the Uzbek language "[Proletarians of All Countries, Unite!]", and on the right—in the Russian language—"Proletarians of All Countries, Unite!". At the bottom on the bow of the ribbon is an inscription: "UzSSR". **Az180** The state arms of the Azerbaidzhan Soviet Socialist Republic consist of a representation of a sickle and hammer, and an oil derrick against the background of a rising sun framed by a wreath of cotton and ears of grain with an inscription in the Azerbaidzhan language: "Azerbaidzhan Soviet Socialist Republic", and "Proletarians of All Countries, Unite!", and in the Russian language: "Azerbaidzhan Soviet Socialist Republic", and "Proletarians of All Countries, Unite!". There is a five-pointed star in the upper part of the arms. **G180** The state arms of the Georgian Soviet Socialist Republic consist of a circle, in the upper part of which against a red background is represented a shining five-pointed star with spreading rays; below, covered by snow, is a light-blue mountain range and, arising out of the center, the snow-covered summit; in the lower part of the circle are represented: on the right, a golden cluster of a bunch of grapes, and, on the left, three golden sheaves, the ends of the ears and the cluster are bound together at the lower part of the circle; the larger part of the center is occupied by the representation of a golden sickle and hammer, which are upright; above—in the spreading rays of the star, below—on the mountain peak, and on the sides—in the ears of grain and the cluster; over the sickle and hammer there is the inscription [in Georgian]: "GSSR"; the circle is decorated with a border with a pattern of Georgian decorations, on the inner ring of which, against a white background, and separated by two small stars, there is an inscription in two languages—Georgian and Russian: "Proletarians of All Countries, Unite!".

Article 181. The state flag of the Russian Soviet Federative Socialist Republic consists of a rectangular red cloth with a light-blue band near the staff, the entire width of the flag, comprising one-eighth of the length of the flag. In the left upper corner of the red cloth are represented a golden sickle and hammer, and over them a red five-pointed star, edged in gold. The ratio of the width of the flag to its length is 1:2.[1]

Ar,E,Uk167, B,Ki,Li,M168, Ka,La,Tu169, Ta170, Uz179; [1]**Ar167** The state flag of the Armenian Soviet Socialist Republic consists of a rectangular red cloth with a blue band in the middle running the entire length of the flag. At the upper red part of the cloth of the flag, near the staff, there are depicted a golden sickle and hammer, and over them a red five-pointed star, edged in gold. The ratio of the width of the flag to its length is 1:2. **E167** The state flag of the Estonian SSR consists of a red rectangular cloth, across which runs a light-blue wavy line with two white strips above, which form six sharp-pointed waves across the length of the flag. The light-blue wavy band together with the white strips comprise three-tenths of the width of the flag. The upper red band comprises one-half of the width of the flag. In the upper red part of the cloth of the flag, in the upper left corner, at a distance of one-sixth of the length of the flag from the staff, there are represented a golden sickle and hammer, and above them a red five-pointed star, edged in gold. The ratio of the width of the flag to its length is 1:2. **Uk167** The state flag of the Ukrainian SSR consists of a rectangular cloth made up of two horizontal colored bands: the upper is red, and comprises two-third of the width of the flag, and the lower is sky-blue, and comprises one-third of the width of the flag, with a representation in the upper part, at a distance of one-third of the length of the flag from the staff, of a golden sickle and hammer, and over them a red five-pointed star, edged in gold. The ratio of the width of the flag to its length is 1:2. **B168** The state flag of the Belorussian Soviet Socialist Republic consists of a cloth made up of two horizontally placed colored bands: the upper, of red, comprises two-thirds of the width, and the lower, of green, comprises one-third of the width of the flag, with the representation in the upper left corner of the red band of a golden sickle and hammer, and over them a five-pointed star, edged in gold. Near the staff, there is a vertically placed Belorussian national decoration of white on a red field, comprising 1/9 of the length of the flag. The ratio of the width of the flag to its length is 1:2. **Ki168** The state flag of the Kirgiz Soviet Socialist Republic consists of a red cloth with a blue band in the center throughout the length of the flag. Along the blue band in the center there is a white band, equal to one-twentieth of the width of the flag. On the upper red part of the cloth of the flag at the staff are represented a golden sickle and hammer, and over them a red five-pointed star, edged in gold. The ratio of the width of the flag to its length is 1:2. **Li168** The state flag of the Lithuanian Soviet Socialist Republic consists of a cloth made up of three horizontal colored bands: the upper is red and comprises eight-twelfths of the width of the flat; the center is white and comprises one-twelfth of the width of the flag; and the lower is green and comprises three-twelfths of the width of the flag. In the upper left corner of the red part of the cloth there are represented a golden sickle and hammer, and over them is a red five-pointed star, edged in gold. The ratio of the width of the flag to its length is 1:2. **M168** The state flag of the Moldavian Soviet Socialist Republic consists of a red rectangular cloth with a green band in the center throughout the entire length of the flag, and with the representation in the corner of the upper part of the cloth, near the staff, of a golden sickle and hammer, and over them a red five-pointed star, edged in gold. The green band comprises one-fourth of the width of the flag. The ratio of the width of the flag to its length is 1:2. **Ka169** The state flag of the Kazakh Soviet Socialist Republic consists of a cloth comprised of three horizontal colored bands: the upper is red and comprises two-thirds of the width of the flag; the center is sky-blue and comprises two-ninths of the width of the flag; and the lower is red and comprises one-ninth of the width of the flag. On the upper red part of the cloth of the flag, at a distance of one-fourth the length of the flag from the staff, there are represented a sickle and hammer, and over them a red five-pointed star, edged in gold. The ratio of the width of the flag to its length is 1:2. **La169** The state flag of the Latvian Soviet Socialist Republic consists of a rectanguar cloth made up of five horizontal colored bands: the upper band in red comprises two-thirds of the width of the flag, and two white and two blue alternating wavy bands, representing the sea, comprise one-third of the width of the flag. In the upper corner of the red band of the cloth near the staff, at a distance of one-fifth of the flag from the staff, are represented a golden sickle and hammer, and over them a red five-pointed star, edged in gold. The ratio of the width of the flag to its length is 1:2. **Tu169** The state flag of the Turkmen SSR consists of a red rectangular cloth with a light-blue band in the center throughout the entire length of the flag. The light-blue band comprises one-third of the width of the flag. Along the light-blue band, in the center, runs a red strip equal to one-twentieth of the width of the flag. On the upper red part of the cloth of the flag, near the staff, there are represented a golden sickle and hammer, and over them a red five-pointed star, edged in gold. The ratio of the width of the flag to its length is 1:2. **Ta170** The state flag of the Tadzhik SSR consists of a rectangular cloth made up of four horizontal colored bands: the upper band is red, and comprises one-half of the width of the flag; there is a white band comprising one-fifth of the width of the flag; there is a green band comprising one-tenth of the width of the flag, and the lower band of red comprising one-fifth of the width of the flag. On the upper red part of the cloth of the flag, near the staff, there are represented a golden sickle and hammer, and over them a red five-pointed star, edged in gold. The ratio of the width of the flag to its length is 1:2. **Uz179** The state flag of the Uzbek Soviet Socialist Republic consists of a red rectangular cloth with a blue band in the center throughout the entire length of the flag. Along the edges of the blue band run narrow white borders. The blue band together with the white borders comprise one-fifth of the width of the flag. [para.2] On the upper red part of the cloth of the flag, near the staff, are represented a golden sickle and hammer, and over them edged in gold a five-pointed star. The ratio of the width of the flag to its length is 1:2. **Az181** The state flag of the Azerbaidzhan Soviet Socialist Republic consists of a rectangular cloth, made up of two horizontal colored bands: the upper, of red, comprises three-fourths of the width, and the lower, of blue, comprises one-fourth of the width of the flag, with the representation in the upper left corner of the red band, near the staff, of a golden sickle and hammer, and over them a red five-pointed star, edged in gold. The ratio of the width of the flag to its length is 1:2. **G181** The state flag of the Georgian Soviet Socialist Republic consists of a rectangular red cloth. The relation of the width to the length is 1:2. In the upper corner near the staff there is a square of light blue, the sides of which are equal to one-half of the width of the flag. In the center of the square there is a circle, the radius of which is equal to one-third of a side of the square. In the circle there are a sickle and hammer, and over them a five-pointed star, from the sides of which to the sides of the square there are 24 rays. The sickle, hammer, star, and rays are red. From the center of the right side of the square, there is a light blue band which runs the entire length of the flag, and the width of which is one-third of a side of the square.

Article 182. The state anthem of the Russian Soviet Federative Socialist Republic is confirmed by the Presidium of the Supreme Soviet of the RSFSR.

Ar,E,Uk168, B,Ki,Li,M169, Ka,La,Tu170, Ta171, Uz180

Article 183. The capital of the Russian Soviet Federative Socialist Republic is the city of Moscow.[1]

Ar,E,Uk169, B,Ki,Li,M170, Ka,La,Tu171, Ta172, Uz181; [1]**Ar169** Erevan **E169** Tallinn **Uk169** Kiev **B170** Minsk **Ki170** Frunze **Li170** Vilnius **M170** Kishinev **Ka171** Alma-Ata **La171** Riga **Tu171** Ashkhabad **Ta172** Dushanbe **Uz181** Tashkent **Az183** Baku **G183** Tbilisi

XI. THE OPERATION OF THE CONSTITUTION OF THE RSFSR AND THE PROCEDURE FOR ITS AMENDMENT

Ar,B,E,Ka,Ki,La,Li,M,Ta,Tu,Uk = PART X.

Article 184. All laws and other acts of state organs of the RSFSR are issued on the basis of and in accordance with the Constitution of the RSFSR.[1]

Ar,E,Uk170, B,Ki,Li,M171, Ka,La,Tu172, Ta173, Uz182; [1]**Uk170, Ki,Li171, Ka,Tu172** and in accordance with the present Constitution.

Article 185. The Constitution of the RSFSR is amended by a decision of the Supreme Soviet of the RSFSR, adopted by a majority of not less than two-thirds of the total number of deputies of the Supreme Soviet of the RSFSR.[1]

Ar,E,Uk171, B,Ki,Li,M172, Ka,La,Tu173, Ta174, Uz183; [1]**E171** of the total number of deputies of the Supreme Soviet. **Uk171, Ta174, Uz183** of the total number of deputies.

STATE ARMS AND FLAGS OF THE USSR

State Arms of the Union of Soviet Socialist Republics

State Arms of the RSFSR

State Arms of the Ukrainian SSR

State Arms of the Belorussian SSR

State Arms of the Uzbek SSR

State Arms of the Kazakh SSR

State Arms of the Georgian SSR

State Arms of the Azerbaidzhan SSR

State Arms of the Lithuanian SSR

State Arms of the Moldavian SSR

State Arms of the Latvian SSR

State Arms of the Kirgiz SSR

State Arms of the Tadzhik SSR

State Arms of the Armenian SSR

State Arms of the Turkmen SSR

State Arms of the Estonian SSR

State Flag of the Union of Soviet Socialist Republics

State Flag of the RSFSR

State Flag of the Ukrainian SSR

State Flag of the Belorussian SSR

State Flag of the Uzbek SSR

State Flag of the Kazakh SSR

State Flag of the Georgian SSR

State Flag of the Azerbaidzhan SSR

State Flag of the Lithuanian SSR

State Flag of the Moldavian SSR

State Flag of the Latvian SSR

State Flag of the Kirgiz SSR

State Flag of the Tadzhik SSR

State Flag of the Armenian SSR

State Flag of the Turkmen SSR

State Flag of the Estonian SSR

INDEX

COLOPHON

letter: baskerville 10/12 and 8/10
setter: The European Printing Corporation Limited
printer: Samsom Sijthoff Grafische Bedrijven
binder: binderij Callenbach
cover-design: Wim Bottenheft